WOMEN PHYSICIANS
OF THE WORLD

In Memory

Leone McGregor Hellstedt, M.D., Ph.D., D.Sc.

January 19, 1900–July 2, 1977

Dr. Leone Hellstedt dedicated her life to excellence in all aspects of her medical profession. It was a life rich in success, high honors, and well-deserved international recognition.

Dr. Hellstedt, past president of the Medical Women's International Association, devoted several years of her life to collecting the memoirs of prominent pioneer women physicians from many nations. This great woman was gratified to know that her efforts were to materialize and would be published. Members and friends of the Medical Women's International Association remember Dr. Hellstedt with the greatest affection and respect. We dedicate this volume to the memory of Leone McGregor Hellstedt, whose work will serve as a beacon to the future generations of medical women of the world.

WOMEN PHYSICIANS OF THE WORLD

autobiographies of medical pioneers

Editor

Leone McGregor Hellstedt, M.D., Ph.D., D.Sc.
Medical Women's International Association

HEMISPHERE PUBLISHING CORPORATION

Washington   London

McGRAW-HILL BOOK COMPANY

New York   St. Louis   San Francisco   Auckland   Bogotá
Düsseldorf   Johannesburg   London   Madrid   Mexico
Montreal   New Delhi   Panama   Paris   São Paulo
Singapore   Sydney   Tokyo   Toronto

WOMEN PHYSICIANS OF THE WORLD

1 2 3 4 5 6 7 8 9 0   D O D O   7 8 3 2 1 0 9 8

This book was set in Theme by Hemisphere Publishing Corporation. The
editors were Sally J. Barhydt, Judith B. Gandy, and Martha Leff; the
designer was Lilia N. Guerrero; the production supervisor was
Rebekah McKinney; and the typesetter was Peggy M. Rote.
R. R. Donnelley & Sons Company was printer and binder.

Library of Congress Cataloging in Publication Data

Main entry under title:

Women physicians of the world.

    1. Women physicians—Biography. 2. Physicians—
Biography. I. Hellstedt, Leone McGregor, 1900–1977.
R692.W68   610'.92'2 [B]   78-9790
ISBN 0-07-027954-3

This book is dedicated to the twelve founders of the
Medical Women's International Association founded in 1919

Esther Pohl Lovejoy	United States
Alma Sundquist	Sweden
Clelia Lollini	Italy
Tomo Inouye	Japan
Yvonne Pouzin	France
Martha Welpton	United States
Grace Ritchie	England
Christine Munch	Norway
Regina Stang	Norway
L. Thuillier-Landry	France
Maria Feyler	Switzerland
Radmila Lazarevitch	Serbia

Contents

CONTENTS

A Message from the President of the MWIA

This book of ninety-one autobiographies of pioneer medical women from twenty-seven nations is a unique documentation. The autobiographers relate the stimuli influencing their pursuit of the study of medicine, the difficulties they had to overcome, and the sacrifices they had to make in order to reach their goals. These physicians lived when women first began to gain access to the lecture halls of professional faculties—at the beginning of the twentieth century. The backgrounds, upbringing, education, and university studies of these medical women are extremely variable and reflect their respective cultures. Although most of these women had to fight a world of obstacles to accomplish their aims, all conclude that if they had the choice again, they would choose a medical career.

We are indebted to Dr. Leone Hellstedt of Stockholm, Sweden, who conceived the idea of this historic edition. It is because of her vision, energy, and personal initiative that these memoirs are recorded and not forever lost.

In editing this book, Dr. Hellstedt was assisted by Dr. Isobel Russell Robertson and her medical colleagues of South Africa, and by Dr. Minerva Smith Buerk of the United States.

The Medical Women's International Association hopes that these autobiographies will have a twofold purpose: to stimulate all qualified women who wish to study medicine to pursue their goals despite seemingly insurmountable obstacles, and to heighten the respect for the outgoing generation of medical women, many of whom are archetypal in their native countries.

Helga Thieme, *President 1976–1978*
Medical Women's International Association

Preface

The Medical Women's International Association (MWIA) came into being in New York on October 19, 1919. Esther Pohl Lovejoy proposed the founding of the association at a dinner in the Waldorf Astoria, where 140 women were assembled to honor distinguished medical women who had just returned from war service in Europe. A committee of twelve drew up the constitution, and Esther Pohl Lovejoy was elected president. The MWIA was the first international medical association in the world. None of our founders is alive today, but the organization has flourished, giving internationally minded medical women a biennial forum to report scientific studies and providing a social milieu where the 13,000 members can meet and discuss common problems with colleagues from all our 40 affiliated nations.

In 1962 in Manila, Philippines, at our MWIA congress organized by Dr. Fe del Mundo (the first international medical congress of any kind to be held in Asia), I encountered for the first time a great number of our Asian women colleagues. The great success of these MWIA congresses, particularly the one held in Manila, led us all to realize how much medical women all over the world have in common. Our curiosity was aroused as to the factors that had made it possible for women in so many countries to break down the barriers that had kept them out of medical schools for such a long time. It is obvious that the social, economic, and educational revolution of the first half of the nineteenth century had led to the founding in 1850 of the Woman's Medical College of Pennsylvania, in Philadelphia, the first women's medical school in the world. What, however, were the inner motivations of the women from all these countries who flocked to this school? There exists almost no such documentation from these pioneer women themselves.

In 1974, when International Women's Year was approaching and I was past president of MWIA and chairperson of the Project Committee, it seemed to me that it was time to investigate the cultural, historical, and familial factors in the lives of our oldest pioneers.

I decided to initiate by means of autobiographies a study of the motives and the emergence of these women in medicine. As all born before 1878 were deceased, I chose the next group, with birth dates between 1878 and 1911. The officers in each national association were asked to select the outstanding pioneers suitable and willing to undertake the duty and honor of writing their autobiographies for this project. Each contributor was requested to stress in her story her family background and the factors, from early childhood on, that would seem to have led to her determination to become a physician. The stories have all been written in the women's native languages, and they have been translated into

English by their native-English-speaking colleagues. None of these women are professional writers. The autobiographies now presented have been edited with great care in order to preserve the charm of the writers' expressions and the particular sequence of thought of the period.

A preliminary, purely descriptive study of the manuscripts reveals how these physicians were already observant, ambitious, and courageous in childhood. The majority of them had come into close contact with serious illness and even with death, affecting chiefly mothers and siblings. Most of these women had chosen their future occupation before or around puberty. With few exceptions, their parents had encouraged them. They have made splendid careers and have been happy and fulfilled in the practice of medicine, usually in the fields of mother and child care, which had been their aim from the beginning.

The response of our pioneers to this project has been overwhelming. I have succeeded in collecting ninety-one autobiographies from twenty-seven nations. All these women have gladly made a unique effort in giving us precious records of their lives as they recall them, in order to help and encourage other women aspiring to or already launched on a medical career. In so doing, our pioneers have also provided us with a picture of a section of the cultural history of women in general and of medical women in particular.

In our affiliated countries there are obviously many other distinguished women physicians of accomplishment who could have been nominated to be a part of this historical and sociological record, but our choice was limited to the MWIA membership—and of course to those who were willing to participate.

Now that the material has been assembled, the contributors themselves, as well as our general membership, have become eager to have access to the autobiographies of their colleagues in affiliated countries. In addition, the intellectual, well-informed reading public has shown great interest in the project. As a result, MWIA has decided to publish the manuscripts in this book, hoping that these records of some of the joys and sorrows that ninety-one pioneer medical women encountered along their medical paths will enrich the outlook of readers in regard to the education and possibilities of women in medicine.

In publishing this book, the MWIA presents the only collection of autobiographies of any profession from international sources and from a specific period of history.

Leone McGregor Hellstedt

Acknowledgments

Although the plan to inspire senior pioneer members of the Medical Women's International Association (MWIA) to write their autobiographies was my own idea, the result, as evidenced in this book, is greatly dependent on the splendid cooperation and expert assistance of two medical friends, Dr. Minerva Smith Buerk, of the United States, and Dr. Isobel Russell Robertson, of South Africa. Both have collaborated with many original ideas, contributed innumerable hours of work, and traveled thousands of miles to Sweden on several occasions in the interest of this endeavor. To both these colleagues and to several editors from South Africa, I extend my deepest gratitude.

The publication of the book has been made possible by the liberal support of the Japanese Medical Women's Association, particularly through the major efforts of Dr. Ayako Sano, of Tokyo, and of the American Medical Women's Association and many other medical colleagues.

I wish to express special thanks for the constant encouragement and aid I received from my MWIA colleagues Dr. Marta Holmstrom, of Sweden; Dr. Helga Thieme, of Germany; Dr. Alma Morani, of the United States; Dr. Ayako Sano, of Japan; Dr. Marta Kyrle, of Austria; Dr. Lola Vilar, of Spain; Dr. Enid MacLeod, of Canada; and Dr. Joan Redshaw, of Australia. I am extremely indebted to my loyal nonmedical friends, Catherine Djurklou, Helen Frey, and Friedel Lehmann, of Sweden; and Herta Dax, of Austria, for generous participation in the many hours devoted to the preparation of the manuscripts.

Leone McGregor Hellstedt

WOMEN PHYSICIANS
OF THE WORLD

CANADA

Jeannie Smillie Robertson
b. February 10, 1878

I was born in Tuckersmith Township, Huron County, Ontario, near what is now the town of Hensall. At that time it was pioneer country and there were still wild animals in the bush. My mother and father, both born in Canada of Irish and Scottish descent, respectively, were living on a farm, in beautiful fertile country that produced wonderful grain and other crops. My parents never went beyond the public school because in their time there was no opportunity to go further. But they were interested in education, and five of the seven of us children had secondary education. My father died when I was six, and my mother died when I was twenty-five. My older brother took over the farm and was like a father to us. Mary, my older sister, married a farmer. I was the third in the family. Margaret, who was next to me, became a public-school teacher. I had two younger brothers, Alex, who became a doctor in Niagara Falls, and Ben, the baby, who became a minister and went to India as a missionary. My younger sister Emmaline became a nurse and was on a hospital ship working out of India during World War I. Later she went back to the university for her M.A. and taught high-school English until her retirement. Margaret, Emmaline, and I lived together for many years.

I was three when I first thought of going into medicine. I had been told about a woman doctor (who was planning to go to India as a missionary), kneeling on a velvet cushion to get her medical degree, and I thought it would be nice if I too could kneel on a velvet cushion! When I was five years old, I asked my mother, "Mother, can girls be doctors?" and when she smiled and said, "Yes", I told her, "Then, I'm going to be a doctor." I was fifteen when I made the definite decision to study medicine, but I could not start medical school until I was twenty-five because I first had to earn the money. I never particularly wanted to do research or medical teaching, but I did want to help people.

When I started my education, I walked two and a half miles each day to the nearest school, until I had finished the third book. (In bad weather a bunch of us students might be driven by ourselves or the neighbors.) Then I had two years in the public school in Hensall, where I learned a great deal from a very wonderful teacher, Miss Jennie Murray. I went to high school in Seaforth, paying three dollars a week for room and board.

When I was eighteen, I got my teacher's certificate and taught first in a school just across the road from the place where I had been born and later in the town of Drayton. There I first met the man I would marry many years later, but at that time I was planning on medicine, not marriage, and didn't think I could have both.

When I began to teach, I earned only about $300 a year; so as I said before, I could not save enough to enter medical school until I was twenty-five. I was one of three members of the last class to attend the women's medical school in Toronto. When I went to apply, I was told that, for the first time, the women students would be taking many of their lectures with the men students at the University of Toronto, although we still did our anatomy classes and dissections separately.

At the end of that year, the women's medical college was closed, and the women were taken into the university medical school. The reason for that was very interesting. The professors had been having difficulty keeping the mischievous and obstreperous boys in order and had noted that the gentlemen behaved better when the ladies were present in the classes; so they decided to take the women into all the classes! We were delighted to be admitted to the university, and we got along very well.

I graduated in 1909. At that time there were very few internships for women in Toronto hospitals, but I knew there were a lot of women doctors in the United States and that there was a women's medical school in Philadelphia. I was able to intern there for a year, in the hospital connected with the Women's Medical College of Pennsylvania. It was a good year. The people were very nice to me, and everything was lovely.

I started solo practice in Toronto in 1910. Although there weren't many women practicing in Toronto, we got a fair share of work to do—but none in surgery. I thought we women would never amount to anything in medicine as long as we had to hand over our surgery to the men. So I tried to coax some of the women to specialize in surgery, but I couldn't find anyone willing to spend the time and money to do so. I decided if no one else would, I would have to do it myself. I had some difficulty finding a place. No one in Toronto would accept a woman. However, I knew that the chief surgeon at the Women's Medical College of Pennsylvania was very good (although nobody really liked her because she was cross). I wrote and explained that Toronto needed some women surgeons and that I would like to get some training. The hospital needed interns at the time, and the professors knew that I would work hard; so they agreed to let me live in the hospital if I would do a certain amount of general work, as well as surgery. I got on very well with the chief surgeon, and she taught me a lot and let me do everything. At first I just helped her with the operations, but toward the end of my six months there, she left me in charge for a week while she was out of town and I did some operations on my own. That helped my self-confidence a lot when I first started to do surgery in Toronto. Six months does not sound like much, compared to the five years of special training required now, but it was concentrated practical work and was, I think, average at that time.

When I came back to Toronto, we women didn't have a hospital in which to do surgery. The first operation I did, for a diseased ovary, was on a kitchen table in an ordinary house. I had several women doctors watching me, as well as one or two kind old medical men, who were encouraging us women.

As time went on, there were more women in medicine and more women specializing in various other fields. We felt the need for a hospital of our own in which to do our work. With a lot of hard work on the part of the women doctors and with the generous financial and other help of friends, we first rented a house on Seaton Street, and some years later we moved to a bigger one on Rusholme Road. Finally, the Women's College Hospital was built on its present site, on Grenville Street. It was very hard going in the early days. I remember once when we women doctors sat at a meeting of farmers' wives, collecting vegetables with which to feed our patients.

I was associated with Women's College Hospital for most of my forty years of practice, doing mostly abdominal, especially gynecological, surgery, and I was chief of the Department of Gynecology for some years. There were a lot of women who had ovarian cysts and had to have operations. I also did a lot of appendectomies, and of course I did maternity work, too. I was greatly helped when Dr. Grace Richardson began acting first as my assistant and later as anesthetist at my operations. She was a great woman and a very valuable assistant.

I was a charter member of the Federation of Medical Women of Canada. Although I was so busy with my surgery that I didn't have much time for committee work, I was interested in women in medicine and glad to do anything I could to help.

Shortly after I started to practice in Toronto, I began to realize the importance of good government, and I became a member of the Women's Liberal Association and later its president. I suppose it was just a chance that I happened to be a liberal; my people were all liberals.

I spent forty years practicing surgery, and by the time I was seventy, I was getting awfully tired because I didn't rest as much as people should; so I retired. But then I thought it was a queer thing to have nothing to do—that I'd have to get another job! So it seemed providential that a man (Alex Robertson) I had met forty years before in Drayton, where I had taught and he had worked in the bank, came into my life again. I had liked him then but had believed he was much younger than I, and I never thought then of falling in love with him. He had married in the meantime, but his wife had died. One year after her death, he began calling on me. He was just the same jolly boy he had been when I first knew him, but now he had become a polished gentleman as well and I was surprised to find that our age was the same. I knew soon that I would marry him—he was too good to miss! We were very happy for the ten years of our marriage.

But now I've reached the place in life where I'm not looking back very much—I'm looking ahead. I'm glad I was brought up in a good Christian home. We always had family worship; mother kept it up even after father died. Very good things have happened to me, but I feel that it is because the Lord has watched over me and has done wonderful things. I give God the glory.

Shigeyo Takeuchi
b. August 3, 1881

My birthplace is in the central highlands of Japan 1000 meters above sea level. The temperature falls to 20 degrees Celsius below zero in the winter. My ancestors came to these backwoods of Shinshu, in the Nagano Prefecture, centuries ago, after being defeated in a civil war in another province. Since then they have been rulers here, handing down their authority from father to son. I was born, the eldest daughter and first of six siblings, to the well-to-do Ide family in 1881.

In order to help you understand my background, I must explain the social situation of the Tokugawa era (1600–1868). During this period Japan was a very peaceable country, with a population of about 25 million. Some 2 million of the people used to travel annually between Tokyo and Osaka, a distance of 550 kilometers, for business and sightseeing. The citizens were law-abiding. Japanese culture was developed under the united effort of one nation, one race, and one language. Trade within the country was promoted and encouraged. There were many schools, both in the towns and in the country, and at that time Japan was among the developed nations with the lowest percentage of illiteracy. During this period European culture, especially medical scientific knowledge, came to Japan by way of Holland, the only country licensed by the Taikun government to carry on commerce with Japan. A change in the international political situation in Asia forced Japan to open her harbors in 1868 and to change her government. Soon afterward European civilization quickly penetrated Japan and the people began to absorb and integrate it into their traditional culture.

I was born some years after these great changes. My father was a highly educated man, held in great esteem in our district. When I entered primary school, at six years of age, the education of women was unheard of and I was the only girl among 100 boys, even though the Compulsory Education Act was already in force. After four years at this school I had to give up the idea of going to a girls' high school because even the nearest one was too far from our village. Instead I helped my ailing mother to take care of the five brothers born after me. As I could not go to school, my father taught me Japanese history,

5

foreign history, and the difficult Chinese "kanbun" characters every day from 4:00 to 6:00 in the morning. From 9:00 in the evening until midnight I studied Utako Shimada's correspondence course for the education of women. Ever since those early years I have advocated four hours of sleep as sufficient for each day, a pattern I have followed throughout my life.

As my life was planned at that time, I would have ended up as an elderly, well-educated woman living in the country. However, at fifteen years of age I developed that rare malady alopecia (baldness), which was a great shock to me. I had to go to Tokyo for treatment and was taken care of in the Red Cross Hospital. There I was very surprised to meet a Japanese woman doctor with a visiting American woman physician. Until then I had never dreamed of the possibility of a woman's becoming a medical doctor, but I decided at once that I also would study for this profession. I asked a nurse many questions about the medical schools in Japan and found out that the Tokyo Women's Medical School had just been established by Dr. Yayoi Yoshioka. Later, when my father saw how determined I was to pursue this career, he went with me to visit Dr. Yoshioka in her home. Thus began my new life.

I entered the school in 1902. It was then of course like a private tutoring school and had been founded only two years previously, but it was a place where I could study medicine. After that it was necessary to pass the national medical examination in order to get a license to practice. I had to work very hard because, after four years of grammar school, I had only been tutored by my father. However, I was accustomed to a strict regimen and only four hours' sleep a night. I graduated after five years, in 1908, and passed the national examination, as well. Dr. Yoshioka celebrated my success with a big party attended by many eminent people, among whom was the late prime minister, the marquis of O-kuma, who had founded the Waseda University. In his speech on this occasion he said, "Nowadays there is a great deal of discussion as to the merits and drawbacks of higher education for women. We expect this young woman to solve these problems within the next ten or fifteen years." Thus, on assuming my role as a doctor, I had the additional burden of this heavy responsibility of women's rights. I became Dr. Yoshioka's assistant and did all I could for the advancement of the Tokyo Women's Medical School.

When I married my husband, Kohei Takeuchi, he was studying pathology at Tokyo University and I had already opened my own practice, in 1913. After he became a doctor of medicine, I began to study again, this time under Professor Nagai, of Tokyo University. I worked in my practice every day from early morning until 3:00 in the afternoon. I then studied at the university and in my own home until 2:00 a.m.

My younger brother and his wife also became doctors of medicine, and thus we had two medical couples in the same family until my husband died in 1951 of lung cancer, a disease that had been his specialty.

Several years after I had opened my practice, I became involved in a tragedy. This caused me so much mental suffering that I consulted Dr. Uchimura, the most famous educationalist and moral leader in Japan. At his institution I met many wise persons who later became leaders in their respective fields. It was a very happy experience, which enabled me to get to know a group of interesting people outside the medical world.

I was always active in women's organizations, especially those for women's rights. I worked for women's suffrage, and when this was granted, I became the first woman to be elected to Parliament, in 1945. I had been engaged in and had headed many women's organizations, and during the war I had done some voluntary service, with the result that after the war I was excluded from public service. I then resigned from Parliament. After being rehabilitated in 1959, I became president of the alumni association of the Tokyo Women's Medical School. In 1964 the government awarded me the decoration of the Third Order of the Sacred Treasure.

I have published books on home nursing, child care, and child rearing. In my spare time my hobby has been embroidery.

I retired in 1965 to live just north of Tokyo with the family of my youngest brother. In the large garden we have 500 plum trees, which make a wonderful picture when they are in bloom. Now, at ninety-four, looking back over my long life, I must say that I have been happy to have had so many good friends and excellent teachers. I believe that life is precious, and in spite of the disabilities natural to my great age, I still enjoy the peace and serene beauty of our White Plum Villa.

CANADA

Elizabeth Catherine Bagshaw

b. October 19, 1881

I was born on a farm on the Twelfth Concession, Mariposa Township, Victoria County, Canada. At that time there was no rural mail, no telephone, no oil—just wood fires. My parents were farmers. We had a bush of nearly 50 acres, and 100 acres besides for pasture and grain farming. The church we belonged to was three miles away, and the school was two miles away. Being in the snow belt, the one-mile side road to the school closed with the first snow storm, which came in early December, and usually stayed closed until spring, frequently until after Easter. This did not give me a good grounding in grammar, but even so, I managed to pass every year with the class. When I got my entrance to high school, my sister and I drove three miles to Cannington, where they gave first- and second-form exams but no languages. Then we went to Lindsay Collegiate for three years, where I took mathematics, history, chemistry, English, Latin, French, and German, although I did not learn much in either the French or German classes.

I was the fourth in a family of four girls, with no brothers. As a child I was very venturesome. I could climb before I could walk; I played on a barn roof at four years of age and rode horseback at nine. When I got older, I had plenty of boy friends, but I did not wish to get married; I wanted a career of my own. At about sixteen, when I was attending Collegiate, I decided to go to medical school. My mother did not want me to study medicine, but father was in favor of it. Unfortunately, a year before I graduated, he died of paralysis three days after breaking his neck in a fall from a ladder in the barn.

I did not have any particular friends to encourage me to go into medicine, but I had read about some medical women. I did not tell any of my friends what I was going to study. When I went to Toronto to register, one of the boys who had been at Collegiate with me came up to me and said, "You are in the wrong place to register. This is only for men."

I replied, "I think I shall stay here; I don't want a B.A. course." Actually, I worked at the women's medical college, starting in 1901 and graduating in 1905. There were eight in my class. Lillian Longstaff and I are the only ones living now.

I did not go to a hospital for internship; such positions were very scarce for women then. Helen McMurchy of Toronto was the first woman to have an internship in a Toronto Hospital, and Maude Abbott was on the staff of McGill Medical School for years before they took girls as students. (Both these women were friends of mine.)

I came to Hamilton in 1906 to take over the practice of Mabel Henderson, one of the early women medical graduates of Queen's University. I liked it here and stayed, continuing in practice until 1976, when, at the age of ninety-five, I decided it was time to retire!

When I graduated and started practicing, we did not have the drugs we do now. Aspirin was new; diphtheria antitoxin was new; there was no chlorine in the water. Typhoid was very common, as were syphilis and gonorrhea and the children's diseases—scarlet fever, measles, mumps, whopping cough, and chicken pox. I had a lot of maternity cases, about 3000; most of them were home deliveries. I was on the staff of the Hamilton Civic (General) Hospital Skin Clinic for about ten years, and for thirty years I was the medical director of the Planned Parenthood Association in Hamilton. This was the first birth-control clinic in Canada, and it caused great controversy in Hamilton; it was actually considered illegal until 1969! When I graduated in 1906, there were very few chances for women to specialize. We just did general practice. If practicing in a city, we could get a specialist to do major operations, and usually the general practitioner either assisted at operations or gave the anesthetics. We did have a few women specialists in eye, nose, and throat.

When I was forty-two, I adopted my first two children, a boy and a girl. The boy was the son of a distant cousin and was only six months old when he came to me. This was excellent for me, as it gave me more home life. The boy studied medicine. He has practiced with me for many years and has been president of the Hamilton Academy of Medicine. He has three children, either attending or having graduated from McMaster University. None of them have gone into medicine, although the wife of one is now a medical student.

I have had diphtheria and rheumatism, and I had a coronary attack ten years ago, but in spite of this I am quite well, except that I cannot walk very far.

I have been active in many medical and nonmedical organizations. I am a charter and honorary member of the Glendale Golf Club and an honorary member of the Victoria Curling Club, the YWCA, the Business and Professional Women's Club, and the Zonta International Club. I am also a member of the First United Church.

In recent years I have received many honors: Citizen of the Year for Hamilton, 1970; Order of Canada Medal, 1973; and LL.D. degree (McMaster), 1974. I am also an honorary member of the Hamilton Academy of Medicine, a senior member of the Canadian Medical Association, a life member of the College of Family Physicians of Canada, and a charter and honorary member of the Canadian Federation of Medical Women.

I think women in medicine have a good life. Certainly, I have had an active and happy life and have always had the support of other medical women. I have never felt my sex was a handicap. If I had it to do all over again, I would still do the same thing and enter medicine.

Elsa Winokurow
b. April 20, 1883

I was born in Moscow of German parents and grew up with three brothers. I attended the German Petri-Pauli girls' school and ended my studies there in the year 1899, taking an additional examination that qualified me to teach the German language as a private tutor. The atmosphere at home was typical of the middle class of the era: clothes, children, church, kitchen, and a natural adjustment and submission to men.

How was it, then, that I, a girl, decided to become a doctor? Above all, it was the zeitgeist of the Russian youth, who wanted to help the humble people, to sacrifice themselves, and to accomplish something in the world. At that time I was full of enthusiasm for the novel *Fathers and Sons* by Turgenev, especially for the country doctor Bazarov, with his criticism of his environment. When I was thirteen years old, I saw an accident in which a man's arm was severed, and the help the doctor gave him made a profound impression on me. I wanted to save life, too. My parents were, however, completely opposed to my wishes. Their argument was, "You are a girl." It was not until the book *The Woman* by August Bebel fell into my hands that I acquired the mental equipment to fight for my idea—to become a doctor.

In 1901, when I was eighteen, I married Dimitri Winokurow, a childhood friend of mine and of my brother's. Dimitri was a graduate of the Academy of Commercial Science, and as such, was already an honorary citizen of Moscow. This marriage gave me Russian nationality and thus the possibility of official admission to the women's university. Together with my friend Katharina von Sawalischen, daughter of the Decembrist D. J. Sawalischen, I first attended the lectures in the Department of Natural Sciences, as there was no medical faculty for women.

At that time there were far too few schools in Russia, and to be allowed to study was a privilege young people really appreciated. In my time there were eight universities for the whole country, with its population of about 150 million. The young women, particularly, took their studies very seriously. It was not until I went to the university that I really learned what it meant to study and to cram for the colloquiums with the teachers from the men's university and for the inevitable spring examinations.

In 1903, after passing the examinations for the natural sciences, we saw no possibility of beginning medical studies in Moscow. Although it was said that a medical institute for women was to be opened, this was very uncertain. So-called revolutionary activities occurred in the form of lecture strikes and meetings with anticzarist slogans. As a result, many students were arrested and the university was closed. Our college was also closed.

My friend and I then decided to take up our medical education abroad. We chose Zurich. Our preliminary studies at Moscow were credited, and we were accepted in the third year. After our fourth term we passed our premedical exams.

The spirit of comradeship among the Russian students in Zurich was perhaps even greater than in Russia. We all felt far from home and were homesick. We had a common meeting place for theatrical and musical performances. It was there that I heard a dispute between Social Revolutionaries and Social Democrats. I remember a brilliant speaker, about twenty-eight years old, with a pince-nez on his pointed nose—Leon Trotsky.

The Swiss universities had long been used to women students, but the citizens did not try to hide their disapproval, especially when these students were foreigners. Swiss students and some of the professors spoke a terrible dialect. The auditorium held about 200 people. It was a room with a wood stove, bare tables, and seats like old school benches. The lecture rooms were filled with foreigners, mainly Jews from Poland, Russia, Yugoslavia, and Bulgaria, who were not allowed to study in their own countries. Foreigners were not permitted to practice in Switzerland, as the university did not want to be held responsible for their scientific standard.

In 1905 and 1906 we continued our studies in Berlin. Professor Ernst Bergmann, a surgeon, refused to tolerate the presence of women students, but we were accepted by Professors Hildebrand and Pels-Leusden. Meanwhile, in Russia the waves of revolution were mounting. Professional revolutionaries were agitating the rural population. There were strikes and riots in all the universities. In February 1906 I received a telegram from Moscow, saying, "Your presence urgently needed." It was not easy to get a premature certificate for my term in Berlin. The chief, Professor de la Camp, gave me an unexpected smile, said, "For you I am prepared to commit any crime," and signed. The other professors followed suit.

On my return to Moscow there was at first no possibility of my being accepted at the university. To widen my knowledge, I offered to work as an assistant in Basmany, one of the municipal hospitals under Dr. von Schiemann, a surgeon. The political scene was changing rapidly. Liberal ministers came into the government, and my friend and I managed to be admitted to the university in Moscow. We had completed nine written final examinations when there came a new political change. Under the new minister of education, Schwarz, there was no question of a woman's being allowed to study unless, according to a law passed in 1861, she had Russian nationality and could produce a doctor's diploma from a recognized foreign university. Although we had all the certificates required and had paid our fees, we were exposed to a wholesale swindle. Nothing could help us. Altogether, there were 12 women (among 350 men) who were facing their final examinations and who had to go abroad once more.

An attempt to go to Munich failed because the rector at that time, a theologian, was opposed to women in a university. We telegraphed Bonn and received the following answer: "Welcome to Bonn." We set out happily. At that time Bonn had brilliant scholars. The summer term of 1907 began with a torchlight procession organized by a student corps to bid farewell to the famous surgeon Professor Bier, who had been called to Berlin. In 1907 and 1908, during two clinical terms, I wrote my dissertation in the Pathology Institute. The title of this histological work was "Some Rare Growths in Animals." My final licensing examination was carried out strictly according to the specifications the deacon had procured from the capital, or rather from the ministry, and included the premedical examination that I had already passed in Zurich but had not received credit for. In gynecology and obstetrics a woman's name, Dr. H. Edenhuizen, was just emerging—a great sensation. She became head physician under Privy Councillor Professor Fritsch. It is well known that Dr. Edenhuizen's confirmation as head physician was successful only because the ministry had printed the initial letter and not her entire feminine given name.

In 1908, after passing the degree examinations, we returned to Moscow via Warsaw. With these certificates in our hands, we began immediately to prepare for our Russian finals. In spite of the hard work we never laughed, danced, or enjoyed ourselves so much as in that year! In 1908 we passed our Russian finals at the university in Moscow. There were twenty-eight special fields and also the premedical examination. The anatomist could not resist asking my friend, "Tell me the names of the female sexual organs." Confused silence. "Come back in a fortnight." After that she passed.

Before receiving my Russian medical degree in the Moscow office of the Ministry of Education, I had first to pay nine rubles to the high official in uniform. On reading through the certificate, I discovered that I was listed as a Roman Catholic (instead of a Lutheran), and I refused to sign. This created great confusion because a second printing was impossible. Then someone discovered that Her Highness, Grand Duchess Elisaveta Feodorovna, sister of the czarina, had recently turned a house of the honorable citizen D. Winokurow into an old people's home and frequently visited it. The reprinting of the degree followed without further ado.

And then came the good years, from 1909 until the outbreak of World War I. I did my surgical training in one of the big municipal hospitals in the part of Moscow called Basmany. I was a junior assistant and was of course unpaid. [Incidently, the heads of departments were paid only 125 rubles a month, and when one died, we collected contributions for the funeral. The daily hospitalization cost per patient (worker) was nineteen kopecks.]

Simultaneously I worked from 1909 to 1921 in the medical laboratory of the Research Institute. I was paid well for this work.

In 1911 my only daughter was born, and in August 1914 the war broke out. The authorities ordered me to convert a school building into a military hospital with 200 beds for the seriously wounded. I was head physician, and I worked there for the duration of the war. My hospital was run by women. Two women surgeons and women specialists in internal medicine volunteered to work with me. The staff of nurses consisted of twelve female students in their first year at the newly founded medical college for women. We also had an office staff, stretcher-bearers, two cooks, and so forth. This period of duty lasted three full years. We treated 4000 wounded soldiers from all parts of Russia. There were men from Greater Russia, the Ukraine, the Tatar Republic, Caucasia, the Baltic, Karelia, German Volga, Poland, and Siberia (the last were, as human beings, the best).

Looking back on that period I must state that all my colleagues, my whole staff, and all the wounded soldiers behaved admirably during those three years of war. This must now seem like a fairy story, since the following disintegration of the government, as well as the proliferation of revolutionary propaganda, caused an abysmal decay of all ethics in the whole nation. As a result of the war, all Germans living on Russian soil—including of course all the members of my German family—were dispossessed and sent to remote regions. The fighting diminished, and there were hardly any wounded needing surgical treatment. The military hospitals set up by Moscow, with their 60,000 beds, were closed. My hospital then had to look after patients suffering from erysipelas, and it later became the distribution center for pulmonary patients who were being sent to health resorts. In 1917 came the disintegration of the front, with chaotic conditions and the destruction of the municipality. For this reason I handed over all the equipment of the hospital to my old, trusted municipal hospital in Basmany, and withdrew to continue my work in the Scientific Institute of the Soviet Union.

Hunger, cold, epidemics, and increasing terror on an incredible scale forced my husband and me to dissolve our marriage in order to avoid the risk of losing our child. The divorce allowed our daughter and me to become German nationals, which alone made it possible for us to leave Russia. My husband and I hoped that the regime would change in six years, at the latest. As we all know now, nothing came of this hope, and my husband and I did not see each other again.

I shall pass over the length of time it took before my daughter and I could finally leave. Our departure was almost prevented at the last minute by guards in the railway carriages. Our journey was a period of suffering lasting almost two months. We traveled via Riga in an empty coal cargo ship *Carbo II* through mine-infested areas to Swinemünde. Later we reached Upper Silesia, Berlin, and finally Frankfurt am Main, where I was told that, to practice, I must pass the German medical-degree examination.

From the autumn of 1921 I worked very hard, and in 1922 I completed two clinical terms. I had to learn 5000 pages in compendium form, as I had to catch up on a fourteen-year scientific gap in all subjects. In the autumn of 1922 I received my medical degree in Frankfurt. I did not have to do a one-year internship, as my former medical activities could be proved and were credited.

At that time, when inflation was developing erratically and permission to open a panel practice was so restricted, it was hopeless for me to attempt it. My brother very kindly offered my daughter and me a home with him in Heidelberg, and there my daughter was put into the school class appropriate for her age, even though she had no knowledge of German. My attempt to be allowed to do voluntary work in the surgical clinic under Privy Councillor Enderlen was refused; a woman was out of the question. Through Professor Neu, a gynecologist whom I assisted for a short time as a substitute, I came into contact with Professor Valentin and his wife. Shortly after that, Dr. Valentin was appointed head physician at the Anna Foundation in Hannover. The Anna Foundation was at that time the second largest orthopedic clinic in Germany. In January 1925 I went to Hannover as first assistant and the head physician's deputy. To my intimate knowledge of surgery of the extremities I added experience in the broader area of orthopedics, which at that time encompassed the gravest results of poliomyelitis, osteomyelitis, bone and joint tuberculosis, and congenital deformity. In 1930 I opened my own practice as an orthopedic specialist in Hannover. I had just paid the last installments on the necessary equipment when the bombs began to fall.

In 1943, in a major air attack on Hannover, I suffered the total loss of my office, as well as of my home. I reported for duty in Goslar, where I was made deputy to the head physician of the surgical ward in the municipal hospital. From 1944 to 1955 I had an orthopedic panel practice in Goslar. I then returned to Hannover for three reasons: first, the population of Goslar, although increased by the war, was decreasing in the postwar years; second, the living conditions were unfavorable; and third, my gifted granddaughter needed better educational possibilities. Once again I had to build up a new orthopedic practice, and these were difficult years. In 1958 on my seventy-fifth birthday I had a surprise. The Hannover newspaper *Allgemeine* published "Annotations to a Golden Hat" (a charming idea by the famous and popular author Erna Doant). "Doctor Elsa Winokurow, Hannover, has been a medical doctor for fifty years!" A flood of congratulations came. From Bonn there came a renewed certificate of my doctor's diploma, and I received congratulations from the German orthopedic association, from the Goslar medical association, from the Panel Doctor's Union of Hannover, and from the German Women Doctor's Association (founded by Dr. H. Edenhuizen). All this moved me deeply. The day ended in gay celebration, with my dear colleagues and my small family surrounding me, Chopin's "Polonaise" sounding through all the rooms, everyone drinking tea around the samovar, and the German Medical Women's Association presenting me with a charming, amusing poem and a gold hat with double contents. In 1961 I handed over my practice to a fellow specialist.

Looking back on my professional life, I must say that an educated woman was shown more comradeship and courtesy in Russia than in Germany. I would like to emphasize here how grateful I am to Professor Valentin for his decision to accept me, a woman, as his colleague.

I fear for my second home, Germany, and the road its youth are taking into the future. Men lead the world. Whither are they leading it? This leadership is one-sided and will not work.

Toni von Langsdorff
b. September 30, 1884

I am a little embarrassed by the request of the Medical Women's International Association that I contribute to this study. On one hand, I can no longer fully rely on my memory—I am ninety—and besides, I have never been much of a writer. But on the other hand, I feel an obligation to help preserve the knowledge of certain facts and developments that may perhaps be of importance to coming generations.

I was the eldest of four children. My father was an officer in the Prussian army, and my ancestors were mainly men of learning—theologians, physicians, and jurists. Special mention may be made of a scientist who took part in great expeditions. Perhaps I inherited from him some of the daring that was necessary for a young woman to study medicine and become a doctor at the beginning of this century.

Being an officer, father was often transferred from one district to another, which meant new homes, new schools, and not many permanent friends. I don't remember any person except my mother who influenced me much during my adolescence. After the birth of her third child, mother was not in good health, but she had exceptional willpower and self-discipline and was a highly cultured, open-minded, and well-read woman.

It was from her that I first learned about the new ideas regarding higher education for women. These ideas, expounded at the turn of the century by such women as Helene Lange, Gertrud Bäumer, and Franziska Tiburtinus, moved women's minds and fitted in with my own urge for independence. The prospect of either having to wait for a man to marry me or living the life of a dependent single woman without work of my own was unbearable to me. As a child, I often drove my family and our domestic staff to despair because I did not allow them to lead or even touch me in the street. My desire for independence later on must also have caused my parents a great deal of trouble and anxiety.

Against all conventions, I was determined to have a career that would render me independent. My choice of the medical profession may be related to the facts that mother was chronically ill and one of my sisters at the age of six had contracted tuberculosis from a maid, and had been confined to bed for years. After several operations my sister was finally cured, but she was left with a considerable handicap. I witnessed pain and grief every day, and the doctor was a frequent visitor at our house. Thus the figure of the doctor, whose mission it is to help and cure, must have become the model on which I shaped the plans for my future work.

My wish to study medicine met with no difficulties at home. Mother supported me, and father had no objections, though he was exposed to the derision and disapproval of his colleagues. Outside my family I encountered an utter lack of comprehension; this of course led to a certain degree of isolation, which was painful for me at that age.

The difficulties of preparing for a university education were enormous. First, it was necessary to have passed the *Abitur*, or matriculation examination. It was possible to take this examination only after nine years at a gymnasium, or secondary school, but at that time no gymnasium accepted girls as pupils. My only option was the difficult and expensive path of private tutoring.

It was a piece of good luck that my father was transferred to Cologne just as I finished at a so-called girl's high school, which provided a general education up to the age of sixteen. In Cologne some interested women had formed a group whose aim it was to encourage and to support financially those girls who wished to take up university studies.

A preparatory course was arranged for five female participants. It was only with great difficulty that a few grammar school teachers were found who were willing to teach us. Most educators considered it beneath their dignity to teach girls, who they believed had an "inferior" intellect, such subjects as Greek, Latin, and mathematics, which were generally reserved for the "superior" male mind. Our lessons did not prove to be quite satisfactory, as the teachers demanded either too much, making our courses very hard, or too little, making our final examinations more difficult.

In order for me to remember what I had already learned but was no longer being taught in this preparatory course, my parents sent me to additional classes at the girl's high school in Cologne. If ever I had difficulties, it was there. The headmaster thought that my studying Latin elsewhere was an insult and a provocation, and he did everything he could to make life still more difficult for me and to find some reason to expel me. He took me for a revolutionary element, doing harm to his school. Once he even went so far as to tell my mother that in my case he would like to follow the lesson in the Bible that says, "If thy right eye offends thee, pluck it out, and cast it from thee." This incident shows clearly the impediments that had to be overcome by those seeking new ways in the education of women.

The finals, the so-called *Abitur*, turned out to be especially hard, as we girls were sent to a school in another town, the Emperor Charlemagne Gymnasium, at Aix-la-Chapelle and were examined under entirely different circumstances. Our reception there was disheartening. We were greeted with the words, "Oh, that it should be our fate to be examiners of girls!" This hostile attitude made me lose my head; I failed so badly in the written examination that the examiners were not willing to admit me to the orals. It took the personal intervention of one of my former teachers to have me admitted. Happily, I passed and was awarded the *Abitur*.

On May 1, 1905, I began my studies at Bonn University because that city was closest to my parents' home. I had not known at that time that Prussia, the state in which Bonn was located, did not allow the enrollment of women as full students. They were only allowed as visiting students or observers. Thus if you wished to attend a lecture, you had to ask the professor for his permission in advance.

During my first semester in anatomy I was the only woman. The course caused me some trouble not only because of the new subject but because I was not accustomed to studying with men, the majority of whom were hostile toward the "female intruder." Paradoxically enough, the gravest annoyance came from the director of the Institute of Anatomy, a courteous old gentleman who hoped for an amorous adventure with me. I decided that I had to leave Bonn in spite of the advantages I might have had through his favor.

I left for Heidelberg because in the southern state of Germany in which this city was located, women who were matriculated were accorded equal rights. However, this equality had not yet been fully realized, as I was to learn by painful experience later on, during my final examinatin in medicine. Female students were more numerous here, and I was no longer so isolated. There were even lodgings for women, and we were not treated like lepers.

In 1908 Prussia granted full matriculation to women, so I decided to attend Marburg University. There, quite unexpectedly, I met with further difficulties because the professors who were against women studying at a university had the right to refuse them permission to attend their lectures. Each woman had to apply in person for such permission. The attitude of the general public in Marburg toward female students followed suit. We could hardly get rooms; the male students often behaved most rudely toward us; and we were exposed to general suspicion, disapproval, and dislike. At Marburg I made the acquaintance of an official of the police department in charge of public morals. He came to my room one day, evidently as a result of some denunciation! My genuine perplexity must have been convincing, for he soon left.

In the autumn of 1908 I passed my preliminary medical examination in basic sciences at Marburg, despite the prejudiced examiners. I then returned to Heidelberg, where I hoped to find relief from the oppressive atmosphere in which I had been compelled to live and work. I made friends with male and female students and no longer led a life of isolation.

At this time I took part in a competition arranged by the department of internal medicine. My essay got high praise and acknowledgement, but I never saw it again in spite of my efforts to retrieve it. I was told that my paper and some others had been lost during renovation work in the institute. I do not know whether this loss was a result of carelessness or intent, but it was a painful experience for me, since I had planned to use the essay as the basis for my doctoral thesis.

On the whole, the final medical examination went all right. The leading ophthalmologist was a fierce enemy of women students. He treated me very badly, but despite his antagonism, I passed. In general, a change of attitude regarding women students had taken place at the university in southern Germany. In May of 1910 I finished my university studies and earned my doctor's degree.

Before I could get a medical license, however, it was necessary for me to work for one year as a medical assistant in a hospital. From May to August I made every possible effort to find such a position but received only negative replies. Thanks to the energetic support and recommendation of the professor under whom I had worked for my doctorate, I was given a job at the municipal clinic in Essen. This marked the beginning of a hard but at any rate normal professional career. The present generation can scarcely conceive of the mental and physical strength it took to achieve my goal.

I should like to mention another great disappointment because the incident is typical of the difficulties that again and again barred the way of women doctors who had long since finished their training and were already established in the profession. After seven years at the Essen gynecological clinic, I settled down in a practice of my own, as a specialist in gynecology and obstetrics. Shortly thereafter, the gynecologist at another hospital died. My former chief advised me to apply for the vacancy and supported my application. The hospital board agreed that I should have the position; however, the surgeon of the hospital declared that he had no objections to me as a person but that he could not be expected to work on the same level with a woman! If I were given the position, he would resign. This being the alternative, the decision in my favor was reversed.

Gradually I was accepted as a doctor by the population of Essen, and I must say it is with satisfaction that I look back on the many years I was able to enjoy a private medical practice—up to the age of eighty.

Helena Klein

b. January 14, 1885

Why did I become a doctor? This is not the easiest question in the world to answer. When I was still a young girl, I knew I wanted to be "somebody," not just to stay at home and wait for my fate to be decided for me. At first I thought of becoming a teacher, but I gave up the idea when I realized I did not have the kind of patience required for such work.

My father, Professor G. Klein, was the chief rabbi in Stockholm and was an internationally recognized scholar in the field of comparative religion. My mother was the daughter of a professor at the old and distinguished German University of Breslau. My parents had six children, of whom I was the third. Mother used to read to us children. Once, when she was reading Viktor Rydberg's *Singoalla* to my brothers and sister, I overheard her from my bed in an adjoining room. The light was out, but the door was ajar as a concession to my fear of the dark. I was about six or seven at the time. Mother was reading the horrible part of the story in which Aslak murders Scapegrace. He turns the body over to make sure the boy is really dead. Suddenly a ray of light illuminates the body he believes to be Scapegrace's, but instead it is the corpse of a man of his own tribe, dead of the pestilence. The Great Plague has come! This was an intensely vivid scene, which I can still visualize and recall. I was terrified, and for a long time afterward, I used to inspect my body to see whether any buboes had developed on it. I have often wondered if this interest in the body and its diseases had any significance in my choice of the medical profession.

From the age of about six I attended a school in Stockholm owned and operated by two sisters, Marie and Ida Salmonsson. The school had a total of only twenty students, from children to young teenagers. From there I moved into the coeducational Whitlock School, where I remained for seven years, until I was ready to matriculate for university studies. This school was very progressive, as evidenced by the fact that it introduced sex education as early as 1900. I took my matriculation in 1903 as a private candidate in the sciences, and I passed the final examination in Latin, which was a requirement for medical education, in 1904.

While I had not been absolutely sure of my choice of profession until that time, I now knew that I wanted to study medicine. At that time premedical training within the faculty of philosophy at either Uppsala or Lund was a prerequisite for medical studies. The required subjects were zoology, chemistry, physics, and botany, and the period of study varied between two and four semesters. I successfully completed the courses within one year and began my medical studies at the University of Uppsala in 1905.

I completed the "candidate in medicine" (basic science) requirements in 1910, having lost two spring semesters due to illness. The theoretical part of my studies caused me considerable difficulty, since I had concentration problems. But when the practical clinical training began, I realized that I had made the right choice. The diagnostic and therapeutic aspects—working with patients—were exactly what I was looking for and gave me immense satisfaction.

The time had now come to leave Uppsala, where everything had been so positive, especially my circle of friends. And in those days student life was very active and stimulating. We organized dance clubs, student balls, sleigh rides, and Sunday hikes and excursions in the countryside, the activities that I perhaps enjoyed most of all. We also did a great deal of community work in addition to our studies. For example, I was secretary of the student teetotaler association for several years and was also a member of Verdandi, which was a student political association.

I now returned to Stockholm, where I earned my medical degree in 1916. During the intervening years I had held several substitute positions in hospitals. As a qualified physician in 1916, I was acting physician-in-chief at Stora Ekbergs Sanatorium for about ten months. Since women were then not eligible for the position of physician-in-chief, my permission to take this responsibility had to be renewed every two months. After working in the department of internal medicine at Sabbatsberg Hospital in Stockholm, where I was finally able to get the special training that I required, I opened a practice in Stockholm, as a specialist in diseases of the digestive tract and the lungs. This was an unusual combination in those days.

I was not particularly interested in private practice, having been spoiled by the more efficient working conditions in a hospital. Thus, when the position of physician-in-chief at the Garphyttan Sanatorium became available, I decided to apply, partly because I wanted to find out how they would react, since no woman had ever been given a permanent position at this level. Suffice it to say that I was summoned to the minister for social welfare, after which meeting I was sure that my goose was cooked. But several weeks later the minister himself telephoned me. "Congratulations, Doctor!" he said. "The government has appointed you physician-in-chief of the Garphyttan Sanatorium, contrary to the recommendation of the board of directors."

There I remained for twenty-four years, on the whole very happy working years. I have now been pensioned for twenty-five years.

During my entire tenure as physician-in-chief I was a dispensary officer, first for a local dispensary and later for the region of Vasternarke. I was regional school doctor for a number of years, and in addition, in the 1930s and 1940s, I was X-ray consultant for the Bofors Company in silicosis and did studies on men working with dangerous quartz molds.

During my first years at Garphyttan I lectured to the student nurses and other groups. I gave talks on tuberculosis throughout the province. Lectures on dietary problems were also in demand, since the vitamin theory was then relatively new and there was a great need for information and education on the subject.

I gave numerous speeches to women's organizations on a variety of topics, including the problems of aging; addressed several meetings of the Örebro Medical Association; and published a number of medical papers.

In 1937 I founded a Red Cross chapter in Garphyttan and served as its president for seventeen years. I was one of the founders of a branch of the International Federation of Business and Professional Women in Örebro and was its president for the first ten years of its existence.

Janet Aitken
b. January 3, 1886

I was born in Buenos Aires of Scottish parents, and I had four sisters, one older and three younger than myself. I had an exceptionally happy childhood, since I adored my father and was spoiled by my elder sister. She and I were close friends, as we were nearer in age to each other than we were to the other three. My father shipped goods to Argentina, and I recall—although this seems quite astonishing today—that his transactions were all carried out without any signed agreement. It was a matter of father's honor and the other party's honor, and no one cheated. My only memories of Argentina are of a large tree in the garden and a man who looked after us and spoke Spanish.

We came home to England and settled in Lancashire in 1890. We were well-to-do, and there was no talk of taking up any career. Three of my sisters married, and the youngest, whom we all loved greatly, died at the age of seventeen years from rheumatic heart disease.

I enjoyed music and played the piano well, so well that my older sister liked to show me off. I remember we had a woman general practitioner for the family, but I had no interest whatever in medicine. I went to St. Leonard's School, St. Andrew's, in 1899 and enjoyed it immensely. I had no worry about leaving home, as my sister was also at the school. I became captain and head of house.

I continued my interest in music and received my L.R.A.M. (piano) in 1905. Then I went to Paris to study French and singing under a pupil of the famous Mme. Marchese. Eventually I attended Manchester College of Music to study under Mme. Fillunger, a friend of Schumann's, and there I was awarded the gold medal for singing. In 1913 I left for London and started a singing career. I had quite a few engagements including that of soloist at Queen's Hall (in the Promenade Concerts of those days).

When war broke out in 1914, I felt I must do something to help and decided to become a masseur. All the young men of our acquaintance were in the armed services, and I lost many friends. Some were wounded and in need of treatment, and this greatly influenced me in my decision to change my profession. The newspapers were also full of the news that young men doctors were being killed and that women doctors would be needed. I passed the examination of the Incorporated Society of Masseurs and became very interested in anatomy and physiology. It was then that I decided to change my career again and to become a doctor.

I was twenty-eight years of age. I consulted Professor Cullis of the London School of Medicine for Women, and she encouraged me to go ahead. By then my father had died and my sisters had married and had families. There was no discouragement from anyone. My higher certificate did not include Latin or science subjects; so I feared that I might find academic work difficult. However, I attended a "crammer" and passed my matriculation easily. I did not find my age any handicap, and I qualified in 1922, at thirty-six years of age.

My original intention had been to become a gynecologist, but while I was house physician at the Elizabeth Garrett Anderson Hospital, I decided that I would rather be an internist. I had a particular interest in rheumatic hearts, as my youngest sister had died of this disease.

I did general practice for two years, and this was a good idea for a consultant physician. Nowadays, however, there are infinitely more elaborate investigations with which one must become familiar as a consultant, so that it is impossible to take the time for general practice. Meanwhile I kept up some hospital work, as what was then called a clinical assistant at the Elizabeth Garrett Anderson Hospital and at the Heart Hospital. I acquired my M.D. in 1924 and my M.R.C.P. (Member of the Royal College of Physicians) in 1926. I was then appointed physician to Elizabeth Garrett Anderson Hospital and later to Princess Louise Hospital for Children, as well as to the Mother's Hospital (Salvation Army).

During the 1919 war for Irish independence I was in charge at the E.G.A. Hospital casualty clearing station. The comradeship between people in all walks of life at that time was a wonderful and unique experience. Any patients needing more than the minimum of X-ray and pathological advice had to be sent out of London; so for five or six years, at a time when medical advances were rapid, I was doing little but administration. This altered the direction of my career, so that after the war I was on the management committees of four hospitals. I was also on the Central Health Services Council of the Ministry of Health and was the first woman to be elected by the profession to sit on the General Medical Council.

I joined the Medical Women's International Association (MWIA) after the war and became honorary secretary in 1950 and president from 1958 to 1962. I had a most interesting trip around the world on the way to the MWIA congress in the Philippines in 1962, during my presidency. I met doctors, mainly women from many lands. In San Francisco I was invited to talk about the MWIA on television. We visited Japan, Saigon, India, Beirut, and many other places. In Manila we were treated most royally, going about in cars with police outriders escorting us and dining with the president of the country. I was then approaching the end of my active life.

I have always had warm family relationships, and I am very interested in the careers of the younger members; they live in such a different world from the one in which I grew up. I think that medicine is a very satisfying career for a woman. I realize that there are difficulties for the married woman doctor with children, but these problems can be solved.

I have no regrets whatever over changing my career from music to medicine. I suppose the real reasons for my becoming a doctor were the death of my sister, the interest I discovered in anatomy and physiology when learning to be a masseur to help in World War I, and finally, the desire to help other women in a way that I found interesting.

Now I am over ninety years of age and can walk easily only with two canes. My friends come to see me, and I have a lovely flat with huge windows through which I can see the superb elms, oaks, and limes of Regent's Park.

Frieda Baumann
b. April 28, 1887

My mother, Ida E. Hooker, was a descendant of Reverend Thomas Hooker, who had settled in Hartford, Connecticut. She met my father, a young lawyer named Anthony Baumann, when he was teaching in Pennsylvania. He taught evening courses in German and Spanish, and mother and her friend Eliza Boyce attended his class. He told them that the best way to learn conversational German was to go to a German church. After class mother asked him if his wife would take them to a German church. His reply was, "I have no wife." He, of course, took them himself the next Sunday.

A year later my mother and father were married, and they moved to Scranton, where my father established a practice in law. My brother Carl, a horticulturist and landscape architect, now ninety years old, still lives there. I was born two and a half years later. We lived next door to Dr. Ludwig Wehlau, father's best friend, whose daughter graduated from the Woman's Medical College of Pennsylvania in 1906. Alma Wehlau inspired me, and I decided to study medicine when I was about sixteen years old.

Later we moved to Elmhurst, about ten miles from Scranton, because father wished our family to grow up where we could become familiar with nature. On Saturdays and Sundays he spent much time with us, working out of doors. By this time I had a younger sister Hilda, and we were each responsible for our own little garden patch. We had horses and cows, three large Newfoundland dogs, a little black terrier, and a number of cats.

There was only a country school nearby, so mother was our teacher from kindergarten until I was about eight years old, when father was taken ill with what was diagnosed as "heart disease" and, in order to obtain good medical care for him, we moved back to Scranton. There we went to school. By this time father had only a limited legal practice, with his office at home, where he died in 1900. Mother then moved to Mansfield and became an associate principal in the Model School of the Mansfield State Teachers' College. We children went to the public school until I was sixteen, when I was admitted as a freshman to the teachers' college.

After finishing normal school in 1906, I went to Lancaster County and taught at the Walnut Run Country School for a year. The following year I taught in Shinglehouse, and the third year I went to Punxatawney and taught fifth-grade and high-school English and history. I established self-government in my fifth-grade class, and the children did a wonderful job while I went to teach the advanced classes in the same building.

In those days it was difficult to find summer work and the school term was only eight months. I could not ask mother to care for me all summer, so I found a full-time teaching position at the Pennsylvania State Reformatory at Morganza. The superintendent asked me to select thirty girls to be moved to a new cottage that was being built, where they would have more freedom, variety in their dress, and activity, both social and scholastic. This proved to be a wonderful success. After two years at the cottage, I was made first parole officer for Western Pennsylvania. I placed the girls and followed them after their discharge. Only a couple of my girls returned for a second term.

Soon I felt that I needed to study, since I did not know enough about social conditions to function adequately. On investigating schools of social service, I discovered that there were few in 1911 and that there was little evidence of Christian teaching. A returned Baptist medical missionary drew my attention to the Baptist Institute, now Cushing Junior College. I attended that school for one year and then decided to study medicine, since the girls I had been working with needed physical, as well as spiritual, health.

In the fall of 1913 I entered the Woman's Medical College of Pennsylvania and graduated cum laude in 1917 in a class of seventeen, four of whom became members of the college faculty after postgraduate study. Two of my classmates and I went to the New York Infirmary for Women and Children for our internships. After that I consulted Dr. James Alexander Miller, chief of the tuberculosis service, Columbia division, at Bellevue Hospital, as I was interested in lung diseases. I was given an internship in his service, and in three months was made chief resident. I served there for eighteen months.

Since an internship in Pennsylvania was required if I wished to practice in Scranton, I became surgical resident at Scranton State Hospital. During my first operation the chief surgeon asked, "Are you Anthony Baumann's daughter?" I said, "I am." Then he said, "I was your doctor when you were a little girl." Although I planned to become a specialist in internal medicine, I was glad to have three months of surgery as basic preparation.

In the fall of 1920 I came to Philadelphia to take the Pennsylvania State Board examinations. While walking up North College Avenue on my way to visit the college, I met Ella Everitt, professor of gynecology and she said, "Frieda, are you coming back? We need teachers, and you have a good teaching background." Thus, at her suggestion, I saw the dean. I was appointed instructor in internal medicine and later was made assistant professor of medicine and associate professor of applied therapeutics. This led to my appointment first as professor of therapeutics and then professor of medicine in charge of nutrition and metabolism. During all this time I was an attending physician in the medical wards at the college hospital, and for two years I was with Ward Brinton in the tuberculosis division at Philadelphia General Hospital. I retired at the age limit in 1952. This same year I was made Hannah E. Longshore Professor of Medicine at the Woman's Medical College of Pennsylvania and the first woman president of the medical-department staff of Philadelphia General Hospital.

From 1923 to 1963 I practiced internal medicine in Philadelphia and its suburbs. I was associated with Emily Bacon, professor of pediatrics, and we had an apartment above the offices. In 1925 Jean Crump, who had graduated in 1923, became Emily Bacon's assistant in pediatrics and joined us in our office. While establishing my practice in Philadelphia, I worked as physician for the Bell Telephone Company of Pennsylvania. One day I was assigned to examine the president of A.T.&T. for New York City. Not knowing who he was, I treated him as I would any other employee of the Bell System and gave him some definite instructions concerning his health. A few days later I was asked to become a member of the A.T.&T. medical department, in the Bourse Building in Philadelphia.

In 1950 the Medical Women's International Association (MWIA) met in Philadelphia, and I was asked to take charge of the housing and entertainment of all the visiting physicians. Volunteers from the Woman's Medical College faculty and alumnae acted as hosts. Our guests were short of funds, as World War II had drained Europe of money. The president of the MWIA was Charlotte Ruys, from Holland. I met many physicians from England, Europe, and elsewhere, as thirty countries were represented. When Jean Crump and I spent six weeks abroad in 1956, we were entertained by many of these MWIA colleagues.

I was president of the Beta chapter of the Zeta Phi medical fraternity and national president, following Anna Quincy Churchill of Boston. We had very active chapters at Johns Hopkins, Syracuse University, and the University of Toronto. The women's medical fraternities were very important in my early days, since we were not yet well accepted in the men's organizations and had fewer opportunities to socialize in medicine and to express our opinions.

The Student Health Department of the Woman's Medical College of Pennsylvania was established under Ellen Potter in 1923. When Dr. Potter was appointed head of the state medical department, I was made physician for the students at the college. Our dean Dr. Tracy and I were much interested in preventive medicine, and she obtained money from Washington to help us build up a program. Each student was required to have a physical examination. During this service I treated students having such serious conditions as acute meningitis, pneumonia, and tuberculosis. The department has always functioned well and the students are well supervised. I found that the average student patient had difficulty meeting hospital bills, and I established a fund from which they could borrow. This fund is now available to alumnae physicians of the college. Since the advent of Blue Cross and Blue Shield, the fund is not much needed, although it is still available.

In 1957, when Ada Cree Reed retired as editor of the *Journal of the American Medical Women's Association*, I became editor and served for five years. At the American Medical Women's Association meeting in New Orleans in

1970, I was given the Elizabeth Blackwell Award for "steadfast leadership and life-long service to medicine." In 1967 the Commonwealth Committee of the Woman's Medical College of Pennsylvania presented me with the award for distinguished teaching.

Over these many years, many young women and men physicians—not only students, but interns, residents, and assistants—have inspired me to do what I could to show young people the opportunities of service to the human race that are open to doctors of medicine.

Tamayo Tetsuo
b. January 21, 1888

I was born in Japan, the youngest of three children of the chief Buddhist priest in Okayama Prefecture. When my elder sister was enrolled in grammar school, I went to school with her every day, so naturally, we became second-graders together. When I was fifteen years of age, my teacher advised me to enter the Okayama Prefectural Teacher's School for Girls. After graduating from that school three years later, I became a teacher and taught at the Seion Girl's School. Soon afterward, my parents moved to Kuchinozu, so I was transferred to the grammar school there.

At that time my elder brother had opened his practice in medicine and ophthalmology, and my sister was married to a gynecologist in Nagasaki. The medical care and sanitation situation was very poor in this part of the country, and many mothers died during childbirth. When I saw these conditions, I felt the only way to solve the situation and help the people was to become a doctor. My parents and family were opposed to these aspirations, as it was a profession believed to be too difficult for women. They proposed that I marry instead. Nevertheless, I spent my nights secretly studying in preparation for the examinations. When the time came, I notified my parents that I was set on going to Tokyo to study medicine. They were still opposed, but they changed their minds when they saw how serious I was. They gave me their blessings and encouraged me to study hard and become a good doctor, and they also offered financial support.

I was admitted to the much longed for Dr. Yayoi Yoshioka's Tokyo Women's Medical School in April of 1914. Of course I studied very hard, but I also had the rare opportunity to be with Dr. Yayoi Yoshioka and to learn from her the many aspects of a medical life.

Dr. Yoshioka was a very busy woman, but despite this, she always had a smile and was courteous to everyone. In her home she was a good wife and mother, but in the outside world she always worked for the betterment not only of women doctors but of all women and all people. I always admired her way of life. She made long-range decisions promptly and with good sense. She was a wonderful woman.

After graduating from the Tokyo Women's Medical School, in 1918, I entered the gynecological department of the Tokyo Imperial University for further studies. Then, in 1919, I volunteered for charity work in the Buddhist Medical Hospital in Azabu and became chief of the gynecological department there.

In June of 1920 I started practice and, together with my husband and brother, established the Tetsuo General Hospital, in Kuchinozu. My husband was in charge of surgery and dermatology, my brother of internal medicine and ophthalmology, and I of gynecology and obstetrics.

There were only two gynecologists in this region, which had a population of 10,000 inhabitants, so we were always busy. At that time I noticed that certain special conditions affected pregnancy in this area, and I concentrated my studies on them.

With the help of the practicing doctors I established the Kuchinozu School for Midwives and Nurses in 1927, and twenty pupils graduated within a year. When World War II started, the school was closed.

I had always lived according to the principles of keeping my mind and body healthy and of then doing my best for the welfare of the people. I also worked industriously for various women's organizations. After the war, especially during the transition from imperialism to democracy, there was an opportunity to try to elevate the status and position of women, so I did medical work during the daytime and occupied myself with the Japanese Medical Women's Association (JMWA) at night.

Also, during and after the war, because of the shortage of food, I became interested in the general health of the people, in nutrition for infants, in the prevention of infectious diseases, and in the early detection of cancer. During this period the economic condition of Japan was so poor that many people could not afford an education for their children. I tried to help some of them by contributing anonymously to their schooling and it is a joy to see these children in their later years, in their well-established lives. I have also contributed as much as I could to the village educational fund.

In 1923 I became the school doctor for the Kuchika High School and continued for thirty-nine years, until 1962. I have also done voluntary service for the Kuchinozu Red Cross, and I have served as president of the JMWA for nearly forty years.

My participation as one of the delegates to the 1960 congress of the Medical Women's International Association in Germany remains a vivid memory in my life. There were nineteen of us in our group, and we visited Denmark, Holland, England, France, and Germany.

On October 31, 1968, I was chosen as the first Honorary Citizen of Kuchinozu, and on the emperor's birthday in 1969, I was awarded the Sixth Order of the Sacred Treasure from the government, much to my surprise and elation.

In October of 1969 I suddenly took ill. I have therefore decreased my activities and resigned from various organizations.

I received the Cultural Award from the Nagasaki newspaper in November of 1973. In April of 1974 the beautiful bronze bust of myself, made by our famous sculptor Seiho Kitamura, was unveiled with great ceremony, and it received much praise. This was a gift to me from the JMWA.

I am deeply grateful to all the people for the happy life I am living as I reach my eighty-eighth birthday, and the bronze bust from my colleagues and friends will bask in the sunshine forever.

SWEDEN

Johanna Hellman
b. June 14, 1889

I was born in Nuremberg, Germany, on June 14, 1889. Both my parents came from Franken, where my mother's family had settled around 1600. My father was a businessman, kind and intelligent, a person whose good advice was sought by many. My mother was a capable homemaker who was deeply concerned with the fate of her relatives. She was especially attached to her two brothers, both bachelors, who, apart from running their leather business, supported the arts. My uncles played an important part in my childhood. The younger had a well-known coin collection, and the other had a large picture gallery. The atmosphere in our middle-class home was warm and congenial, and the education of the two girls (myself and my sister, five years younger) was an important issue.

I first attended a public school for girls, which I disliked profoundly. After five years, however, I transferred to a private school, where I soon felt happy and became a first-rate pupil. For many years, a close friendship bound me to the principal, Miss Lohman. My mother has told me that I started operating on my dolls at the age of eight. My sister clearly remembers us making incisions into the abdomen of the dolls. I soon found out that the papier-mâché was readily treatable when water was infused through the doll's mouth.

When, at the age of fourteen, I was confronted with the choice of a career, I decided at once to seek a university education, a decision rather unusual for a girl at the turn of the century. My parents' opposition was soon dissipated by the strong backing of my uncle Kromwell. Since no college for girls existed in Nuremberg, I had to leave for Munich, where I spent four years in the home of a teacher's family. In 1909 I passed the matriculation at a boys' school. In the meantime I had read and heard a great deal about conditions in South-West Africa, and the need of the poor black peoples for medical help impressed me so much that I decided to study medicine.

The best opportunities for the study of anatomy were offered in Berlin, and there I went. Professor Virchow's lectures attracted a large crowd of students, both women and men—but dissection courses for male and female students had to be strictly separate. After one and a half years I moved to Kiel. Out of sheer

33

curiosity I attended a lecture in surgery, and it struck me immediately that surgery was my goal. Although only in my third semester, I called on the director of the University Surgical Hospital to express my wish to work in his clinic. His assistant rejected me with a sarcastic remark, but Professor Anschütz understood the seriousness of my arguments and reluctantly agreed to try me out, still stressing the fact that a woman surgeon had no future whatever. From then on, until 1928, I spent all my time continuing my medical training and devoting every free moment to work in the hospital. For my later activity it was to my great advantage that, in the beginning, I was asked to help the ward nurses and thus received experience in all aspects of patient care. If I had to plan the education of physicians, I would make such work compulsory within the basic training in order that doctors would have a better understanding not only of disease but also of a sick person.

In 1914, with the outbreak of World War I, most assistants were drafted, but I remained at the university surgical hospital. I passed my final licensing examination, wrote my doctoral thesis, and at the same time worked in various wards, taking care of the director's private patients and receiving the soldiers in the infirmary affiliated with the hospital. Together with the head surgeon I was allowed to perform major operations, and I obtained a first-class education in surgery, urology, and orthopedics. Since the chief surgeon was in addition the head of the X-ray department, I also came into close contact with this section, and after a few years, I was able to replace the head technician and later the medical chief of the X-ray clinic. From 1921 through 1929 I spent most vacations as a substitute for the heads of various municipal hospitals. The time at the district hospital in Hameln is among my happiest memories. In 1920, I joined the Northwest German Surgical Society, and in 1925 I became the first female member of the German Society for Surgery.

It was a general rule that the assistants in university hospitals had to live in the hospital proper. Thus, for fifteen years, I lived in almost conventlike seclusion in the Kiel University Surgical Hospital. I wish to mention a perhaps unequaled experience that I had during this time. In 1916 a young woman was hospitalized, fatally ill, bringing along her three month old baby, whom she was nursing. After her death, nobody knew what to do with this child, whose father was at the front. I was bold enough to take the baby to my room, and with the nurses' help and the "closed eyes" of the director, I managed to foster her during the following five years. I became so closely attached to the little person that it was a terrible blow when the father, some time after his return home, rightly claimed his daughter and I was not able to adopt her.

In 1929 I accepted the position of a surgeon in a private hospital in Berlin. This work did not appeal to me, and I was not happy again until the director of the university outpatient clinic, the Charité, called for me. I held the position of Professor Sauerbruch's assistant until 1933. During vacations I acted as a substitute in the municipal hospitals of Lauben and Warmbrunn until I opened my own private practice in Berlin, as a specialist in surgery, urology, and roentgenology. I had applied for top positions in various Berlin municipal hospitals but had been advised to visit the representatives of the political parties. To my amazement, they inquired into my political views and party affiliation and did not pay much attention to my medical abilities. To my mind, the only imperative task of a medical doctor is to cure patients, irrespective of party affiliation. The politicians disapproved of my response, and my name was deleted from the lists of applicants. In 1932 I became the director of the Hospital of the Salvation Army in Berlin, a position I held until 1938, when I had to resign as a consequence of the Nazi discrimination laws.

I understood that I had to prepare for emigration. The decision was painful and beyond my comprehension. How could I be forced to leave my homeland, where my family had lived for more than three centuries? I investigated the possibilities of emigrating to Britain, Sweden, and the United States. Then, while I was visiting my sister in Copenhagen, World War II broke out and it was definitely unfeasible for me to return to Germany. Friends of my sister then brought me to Sweden. As a refugee, I accepted the hospitality of Commander Larssen, the chief of the Salvation Army. I was granted a permit to stay in Sweden but was refused permission to work in my field. It was hard to be confined to a life outside a hospital, not being allowed to practice. I spent the time learning the Swedish language and taking care of other peoples' children. When, in 1940, a fourth child was born to one of these families, I took the baby girl completely to my heart and her family left her upbringing and education to me. Many years later I adopted her, and she and her child are the joy of my old age.

In 1944 I was given the assistantship in the surgical hospital of Eskilstuna, and for a while I felt happy to be back in familiar surroundings. The Swedish law at that time allowed foreigners to keep a position only as long as no Swedish citizen applied. I obtained a Swedish citizenship in 1945. A year earlier I had been given permission to treat refugees, but not until 1947 was I authorized to have a general surgical practice. During the following years my private practice was no bed of roses. Referrals of patients from Swedish colleagues were rare, and the fact that I was a woman surgeon was not greatly appreciated.

Despite many difficulties I slowly succeeded in building up a considerable practice and finding many good friends. In 1950 I bought a house in Lidingö, with a garden in which I work to my heart's delight. There, as well as in my office in downtown Stockholm, I can receive patients. Since 1952 I have also worked as medical consultant and confidential medical officer for the German embassy, which involves extensive activity in connection with the rehabilitation and restitution program. In this way I have had a new chance to help people in distress. A few years ago the municipality of Lidingö appointed me doctor for the community teachers. Thus, at the time of this writing, at 86 years of age, I am still active in my profession.

Helena Kagan
b. September 25, 1889

I was born in Tashkent, Uzbekistan, Asia, to a Jewish family. My father was an engineer and the director of a large glass industry. When he was required to convert to Christianity, he refused and resigned from his position. For a time this caused a very difficult financial situation for the family. My parents were, however, always able to pay for my education and that of my older brother. I went through school in Tashkent up to matriculation at sixteen years of age, in 1905.

As far back as I can remember, I wanted to become a doctor. I wanted to do something for humanity. My mother wished me to study music, which, she believed, would leave more time for my future life. My father felt that I should choose whatever profession I desired. I was always particularly interested in biology, and my scientific heroes were Paul Ehrlich and H. Sahli.

When I was sixteen, my mother took me to Bern, Switzerland, to study medicine, but as I was too young to be registered in the medical school, I simply attended the premedical courses at no cost, and registered at the academy of music. I graduated in medicine from Bern University at twenty-one and continued there for four more years of graduate studies in pediatrics. Then, at twenty-five, I proceeded to Jerusalem, which at that time belonged to the Ottoman Empire. Under Ottoman rule no medical woman was given a license to practice medicine. This was however, 1914 and the beginning of World War I. There was a typhus epidemic, and nurses were badly needed at the Jerusalem Municipal Hospital. When the French nuns departed, I was given the job of training Jewish and Arab girls as nurses. I was also allowed to assist the doctor who made the evening and night rounds. After the death of the physician who headed the typhus ward, the cholera ward, and the prison hospital, I was temporarily appointed to take care of all these jobs.

During this period Dr. Omar Nasha Bey came from Constantinople on an inspection tour of the Near East. He was so impressed with my clinical achievements that, when he returned home, he arranged for me to receive an official work permit.

In 1916 I founded the first daytime creche for working mothers and also the first twelve-bed children's hospital, which was later incorporated into the American Zionist Medical Unit, the predecessor of the Hadassah Medical Organization. Here I was head of the pediatrics department from 1918 to 1925. During this period I was also attached to an Arab Infant Welfare Station and Home (Spafford).

In 1924 I founded the first institution for homeless children in Jerusalem, as well as a number of day nurseries for working mothers. The program was to educate and organize the women of Palestine in social work and self-help, in order to raise the cultural level of the Jewish women. Over the years I supervised mothercraft training centers and day nurseries all over the country.

In 1927 I founded and became chairperson of the Israel Pediatric Association. I was also elected a member of the Jewish National Council. In 1936 I joined the pediatric department of the Bikur Cholim Hospital, where I introduced modern ideas, such as allowing parents to visit their hospitalized children every day, and even to help take care of them. From 1942 on, I was associated with the Hebrew University, first as a member of a standing committee of the medical board and later as governor. In 1947 I gave a paper on rheumatic fever in Jerusalem at the International Pediatric Congress in New York. In 1948, during the siege of Jerusalem in the war of independence, I was made head of the medical services for the Jewish community. From 1953 to 1963 I was chairperson of the Advisory Committee on Child Welfare of the Ministry of Health. In 1958 I received the Medal of the Freedom of Jerusalem, being the first woman to be so honored. I presided in 1961 at the dedication of the Bikur Cholim Hospital's new pediatric department, with a wing for patients with the rheumatic fever. In 1963 I received an award and citation for my contribution to the study and prevention of rheumatic fever from La Robida Hospital, affiliated with the pediatric department of the University of Chicago. At the close of the six-days' war in 1967, I received the honorary doctorate of the Hebrew University. After carefully choosing my successor, I retired in 1968 at seventy-nine years of age, from the pediatric department of the Bikur Hospital. In 1975, on the twenty-sixth anniversary of Israel's independence, I was awarded a special Israel Prize, the highest honor in the country. The prize was given to me in recognition of my life work in preventive medicine and in the education of mothers in hygiene and general child care despite the primitive conditions and the background of poverty. The prize also marks International Women's Year.

Hilda Mary Lazarus

b. January 23, 1890

I was born in India, the ninth of my mother's twelve children. Five boys and four girls survived to grow up. People appreciated the family background and upbringing we had as Christians following in the steps of Christ. My grandfather was one of the earliest Brahmins to be convinced that Christ was the only Savior of the whole world and that God the Creator was a loving father. For changing his faith, his community tried to poison him, brought false charges against him, and threw him into prison. However, God saved him, and he was honorably acquitted. He had attended the same school where my father taught for forty years and where all his grandchildren were educated. My mother and her sisters were taught Telugu, English, and Sanscrit at home, and were among the first Indian women to be highly educated. Mother's second sister and her brother had their medical education in Edinburgh, and her third sister retired as director of female education in Madras Presidency. My father was an excellent administrator, educationalist, scientist, mathematician, artist, and musician, and many of his students became highly prominent officials, educators, and professionals—governors of provinces, college professors, schoolteachers, engineers, and doctors.

Because of ill health, I did not go to school until I was nearly seven years old. A younger brother began with me. We were taught at home by my mother in both English and Telugu, the language of our region. We commenced in the first grade, as there was no kindergarten in those days. My father, principal of the London Mission High School in Visakhapatnam, was the first in South India to introduce the Montessori system. In a class of forty there was often only one girl. In second grade we were seven girls and sixty-five boys. For prompting someone, I was once made to stand on a bench in front of the whole class. Such was the discipline of the school.

I won a few prizes in the ten years I was in grammar school. In the ninth grade I was often absent due to illness, but I still topped the class, to the great disappointment of the boy who was my close rival. This was a mental shock to him, and he ran away to his village. After a few days he returned and we both passed the matriculation at the same time. On another occasion a boy much older than I gave up his studies altogether because I corrected his wrong answer. I did not know this until years later, when I happened to go to his house as a medical woman. All my further education in India and abroad has been coeducational, and I have had no trouble at all except the above minor problems. Even as a woman doctor, I have always been shown the greatest courtesy by my fellow doctors, professors, or consultants.

I had no difficulty in deciding to become a doctor. I joined a local college for the First in Arts and took up physiology in order to go to medical school. Then I went to the Presidency College in Madras for a B.A. in botany and biology, in order to have teaching to fall back on if my health did not permit me to complete my medical course. I am very thankful, however, that my health has been excellent throughout my medical career of thirty years in the Women's Medical Service in India, from which I retired as chief medical officer in 1947; seven years as principal, medical superintendent, and director of the Christian Medical College, in Vellore; and seven years as honorary director of the Institute of Obstetrics and Gynecology, Andhra Medical College, Visakhapatnam.

I was the first Indian woman to be appointed from London to the Women's Medical Service in India. My first posting was as assistant to the obstetrician and gynecologist in the Lady Hardinge Medical College Hospital, New Delhi. After two months I was transferred to Dufferin Hospital, Calcutta, as the first resident medical officer of that hospital. There I had to attend to all emergencies, all special paying patients, outpatients, and a ward of twenty beds, as well as being responsible for all statistics. The only languages I was acquainted with were English, Telugu, and Tamil, but here I was obliged to lecture to midwives in Hindi, to deal with Bengalis, and to study Urdu. It was compulsory for every officer of the Women's Medical Service to pass in Urdu before confirmation of service. I managed this with credit in two and a half months and then began to study Bengali, in order to understand the patients and help them to understand me.

After thirteen months in Calcutta I was transferred to Surat. There I studied Gujarati in order to train nurses and midwives in the regional language. I also had the hospital recognized as a training school by the Bombay Presidency Nursing Association. There also patients were more satisfied when spoken to in their own language. As this hospital admitted only Parsees and the higher classes of Hindu patients, I once experienced difficulty in admitting an accident case with open wounds because she belonged to an untouchable caste. After cleansing and dressing her wounds, I requested the head nurse to prepare a bed for her on the verandah of the ward. The nurse did so with great hesitation, and the stretcher bearers refused to take the patient from the outpatient department to the bed. With the help of my house surgeon I attempted to carry her upstairs. The stretcher bearers then came forward remorsefully and took the patient to her bed. Thereafter I had no trouble in admitting any cases, irrespective of caste or creed, and I was not questioned by any member of the governing body of the hospital.

After a period of three and a half years I was transferred to Visakhapatnam, as the authorities there had asked for me. Although the language there was Telugu, I was obliged to learn Oriya, in order to train midwives and thus to get a grant for running the hospital. Even as early as 1922, Visakhapatnam was an international port, and I found that, in addition to English and Telugu, other languages were helpful, since it pleased my patients when I was able to speak their own languages.

At that time there was only one training school for midwives who spoke the regional languages, who were called Red Jackets, as they wore white saris with red jackets or blouses. The subassistant surgeon who was responsible for their training lectured to them in regional languages for one hour, with results that I found inadequate. Mission hospitals were also training nurses and midwives in the regional languages but could not meet the demand. I had the hospital recognized as a government training school in English for nurses and midwives, and I was also able to influence the government to open up hispitals with sufficient maternity beds for the training of midwives in the regional languages. This training by the government has continued, and I am glad to say that at my suggestion they have introduced domiciliary training as well. This is done at maternity and child-welfare centers in collaboration with city corporations, municipalities, zillah parishes, panchayats, and hill areas—organizations chiefly connected with health measures in rural areas.

With the assistance of the municipal health officer, I undertook the inspection of textbooks for midwives. I helped them with difficult cases and encouraged them to bring patients with abnormalities to hospital in the early stages of the conditions.

After five years I was transferred to the Lady Willingdon Medical School, Madras, to relieve Dr. Beadon, a Woman's Medical Service officer, who was on the Haribilla Sadar's committee to raise the age of young brides. After four years I returned to Visakhapatnam to reorganize the hospital, which was having financial difficulties. I was obliged to delay my furlough for a year. On my return from the furlough I was transferred to Madras, and in 1940 I became principal of the Lady Hardinge Medical College and superintendent of the attached hospital. Three and a half years later I was appointed chief medical officer of the Women's Medical Service of India, and held this post until I retired, in 1947. I then gave my servics to the Christian Medical College, Vellore, as principal and later as superintendent after the resignation of Dr. Cockrane, the man famous for the treatment of lepers in India and the world at large.

I retired from the Christian Medical College in 1950, at the age of sixty. I was, however, appointed honorary director of the Institute of Obstetrics and Gynecology, and professor of obstetrics and gynecology at the Andhra Medical College, Visakhapatnam. I worked there for seven years, reorganizing the whole institute with an adequate lecture gallery, museum, library, and residential quarters for postgraduates, so that they could attend and note special emergencies. In addition, I obtained a well-equipped clinical laboratory and a new outpatient department for obstetrics and gynecology, as well as an outpatient department for sterile women and their husbands. I was obliged to resign, as I found that patients wanted to be examined only by me and had no faith in my young assistants, whom I had trained and who, I believed, would do equally well or even better than I in the course of time. I had then reached my seventy-second year.

I was nominated for membership on the legislative council, by virtue of which I was on the municipal council of the town, a member of the zillah parish, and on the advisory committees of five hospitals. I was renominated for the zillah parish when I had already reached eighty-five years of age, thus keeping my connection with a health organization in the rural area.

Elma Linton Sandford-Morgan
b. February 22, 1890

I was born in Adelaide, South Australia, the youngest of six children, three boys and three girls.

My father emigrated from Scotland with his family at the age of fourteen. Mother's people came from England about two years before she was born. Neither family had any medical background. By the time he was twenty-five, father had founded a successful business, dealing with dairy products and farm machinery. Later he was elected a member of the legislative council in the South Australian Parliament.

My mother was the eldest girl of a large family. As grandmother was widowed young, mother was competent and resourceful by the time she was married. She was deeply religious and always ready to help anyone in trouble or need, but the welfare of her husband and children was her chief interest in life. Sundays were strictly observed, with attendance at Sunday school and twice at church.

Both parents set very high standards for behavior, and we children were strictly disciplined. At the same time, mother and father were fond of fun and very generous, so despite the discipline, we all led happy and carefree lives in a large, hospitable home.

We three youngest children—two boys and myself—formed the nursery group, while the eldest brother and two sisters were "the big ones." As we three little ones attended a "dame's school," my games and pursuits were mainly those of the boys—climbing trees, clambering up on the roof by means of a grapevine to hide behind the chimneys, and performing acrobatic feats on our bicycles—until I joined my sister at a decorous private girls' school.

Our old family doctor, like most others in Adelaide, lived and had his consulting rooms in the city and paid his visits in a dignified brougham with a liveried coachman. Suburban general practitioners were scarce in those days, and when the doctor was needed urgently, one of us children would be dispatched to the chemist's shop, which had the nearest telephone, to ask the chemist to summon the doctor, while mother meanwhile stopped the bleeding or dealt with the convulsions or whatever the emergency was.

Mother had a particularly sensitive nature and was genuinely distressed at the sight of pain and suffering, but this never prevented her from rising to the occasion when confronted by danger or severe illness—and many times in her life she performed amazing feats of bravery when conditions called for a cool head. She was a great source of strength to many neighboring young mothers who, when faced with an alarming illness in their children, always came to her for help or advice. When we met with accidents or became ill, mother never panicked and we for our part were quite confident that she could cope with the situation. Actually, I feel that she—and not I—would have been the medical member of the family had circumstances been different.

Although several women had graduated in medicine in Adelaide after 1890, there was no woman in general practice here until about 1900, and it was not until some years later, when we were living in Victoria, that we became patients of one of the pioneer medical women there.

When I was fourteen, my father, who had gone on a business trip to America, taking with him the elder of my young brothers, found it necessary to go on to England. He cabled mother to join them there and to bring us three girls. After an adventurous voyage—because of monsoons, which held us up for three whole days in Ceylon—my father met us in June, and we spent an unforgettable summer in France, Switzerland, Germany, and Belgium before reaching London. Later visits to Norway and Sweden, as well as to Scotland, Ireland, and Wales followed, with London serving as our headquarters for over a year.

The next year, 1905, I achieved one of my ambitions in life—boarding school—when I entered Cheltenham Ladies' College. It was intended that I should finish my schooling there, but my father, who had meanwhile returned to Australia for a brief visit, again sent for us to join him and my mother could not bring herself to leave me twelve thousand miles away from home and family, so I came home, too.

I arrived in Adelaide in December 1905 to find that father was to enter the hospital the next day for an exploratory laparotomy. It was found that he had inoperable carcinoma, and he died two weeks later. From then on, the whole of our life pattern changed. During the next year or two all my brothers left home for various reasons, and our hospitable home, with the tennis parties and other mixed gatherings, was replaced by an isolated female household; it was not considered necessary for women to have interests outside the home. In fact, my parents held the common view that it was unfair for those from financially secure homes to take up any employment or profession, since they would be "taking the bread out of the mouths of others," for whom employment was financially essential. So our lives ran on unexciting lines. I was still a schoolgirl and also pursuing my musical studies at the conservatorium of music, spending several hours a day practicing the piano. I had a vague idea of wanting to go on to the university, but only an arts course appealed to me, and that led to nothing but teaching. Such interesting professions as journalism or librarianship were almost unknown. I did matriculate, however, in the hope that I might find some course to satisfy me. Some of our friends were medical students. In fact, my Sunday-school teacher was one, but although I admired her greatly, I had no thought of emulating her, as most of her friends seemed to have the idea of becoming medical missionaries.

It was not until the end of 1908 that the idea of medicine as a career first came to me. We were at a holiday resort where we met a doctor who regaled us with tales of his student days in Ireland and lent us medical journals to read, so that for the first time I realized how full a life that of a doctor could be. At the same time we met some Sydney women graduates who told me of the residential women's college within the University of Sydney and how desirable residence in such a college could be.

It was these two influences that suddenly led me to decide that medicine was to be my career and that Sydney, with its women's college (the only one in Australia at the time), was where I wanted to study. My mother was delighted with my decision and kept me to it.

Those years in college were perhaps the most satisfying ones of my life, and the friendships I made then have lasted ever since. I played hockey for the university and entered into so many other activities that, when war broke out in 1914, I was only halfway through my studies. This was not only because I was not an assiduous student but because at the end of my third year, when I arrived home for vacation, I found that my mother and sisters had arranged for a holiday that I could not resist joining—traveling in Ceylon, Burma, and Japan, across Siberia to Russia, and from Germany to England. This meant that I did not return to the university until the beginning of 1913 and did not graduate until 1917. By then, of course, World War I had greatly affected our studies. Many of our lecturers had joined the forces, and there was such a general shortage of medical personnel that the university speeded up the course by cutting out our vacations. On graduation, I was appointed a resident medical officer at the Royal Alexandra Hospital for children in Sydney, where I served for six months, and then a senior medical registrar at our clinical school, the Royal Prince Alfred Hospital (the R.P.A.H.).

During the latter part of my stay at R.P.A.H. I found myself having to undertake the care of patients in the opthalmic wards. I became so interested in the field that I left the hospital early in 1919 and went to England to get further experience in various London eye hospitals.

Having heard of the great amount of eye disease in India and especially of the intracapsular cataract operations by Colonel "Jallunder" Smith of Amritsar, I decided to go to India before returning to Australia. In England I heard by chance of a mission women's hospital at Bhiwani, in the Punjab, which held an annual "eye camp" in the jungle, where great numbers of cataract extractions and remedial operations for trachoma were carried out. In November of 1919 I sailed for India under the agreement that, in return for tuition and experience in eye work, I would help with the general work of the hospital. There was a great shortage of medical personnel in hospitals throughout India at that time. Passages to India were at a premium, and most of the doctors were badly overworked, as no replacements had been possible during the war.

My arrival in Bhiwani was greeted with warmth. The two woman doctors were in very poor health and overdue for leave. One (long past retirement age) was a wonderful clinician—all the more so in that she had absolutely no laboratory facilities to aid her. She was just awaiting my arrival to retire to England. The other doctor, a Scottish graduate, was considered one of the best obstetricians and gynecologists in India, as well as being an excellent eye surgeon. It was she who conducted the annual eye camp. Both doctors had worked under "Jallunder" Smith and promised to arrange for me to do so, too. I did later on.

We worked under unbelievable conditions: water was brought from the communal well in goatskins; sterilization of dressings and instruments was carried out on primus stoves; and in both the hospital and the patients' homes, hurricane lamps or lighted wicks in saucers of oil provided the lighting. The work was of the highest quality, and the results were excellent, even when the operations were carried out in unsanitary mud huts.

After some months I left for Amritsar for cataract experience with Colonel Smith and then, in answer to an SOS, went to a mission hospital in Quetta, where the only British woman doctor had broken down in health. There for some weeks I worked around the clock in the operating theater.

I was planning to return to Australia in June of 1920 when I heard that the British in occupation in Mesopotamia were about to open a hospital for women and children in Baghdad and that they wanted a woman medical director, who would also have the right to a private practice, so I applied for and obtained the post.

The hospital, located on the right bank of the Tigris, was a relic of Turkish days. It was an impressive-looking marble building of 140 beds. Inside, it was primitive. The patients were Arabs, Jews, and Armenians, while the nursing staff consisted of French nuns, who had functioned there in Turkish days. French and Arabic were the official languages spoken, but as the nuns said, it was *un véritable tour de Babylon*. My assistants were all males—Greeks, Arabs, Jews, and Armenians. I conducted all the large outpatient departments myself and did all the surgery. I visited private patients (Arabs and Jews) in their homes and confined most of the British women, many of them coming down from posts in Persia, in the government nursing home.

In early 1921 I married Captain Harry Morgan, a British army officer seconded to the Arab army (where he had to lecture on artillery in Arabic!). I continued with my work until we went to Australia for a brief leave at the end of the year.

Owing to unsatisfactory conditions of service I did not return to the medical service when we went back to Baghdad but practiced privately until my daughter was born in August 1922. I was attended by the only other medical woman in the service, who came from Basra. I continued in private practice until the Arab army was disbanded in 1923, when we left "Mespot" (by then called Iraq) for England.

Postgraduate work in Scotland at the children's and women's hospitals in Glasgow occupied my time until we decided to return and settle in Australia.

On our arrival in Melbourne in 1923, my mother's doctor, a woman, strongly advised me to start general practice in Tasmania, where there had never been a woman physician. We took her advice and stayed there until 1926 (my son having been born meanwhile). Conditions in the medical world in Hobart, the capital city, were very unsatisfactory, because the general hospital was presided over by an unqualified male doctor and was consequently out-of-bounds to us members of the B.M.A. It was interesting to note that nearly all my patients in Hobart were either Victorians or somehow connected with Victoria; women doctors in that state were highly regarded by the public because of the Queen Victoria Memorial Hospital, which they had established in Melbourne.

We moved to Sydney in 1926, and I commenced private practice in one of the suburbs. I was also medical officer of the Mothercraft Training School and an outpatient physician at the Rachel Foster Hospital for Women and Children. I instituted a mothercraft page in a widely circulated magazine and answered several hundreds of letters from mothers all over Australia, as well as the Pacific and South Africa.

In 1928 I was appointed assistant to the director of maternal and baby welfare in the Public Health Department, being responsible for all the baby health centers in New South Wales and conducting prenatal clinics at several centers. In 1929 I became director myself and, as such, was the first woman to hold an executive position in the state public service. I was also expected, because of my sex, to perform many other duties in the Public Health Service, such as examining young women for the public-service or widow's pensions, although I was paid a lower rate than men of equal status.

I stayed in this post, seeing the work grow satisfactorily, until 1937. Meanwhile, I was able to undertake other outside work, such as becoming a district commissioner of the Girl Guides and representing Tasmania on the executive board of the Australian Federation of University Women. These activities and my professional work were possible only because I had the good fortune to have reliable domestic help throughout the childhood of my daughter and son, so that during my enforced absences I knew they were as well cared for as when I was at home. Such is not the condition in Australia today, and most married medical women are hampered by inefficient or indeed unprocurable home help.

After I had had several years of satisfying work in my post in the Public Health Department, I made an important decision. The medical director of the Mother's and Babies' Health Association of South Australia wrote that the association was proposing to start a mothercraft training school in Adelaide and asked me to suggest someone to undertake the project. The letter came at what seemed just the right moment to settle my own personal difficulties. My English husband had never settled very happily in Australia, and we had decided to separate. Moreover, my young son was asthmatic and it had become unwise for him to live in Sydney. He had been a boarder for some time at a preparatory school in the country but was now reaching public-school age. He had recently spent several months with my brother in Adelaide, where he was asthma-free, and we had already decided that it would be desirable for him to attend the college in Adelaide where all my brothers had studied. So in 1937, with many regrets, I relinquished my Sydney post and moved to Adelaide with my daughter and son. I found it very interesting establishing the mothercraft training school "from the ground up," and I also undertook some general practice as a locum tenens.

When war broke out I enlisted in the Royal Australian Air Force Medical Service, but the medical personnel authorities banned my leaving South Australia, so I undertook work with one of the partners in a three-doctor general practice while the other two were absent for military service. I remained there for the duration of the war.

The editor of the paper in which I had conducted the mothercraft page some years before was now editor of Melbourne's chief daily paper, the *Argus*, so in 1947 I contracted with him to conduct a weekly column in the form of a diary of a general practitioner. This I carried on for four years, answering hundreds of letters from readers.

Meanwhile, I had been appointed, as the only woman member, to a parliamentary commission to investigate the health services in South Australia and to recommend whatever innovations might be desirable. This commission functioned for about two years, and much of the present health and allied services in the state are the result of its recommendations.

Anxious to revisit Europe, I applied in answer to an advertisement in the *Australian Medical Journal* for a post as a medical officer at one of the Commonwealth Immigration Camps in Australia. The advertisement stated that such an appointment would make one eligible for a posting under the Department of Immigration in one of the European countries, such as Italy or Germany. I was appointed to the camp at Bathurst, New South Wales, and stayed there for the whole of 1951. The camp held up to 5000 migrants at various times, and I was the only registered medical officer! I had eight unregistrable refugee doctors to assist me. At the end of the year I trustingly applied for a post in Europe, only to be informed by the commonwealth health authorities that this reward for services rendered applied only to *male* doctors and that no medical *women* were employed in the immigration department's overseas recruiting centers. So I sailed independently for Europe in 1952, and on board were no less than four medical men (and their families) being posted to various centers in Europe—none of them having had more than a few weeks' migrant-camp experience in Australia. I made several more attempts in Italy and in London to break down the sex barrier—but to no avail—so after eight months' holiday I returned to Australia.

Back in Adelaide, I acted as locum tenens in several general practices until, in 1954, I was appointed neoplasm registrar to the Anticancer Foundation of the University of Adelaide. I carried out this work in the Radio-Therapy Department of the Royal Adelaide Hospital for eleven years until compulsory retirement at the age of seventy-four, in 1964. Since then I have worked with the Red Cross Blood Transfusion Service.

In 1966 and 1968 I attended the Medical Women's International Association conferences in Rochester and Vienna respectively while I was president of the Australian Federation of Medical Women.

I am still interested in helping to overcome the bias of the Australian medical world toward the inequality of the sexes. Only a few years ago the board of the Royal Adelaide Hospital (the only public general hospital and clinical school in South Australia at that time) suddenly announced that they would not be pursuing their usual policy of appointing women graduates as resident medical officers according to their position in the final examinations. This meant that three women graduates who had always come well up in the pass, or honors, lists in their previous years were not to be appointed to the resident staff at all.

We of the Medical Women's Society of South Australia (of which I was president at the time) at once took up the challenge and demanded equal treatment for the women, and with parliamentary support and gratifying backing in the press from the general public, we obliged the hospital board to reconsider its decision and to appoint all three women to the resident staff. They fully justified the appointments and have all subsequently achieved success in their various branches of the profession in which they are still practicing, two of them having married meanwhile.

In all my years in medicine (at any rate, in Australia) I have found that medical women have had to fight and still have to fight for their rights, especially as far as equal pay for equal work is concerned.

Neither of my children has ever had any desire to adopt medicine as a career. They both served with the Royal Australian Navy during the war, after which my daughter elected to become a medical social worker and my son entered the business world.

How much of the happiness and satisfaction I have in life has been a result of my professional interests—friends I have made, countries I have worked in, and the like? Actually, my background and upbringing played as great a part in assuring me a full and satisfactory life as have my medical training and experience, and it is difficult to separate one influence from the other. With the friendships I formed all over the world and the happiness of seeing my own children and their children develop satisfactorily, I feel I have indeed had the best of two worlds—professional and personal. And I am more than ever of the opinion that the average woman doctor is more single-minded regarding her professional work than is the average male practitioner.

Doris Odlum
b. June 26, 1890

When I was born, my parents had already been married for six years and were both twenty-eight years of age. I was their only child. My mother's father was a civil engineer and had mining interests in South Wales. My father's father owned a chain of hotels in England and southern Ireland. Both came from fairly large families with good medical histories, but none of them took up medicine. Father was an accountant, and he and mother first managed hotels and subsequently became the proprietors of a hotel. I was born and brought up in luxury hotels and therefore had a very unusual background. My parents were devoted to each other and to me, and we were always in harmony with one another. They were good mixers, and so was I, and we had very happy relations with the staff of our hotels, who stayed with us for many years. From early childhood I had the opportunity of meeting and mixing with a great variety of people of the middle and upper classes and also of learning how to behave toward and how to handle staff.

My parents were extremely liberal in their ideas but believed in discipline and order. They believed that true religion was best expressed by living a life of kindness and thought for others and were not interested in dogma or any special creed. They seldom went to church and did not press me to go, but we had a number of friends among the clergy. Up to the age of seven I was brought up by nurses and governesses, although I was always in close contact with my parents. Father was my special hero, and it was not until I was older that I really appreciated mother's fine qualities. They were both warm, outgoing personalities, and we were an affectionate and uninhibited family. As I had no brothers or sisters, my early years were lonely and I became very self-sufficient, living largely in a world of fantasy when I was not with people. When I was seven, a cousin came on holiday and we became so fond of each other that, with the agreement of her parents, it was decided that she should spend the greater part of her time with me. She had a much older brother and therefore was also virtually an only child. Though she was five years older than I, I was very precocious and we were more like contemporaries.

My own health as well as that of my family was excellent, and our relationships remained extremely happy all through my adolescence. I do not recall any basic difference of opinion or attitude between them or my cousin and myself. She married when I was sixteen but lived nearby. I learned to read at five years, and reading has always my greatest pleasure and relaxation. My parents were both great readers, and so was my cousin. Father was especially interested in literature and history, which were also my favorite subjects.

I went to school for a term when I was seven, but owing to my unusual upbringing, I was much more mature than the other children; I aroused their hostility without knowing why and so was very unhappy. For a year father taught me, and then my cousin and I went as day students to a school where I was much happier, but it was not until I was eleven that I was able to have a happy relationship with other children. I then formed my first close friendship, which lasted until my friend's death a few years ago. I was reasonably successful academically but showed no great promise until at fourteen I passed with honors an examination that was usually taken by fifteen-year-olds; from that time onward my headmistress suggested that I pursue an academic career and even go on to a university. At fifteen, I decided to take up Latin and Greek and prepared to enter Oxford to study classics. I was a voracious reader of English and European literature and was also interested in classical and modern history and culture. I was poor in mathematics, so for my entrance for Oxford I decided to do logic and psychology instead, which I thoroughly enjoyed.

At eighteen, I passed the London University intermediate degree in arts, with honors in English. This qualified me for entering Oxford University, which I did when I was nineteen. I read for classical honor moderations and took an honors degree in 1912. At that time women were not allowed to use the title Bachelor or Master of Arts or Sciences, and it was not until 1919 that this right was conceded. I was one of the first seven actually to receive the Master of Arts degree from Oxford, in 1919.

After leaving Oxford in 1912 I lectured for the Workers' Education Association, which brought me into touch with women in the industrial areas of England, the Midlands and the North. Up to that time my whole life had been spent on the south coast in seaside holiday resort towns. I also took part in the suffrage campaign as a member of the party that did not countenance violence. My ancestors on father's side were Quakers, and both my parents were antiviolence. At the time of World War I father was too old for military service. The outbreak of war resulted in a change of direction in my life. I had taken my diploma in education with the idea of teaching, but I decided that this was not the career that I wished to follow. Many of the working women I had met told me how much they wished there were more women doctors to whom they could go for help and advice. Father had always been interested in science and medical matters and had discussed them with me, but I had never thought of being a doctor myself.

My only direct contact with medicine, apart from our friendship with our own doctor, was through a relative of father's who was a patron and a lifelong friend of Dr. Helen Boyle's. As far back as 1905 she and her woman partner realized how many women were suffering from what was then called nervous debility and neurasthenia and how little their difficulties were understood by their men doctors or by their husbands. These two pioneer women started a small home near Brighton for women suffering from "neurasthenia or nervous exhaustion," and by 1920 this had developed into the Lady Chichester Hospital for Nervous Diseases, which charged patients according to their means and which was maintained by voluntary contributions. This was the first hospital of its kind in England and probably in the world, and it was run along lines that are regarded as modern even today, including occupational therapy and what we now call the therapeutic community policy, with psychotherapy as the main form of treatment. I stayed several times with my aunt at Dr. Boyle's private home, where the doctor also had resident patients. Thus, from the age of fifteen I had some interest in the psychological aspects of medicine, although I never thought of it as a career for myself.

Both my parents and my headmistress had a strong sense of social service, and I was brought up to believe that whatever capacities or fortunate circumstances we had in life were in a sense a loan that we were expected to repay in service to others. With my parents' full consent I decided in 1915 to study medicine. By this time our financial situation was such that there was no need for me to earn a living and my parents were able to afford my expenses as a medical student. In those days there were practically no means of obtaining grants or scholarships, and many boys and girls were unable to study medicine for this reason. I started my studies in October 1915 at the London School of Medicine for Women, which was attached to the Royal Free Hospital. At that time the school was largely staffed by women and had no male students. There was no actual prejudice against medical women in this country, and there were already several thousand women on the medical register, mostly working as general practitioners, although some practiced obstetrics and gynecology and other specialties, including general surgery and mental illness.

At the beginning of World War I a volunteer reserve corps of women was started in London by Colonel Charlsworth, herself a pioneer woman in many fields. This was the first corps of women in military uniform in this country, and I joined as soon as I came to London. We undertook various forms of noncombatant war work as a part-time activity, and I did canteen work at Woolwich Arsenal one night a week, as well as drills and route marches, throughout the war. We all had to start in the ranks and earn our commissions, and I became a captain in charge of a company and later in the war did full-time work as commander of a forage guard in the New Forest for eighteen months, from 1917 to 1919. This interrupted my medical studies.

In 1920 St. Mary's Hospital, Paddington, which was a mixed hospital, opened its doors to women. As the intake of medical students at the Royal Free School of Medicine was then greater than the school could cope with, a number of us were offered the chance to go to St. Mary's to complete our hospital training and I decided to avail myself of this opportunity. Hitherto, I had lived and worked predominantly with women, and I welcomed the chance to mix more freely with men students. For years we had very happy relationships with the men, especially participating in amateur theatricals, for which the hospital was noted. I was fortunate enough to leap into fame at an early stage of my career and took prominent parts in acting and producing plays. A group of us used to go camping and were members of a night club, Murray's, in Beak Street, which was one of the most popular night clubs of that period. It may come as something of a surprise to realize that men and women medical students were mixing freely in this way at this period. I had a fairly undistinguished medical career at the hospital but managed to qualify in 1924.

I had had another delay, owing to the death of my father in 1922, which for both me and my mother was a shattering experience. My mother was extremely brave and insisted that I should go on with my medical career. Father and she had been managing their own hotel in Bournemouth since 1912, and she then decided to run it herself. My cousin's mother, who was a widow, went to live with her, so she was not too lonely. My cousin remained very close to me and had two daughters, who were almost like my own children. Mother died in 1942 at the age of eighty-two, and I then became the owner of the hotel and appointed a managing director to run it on my behalf. I sold the hotel in 1961 but am still a director.

When I qualified in 1924, there was a glut of young doctors and many of them found it extremely difficult to get posts. I had always felt a special interest in psychological medicine, then in a very rudimentary state, and had obtained the psychological medicine prize as a student. Fortunately for me, the Lady Chichester Hospital advertized for a resident medical officer in June, and I was appointed and started work there in July 1924. The hospital treated only women and children at that time, and we had about 40 beds and a big outpatient department. After eighteen months I was made an honorary consultant, and Dr. Boyle arranged for me to become assistant medical officer at Camberwell House, a 500-bed private mental hospital in London, while I attended Lady Chichester one day a week. In 1927 I took my diploma in psychological medicine, working part time at Maudsley Hospital. This diploma had been established only a few years previously, and the word *psychiatry* had not yet been invented. Doctors working in the mental-health field were called alienists, and the treatment in mental hospitals consisted almost entirely of custodial care, with a certain amount of drugging for violent and intractable patients. According to the law, patients could only be received in a mental hospital, public or private, with a certificate from two doctors and a legal order from a magistrate, which prevented the patients from leaving of their own free will. This meant that only those who were in such a severe state of mental disorder that they were either a danger to themselves or to others could receive any care or treatment in a hospital. Many of the state mental hospitals were very poorly run, and the conditions under which the patients lived would today excite public horror, although a commission appointed in 1926, at which I gave evidence, did not report evidence of much actual mental cruelty.

In 1928 I was invited by the senior surgeon and physician of the Royal Victoria General Hospital in Bournemouth to join a Dr. Statham in forming a psychiatric department. This was predominantly an outpatient clinic but had the use of beds, and it was a pioneer venture. I applied for the post of consultant physician to my old hospital, St. Mary's in London. I received a letter saying that they would be happy to have appointed me but that this would constitute a precedent, as they had no consultant women on the staff. This was the first time I had actually come up against discrimination. Even in those days women could do quite well in general practice, but it was extremely hard for them to reach higher levels. Despite this discrimination, several women did achieve consultant status.

Dr. Boyle and Dame Evelyn Fox, who was also a pioneer in the field of care for the mentally handicapped, were instrumental in starting the National Association for Mental Hygiene, of which I subsequently became honorary secretary. This brought me into contact with many people in the field of mental health, both in this country and in Europe. Our chief function was the education of the medical profession and the public and an attempt to improve the services available and the attitude toward the mentally ill and subnormal. I subsequently became president of the European League for Mental Hygiene and was the United Kingdom representative on the first executive board of the World Federation for Mental Health. The National Association for Mental Health for England and Wales was formed from an amalgamation of other volunteer mental health associations in 1946, and I became vice-president.

In the meantime social work, as well as occupational therapy and child guidance, was being developed. In all of these I played an active part. In 1937 I was appointed honorary consultant psychiatrist to the West End Hospital for Nervous Diseases, and helped to start the psychiatric department in the Elizabeth Garrett Hospital for Women. In the same year I was coopted onto the London County Council as a member of the Mental Health Committee, which administered all the mental hospitals in the greater London area. I was invited to stand for Parliament but refused, as I wished to remain active in clinical medicine. In 1940 I was elected chairperson of the Psychological Medicine Committee of the British Medical Association (BMA) of which I was the only woman member; I have subsequently been chairperson of a number of their committees, and I was made a fellow in 1958.

I was chairperson for fifteen years of the Joint Doctors' and Magistrates' Committee of the BMA, and during that period my committee promoted the change in the law in 1961 by which suicide and attempted suicide ceased to be criminal offenses. In 1961 I joined the Samaritan movement, which is an entirely voluntary movement conducted by lay people, maintaining a twenty-four-hour telephone and personal service for anyone who is in despair or feeling suicidal. This service has developed, and in its twenty-first year in Great Britain and Northern Ireland, some 1600 volunteers in its 150 branches dealt with more than 170,000 self-referred clients. In 1973 I was elected the group's life president.

In the course of the years I have written various books. My *Psychology, the*

Nurse and the Patient was the required reading for the preliminary nursing examination in mental health, and for fifteen years I was the psychiatric examiner in this subject for the General Nursing Council. I also wrote *Journey through Adolescence* and *The Mind of Your Child*, and I have lectured, given papers, and attended conferences in most parts of the world. I have also done a considerable amount of broadcasting.

It will thus be seen that, although obviously there was some discrimination against me as a woman, I have been able to take a fairly prominent part in pioneering many developments in the field of mental health. I must also say that I have received unfailing kindness and consideration from all my male colleagues and have never met with any personal antagonism or opposition from anyone of either sex.

Although I have had very close men friends, I have never wanted to marry, as I preferred my independence. I am fond of children but did not wish to have any of my own. My life has been so full and satisfying that I should not have had the time or energy to play the part of a wife or a mother. I lived for thirty years with a woman medical friend in London, and for the last nineteen years with another friend in Bournemouth. Fortunately, I have two women housekeepers who have been with my family for over fifty years, so I have never been lonely or had domestic cares to distract me from my work. In 1924, when I qualified, I joined the British Medical Women's Federation and in 1926 the Medical Women's International Association. I was elected a vice-president in 1929 and was treasurer during the war years, 1940–1945, and was then vice-president for a further period. I was president of the British Medical Women's Association from 1950 to 1952.

Nanna Svartz
b. August 1, 1890

I was born in Västerås, a town situated about 110 kilometers to the west of Stockholm. At that time Västerås was a small town of 6000 inhabitants, a place where "everybody knew everybody."

My mother and father were cousins, their mothers being sisters. My mother Anna Moxen was the daughter of a clergyman whose parish was a part of the Stockholm archdiocese. It was said of her that she was always in a good mood even when her father had been drinking a little too much. My father was the son of a merchant in Leksand, Dalecarlia, who died of pneumonia before the birth of his son. My widowed grandmother moved in with her father, an accountant in Falun, 300 kilometers north of Stockholm. My father grew up to be an earnest, somewhat formal, and completely upright man. He was very strict in the upbringing of his children. After studies at the University of Uppsala he was awarded his Ph.D. in Latin. For many years he was the senior teacher of Latin and Greek in the secondary school in Västerås.

I was the fifth child in the family, five years younger than my youngest brother. My eldest brother died some months before I came into the world. I was a very gay child, a pet in the family. My earliest memory is my father's fiftieth birthday. At about five o'clock in the morning the boys whom my father taught came to our home to congratulate him. They were singing very boisterously. I became frightened and began to scream so loudly that I almost drowned out the song.

Until I was eight or nine years old there were nearly always one or two in the family who were ill. My second brother Martin died when I was four. I was told later that, when Martin felt well enough to go to school, he was allowed to go into the classroom at any hour. As long as he was not too short of breath, the teacher let him continue. However, his health deteriorated and he soon passed away. My father, who never got over Martin's death, used to visit the graveyard every day.

The next year my grandmother died suddenly. She had a room in the top floor of the house in which we had an apartment. The family living under her room heard her moaning and reported to mother, who went up at once. Some months later father fell ill with a severe, prolonged attack of typhoid fever. He did not want to go to the hospital for infectious diseases. Instead, he preferred to have mother take care of him at home. The two of them confined themselves for six weeks in two rooms of our flat. In 1896 my third brother Ernst fell ill with pains in the abdomen and diarrhea. The symptoms did not stop; he got worse and worse, and he left us in December of that year.

I heard mother say, "It can't be true." She looked exhausted. To me she said, "Don't mourn, Nanna. You see, your brothers and grandmother are much better off now, with no pain and no breathing difficulties." "If they are in such a nice place," I asked, "why don't we all go there?" Mother explained that we had to wait. I assured her that, no matter what happened, I would stay with her, father, and my sister Lisa. She replied, "Oh Nanna, please be a good girl and do that."

The family then experienced about a year and a half without serious problems. At the end of 1899 my eighteen-year-old sister began to cough and to feel very tired. The diagnosis was pulmonary tuberculosis. From then on, she was almost constantly in tuberculosis sanatoriums in Sweden and Norway. She came home only for Christmases and once in order to be a bridesmaid at a big wedding in the Västerås cathedral. Everyone thought she looked wonderful and healthy. Two or three days later she developed a high fever and pneumonia, after which she never fully recovered. I loved Lisa and was anxious to come home as quickly as possible from school. I wanted to sit at her bedside and tell her all the news. "It can be dangerous to sit here, Nanna," she said, but I did not pay much attention. She told me that she was never going to get better, and in fact she passed away in 1904. By that time I fully understood the seriousness of death; I had matured fast, and I was inconsolable.

I have told all this in order to show how as a child I became accustomed to being constantly among sick people. I came to ponder why all this happened to us. My mother had taken extremely good care of us all, and she had done everything possible for us. It seemed incomprehensible. Could anything have been done to cure my sister and brothers? Was it inevitable that their illnesses should have led to death? Lisa had had tuberculosis, but which diseases had my brothers had? I decided to try to find an answer some day, and I am convinced that my childhood among sick relatives played a large part in my attraction to medicine. After having started my medical studies, I actually was able to diagnose their diseases. Through thorough questioning of my mother and others I could establish that in our apartment house there had also lived two seamstresses who loved the children in our family. When the children went out into the courtyard, the seamstresses immediately went out to them and began to play with them. These ladies coughed and expectorated on the ground. That my brothers also suffered from tuberculosis fitted well with the symptoms they had shown. I was the only one of the children not to be infected, undoubtedly because we moved to another house when I was a month or so old. At that time infants were never taken out in the open air during the first few months of life.

There is no doubt that the illnesses of my brothers and sister formed the basis for my growing interest in biology and medicine. But there was also another factor that contributed to my interest in medicine. When I was about fifteen, I often took walks in the afternoon with classmates, as did the boys from the gymnasium. They frequently discussed with us what kind of work they would choose when they had finished school. Some of them felt attracted by the medical profession, and this was the case with Nils Malmberg, whom I married twelve years later.

My father was doubtful about my pursuing such a long course as the medical one. He would have preferred for me to continue my Latin, which was his main subject and of which he had taught me so very much when I was studying for my matriculation. In addition, he considered medical studies too expensive, and he also implied that I was a little too interested in dancing and other pleasures. However, I was determined to study medicine, and I have not for one second regretted this decision.

When I started at the medical school in Stockholm in 1911, there were two girls in my first-year class. When we were asked to take our seats in the dissecting room, I heard a boy say to his friend, "Hurry up and take a seat so that we don't have to sit beside the girls." However, we gradually became quite well accepted. During the microanatomy course I was invited to do extra work in the laboratory. This was my first attempt at research.

A year and a half later the professor of pathology offered me a post as extra assistant. I was most grateful and rushed off to get permission to postpone my course in physiology. When I returned to the pathology institute about one hour later, there was a male student sitting in my chair. "What are you doing here?" I asked. He answered, "I need this assistantship for my future. You're a girl; you don't need it. Therefore, I am staying here." Nobody helped me to displace him.

From 1913 through 1914 I took part in the compulsory preliminary instruction at Uppsala. During these courses I decided to try to specialize in internal medicine. An amusing thing happened one day. I had been assigned a patient suffering from pernicious anemia. This patient was to be demonstrated on in a lecture. Professor Forssner wanted to demonstrate hemorrhages on the feet of the patient, but had trouble taking off the stockings. Suddenly the patient said in a loud voice, "This is something Miss Svartz can do much better." Everybody laughed. The professor said, "If she is so clever, she can now show us whether she is also able to teach. Please, take my seat." I dared not make a fool of myself; I had to do my best, and it went reasonably well. In fact, this event had a certain influence on my reputation.

My woman colleague had been overworked, and I was now the only female in the group. Gradually I became good friends with all the men in the class. Perhaps a contributing factor was what happened one day when one of them was somewhat under the influence of alcohol on his arrival at the morning lecture. I lured him into a distant room and bolted the door, so that our teacher would not see him in that condition.

After the preliminary course in Uppsala our group returned to Stockholm for continued clinical courses. More and more interested in internal medicine, I worked particularly hard before my examination in this specialty. Professor Israel Holmgren, head of the department and son of a woman deeply involved in work for women's rights, promised me a job when I had passed all my examinations.

Meanwhile, I had become engaged to Nils Malmberg, who intended to specialize in pediatrics. We often met in the evenings and had decided not to marry before both of us had taken our final examinations. I had started my medical studies later than he because I had had to take some extra courses before entering the gymnasium in Stockholm. I received my licensing certificate in the spring of 1918, and we were married in October of that year.

In January of 1919 I started as assistant in the Department of Medicine headed by Professor Holmgren at the Serafimerlasarettet. I remained there in different positions for about nine years, during the last two of which I was head of the central laboratories.

Once, when I was promised a more attractive appointment in the hospital, a member of the board questioned whether it would be suitable to give me such a position, as I was living with a man without being married to him. I was in fact married, but I had continued to use my maiden name at a time when this was not legally sanctioned. Holmgren replied, rightly, "What has that to do with her capacity in the hospital?" In addition to my duties in the wards, I made a series of scientific investigations, chiefly on intestinal diseases. In 1927 I presented my doctoral thesis on iodophile bacteria in intestinal contents. After the acceptance of my thesis I became assistant professor of medicine.

I had a very pleasant time at Serafimerlasarettet. It was hard work but extremely interesting. There was always good and pleasant comradeship. At the end of the Serafimer period I took a leave for about six months. I went abroad "for studies," as I said, but the real reason was that I was expecting a much desired baby. I was overjoyed to see my little girl child in the beginning of August in 1929. Israel Holmgren wanted me to start teaching students in September. At that time it was actually easy to get excellent help in the home and a competent nurse, in contrast to the great difficulty or even impossibility of obtaining help nowadays.

Israel Holmgren was to retire in 1936. I decided to apply for his chair, as did nine male assistant professors. The competition lasted two years, probably because of my application for the chair and the difficulty many experts had regarding my ranking. The period of competition was rather troublesome. It was said that the work would be too hard for a woman, particularly one approaching menopause! During this period I thought it would be wisest to be very cautious in my fight. It was a disagreeable surprise for many that I was placed high on the list of applicants by the committee of experts. One of the applicants became furious. He wrote a long paper complaining about my ranking and criticizing my publications in detail. I had to answer carefully. After a further two or three months the appointment to the chair was discussed at great length at the Karolinska Institute. Professor H. C. Jacobaeus, who acted for me, had to answer the often very irritating questions of his colleagues. At last he called me by telephone and told me that I had been put at the top of the list for the chair. My family opened a bottle of champagne. We had just started to sip the wine when a telephone call came again to tell me that Professor Jacobaeus had been admitted to the hospital in very serious condition as a result of a heart attack. It was a shock, and I realized that I must take a cab to the hospital immediately. On arriving there, I tried to behave as calmly as possible. When I entered the room and saw that Professor Jacobaeus was extremely ill, I tried to do everything I could for him, and after about two hours his symptoms were less pronounced. He began to speak and soon got on to the subject of the conference that had just ended. I tried to stop him from talking, but he persisted. A new attack of cardiac pain soon occurred, and he became unconscious. He passed away in the morning of October 29, 1937. This event was the hardest of my professional life.

I then had to arrange a great number of things. I had to inform the rector of the medical school and the dean of the Karolinska Institute, arrange for a locum tenens for Professor Jacobaeus, and prepare a speech for the funeral service.

My definite appointment to the chair of Israel Holmgren was expected to take place in December of 1937. At that time there were two chairs of internal medicine in Stockholm, and both of them had been held by deputies for six weeks. Finally I was appointed professor of medicine in the middle of December 1937.

Professor Jacobaeus had intended to move from Serafimerlasarettet to the new university hospital (Karolinska Hospital) in 1940. Because of his death it became my duty to make the move. This professorship was located in Serafimer-lasarettet for two years and in the Department of Internal Medicine of Karolinska Hospital for eighteen years. I had to organize the latter department, including the planning of the daily work. It was highly interesting, and the only difficulties arose when I presented new plans of importance for my department. At times it was not easy to obtain a majority vote for them. Such, for instance, was the case when I proposed the construction of a new research institute on the grounds of the Karolinska Hospital with the funds collected by the Swedish people on the eightieth birthday of King Gustaf V. This was, of course, an extensive and important project. Some of my older colleagues came to my aid and made it possible for me to carry through with the plan. I had the privilege of planning the new research institute in collaboration with the architect. The plans included four large laboratory departments and a special wing for the animals. The inauguration took place in May of 1948.

After the opening, I was subjected to ghastly accusations by a colleague. I was said to have surreptitiously received a double salary and was accused of being incompetent to manage this big research institute. The author of the accusations compelled me to defend my activities before the Swedish Medical Council, which was a distressing experience. I told the council, among other things, that I had lost 35,000 Swedish kronor by not demanding compensation for the time I had been off duty, performing my part in the planning of the research institute. I was supported by the Swedish lord high steward, and all ended well. After winning this battle, I was able to work in peace.

The institute was intended for research on crippling diseases, including primarily rheumatic conditions. Successful scientific work has been done there not only on rheumatic diseases but on atherosclerosis, diseases of the blood, the treatment of severe burns, and auditory disturbances. My period as chief of the Department of Internal Medicine involved me in many duties, and I often had to work twelve to sixteen hours a day.

I had been much interested in the arts, especially painting and the theater. I decided to give up most of these outside interests, and I became more and more a so-called professional idiot. I also abstained from taking much part in conferences other than medical ones. I was so happy with hospital and research work and with my private practice that I did not miss the things that I had to sacrifice.

One of my duties was to promote the scientific activity of the department, most of the assistants being engaged in some kind of research. An extra task was membership on the board of the hospital, as well as on the National Board of Health. As a member of the faculty of the medical school, I had many special commissions. Of particular interest was my being chosen as a member of the small committees who prepare judgments regarding those scientists proposed for the Nobel Prize. I was a member of such a committee four times, regarding the awards to Gerhard Domagk, Alexander Fleming, Sir Howard Florey, Ernst Chain, Philip Hench, Edward Kendall, and Tadeus Reichstein, among others. It was fascinating to follow the paths of their great discoveries.

During World War II, I initiated the formation of an international society of internal medicine, with the stipulation that it be strictly nonpolitical. Professor Gion of Switzerland became enthusiastic, as did Professor Roskam of Belgium and Professor Justin-Besancon of France. As colleagues in most other countries thought it impossible to found a new society during a world war, the project was postponed until 1948.

Since retirement from my chair I have carried on a restricted private practice, at first three or four days weekly and since May of 1975, only once a week. My main activity at present is daily work in the King Gustaf V Research Institute on the primary cause of rheumatoid arthritis and on the rheumatoid factor. I have had the good fortune to be self-supporting in the institute, thanks to most generous donations from the Wessen Foundation. The main results of my scientific writings total about four hundred papers. The second milestone in my work was the introduction of the drug salicylazosulfapyridine in 1938 through 1939. This medication is nowadays widely used.

For many years I have taken great interest in the origin of rheumatoid arthritis. At the International Congress on Rheumatic Diseases in 1936 I discussed this problem, as well as experimentally produced arthritis, in order to elucidate different possibilities. It was decided at the congress that the different opinions should be published in one volume. We sent the papers to the secretary, Professor Ginzburg of Belgium, but unfortunately, he was arrested in his home at the beginning of World War II and all his documents disappeared. A large number of investigations were made as a continuation of the research discussed at the above-mentioned congress. I came more and more to the conclusion that rheumatoid arthritis, like rheumatic fever, is a streptococcal disease, although the types of streptococci are different in the two diseases. I have discussed this theory at many congresses and symposia.

Except for my family, research has been my greatest interest and pleasure. It has sometimes been a little difficult to achieve recognition for my scientific results, and this may have something to do with my sex. Perhaps the results were not interesting enough; if this is the case, I find consolation in the words of an outstanding man who said that a woman has to be ten times as clever as a man to receive recognition for a piece of work. Even if this is an overstatement, it nevertheless contains some truth.

I should like to finish this autobiography by emphasizing that I have every reason to be deeply grateful in the first place to my family—particularly my husband, pediatrician Nils Malmberg, and my daughter Gunvor Svartz-Malmberg, also a doctor—for their unselfish and wonderful help. I am also much indebted to my co-workers and other friends for their great readiness to give support. On the whole, I have had a glorious life, with good health, much work, and great satisfaction. Gradually I have acquired a certain instinct of self-preservation and have tried to avoid plunging too deeply into difficulties and simply to concentrate on my work. At eighty-five I eagerly hope that I may be able to continue my activities.

Kunie Miyaji
b. March 1, 1891

I was born in a little fishing village called Suzaki in the Kochi Prefecture in 1891. After graduating from grammar school there, I entered the only prefectural girls' high school in Kochi. At that time it took a whole day on the tiny ferry boat, plus a ride on a jinrikisha and a horse carriage to reach Kochi from Suzaki. Now a round trip takes only two hours by bus. Most of the students walked the whole distance, but I was placed in a boarding school. I was the elder of two children.

Since I was born into a family of doctors, I aspired to become one myself. After gaining this difficult permission from my family, I set forth to Tokyo to enter Dr. Yayoi Yoshioka's school of medicine in 1909, the year I graduated from the girls' high school. We studied only medical subjects at the medical school, and after that we had to pass the National Practitioner's Examination in order to be licensed. We had to be tested in basic sciences, clinical medicine, and in the practical examination of patients. After passing all these subjects, a doctor's license and a graduation certificate were awarded. The final tests could be taken at any time when the student felt prepared.

At that time there were many national and private medical colleges, but women students were not allowed to enter any of them. The only way for a woman to become a doctor was to study very hard and to pass the national licensing examination. Dr. Ginko Ogino, who was the first woman to do this, made it possible for other women to do the same and thus to become doctors.

In November of 1914 I graduated from the Tokyo Women's Medical School and passed my national licensing examination. I then remained at the medical school for about two years, for further studies and experience in the gynecological department.

During 1915 through 1916 the pro-Japanese Mohammedan Indian Mr. Suttermall of Rangoon, Burma, suggested to his friend the Marquis Ohkuma that the Burmese would like to have some women doctors from Japan, in addition to the English and Burmese women physicians who had studied in England. Burma is a country where the sexes are segregated, so when a woman becomes ill, a woman doctor has to attend her. Dr. Yayoi Yoshioka, founder of the Tokyo Women's Medical School, was much in favor of the idea of sending women doctors abroad, especially to Southeast Asia. When this offer came, I was chosen, together with Dr. Matsuno Yoda and two midwives, to go to Burma. We made headlines in the newspapers, since going abroad sixty years ago was like going to the moon, although London or Paris would have been more usual than Rangoon. The most difficult part was obtaining permission from my family. This was during the middle of World War I, and it was complicated to obtain passports from the British embassy. The passage to Rangoon took twenty-three days on a freighter, which stopped at every seaport.

I worked for three years in Burma. The patients were very friendly, and we used Japanese medication and techniques. The war ended just as my three-year contract also came to an end. When my replacement arrived, I returned to Japan, but Dr. Yoda and a nurse remained. Unfortunately, this hospital was destroyed during World War II.

On my return to my home country there was again much sensation in the newspapers, and I was asked to give lectures here and there. Also, many offers came from different hospitals, but I decided to practice in my home town of Suzaki, according to my father's wishes. I was the first woman doctor to practice in the Kochi Prefecture. The following year I married Dr. Katsuro Miyaji.

As yet no women were admitted to the medical universities. I managed, however, to enter the gynecological department of the Kyushu University for a year's further training, and then I returned to Kochi to resume practice and to build a hospital with modern surgical equipment. People did not believe that a woman doctor could do a laparotomy. My first patient had "blasenmole." I prayed earnestly and did the operation, which was a success, and my patient lived to be seventy years of age.

After practicing for twenty years, we founded the Kochi Women's Medical Association, with twenty-five women doctors. It is at present a very active group with more than eighty members.

In 1941 I decided to pursue my studies again at the gynecological department of the Tokyo Imperial University School of Medicine and to work for my doctorate. I was fifty years old, but Dr. Yayoi Yoshioka severely reprimanded me for giving up a good practice and my family to go into research. Nothing, however, could stop me, so I began my research secretly.

World War II started that year, and more than half my colleagues at Tokyo University were recruited one by one. Two of the best ones were killed in the Midway battle. As the war became worse, we had much difficulty in keeping our experimental animals alive because of a lack of food for both animals and human beings. However, I took my doctorate in 1945.

In August of 1945 World War II ended and women gained their rights by changes in the Japanese constitution. When women's suffrage was granted, several women were elected to the House of Representatives, including Dr. Shigeyo Takeuchi, one of our pioneer women.

After the war great changes in the entire school system followed, and women were allowed, on the same competitive basis as the men, to enter the universities that had been closed to them. At present there remains only one women's medical school, the Tokyo Women's Medical School, founded by Dr. Yoshioka seventy-five years ago.

The Japanese Women's Medical Association was revived in 1955 and in 1957 was again formally admitted to the Medical Women's International Association (MWIA). Since then membership has increased yearly. Attending the MWIA meetings held every two years in different countries has been a popular asset to the association, and national general meetings are held yearly in different prefectures, always with membership on the increase.

At present I am retired, and my practice is being carried on by my daughter and her husband.

Jerusha Jhirad
b. March 21, 1891

I was born in the Bene-Israel community of India. This is an obscure Jewish group that was identified in about the twelfth century A.D. According to legend it is one of the lost tribes of Israel, whose ships were wrecked on the shores of Konkan district, south of Bombay, about 2000 years ago. There is a cemetery in one of the villages where the bodies of those washed ashore were buried. The survivors are said to have settled in neighboring villages and are reported to have taken at first to oil pressing, and as they refrained from working on Saturdays, they were known among the other residents as Saturday oil pressers. Later they also became farmers. Families in each village took the name of the village. My ancestors lived in the village of Jhirad and were called Jhiradkars. With the advent of the British a number of Bene-Israelites migrated to the towns and were enlisted in the army. India is a country where Jews have never been persecuted.

My great-grandfather served in the British army during the Indian Mutiny in 1857, and in recognition of his services, he was awarded the Star of India and a stretch of land at Poona, about 120 miles from Bombay. This was our family home until about fifty years ago. My two sisters were married from the house, and my children spent many happy holidays there. A Bene-Israel synagogue now sanctifies the grounds.

My mother came from Thana, about forty miles from Bombay, where her grandfather, who had also served in the British army, built a synagogue. She was one of a large family, which used to gather particularly on high holidays, when my father would conduct the services. My mother's youngest sister was the first university graduate among the women of our community, while I was the third—but the first to take up medicine.

My father was studying at the medical college when he married, at the age of eighteen years. My mother was only fourteen years old, and as the children started arriving, father had to give up his studies. I had four sisters and three brothers, one of whom died young. I was the fourth child in the family.

About this time my grandfather acquired a coffee estate in Mysore state, and father was put in charge of it. We had wonderful times there, roaming through the plantation and chewing sweet, ripe coffee berries, paddling in the streams, or watching the crushing process. All went well for some years until suddenly the "planter's pest" overran our plantation, as well as those surrounding it. Our circumstances changed; father had to go north to secure employment on the railway. Meanwhile mother, who had never been very strong, developed rheumatoid arthritis, from which she eventually became crippled. She remained so for about twenty years, but she was always cheerful and helpful. For my education up to matriculation I was sent to a high school for girls at Poona. I was already at boarding school when mother took ill. My two older sisters married young, and in 1902, while I was at school and about eleven years old, my second sister, who was only seventeen, delivered twins prematurely and was seriously ill. Her life was saved by a woman doctor, Dr. Benson, who was in charge of the Cama Hospital, one of the first government hospitals for women, entirely staffed by women. This event struck my fancy, and as my elder brother was studying medicine, I wished that I could also be a doctor, study in London, and be in charge of Cama Hospital—a daydream that I never mentioned to anyone.

My schooling was entirely dependent on merit scholarships, and I won enough of these to put me through my medical studies. I qualified in 1912 and set up in private practice in Bombay. A group of young teachers and college students arranged a gathering in my honor, which was the first of its kind among our community. This inspired me to organize a Jewish women's association for cultural and social advancement. This society has recently celebrated its diamond jubilee.

Early in 1914 I was awarded a Tata loan scholarship to study in London, and six months later, I became the first woman to be awarded, in addition, the Government of India Scholarship. I registered at the London School of Medicine for Women. After obtaining the degree of M.B.,B.S., I was keen to take an M.D. degree in obstetrics and gynecology at London University. This meant a resident post for at least six months. London was very conservative in those days; women were admitted only to the Royal Free and the Elizabeth Garrett Anderson hospitals, and British women got the first chance. However, with the outbreak of World War I, medical men were called up and women were welcomed at the general hospitals. I was taken on at the Elizabeth Garrett Anderson Hospital, where I spent nearly two years receiving valuable training in obstetrics and gynecology. I qualified for the M.D. in 1919 and returned to India.

The last part of my daydream remained to be realized. I offered to do honorary (voluntary) work at the Cama Hospital, but there was no opening at the time, so I set up in consultant practice in Bombay. In 1920 I went to a small hospital in Gangalore, where I was in charge of the maternity unit. While there, I interested the social workers and we formed a child-welfare council to organize clinics and feeding centers.

In 1924 I returned to Bombay, where honorary posts had been sanctioned at Cama Hospital, and I was taken on. In 1928 I was appointed medical officer of the hospital. I was the first Indian to be given the post. This was a real fulfillment of my childhood dream. In my new post I reorganized work in the delivery ward.

Osteomalacia was common, especially in purdah women (mostly Muslims) and it was quite a task to persuade their menfolk to consent to Caesarian sections.

I was very fond of teaching and used to hold special sessions in the evenings and even on Sunday mornings; these classes were attended by postgraduates, many of whom, including a number of women, came from other centers. These women needed residential accommodation, so among the extensions that were built was a postgraduate hostel. These extensions wery made possible by donations made during the golden jubilee of the hospital in 1936.

Cama Hospital hardly had any library to speak of when I took over. As I was keen on keeping up with the times, I subscribed to various journals and purchased some of the latest publications. These I lent to my residents and postgraduate students until I was able to persuade the government to sanction grants for subscriptions to the journals. My residents and students were really appreciative of my interest in them. Some of them, now senior honoraries, collected funds and obtained government sanction to open a post-graduate library at Cama Hospital that was named after me on my eightieth birthday, in 1971.

On my retirement from Cama Hospital I settled at a quiet and picturesque village named Dahisar, which is twenty-five miles from Bombay. At that time, 1953, the village had a scattered population, only well water, and no street lights. Country midwives were attending confinements with dire results. When Dahisar became part of Bombay, I began agitating with the municipal health authorities, requesting them to open a small maternity home for our poor patients. This has not yet materialized, but we live in hope.

I was examiner for the M.D. degree at Bombay, Poona, and Madras universities for many years and was first a member and then chairperson of the Maternity and Child Welfare Committee of the I.R.F.A. I became a member of the Association of Medical Women in India soon after my return from England in 1919. Established in 1907, this was the first medical association in India. Its first meeting was held at Cama Hospital, and the first president was Dr. Benson, who was then in charge of the hospital. I served on the executive committee of the Medical Women's International Association for several years. My interests have made me take a leading part in organizing and encouraging work for general welfare, particularly among mothers and children in this state.

We women in India have not needed to struggle for our rights. Men, with the incentive for social improvement, helped generously to bring women out of their bondage, to promote education, to abolish suttee (immolation of the widow on the husband's funeral pyre), and to encourage widows to remarry. Marriages used to be contracted at a very early age, and therefore there were many child widows. Medical colleges in India were open to women students from the date of their inception. Women have been welcome in all professions, particularly in medicine, as women from most families were reluctant to be examined by men.

Nine years ago I was awarded the Padma Shree, an Indian distinction. If I have helped to achieve some advancement in various fields, I am conscious of and grateful for the cooperation of my colleagues and above all for the inspiration and guidance from God, omnipotent and omniscient.

Hjördis Lind-Campbell

b. June 27, 1891

It was a summer day, and we had just moved to the country. I was seven years old. I wandered around in the sun and watched its reflection in the wooden barrel filled with water. A bumblebee lay there dead. No, it moved a little. I picked it up, dried and warmed it, and saw it gradually come to life, start crawling, and then fly away, its life saved—by me! It made my day.

When I was twelve years old, I was invited to stay for a month with my uncle, an elderly doctor who lived in a small town without any children. It was so boring that the days just crept past. There was a library on the top floor and looking for something worth reading there, I came across my uncle's books from his days as a medical student. Cheeks burning, I read about anatomy, studied the pictures, and gorged myself on descriptions of various diseases. The days flew past as I read book after book. Finally my aunt wondered whatever I was up to and came up and surprised me. The library was locked, and my wonderful time was over.

At the age of seventeen I got to know a district nurse whom I admired, and when she noticed my interest in her work, she invited me to accompany her on her calls one day. One of the people we visited was an elderly widow who supported herself by taking in illegitimate children and looking after them for a small fee. The mothers, often very young, had difficulty in keeping up the payments—and the care of the children lapsed accordingly. On the bed and sofa in the single room lay five small, frail, pale babies with their bottles. There was a terrible stench, and it was a sight I have never been able to forget. Naturally, the death rate among these children was high. In due course it was discovered that a social injustice existed—"baby farming." A society known as the Milk Drop was initiated, and with it a certain check could be kept on infants.

A year or so later I met a nurse with whom I became very friendly. She was employed at a hospital in Stockholm that dealt with women having venereal disease. They were prostitutes, and the aim was to protect men by keeping these women under careful medical surveillance with regular check-ups. If a venereal disease was detected, the infected women were sent to a hospital where they were treated and isolated until all the symptoms had disappeared, after which time they were allowed to return to their "work." There were a mixed bunch of women, from pretty young girls to aged, toothless "mountain larks," so called because they "received" in the hills around Stockholm. I often visited them there, and they were pleased to have a break in their isolation and to show me their best side.

I was the third of four children in a middle-class family. I attended a girls' school for eight years, until I was seventeen. Of course, I had dreamed about becoming a doctor, but the goal was so unattainable that I never dared to mention the idea. One day I noticed an advertisement offering a position for six months as trainee in a maternity home. I applied for the job and was able to start immediately. It was interesting and instructive to help with the deliveries and look after the mothers and the newborn babies. I was full of questions, such as, "Why do you do this or that?" and always the answer was the same: "The doctor said so."

After a few months the matron wanted to talk to me. She was an elderly, kindly woman. She was very pleased with my efforts and wondered if I intended to go on and become a nurse. I answered that I wasn't sure what I was going to be. "Have you considered becoming a doctor?" she asked. "I think you would make a good doctor, and I would advise you to think seriously about it." This was the first time I had received any encouragement in my plans, and now that somebody believed in me, I decided to take the plunge immediately. At the first opportunity when I was free, I went to the higher secondary school with my reports from the girls' school, and was admitted for the next term. I took my higher examinations in the Latin line, and by the new year of 1911 I had completed physics and chemistry and could send in my application to the Karolinska Institute, in Stockholm. There I started my medical studies.

I met neither resistance nor encouragement from my family concerning my choice of profession. We were seldom ill, and on the occasions we were, an old family doctor came in and treated us. Neither the family nor I had met a woman doctor. My father had died suddenly of pneumonia when I was seventeen. I continued to live with my mother. My studies were free, so there were no financial obstacles.

From the first day, I knew I had made the right choice. Everything was of vital interest. I received answers to all my questions. I had always been in a girls' school and had never had any male friends. Now I was the only woman in a class of twenty men, and I felt I would never be able to manage. However, the men were all friendly and courteous and I got used to them during the two and a half years it took to learn the basic science. After that some women colleagues gradually joined me. At the final examination in the course our impressive professor turned to his pupils and said, "You haven't understood very much of this course. Only one of you has grasped the idea of it and given the answer I wanted, and that is graduate Lind." I shall never forget that episode.

After the examination we dispersed. Places were to be made for us at various hospitals. Some stayed in Stockholm, some went to Uppsala, and some chose

Lund. I was among the last group. A new and wonderful world was now opening before us. We were about to work in a hospital, learn to recognize symptoms and to diagnose surgical and medical illnesses. At the same time we spent a few weeks learning to listen to hearts and lungs, to perform laboratory analyses on all types of human secretions, and to question patients about their symptoms. Everything had to be written up in journals, which were the basis of all therapy. In due course we advanced to going on the rounds. In white coats we glided through the wards, first the professor and chief physician or surgeon, next the assistant physician or surgeon, and then we undergraduates. We made a short or longer stop at each bed. Someone responsible for the patient had to give an account of the symptoms, the results of the examination, and suggestions for therapy.

After six months I had come to the same conclusion as a well-known professor. Years after he qualified, he found a letter he had written after six months of practical hospital studies. "I now recognize all diseases and can cure most of them," he had claimed.

After the intensive period of studying before our examination we were now comparatively free and had time to experience the atmosphere of Lund. Between the morning rounds and the afternoon work we had a few hours off. The lectures at the university were inviting, and I sampled those given on various subjects before deciding on the psychology course given by the famous professor Hans Laesson. It was fascinating, and I continued up to the examination in this subject. I now had the opportunity of meeting fellow students from other fields of study, and in this way I met my husband, who at that time was assistant at the museum and later became professor of ethnology at Uppsala.

I continued my medical studies until I attained my medical degree in 1922. It was usual after a number of examinations in the main subjects to take a break in one's studies in order to act as locum tenens. I had been employed as a provincial doctor, I had worked in hospitals and sanatoriums for longer or shorter periods, and I had had time to get married and have two children before taking the examination to become a licensed doctor of medicine in 1922.

Eight days after graduation I was offered employment as a doctor at the sanatorium in Västerås. I took care of the job, and when the usual doctor returned, he made me promise to stand in for him the next time he was away. Off and on for the next eighteen years I was on duty there for shorter or longer periods as assistant doctor and acting chief physician. During these years I also acquired experience by various appointments. I was a doctor in the medical ward for one year, a condition for obtaining specialist competence in pulmonary disease. I was a doctor at an outpatient department for gynecology. I served in a children's hospital and was employed as a provincial doctor. Once, when I was working in a remote place in Varmland, I emerged from the house of a patient who lived out in the backwoods. In the courtyard stood crowds of people and jalopies of all kinds. I turned back in the door and asked whether there was an auction on or why so many people had gathered. "They have come to see the doctor," the patient explained. "None of us has ever seen a woman doctor before!"

In 1940 I started a practice of my own in Västerås, which I carried on for thirty-three years. Besides that, I was a school doctor, a member of the city council for ten years, a member of the board of the central hospital, and a member of the Maternity Assistance Board.

A lucky chance led me to Elise Ottesen-Jensen, who had recently started the National Swedish Association for Sexual Information, and I was invited to be her colleague. For twenty years I traveled to Stockholm every Wednesday and took care of the advisory service there. It was an interesting and varied job. People with sexual problems came to us from all over the country, sometimes even from abroad. We carried on intensive informational activities with lectures and courses. I was especially interested in pregnant women who wanted to have abortions. The initial laws concerning abortion had come out but were very restrictive. Only in the case of mental illness or some other serious disease was an abortion permitted. We decided we had to take care of these women, who were in real difficulty. The association started a pleasant and well-run home where those women who wished could live. When we had applied for an abortion through our welfare officer and the application had been rejected, we had to help these pregnant women to get through the pregnancy and arrange for the expected child. At the same time I often had visits from married women who had not managed to have children despite all the usual examinations and treatments. This led to the idea of starting an adoption agency.

I looked after the adoption agency with the help of the welfare officers. Each expectant mother who wished to have her child adopted was carefully questioned as to ancestry, diseases, characteristics, professions of parents, brothers, sisters, and grandparents on both sides. I generally managed to obtain the same information from the child's father. Only if the child was likely to be normally talented did I dare to take the responsibility of recommending it for adoption. We recommended a foster home for those children we felt doubtful about, and this was taken care of by other organizations. Families wishing to adopt children obtained a testimonial of suitability from the Child Welfare Committee. I repeatedly contacted the families who had been approved, and in this way I gained an impression as to their suitability to take care of a child and bring it up. About 300 children found homes through our efforts during the twenty years I was involved. I am still in touch with parents and children and receive letters and visits from near and far.

During my life as a doctor I have never noticed any signs of sex discrimination, either from colleagues or from the general public. Colleagues have always been friendly and positive in their cooperation. It has often happened that patients in a hospital ward said spontaneously, "What luck that I came to a ward with a woman doctor!"

During my time in private practice almost every day patients have expressed their thankfulness that they have a woman doctor to consult. I feel an enormous sense of gratitude to the fate that gave me the privilege of serving as a doctor. Every day has brought me great satisfaction in being of some use in this field.

As I now finish my life's work, I am pleased that two of my four children have chosen to be physicians.

Giuseppina Pastori
b. October 12, 1891

There was no one remarkable among my ancestors, no famous personage, no doctor, and no cultural tradition in my family. My father and mother were country people. My paternal grandfather and grandmother, as well as my maternal grandfather, had died of typhoid fever during one of the terrible epidemics that often devastated our villages at that time. My parents went to live in Milan, and my father found work at a religious institution. His job was to see to the garden, the vineyard, and the stable. To help with the family budget, my mother became a lace maker. She carried the burden of eight pregnancies. Two of the babies died, so we were six children: the eldest, my sister Louise; I, the second one, the frailest, almost always sickly and often ill; Mary, third; then Charles; Theresa; and finally, Graziano, who became a bank director, alpinist, and mountain poet.

When I attended primary school, each child had to learn by heart a stanza of a poem that was to be recited at the party at the end of the school year. Two children fell ill, and I happened to replace them. I recited three stanzas and received three prizes—that is to say, three nice holy pictures. I realized then that I had a good memory. At the primary school my teacher said to me, "You have shown no merit in being the best because you learn with no effort whatever." In those times children were compelled to go to school until they were eight, but our parents wanted us to go on learning until we were thirteen and we attended a technical school that prepared us for office work. We had to study literature, arithmetic, accounting, history, geography, French, and a little elementary German.

Having finished her schooling successfully, my elder sister Louise took an office job. To my deep regret, the same fate awaited me. But when Mary was about to finish, the principal of the technical school called my mother and said, "Your child is very intelligent; she possesses a mathematical talent and should not drop her schooling. It would be a great pity." She was quite right, as Mary became a professor at the University of Milan and an illustrious member of three academies, including the Academia Nazionale dei Lincei.

One Sunday during the parish catechism I heard some strict judgments about girls who expected to become what only men are fit for. It was declared that the polytechnic school, the scientific faculties, the law school, and so on were for men and not for women, although despite this judgment, the study of medicine was allowed for women because "medicine is a work of charity." Coming back from the church, I confided to my mother, "I shall study medicine." "Just listen to this," she scolded me. "What a foolish thing to say! Your family will never be able to maintain you for six years at the university. You must not dream of it, never even mention it. I forbid you." I never spoke about it, but I always thought and dreamed of it. I spent my day in the office, but in the evening, when my family was assembled in the only room that was kept warm, Mary and I took refuge in our cold rooms. She taught me, without any books, mathematics, physics, and chemistry, and she lent me her own books on other subjects. She obtained her degree with very good marks. I had the courage to sit for the same examination as an external candidate and passed.

Thus, I could leave the office job and teach in a primary school. This success gave me great encouragement. During my teaching I began to learn Latin and Greek, aiming at the Maturita Classica, the degree with which I could have been admitted to the university. Mary, still without books, taught me algebra and trigonometry. Two years later, again as an external candidate, I received my diploma. I was so happy!

In Milan there were still no scientific faculties. To study medicine I had to go to Pavia. I was awarded a scholarship. In Pavia there was a student hostel run by nuns, but they did not accept any medical students, as some had behaved badly. What a change in half a century! The very same religious convent can now boast a dozen nun-doctors, who work in Catholic missions. I rented a room with a very small kitchen and a fireplace. After my lessons at the laboratory or clinic I bought bread, milk, cheese, sausages, sometimes a small piece of goose, and in the spring I bought frogs, which were cheap.

I attended the laboratory of histology, directed by Camillo Golgi, who enchanted us with his histological methods in research on the nervous tissue. That was the heroic period of histology. From the third year onward, the charm of the microscope gave way to the charm of the hospital and working with patients. Research and discussion leading to the diagnosis excited me more and more. I found no examination really difficult, but obstacles were not lacking. During the sixth year, to be admitted to the obstetrics examination, we were obliged to have assisted twice at a delivery. They took place during the day and the night—but more often at night. The male students had a six-bed room at their disposal, and they could sleep there, six in turn every night, to get up when the delivery seemed imminent. And I? I was the only woman. "You will assist at the deliveries that take place during the day." Every night I was sent away—and the naughty babies preferred to be born at night. Days and weeks passed and the examination drew near. I begged the director of the clinic, "Do not send me away again tonight. I can remain here, even if I have to stand." I was lodged in a room with patients.

Exactly at the end of the sixth year, on July 17, 1921, I became a doctor in medicine and surgery. I was offered a job as assistant at the Catholic University of Milan, due to open its courses in December. As the Faculty of Medicine did not exist, I was appointed to the Faculty of Philosophy. I joined the laboratory of psychology and biology and began my histological research. I wanted, however, to be a practitioner. To register in the professional list, I submitted my signature regularly at the health department in my town. Soon after having signed a prescription, I was called to the department and told, "You are not registered." I protested warmly, and they discovered that I had been registered as a midwife, owing to my female name. Without leaving the laboratory at the university, I practiced medicine as a voluntary house officer in the hospital in Milan and was finally offered a job as house officer in a nursing home for chronic patients. My appointment had been discussed by the members of the administrative council, and I was to be given a two-week's trial without remuneration. I made my counterproposal: should my trial period be a failure, I would receive nothing, but if it were a success, I would receive payment. And so it turned out.

Every morning at 8 o'clock I was with my patients. After my rounds I devoted myself to research in medical chemistry, and after that I went to the university. In the afternoons I went back to the nursing home for my rounds again and then on to the laboratory at the university. I had night duty every ten days. My histological research made progress. The Italian Medical Women's Association granted me a scholarship that permitted me to frequent the histological laboratory of the neurological institute at the University of Rome for over six months. During the hospital vacations I studied at the university clinics in Rome, Bologna, and Modena. The chancellor of the Catholic University, Father Gemelli, who was also an old pupil of Camillo Golgi and a worthy histologist, encouraged my histological research.

In the year 1930 I became *libero docente* (that is, a fully established university lecturer) in histology. This degree authorized me to teach biology in the Faculty of Philosophy in my university. However, I needed the nihil obstat of the Holy See. As they did not want to create a precedent by granting a woman a doctorate, this was refused. I was about to leave the university and continue my work in the hospital when my sister Mary reminded me that a famous mathematician, Maria Gaetana Agnesi of Milan (1718–1799), although a woman, had been called to the University of Bologna by an apostolic brief. Among the documents in the Ambrosiana Library in Milan I found this paper signed by Pope Benedict XIV in 1750. There was my precedent. The refusal was withdrawn. How times have changed! Now a lot of women teach at the Catholic University, and they surely have the obstat from the Holy See.

As soon as *Roma locuta est* ("Rome had spoken"), I left the hospital in tears. I had given much attention to my course in biology for philosophers, and my pupils who belonged to the clergy or laity asked me many questions. We discussed and learned together, with a rich library and a good laboratory at our disposal. With the aid of a very intelligent and devoted laboratory technician, I organized some simple experiments, such as microscope observations of tissue sections, bacteria, protozoa, and cultures *in vitro*, verifications of physiological laws in the nerves and muscles of frogs, studies of the myonemes of protozoa, and a thousand other experiments that were very useful for opening our discussions on the phenomena and properties of life. I shall never forget my pupils' fascination with the registration of the movements of an isolated frog or tortoise heart. We fell to speaking about biological problems related to philosophy, the origin of life, the evolution of living species, genetic laws, and the connection between soul and body. I taught hygiene, too, to the *Magistero* classes. I gave the public lectures and published several scientific papers and informative articles, as well as some books for students: *Il substrato biologico della personalita, Le leggi dell'eredita'biologica, La mensa sana,* and *Le origini della vita.*

During World War II my flat was bombed. I slept in a little village at night and came to Milan three times a week to give my lessons. There was no practitioner in the village. I was often summoned for hatchet wounds, pneumonia, and infections, and I helped as well as I could. The peasants thanked me and gave me milk, eggs, and mushrooms as presents. After the war, under the guidance of Professor Herlitzka, the director of the Institute of Physiology at the University of Turin, I began my research on the vital functions of protozoa, the most fascinating of all the subjects I had selected for research.

In 1961 the Catholic University opened its Faculty of Medicine in Rome. I was seventy years old, tired and exhausted, so I retired. I still published articles and gave lectures. I occasionally happen to meet a few old and grateful pupils, which is a great pleasure for me. Now, however, it is right to leave my place to young people. On the day of my last farewell my pupils gave me a big medical encyclopedia as a souvenir.

I never married, and I admire my many colleagues who have accomplished so well the double function of doctor and mother. My too-modest resources did not allow me to do the same. Of the two possibilities, I chose one, and it has been enough for me.

Ellen Balaam
b. November 30, 1891

I was born in Melbourne, in the state of Victoria, in Australia. My grandparents were all of British stock and were pioneer settlers in Victoria early in the 1850s. My paternal grandparents were English, from London and its environs. My grandfather was a wheelright, and my grandmother was a teacher. They settled in the country area of Victoria and lived there all their lives. They had a family of ten, eight of whom grew up into fine adults. My maternal grandfather was a Scot from the north of Sutherlandshire, who had been well educated in Edinburgh. He married an Irishwoman from County Clare, and it was a marvelous union. They settled in Australia on the land just out of Ballarat and later were very early pioneers in the virgin Mallee country, finally becoming successful wheat farmers. They too had a family of ten, eight of whom became adults and enjoyed long lives. The men in my father's family have all been in the engineering and allied industries. Most of the men in my mother's family have stayed on the land, either as wheat or sheep farmers.

Mother and father had a family of nine children, including a set of twins, but they lost a baby; so we were eight children, all of whom grew to adulthood, and there are five girls living, the youngest aged sixty-eight. My elder brother was born in 1889, and I arrived in 1891, the eldest of six girls. We had a healthy childhood in a home with a moderate family income but with good, thrifty parents who had no vices, such as drinking and gambling.

I was reported to have said at the age of seven that I had three ambitions: to be a doctor, to own my own home, and to see the world. All of these, I have achieved. At about that time three young women university students who lived in the next street used to pass our home on their way to church each Sunday. My parents used to point them out, to show me what could be done. Two of these girls became medical practitioners, and the third became one of our first women lawyers. Looking back over the years, I think this may have been one of the early influences that led me into medicine.

In my eighth year we moved, but I still attended the same primary school. I had to walk a long way to do so, but it was considered to be one of the best primary schools at that time. In my final year my teacher was a very good man, of excellent character, and also an outstanding teacher. He was noted for the number of his very successful pupils, many of whom entered the medical profession. He had three sons who became doctors, one of whom was a classmate of mine and who was my chief rival for the top of the class each week. This teacher gave me every encouragement and had a great influence on my entrance into medicine. He knew I was the second eldest of a family of eight children, with a very moderate family income; so when I won a junior scholarship worth ten pounds at the end of the primary year at the age of fourteen, he sent for my mother and begged her to let me take up the scholarship and go on to secondary school. I might mention that this was at the end of 1905, just after a worldwide depression, and my parents, after much thought, finally agreed to allow me to go on.

In Melbourne in 1903 a new type of school, with teachers selected for their pedagogic ability, had been established by the state Department of Education. It was called the Continuation School. My teacher advised my parents to send me to this school after I had won the junior scholarship. I transferred there in February of 1906 and continued there for four years. My teachers were excellent and helped me very much by giving me every encouragement once they knew that my goal was to go to the university and to enter medicine. At the end of the third year I won a senior scholarship for entrance to the university. Only twenty of these were available in the entire state—and only after a special examination. They were worth twenty pounds for each year at the university. I continued for one year in this school and was then awarded a scholarship that entitled me to tutorials in all subjects in first-year medicine.

I entered medicine in 1910 at Melbourne University. The tutorials were a great help to me in my first year, but I could not continue them after that year because my scholarship was a nonresident one at a main college for men students. My senior scholarship allowance of forty pounds per annum did not cover all the fees and books at the medical school; so in order to help my family financially, I did some tutoring in senior general mathematics. I worked during the week and on Saturday afternoons at one of the public schools in Melbourne for the first three years of the course. From then on, I concentrated on my studies, with the result that I finished the five-year course without any failures at all and gained second class honors in all subjects in the final examinations in 1915. My good marks enabled me to be appointed as resident medical officer at Melbourne Hospital for twelve months.

As there was no money available for travel overseas to do postgraduate study, I decided to start in practice. I married a classmate, who had finished as top student, with first class final honors, and had also been appointed as resident medical officer. We were married in June of 1916 and we both started in individual practice.

I was appointed clinical assistant to Queen Victoria Hospital in July of 1917, then full member of the staff in April of 1917, and honorary surgeon to inpatients in January of 1924, from which position I retired some years later.

The Queen Victoria Hospital had been established by the pioneer medical women of Victoria in 1895, to be managed and staffed by women for the women of the state.

I developed a good general practice, including considerable surgery. I was the first woman to do general surgery in Melbourne. During my years in practice I was very thrilled, as well as humbled, by the support and confidence placed in me by my parents and family, my old teachers, friends of my parents, my old schoolmates, and people who had known me as a child and watched my progress through life. I can honestly state that I never came up against any prejudice on account of my sex. I had many men patients, even for surgery. To the best of my knowledge, I did not experience any prejudice among my colleagues, men or women. In fact, when I commenced in private practice, most of the older women colleagues gave me every encouragement and support.

I retired at sixty, after thirty-five very busy years full of work and happiness because I was able to help people. I enjoyed every minute of those years and have no regrets or grievances. My husband died in 1964, at the age of seventy-eight, and unfortunately, we had no children. Since my retirement I have cared for my house and garden. I enjoy reading, music, the theater, opera, ballet, and travel when possible.

A niece and two grandnieces have gone into medicine, without being actively influenced by me, and there is the possibility of another grandniece's following them. It gives me great pleasure to think that I may have been the inspiration for their decision to enter this profession, and I sincerely hope that they will find as much happiness in their chosen career as I did.

CANADA

Margaret Owens
b. January 11, 1892

Great-grandfather was a merchant in Boston and a United Empire Loyalist who, when his business went into a decline, moved to the Ottawa Valley in 1818 and settled on a farm near Lachute in Quebec. His descendants still till those acres. Great-grandfather's log house was built on the bank of the Ottawa River, and in the year of the "high water," it was carried away in the flood. Great-grandmother was taken away on a raft; her baby (my grandfather) had to be delivered in a barn, and she died. Great-grandfather sent to Yorkshire, England, to ask his wife's widowed sister to come out to Canada to look after the new baby and the other children. She came, with her own two children, and three years later she and my great-grandfather married.

My grandfather farmed the land, but while his brothers did the actual farming, he became a carpenter and cabinet maker. I rmember him well. He was almost blind, and I used to pass the tools to him to help with his cabinet making. All our sleighs, wagons, and furniture were made by hand, and much of this is still in my sister's house. My father grew up on the family property and remained there after his brothers and sisters went west and settled in Manitoba in 1877.

We children went to school in Hotspur, Ontario, five miles from our home. To get there, we had to cross an interprovincial railway bridge. We walked over on Sunday night and came back on Friday night. We took our food with us, and our landlady prepared our meals. There were seven of us, and I was the second eldest. I have happy memories of life on that remote Quebec farm. All seven children loved to help with the maple-syrup production. We used to tap about 300 trees, and on such occasions all the neighbors helped with the "sugaring-off." I drove and rode horses from the time I was six years old.

The year I graduated from high school in Ontario, our home was destroyed by fire. I taught in a country school for a year, with pupils ranging from six to twenty-one years of age, at a salary of thirty dollars per month. I then went to normal school in Ottawa, and taught until 1918. My two sisters also attended normal school, after which one went to Queen's University and one to McMaster.

I, however, wanted to study medicine. I was the only one in the family with this desire. Both father and mother had had acute rheumatic fever in their teens, and an uncle had died of the same disease at twenty-one. Thus, my earliest childhood was associated with illness. When my youngest brother was born, both father and mother had rheumatic fever again, and they were very ill for three months. The next year mother had lobar pneumonia. I heard the doctor tell father, "Your wife is very ill, and there is so little we can do, but if you could get help to keep flax-seed poultices applied twenty-four hours a day until the crisis comes, then she has a good chance of survival." A neighbor was asked and came. This was my first experience of being in attendance throughout an illness. The neighbor kept the poultices hot downstairs, and I carried them upstairs to my grandmother, who attended my mother. Although mother recovered, she was left with severe mitral stenosis. I remember how frightened I was. The doctor could only make one trip, a twelve-mile drive behind a horse in winter, which took a whole day. The care of the patient was left to the neighbor and my grandmother. This may have influenced me to become a doctor.

My father thought it was unwise for a woman to take up medicine but left the decision to me. Neither did my high-school principal approve of my choice. I had never seen a medical woman. However, I applied to McGill, and they turned me down, as they had not yet accepted women in medicine. My next application was to Toronto University because I had taken my matriculation in Ontario with honors, which was a prerequisite for entrance to Toronto. They accepted me. Ellen Douglas had graduated from Toronto in 1905, and there had been other women after her, but I did not know any of them. Neither had I yet heard of Maude Abbott, who had gone to Bishop's College in Lennoxville, the only medical school in Quebec that accepted women.

During the war years everybody was called up to help in the Niagara belt at harvest time. I went to a large tomato-canning factory and worked with all the women employees. This was a national war effort, as the canned tomatoes went overseas to the soldiers. We also picked peaches, pears, and grapes until it was time to go back to the university. One week after my return I came down with influenza and was seriously ill. The next thing I remember was the noise made on November 11 by students celebrating Armistice Day. Across the hall was another medical student who was so ill that she became deaf and had to give up medicine and go into science.

By January I was well enough to enter a class with the returned soldiers. We were the largest group ever to register at Toronto University. Many were older and already had other degrees. I was still in poor health and found the courses difficult, but with the help of iron injections, I managed to keep going. That summer I went to Muskoko and lived there with little to do but look after four children along with another student. I returned there the next summer as a waitress and averaged $200 per month.

There were seventeen women in my class, which entered in 1918. Charles Best, Clark Noble, and Bess Chant Robertson were among classmates who became famous. Frederick Banting was one of our teachers.

When 266 of us graduated in 1923, it was a rule that only two were privileged to intern in the Montreal General Hospital. I applied and was fortunate to be the first woman intern to be accepted there. Since the hospital would not let me room there, on the excuse that there was no space, I lived in the home of Dr. Mary Bird. I spent four months in the outdoor clinic in emergency surgery, six months in medicine, and three months in anesthesia. That year I met and worked with Maude Abbott.

The following year I was the first woman to be accepted at the Royal Victoria Hospital, with Dr. Chipman as my chief in obstetrics and gynecology. He insisted that I do clerical work at first because he was president of the America College of Surgery and he needed his records surveyed for a paper he was to give at their next meeting. While I was an intern, I had checked the galley proofs of the bibliography of Sir William Osler on behalf of Maude Abbott, and she told this to Dr. Chipman; so I had to work up his clinical records and was not taken on in gynecology. I went over to pharmacology, as I could fit this in with the work on the records. When these were finished, Dr. Chipman gave me my appointment as an intern, prompting a member of the staff to say, "I don't believe it. There will be two moons in the heavens before our chief gives a woman an appointment. He has no use for women doctors. She will not last six months in his service." As it turned out, Dr. Chipman and I became the best of friends, and I worked with him both in surgery and in gynecology. He was a wonderful man to work for. We did special rounds on Sundays, after which he would sometimes ask me home for lunch. Mrs. Chipman was a fine woman, totally blind. At that time radium seeds were used in gynecology, and she had donated $15,000 for radium.

After two years I went to Philadelphia to study pathology with Lola McLatchie, then spent a month doing radium treatment of carcinoma of the cervix before returning to Canada.

When I think of heroic women, my first choice is Maude Abbott. She was such a marvelous woman. My other choice would be Miss Webster, night supervisor at Montreal General. I was in acute surgery, and all sorts of emergencies came in from the streets. I never knew anyone so like Florence Nightingale as Miss Webster; she was actually in charge of that hospital at night for twenty-five years.

In 1929 I went out west to work for the Alberta Public Health Department, arriving in Edmonton on St. Patrick's Day. I was the first woman to join the public health staff. At that time our program included going to the outlying districts where the department had organized nursing services. One of the first calls to reach Edmonton was because of an outbreak of diphtheria at Fort Vermilion. In order to get the toxoid there as quickly as possible, Wop May, who had been a famous war pilot, flew the first commercial plane to the north.

I then visited Jarvie, the first area to be served by a district nurse. I observed her work for about two months, giving consultations when her patients required medical care or hospitalization. In Wanham, my second district, I had several interesting experiences. I was called to attend a maternity case in the direction in which a forest fire had been burning the previous day. Arriving by train, I found twenty-two men guarding the grain elevator and other buildings. I proceeded on horseback through the burned-out area to confine the woman, who was living in a cabin that had been surrounded by fire the day before. Not far away, I found another woman, a mother of four children, lying on the floor of a burned-out cabin, and I confined her, too. As the fire was still smoldering in some areas, I decided to send a mounted policeman as soon as I could to guard these two families in case of a new flare-up. The Mountie found the second woman up, doing her work with the help of the first. These were immigrants. There was no food for them, so I reported that they needed relief. It is hard to picture the pioneer situation of these people, who could speak no English and had no interpreter. In one instance, when I asked a husband to hold a lamp so that I could see to cut a baby's cord, he collapsed in his chair at the sight of blood. The lamp went out, and I had to continue in the dark. Since I had been trained in sterile technique, conducting deliveries under these conditions really tested my powers of adaptation. I never heard of a single case of infection in all the strange circumstances under which I did maternity work. The women took the matter so calmly that there was never a sound in the house. The children were in bed a few feet from their mother and never knew that I was there. In the morning they would find a new brother or sister.

I was sent out with a traveling clinic every summer for six years. I had a trained staff of nurses, a surgeon, and two dentists. I found this work extremely interesting. We visited only outlying districts where children had no opportunity to have medical or dental examinations. District nurses did an inspection of the district before our arrival, appointments were made, and the local people, who were very cooperative, chose a hall, had it cleaned, collected cots and tables, and set up a separate room for operations. As the children arrived, histories were taken; then the children were undressed, and they filed past us for examination. They were first seen by the dentists, then by the ear, nose, and throat specialist, and then by me for a general medical examination. These were the depression years, which meant poverty and malnutrition and thus an extreme effect on dentition and vision, as the children were without vegetables, milk, or fruit. The only thing that the mothers could get was cod-liver oil. Vitamin deficiencies were common, and in one clinic 25 percent of the girls had adolescent goiters. We had the water examined, and it was totally devoid of iodine.

The clinic traveled as far north as Grande Prairie, 500 miles beyond Edmonton. The nurses and I lived there in cabins. Our food was brought to us by truck. Horseback riding was no trouble for me on these trips, even when it involved my being thrown off in muskegs and having to creep to safe ground to remount.

I have never myself driven a dog team, although I have often been transported on the sled, warmly wrapped up, with my bag on my knees and the driver calling out, "Mush!" Dog teams are best for crossing lakes, as horses insist on going around. The Indians, who are excellent mushers, have three to five dogs in a team.

Whenever a Mountie reported that an Indian woman needed medical attention, we had to fetch her out to some place where I could give this care. One such case was that of a pregnant Indian girl, only seventeen years old, living on the sixty-mile-long trail to Battle River, without any real road or any place to stop overnight. With a dog team and sleigh the Mountie and I found her in two days, and I decided that she was almost at term. The Mountie had to proceed farther to fetch a prisoner. I was fortunate to be able to stay with Dr. Mary Percy Jackson and her trader husband. On Christmas morning, the very next day, he presented each of us with a large flour sack filled with a beautiful black bearskin. The postman who brought the mail once a year from Fort Vermilion arrived with his wife and nine horses, after which we all set off for Battle River, traveling with three sleighs and two tons of mail. We first picked up my patient, as well as the body of her fifteen-year-old brother, who had frozen to death the day before. Her father and the two younger children had to be taken along, as her father had to report the death and bury the boy.

On one sleigh the postman had a small stove, on which he melted snow while I cooked oatmeal porridge and dried out wet socks and mittens. I creamed everyone's face with cold cream to prevent frostbite. The men walked all the way on snowshoes. The horses suffered terribly and could scarcely breathe, let alone pull the mail. It was then 72 degrees below zero. After five days and nights on the trail we got back to Battle River, and the baby was born two days later. The mother had a severe postpartum hemorrhage. None of us could have survived had it not been for the knowledge of these northern men as to how to manage in such extreme cold.

In 1936 the new premier of Alberta, Mr. Eberhart, who did not approve of women doctors, made things so uncomfortable for me that I felt compelled to resign. I went to Winnipeg, bought a home, and set up a practice in obstetrics and gynecology. Because I had always admired hand-crafted furniture, I hired an expert local craftsman to make furniture for my home, and I still have many of these pieces. This home was destroyed when the Red River overflowed in 1950.

I started teaching about contraceptives when I came to Winnipeg, chiefly because of an experience with a woman on a homestead in Alberta. She had been confined in Edmonton and was kept in the hospital for five days, after which she traveled with her new baby 500 miles to her homestead. Not long afterward, her husband came 25 miles to fetch me to see his wife, and we arrived just as she died, leaving him with eight children, the eldest a girl of fourteen years. The mother had told her husband that she would never live to have another child. I have never seen children so terrified as those eight, and their faces still haunt me. Never after did I want to see a woman bring a child into the world against her will. I practiced in Winnipeg for nearly forty years and was instrumental in starting planned parenthood clinics in the city. Many of my gynecological colleagues opposed me in this work, but I had seen too many tragedies where women perished from repeated childbearing, leaving numbers of children with no one to care for them, so I continued with family planning.

In 1939 I married Alfred Waite, whom I had met while working up in the north. He had been brought to me as a patient when he was working with an aerial-photographic survey crew and was unconscious from exposure to high altitudes for too long a time. In the following years we saw each other frequently, and when his work brought him to Winnipeg to set up a training school for aircraft mechanics and pilots, we decided to marry.

I have attended many meetings of the Medical Women's International Association, and I have been secretary, treasurer, and president of the Federation of Medical Women of Canada. It was during my presidency that Queen Wilhelmina of the Netherlands presented us with the Arnhem Medal. Since that time it has been used as the badge of office for the presidents of our association.

BRAZIL

Carlota Pereira de Queiroz
b. February 13, 1892

I was born in São Paulo, Brazil, and until I was eight years old I led a happy life, free of worry. I lived in a typical country house in the residential part of the city with my parents, grandmother, and Manuel Elpidio, my brother. As was usual in those days, we had household help and even old slaves who had remained faithful to the family. Family reunions were common, as were parties on special occasions.

I was a delicate child until the age of six, thus causing my parents and grandmother a good deal of worry. From then on, however, I flourished and, because of my size, appeared to be older than my age. Dolls were my favorite toys. I had a number of "children," and what pleased me most was being their "doctor." This was a reason for constant quarrels with my older brother, who used to make fun of me by saying, "That is not a profession for a woman, and when I grow up, I will become a doctor and take away all your patients. Who will choose a woman when they can call a male doctor?"—a statement both irritating and challenging!

I started school when I was four in the recently opened kindergarten. My stay was short, as I was not able to adjust to the discipline and make contact with so many children. Two years later I went to the Prudents de Moraes Model School, where I fitted in very well. I learned to read without difficulty, was always a good pupil, and studied with pleasure. I made close friends among my schoolmates and have retained the friendship of some ever since.

When I was about eight years of age, two significant events took place. The first was a visit with my mother to a woman doctor's office. Dr. Renotte was the first woman doctor I had ever met. She was Belgian by birth and had already qualified when she arrived in São Paulo. She had a large practice, and I saw then how a woman could be a successful doctor. The second event was having to leave our home, which for my brother and me had been a real paradise. Economic reasons demanded changes in our style of living and a reduction in all types of expenditure.

I went to a different public school, closer to the new house. At this time one of my teachers noticed that I could not see well from a distance. She warned my father, who took me to an occulist. The diagnosis was myopia, and I have worn spectacles ever since.

In 1904 I took a teachers' training course in order to become a primary-school teacher. I firmly intended to work, as our economic situation demanded it. The courses were in the same school I was attending and were considered the highest possible level of education for a girl.

That same year, 1904, my mother gave birth to a girl named Maria and two years later to a boy, Alfredo. These two additions provided the family with much excitement and happiness.

I obtained my primary-school teaching diploma in 1909, and in view of my high marks, the director invited me to work in the same school. Overcoming family resistance, I accepted the offer and was appointed primary-school inspector. After two years the director suggested that I teach in the kindergarten, and my knowledge of the Froebel and Montessori systems dates from that period. Being with children, I began to realize the importance a child's health has on his or her schoolwork.

Our life improved from an economic point of view and in 1912 we moved to our own home, built by my father in a new residential district. Even so, I paid my own way with the money I earned from my work. My education was no longer limited to school studies; I took private lessons in music, languages, and painting, given by able teachers, all at my own expense, and I also paid other personal expenses. I learned to read, write, and speak French and English with ease, especially French. I took part in social and sporting activities, learned to play tennis, and used to go to dancing parties at the homes of friends and relatives. I was, however, disillusioned with my career as a teacher. The prospects were poor, with little hope of advancement and with the best jobs going to men. I left teaching but continued to give private lessons in order to maintain a certain economic independence. At that time, despite the fact that a woman could have an excellent level of education, as in my case, there was no access to the majority of the professions, which were exclusively filled by men. I was dissatisfied with this situation and believed that a woman had to develop her spirit and her abilities, becoming more active and more productive in society, as well as in the family. There was nothing to prevent women from performing jobs that until then had been reserved for men, as long as women could demonstrate equal ability. Therefore, I started to favor coeducation, as the close companionship and mutual influences could only benefit the future lives of both sexes.

During that time I suffered from a stubborn sinus infection, and my parents took me to Rio de Janeiro to consult Professor Miguel Couto, a man well known throughout the country and abroad as a physician and scientist. It was my first contact with this expert, who was also a man of great insight into human character and who had a very important influence on me at that period of my life. Apart from treating my health, he noticed my state of mind: the disenchantment with my profession and the prejudice I faced when I planned new ventures, for example, the study of medicine, which attracted me so much. I could see a vast, rich field in medical science, where, with dedication, I could develop useful activities throughout my life. Having evaluated my ability during several discussions, Professor Couto promised me that, once I graduated, he would take me as his assistant. The idea was not well received by my family, especially my father, who however conceded that he no longer had the right to interfere with any of my decisions. Miguel Couto's stimulus was decisive, and in 1920, after studying alone for two months, I took the entrance examination at the Faculty of Medicine of São Paulo and was accepted.

There were only three women in my group. I attended this faculty until my third year, 1923, when I moved to the Medical School of Rio de Janeiro.

In the Faculty of Medicine of Rio de Janeiro I really found a different atmosphere among the students. There were only five women in the whole group; one died during the course, and the other four graduated. Of these, two never practiced their profession and a third became a medical hygienist; she is now retired and still my friend. I am the only one who practiced medicine. In my fifth year I was already an active intern for Professor Couto. My introduction to hematology dates from that time, as Professor Couto required a hematological examination of patients in his ward. During that year I chose the subject of my thesis with his help. It was entitled "Cancer in Children."

Toward the end of 1925, taking advantage of my holidays, I made my first trip abroad and, together with a group of friends, took a cruise to the Orient followed by a few days in Paris and London. My interest in visiting London was connected with research for my thesis. It was there that Peyton Rous was developing his detailed studies on cancer in rats, and I had the opportunity of meeting him and knowing his work. On my return a happy coincidence helped me. Madame Curie visited Brazil, and I was chosen to accompany her to see the old cities of Minas Gerais.

In my sixth year I registered as a resident intern at the Artur Bernardes Hospital, specializing in newborn babies, under the direction of Professor Figueira. There I held the position of director of the school for young mothers, to whom we gave lessons on child care. I continued working on my thesis, and having reached the conclusion that there was no difference between cancer in children and in adults, I changed the title, making it more general: "Studies on Cancer." When I presented my thesis, it was passed with distinction by the examining board, and I was presented with the Miguel Couto Prize, which had just been created. I also received honorary mention from the Cancer Institute for having been the first person in Brazil to have done experimental studies on live animals in this specialty. All my family—my parents, my older brother and his wife, and my younger brother and sister—came to my graduation, traveling from São Paulo for the occasion.

As a result of the success of my thesis I was contacted by a group that was planning to found an institute for the study of cancer and wanted me to work in it. Interested, I decided to go to Europe to look for more advanced centers where I could study, and I took courses in Paris, Italy, Switzerland, and Germany. In Paris I was made a member of the French Society for Studies on

Cancer. I returned at the end of a year to be greeted by the disappointing news that the institute did not yet exist, and in fact, it was never created. I went to São Paulo, where, not finding any research work available, I decided to open my own consulting rooms, together with three male colleagues. At that time (1928) I was appointed laboratory chief of the pediatrics clinic of Professor Pinheiro Cintra in the charity hospital of São Paulo. As the professor was a serious student of hematology, he always encouraged me to continue my work in that specialty. This I did, and I always had a large number of patients, especially women and girls.

Since 1930 the country had been living through great political turmoil. In 1932 the Constitutionalist revolution broke out in São Paulo. Its aim was to reconstitute the country, which had been under a special regime for two years, and the atmosphere was one of civic enthusiasm. Giving my support to the movement, I became part of the organizational commission of the Department of Assistance to the Wounded. The federal government managed to defeat the movement but also decided to promulgate a new constitution, under which women were given the right to vote. The Federation of Volunteers decided to appoint a woman, thus paying homage to the women who had helped during the revolution. My name was chosen, and I was elected, becoming the first congresswoman in Brazil—and in all South America. I took part in the Constituent Assembly, which gave the new constitution to the country. In the Chamber of Deputies, in view of my background as a teacher and a doctor, I concentrated on health and educational problems. As a member of the Commission on Health and Education I paid special attention to literacy, to education in general, and to improving conditions for mothers and children, particularly the poor and abandoned. Projects that were my own were the creation of social-service schools, the creation of a laboratory for child biology in Rio de Janeiro, where an abandoned child would be fully examined before being passed on to the appropriate educational authority, and the establishment of Child Welfare Week.

In 1937, with the close of the Congress and the establishment of the new dictatorial regime, my political career was finished. I returned to São Paulo to reopen my surgical practice and take up again my specialty in hematology. Next to my surgery, I established a clinical laboratory, where, apart from hematological tests, I performed various preoperative tests. My surgical colleagues began to send me patients so that I could prepare them for any surgery they required.

My father died in 1940 at the age of seventy-eight. My mother, my youngest brother, and I continued living in the same house. In 1941 I was unanimously elected honorary member of the Society of Medicine and Surgery of São Paulo.

The years of 1942 and 1944 were notable for my entry into the Brazilian Academy of Medicine and into the National Academy of Medicine of Buenos Aires, respectively. In both academies I was the first woman elected, and in our Brazilian academy only two women—Madame Curie and Madame Durocher—had previously appeared as honorary members.

I could not renounce my interest in national politics after having participated so intensely. I worked actively in the movement for the redemocratization of the country, which took place in 1945. The dictator was deposed, and general elections were called with the proclamation of the new constitution.

When a teaching hospital, attached to the Faculty of Medicine, was built in São Paulo, I was transferred there to work as the technical assistant in hematology. I retired from public service some years later. In 1950 I received the Legion of Honor of France.

My brother Alfredo married in 1957, when he was already regarded as a confirmed bachelor, leaving only my mother and me in our house, which then seemed very large. My mother died toward the end of that year, when she was nearly ninety. As I was all alone, I moved in 1960 to an apartment building in the same area, leaving the home I had lived in for fifty years. I also opened my surgery, but without a laboratory, in the same building.

It was about this time that the Brazilian Association of Medical Women was formed, and I played an active and enthusiastic part from the beginning. On September 16, 1961, the election of the first board of directors was held, and I was elected president with a two-year mandate. I was reelected for the second and third two-year periods, and in 1967 I received the title of honorary president. I was always very interested in the problems of the association, fighting to the best of my ability for its growth, taking part in its programs and meetings, and attending national and international congresses.

In 1963 I had my first serious health problem. After a successful operation, I recovered and quickly returned to a normal life. I was able to accompany some friends to Europe, where I had not been since 1930.

In December of 1964 the São Paulo City Council awarded me the title of Honorary Citizen.

Having reduced my professional activities, I turned to the study of family documents that had been in my hands for many years and that I had always wanted to investigate. I then published a book on my paternal grandfather entitled *A Paulista Farmer of the XIX Century*. That same year (1965) I closed my surgery for good.

In 1967 my brother Alfredo died in an automobile accident. I was so shocked that I acquired a diabetic disorder and also began to have problems with my vision. In 1968 I went with some colleagues to the Eleventh Congress of Medical Women, which was held in Vienna. The fact that I was able to take part in such a large gathering cheered me up, and I was very enthusiastic about the congress.

My sight became worse, with the occurrence first of a retinal hemorrhage and then glaucoma, requiring the removal of my left eye. The operation was successful, but I was very depressed.

On reaching my eightieth birthday, in 1972, the São Paulo State Legislative Chamber honored me with a special commemorative session.

My right eye showed signs of a cataract and glaucoma and was under constant treatment. Finally, in 1973, I had a cataract operation, resulting in little improvement in my vision because of the glaucoma. In fact, at present I cannot read or write.

In 1974 I had the pleasure of participating in the Fourteenth Congress of the Medical Women's International Association, which took place in Rio de Janeiro. I was present at the inaugural session and took part in the closing banquet with 400 women doctors from various countries. My enthusiasm for my profession and for the association is still very much alive.

In closing I would like to quote parts of the speech I made in 1961, when I accepted the position of president of the Brazilian Association of Medical Women, as it expresses my way of thinking.

When I started my medical studies, more than forty years ago, it was an effrontery and almost an adventure for a woman to want to be a doctor. Today the student groups in the school are more than 30 percent women. Once this association was founded, it very soon gathered, as members, more than 200 professional women in the medical field, from all parts of this vast territory, which is Brazil. They came together to get to know one another and to discuss their common problems. This is the greatest proof of the usefulness of its foundation.

Aware of her rights and her duties and deeply convinced of her professional responsibility, the medical woman will have to be respected for her own worth and her moral competence. She should not give up her female personality; neither should she try to imitate men or aim to replace them.

Our association, with a true social spirit, wishes to gather medical women together to give them more awareness of their role, so that they may serve their profession better and make it more noble in every way.

Having graduated thirty-five years ago, I cannot hope for a better prize at the end of this career than to see gathered together in a meeting around me, as my successors, this new generation of medical women, who represent many hundreds of others scattered throughout Brazil and who also represent the realization of my old ideals.

Anna Maria Dengel
b. March 16, 1892

The memories I recall of the happy days of my early childhood with my beloved parents, grandparents, and other relatives, including of course my brothers and sisters, produce a warm glow in my heart and will never be erased from my mind. I was the eldest of nine children.

It was in the lovely Tyrol of Austria that I was born on a cold winter day, in Steeg in the Lechtal. In recalling my early years, the beautiful setting of mountains, meadows, and trees brings into my heart feelings that cannot be described but have to be felt to be appreciated. My father inherited the ancestral house, with its farm and grocery store, from my grandfather. Father was educated in the famous commercial school (*Handelsschule*) of Kempten in nearby Bavaria. The school exists to this day. On returning to the Tyrol, he met my mother who was the daughter of a church decorator from a neighboring village. She had inherited the artistic talents of her father and was trained as a professional embroiderer of church vestments and banners. When my parents had been married for a while and children had been born to them, they decided, for the sake of educating us, to give up the farm and store and to take up the church-vestment business in a city in a more central part of the Tyrol, since our village Steeg was very isolated. I had one year of schooling in Steeg and then attended school in Hall, near Innsbruck. I entered the regular city school and was able to follow without any difficulty.

The school system in Austria had been inaugurated by Empress Maria Theresa (1717–1780), and even the village schools were good. Prior to our move from the village I had my first experience of illness in our family. My father had contracted Russian influenza, which did not seem to want to leave him and had made him very weak. My mother therefore went with him to the famous Father Kneipp in Wörishofen, Germany, for the then much dispited "water cure." Father Kneipp personally took care of father, and my family attributed his recovery to this man. For years afterward father returned annually to Wörishofen for treatment. Once, when I was a little older, he took me with him, and I learned to like and appreciate this natural cure. As a result of my father's recovery by "natural means," the use of medicines in our family was minimal and we believed in simple and wholesome food.

My other experience with illness was the early death of my mother, when I was about eight years old. Her demise caused me terrible suffering, and I attribute to this pain the compassion I later had for the women and children of India.

After the death of my mother, father sent me and one of my sisters to the boarding school of the Visitation Sisters in Hall, where we received a commendable education, not only in academics but in character. We were minutely cared for in every aspect. Christian ideals were instilled in us. At that time Countess Theresa Ledochowska, who eventually founded the Sisters of St. Peter Claver, was active in speaking and writing on behalf of the African slaves. Her fire for the good cause caught my heart, and I resolved to study languages in order to be able to be involved in missionary activity, in helping the needy, and in spreading the word of God. I wished to bring joy to the sorrowing and light into the darkness.

To perfect my French, I seized the opportunity of going to Lyons, where I helped with the teaching of German. I stayed there for two years, but teaching was not what I had in mind for my life. The thought of missions would not leave me, and when by a coincidence, after having returned to Austria, I read about a nursing school in Lyons where young women would be prepared for nursing service in mission territories, I asked a friend to inquire about this school for me.

This led to something very important in my life, for I came in touch with a great woman doctor. Instead of telling me more about the nursing school, my friend told me of a certain Dr. Agnes McLaren. It would take pages to describe her worth. Agnes McLaren was born in Edinburgh in 1837. She studied medicine in Montpellier, France, as the medical schools in Britain were not open to women at that time. She then practiced medicine in the South of France. She had a high ideal of the mission of Christian women. To uphold the dignity and rights of women, she prayed, wrote, and traveled throughout Europe. Imbued with the spirit of a true crusader, she even brought the needs of women to the heads of state. Great was her endeavor for the abolition of the white-slave trade. Her life was spent for the cause of Christian morals and the worldwide reign of social justice.

The women of India claimed her special attention. She had heard of their medical needs, their misery and helplessness, which resulted from the purdah system of the Orient. For medical aid, they depended on women doctors, who in those days were few and far between. The mortality of young mothers and children was pitifully high. Agnes McLaren's heart was so moved by their plight that she resolved to do her share in lifting their burden of unnecessary and preventable suffering. In a providential way she met Monsignor Dominic Wagenaar of Mill Hill, who had spent many years in the north of India, now Pakistan. He had long realized the need for Catholic hospitals for women and staffed by women! At the age of seventy-two the ardent Dr. McLaren traveled to

Rawalpindi, now Pakistan, where she founded a hospital for women and children. She did this with the help of Monsignor Wagenaar and a committee of Englishwomen in London. Agnes McLaren pleaded for young women to study medicine and then come to the aid of the purdah woman. She even offered to help with their expenses in a small way. Her call came to my ears and kindled a fire in my heart that has not been extinguished to this day.

Through her suggestion I applied for admission to University College, Cork, Ireland, since I needed a British diploma in order to practice medicine in India. Sir Bertram Windle, then the president of the medical school, was much interested in Dr. McLaren's ideas. He encouraged me to take up the study of medicine at Queen's College. Having passed my premedical courses, I entered the college in October of 1913. Alas, World War I broke out in 1914, leaving me without help from my family in Austria and without contact with them. These were hard years for me. I was poor and had to do all sorts of work to pay the tuition, but kind people and my own determination saw me through to graduation with honors. It was 1919 by then. I needed a fee of five pounds in order to sit for the final examination. The sum was lent to me by Professor Mary Ryan, whose brother later became bishop of Trinidad. This was the only debt I incurred, and I repaid it with part of my first salary. Agnes McLaren died in April of 1913. To my great disappointment, I never met her personally.

I now turned my attention to securing a position, in order to gain experience for future mission work and to spend my time profitably while awaiting my visa for India. It was supposed to take five years for a non-British subject to obtain one! Ireland had sufficient doctors, so I wrote many letters to various prospects in England. Through a friend I was accepted as assistant to two doctors in private practice at Claycross, near Nottingham. One of them told me later that he knew I was a foreigner by the small tail I added to the D in my name, then added, "Queens College always turns out good doctors." The position was on a salary basis of 500 pounds a year, and I had to take all the night calls and a turn at the surgery each day. This was a mining district, and attempted suicide was not uncommon. During an influenza epidemic I once made sixty-two calls in one day. It was here I learned to master a bicycle, which was to stand me in good stead in India.

The visa for India came unexpectedly fast. The committee that worked for the little hospital that Agnes McLaren had founded in Rawalpindi used their influence to speed up the visa, since there was no doctor in the Rawalpindi hospital for which I was destined. After a short visit home to my family in the Tyrol, I took the boat for India.

This was in October of 1920. I then took up duty at St. Catherine's Hospital. The work was overwhelming. Besides the study of language, there was hospital work, the dispensary, and home visits. I quickly realized that this was a task for many and not for one. I could not have endured it longer than the four years I was there. No matter where I looked, I saw unrelieved, although preventable, suffering. Malaria was common, epidemics were a constant threat, and government facilities were very limited. The marriage age was about fifteen, and the mortality of young mothers was very high, as midwifery was just being introduced. The awareness of the need for cleanliness was still rare. The hospital, although small, was not always full because the women, especially the Moslem women, could not easily come to stay. We had many obstetric cases, very often complicated ones. The few sisters present in the hospital were, owing to Church laws, prevented from assisting in midwifery, which in view of the haphazard care of women in childbirth, presented a serious gap in a women's hospital. This attitude, as well as our inability to help mothers in their hour of need under the prevailing conditions in India, touched me deeply and spurred me on to find a solution.

I was determined to return to the Western world to make these things known and to bring them to the attention of my fellow Christians and the Church. In England I made my intention known to one of the members of the committee, Miss Pauline Willis, who was a most wonderfully zealous worker for any good cause. Given the poverty of Europe after World War I, there seemed to be no sense in speaking there; so I was—I do not know how—urged to go to America, which I did in the company of Miss Willis, A Bostonian of great influence. She introduced me to bishops, priests, religious superiors, women's leagues, and influential charitable women and clubs. The generosity of the Americans equaled my fire, and by the grace of God, within a year I had founded what was then the only possibility for my purpose—a missionary medical sisterhood—because the practice of medicine in its full scope was not permitted to nuns.

I knew the Church would see the great need and would eventually permit nuns to become medical doctors, and so it turned out. In the year 1936, eleven years after we had formed the Pious Society, not only was the permission given by the Church but religious congregations of women were encouraged to train medical people for this important work.

Fifty years have now gone by, and seven hundred co-workers are my consolation; they will carry on the mission started in 1925. The reports that come from far and wide of the work of our sisters amaze me and make me grateful to God that He let the seed fall and let fruit spring forth.

In 1975, the year of the jubilee of the Missionary Medical Sisters, I received wonderful letters from our sisters, commenting on their happiness in being called to serve the sick and the suffering, to heal and comfort them, to help raise womanhood to the dignity due it, and to aid in bringing peace and justice into this world.

This is in a few words what could be told in a few thousand words, but all is written in the "book of life."

May Ratnayake
b. May 31, 1892

Our ancient system of *Ayurveda*, although the preserve of "learned pundits," was taught and handed down as a family secret. When, as sometimes happened, a daughter was the only candidate for studies in medicine, the female physician was accepted with full honors. Thus, for a woman to become a doctor was not prohibited. The training of women, along with men, at the medical college was, however, a bit of a hurdle.

When in 1896 the government called for women medical students to be trained as doctors in order to staff the newly built Lady Havelock Hospital for Women, Dutch burgher women were the first to respond. There was, however, one Sinhalese woman student, Lucy de Abrew. She came from a family of scholars. The first girls' school in Colombo, now over a century old, was built and endowed by her father, a German educationalist. Lucy was a brilliant scholar, but unfortunately, she succumbed to cerebral malaria while on a pilgrimage to Anuradhapura.

I was born at Kandy, Ceylon (now Sri Lanka). My father, Dr. John de Livera, having worked at the general hospital in Colombo and at Kandy, was due to take his turn at one of the less popular hospitals along the great white road that then linked the upcountry forest with the towns. Thus, my earliest and happiest memories are of forested hills and wide open spaces where we roamed at will. Our garden was full of roses. A great passion-fruit creeper grew like a curtain over the front verandah. One day my father sent a note across to us for emergency dressings for a man mauled by a bear. Mother began tearing up old sheets and then decided to go over herself to render first aid. Villagers have their own first-aid remedies; they use opium and ganga for the relief of pain and shock. They had carried the man out of the forest on an improvised stretcher, with his face covered over by tender green leaves. Bears stand up on their hind legs and attack a man's face, gouging out the eyes and tearing the nose and mouth.

I was the fourth of seven children. There was an interval of four years between my younger brother and me because there had been a stillbirth in between. I clearly remember us being called into mother's bedroom to see our baby brother who had died on his journey to this world. We little realized how close we were to losing our dear mother. The rigors of septicemia had already set in. Brave mothers! How risky was childbirth in those days. My elder brother was already a scholar. At the age of seven he had traveled to Kandy by bullock car to enter Trinity College. Father then rented a house for us in Kandy, and we all went to school. Only too soon father was moved to a more distant place, and we went along. Then malaria struck us down, and father brought us to his father's house in Colombo. Grandfather was very old and already in his nineties. He was tall, upright, and stern-looking. His wife, a dainty, small woman, always followed him about. Grandmother was a great woman in her own right, being the daughter of Mudalayar Rajapakse. We next went to live in Matara in a home that had been an old Dutch fortress. We enjoyed going to school and being prepared for the Cambridge local examinations. Then it was decided that, for the sake of the education of our younger brothers, we should all move to Colombo.

There were at least three eminent women doctors in practice in Colombo at that time. Mother was greatly impressed by the efficient work of one who attended the confinement of a neighbor. It was probably then that my fate was sealed. Mother decided that her daughter should become a doctor. Dr. Alice de Boer was one of the first licensed doctors from the Ceylon Medical College. She had gone abroad and had obtained British qualifications, as well. She soon realized that the only post available to her, that of house officer at the Lady Havelock Hospital, was insufficient. With the help of the woman medical officer, appointed from abroad, they organized another post, that of medical officer of the Female Outpatient Department, with the right to private practice.

In 1911, when I applied for admission to the medical college, I was told there was no call for women doctors. There had been no women students for many years. However, I was allowed to take the entrance examination, and I gained admittance. Everyone was most kind. The anatomy lecturer was R. L. Spittel, author and a friend of the Veddas of Ceylon; Dr. Spittel had eradicated the terrible tropical disease of yaws. This great man took the trouble to set up a special women's dissecting room for me, the lone woman student, and he also selected the best students as my dissecting partners. The next year I was joined by Miss Pinto, and two years later by Miss Van Rooyen. In 1916, when I qualified and went for an interview with the principal civil medical officer, I was told that, although I had obtained a "class," and was entitled to a post, there was no vacancy for a woman doctor. However, the medical officer kindly gave me a letter of introduction to Isabel Hardy Curr, a woman doctor at the American Mission Hospital in Jaffna. I spent four years in most varied and fascinating work, both in the hospital and out in the villages. Calls to the villages were almost invariably for midwifery, when the village midwife declared she could do no more. I would set out with a senior Tamil nurse, well trained and efficient. We would travel by pony carriage until the road came to an end; then we would tramp along paths between the fields until a little cottage came into sight. We would creep in to find an exhausted woman squatting on the mud floor being urged to bear down by pulling on a sari suspended from a rafter. The only sedation we had was morphine and atropine, in little tablets to be dissolved and injected. Meanwhile the nurse would send to the village for a wooden bed or table. She would then clean up the patient and prepare for examination and forceps delivery.

During the war years, in about 1918, an influenza epidemic swept across the world. In Ceylon it was called Bombay fever, having reached us from Bombay. It was a most devastating fever, leaving its victims completely prostrate, with a very high mortality rate. The death toll in five months around the world exceeded the total mortality from five years of war.

In 1921 a vacancy occurred for a house officer at the Lady Havelock Hospital. I was too senior for the post but decided to accept it in order to work with Catherine Anderson, a brilliant surgeon. The next year the generous Alice de Boer waved her magic wand and created for me the post of assistant female medical officer, Outpatient Department, entitled to private practice. Dr. Van Rooyen, who had just qualified, found my old job awaiting her. Because of the kindness of Catherine Anderson and Alice de Boer my surgical experience continued. It was no small sacrifice for Alice de Boer to release me from the crowded outpatient department for an hour, two days a week.

In 1925 I went to England on leave for postgraduate studies at the Royal Free Hospital School of Medicine for Women. The professors were mostly women, one of whom, Dame Louise Waebbroy, was outstanding. In addition to laboratory work, there were opportunities for ward experience in the hospital, as well as at the Elizabeth Garrett Anderson Memorial Hospital.

On my return to Ceylon, Alice de Boer retired in order to educate her two grandnephews in England. I succeeded to her post, and she very kindly introduced me to her private patients. Dr. de Boer was a great woman in every way.

All midwifery was conducted in the homes in those days. With the contents of our bags, including sterilized instruments, with courage in our hearts and, most certainly, with the grace of God, we woman doctors went about our life-saving mission.

About this time I met my future husband, who was a brilliant lawyer. His sister and her little daughter were my patients. Mother, who kept house for me and loved children, would enter into conversation with them. She soon heard of the wonderful brother who had taken care of them all when his mother was left a widow at the early age of thirty-two years. My husband was very ambitious for me. He joined forces with Catherine Anderson in persuading me to go abroad once more and obtain a fellowship. Edinburgh is a most delightful city. I returned in 1933 with the requisite fellowship, but Catherine Anderson was no longer there to greet me. She had taken sick leave and had died at sea. A tablet in the entrance hall of the Lady Havelock Hospital commemorates this great woman doctor. Thus, I succeeded to the post that she was so anxious for me to hold.

Soon afterward the university took over the staffing of the children's hospital. Professors of medicine and surgery, as well as numerous house officers and registrars, were appointed. They most kindly shared duties with my two house officers, giving them much needed leisure hours. Thus ended the isolation in which women doctors had worked all those years. Although at first all the university staff were men, women doctors soon began to specialize in children's diseases. They now had a specialist competence, M.B., B.S. (Ceylon), and were appointed to the teaching staff as professors. They also staffed hospitals all over the island.

My daughter Swarna, as a little girl, decided that she was not going to be a doctor and that she would stay at home and look after her large family. She used to say, "Mummie, you don't know how much I love dolls." Her father saw to it that both she and her brother entered the Faculty of Medicine, But—alas!— he did not live to see them graduate. Swarna married a young doctor who did not believe in working mothers. She did not practice medicine but satisfied her heart's desire by waiting on her husband and children. Neither did her husband believe in formal education. He thought children should be set free from the bondage of school to use their senses and to discover everything for themselves. What a wonderful countryside those children had to explore! The children knew every bird and beast by name, and the house was full of wayfarers, both human and forest dwellers. This is part of a long story, but a baby elephant once walked up to Swarna's chair, rested its head against her shoulder, and went to sleep. But Swarna, like her paternal grandmother, whom she greatly resembled, was widowed early in life. She returned home and after a refresher course went into medical practice.

In this mystic land certain persons are credited with possessing the "healing hand." What have I learned from a lifetime of medical practice? In my day women doctors treated only women and children. Of course, our patients expected more of us than of men doctors. We had to be mothers to them, more patient and kinder than men could be. Strictness and firmness were essential, but kindness had to exceed every other quality. When we begin to waver and lose confidence in ourselves, it is the confidence of our patients in us that restores our faith.

It is important to make good contact with a patient. While working at the Outpatient Department, I noticed that, as a patient sat down, she always extended her wrist to me. This is the Ayurvedic custom of offering the pulse to be tested. One of our teachers, Dr. Garvin Mack, used to reprimand his students for not feeling the pulse: "God has given every person two radial arteries, but you donkeys will not raise a finger to feel the pulse. You miss easily available and valuable information about your patient's condition."

The modern doctor does not test the pulse or take the blood pressure. All data are charted by paramedicals. The final diagnosis may be computerized. We of the 1890s are "the stuff that dreams are made of."

Whereas at the beginning of the century women were discouraged by lack of opportunity for hospital experience, today all government hospitals accept women doctors on their staff. We are no longer in purdah. Recently a committee was appointed to decide whether restrictions should be imposed on the admission of women students to medical schools. How, then, are the patients to be taken care of? The men migrate, and the women remain to staff the hospitals. Of course, a bedrock of men doctors is also essential.

Now that the battle between the sexes has been fought and won and that men and women work together, what message may I presume to send to my sisters in the Medical Women's International Association? Both men and women, equal and interdependent, are happiest when working together.

My greetings and best wishes to the brave women doctors all around the world. Greetings and thanks to the men, both doctors and those in every other sphere of life, who have helped and guided us.

> Ring out the old, ring in the new,
> Ring in the thousand years of peace.

Katharine Wright
b. September 17, 1892

I was born at Carroll Springs Sanitarium, Forest Glen, Maryland, on the seventh wedding anniversary of my parents, and mother always said I was the nicest anniversary present she had ever received.

My position in the family was fourth of five siblings; two brothers and a sister were older and one brother younger. My place in the family constellation was similar to that of the middle child, in that I was not the first girl nor the last child. This meant that I always struggled for my position in the family. It has been a real stimulus to my many achievements.

My motivation for studying medicine was derived from the examples of relatives in medicine on both sides of my family. My mother's sister was a gynecologist in Chicago, and their maternal grandfather was also a doctor. Records show that he, Daniel Waite, was the first president of the Cook County (Illinois) Medical Society. More important was the fact that my father was a doctor and also director of a small sanitarium for nervous disorders—neuroses, not psychoses. I learned medicine from father; so I made up my mind early in life to study this profession, and I never wavered.

Father earned a scholarship to Cornell University and graduated with a B.S. degree. He then returned to his home in Washington, D.C., and attended Columbia Medical College (now George Washington University Medical School), where he received his M.D. in 1882. He married in Chicago in 1884 and, through the influence of his mother-in-law, became interested in homeopathy. That led to a two-year postgraduate course at Hanneman Medical College in Chicago for another degree. Father practiced this branch of medicine thereafter. I was brought up on homeopathic remedies, as well as a strict health code.

My mother was an inspiration to me for her achievements. She was one of the first two women to graduate from the University of Chicago. Her graduation thesis in 1877 was entitled "Influence of Plato and Socrates on Modern Thought," and it brought her great honor. She was salutatorian of the class. As my mind ran to science, I was grateful for mother's help with Latin and other languages in my high-school years. She was an outstanding person in club work.

At the time I entered high school, she was president of the Montgomery County (Maryland) Federation of Women's Clubs. Her example of achievement in areas other than the medical profession set a second pattern for me.

I obtained my B.S. degree from the University of Wisconsin in 1916, and the same summer I was married to Lewis A. Wright, who had earned his degree in engineering from Lehigh University the previous year.

My first license to practice medicine was obtained in Washington, D.C., in July of 1918. Then, by reciprocity, I was licensed in Maryland in 1919, at which time I became the first woman member of the Montgomery County (Maryland) Medical Society. I obtained further licenses in Illinois in 1938 and in Wisconsin in 1950.

Since my basic training was in allopathy, I used that system of medicine for my license and continued to study homeopathy with father, helping him in his work. In 1918 I graduated from father's alma mater, now called George Washington University Medical School. In 1920 father took eight months leave of absence to travel in India and the Orient, and I assumed full charge of his private country practice, as well as the position of medical director of the Carroll Springs Sanitarium.

It was at this time that I dealt with many emotionally disturbed individuals, and this experience laid the foundation for my interest in psychiatry. An added factor in my choice of specialty was an excellent course given by William Allen White, an outstanding psychiatrist at St. Elizabeth Hospital in Washington, D.C. The one-year course of lectures and clinic demonstrations of patients at the hospital included a unit for the criminally insane.

Lewis's business as patent attorney took us to Detroit, Michigan, where I spent ten years primarily raising my family of three children, one boy and two girls. Each one graduated from college, married, and became the owner of a home. From their marriages I have eleven grandchildren, and with each one I have a meaningful relationship.

While raising my children in Detroit, I took several graduate correspondence courses in parent education at the University of Michigan. Also, under the auspices of the Detroit Board of Education, I taught classes in parent education and became consultant at the progressive preschool at Merrill Palmer.

On moving to Chicago in 1938, I picked up my medical work again and obtained by reciprocity my Illinois license. In 1940 I renewed my studies by obtaining a position on the staff of Elgin State Hospital, where I studied clinical psychiatry by direct contact with the patients. After three years at Elgin, I obtained a teaching fellowship at Illinois Neuropsychiatric Hospital. The next three years were spent working with junior and senior Northwestern University Medical School students at this institution, as well as serving as a staff member at the Psychopathic Hospital of Cook County. At the outpatient clinic I continued to treat patients and also spent time studying for the boards in neurology and psychiatry.

Since I was interested in group therapy, while at Elgin State Hospital I worked with another doctor, using a nonverbal technique with patients there.

Collaborating with him, I wrote a paper on the subject. Later I used this same technique at the Mental Health Clinic at Mary Thompson Hospital, at the YWCA with groups, and with weight-control groups. I continued to use this approach until 1963, when other interests absorbed my time.

Since 1945 I have been in private practice in psychiatry, together with continuing part-time work in the mental-health field, primarily at the Psychiatric Clinic in Chicago, a facility that I founded in 1947, when I was a staff member at the Mary Thompson Hospital, and that had a medical staff consisting entirely of women doctors. When the clinic outgrew the available space at the hospital, it was moved to larger quarters, and since that time it has been called the Katharine Wright Psychiatric Clinic. It is now located at Illinois Masonic Hospital. My interest in Mary Thompson Hospital continues, and I am psychiatric consultant there. In 1945 I became a diplomate of psychiatry in the American Board of Neurology and Psychiatry.

In addition to the honor of having the Katharine Wright Psychiatric Clinic named for me, other honors bestowed on me include the following: Woman of the Year in 1959, Distinguished Citizen of the Press Club of Chicago, honorary member and one of the founders of the Illinois Group Psychotherapy Society, member of the Pan American Medical Association in 1965. In 1966 I received the Distinguished Service Award of the University of Wisconsin Alumni Association. In 1968 I was appointed to the Fifty-Year Club of the Illinois State Medical Society. In November of 1969 I was presented the Elizabeth Blackwell Award from the American Medical Women's Association (AMWA), which I have served faithfully and in which I have emeritus membership. I also was awarded emeritus membership in the Illinois State Medical Society in April 1975.

I am serving currently on the board of trustees of the American Women's Hospital Service. I am also president of the medical staff of Chicago Lakeshore Psychiatric Hospital. In addition to all this, I have been a lecturer on psychiatry and mental health for community and professional groups and have published a number of professional papers.

My special interest has been in the AMWA. I was first a member in 1935. In 1947 I was president of the local branch in Chicago. In 1958 I had the honor of being president of the AMWA. That same year I accepted the position of vice-president for North America of the Medical Women's International Association, and I served eight years, attending every conference as well as the interim executive meetings. Although this was costly in time and money and in expenditure of personal energy, it was most rewarding in friendship and in results achieved.

My association with outstanding women of high achievement in their individual specialties in many different countries has been of value to me in my personal life development, as well as in my professional field.

Ellen Kent Hughes
b. March 29, 1893

My paternal grandfather was an immigrant to Australia from North Wales. Grandmother came from London and was of Scottish descent. My grandfather was a descendant of Prince Llewellyn, my grandmother of the house of Stuart. She told me that after the battle of Flodden Field, when Prince Charlie fled to the Continent, he tapped her grandfather, the sole survivor of seven brothers, on the shoulder and said, "You shall no longer be called Stuart but the Man," and that surname she bore.

My mother's father was a miller and landowner in Essex, and members of the family were accomplished musicians. My grandfather and his brother came to Melbourne in 1836 but returned to England. Then grandfather came back to Australia in 1848, lived at Hernani, between Armidale and the coast, and eventually settled in Melbourne. The youngest of his three sons was my father, who went to England to study medicine at St. Bartholomew's Hospital in London. There he met and married my mother, who was a nurse at the hospital.

I was the eldest of seven children, two of them brothers and four of them sisters. We were all born in Australia. One brother was Sir Wilfred Kent Hughes, a distinguished soldier, athlete, and politician. My younger brother is a doctor, and he founded and is president of the World Federation of General Practitioners.

In 1895 Gertrude Halley, who was a fourth-year medical student from Tasmania, boarded with us. My father was always sympathetic toward the few women students, and it was he who arranged for Gertrude to live with us. My mother had all seven confinements at home. One brother, who was always in a hurry, was born rapidly. On this occasion Gertrude, still in the fourth year of her medical studies, assisted and welcomed my father with his first-born son in her arms. After that mother insisted on having a woman doctor for her confinements, and I think Gertrude Halley attended her every time.

I had poliomyelitis at the age of fifteen months, and it permanently affected my left ankle, so that I was always rather clumsy at sports. My family experienced no other illnesses of note except serious influenza in 1918.

My first two memories are of acting in a play at the age of four and attending St. Peter's Anglo-Catholic Church, where my uncle was the vicar. I have vague memories of the first kindergarten in Melbourne, which I attended for two years. Later during my school life I always had a leading part in school plays.

My father used to do some operations at his office, and I was allowed to assist by holding basins when I was only six years of age. I can remember father's making an incision over a boy's hip joint and my holding a basin to catch the blood. I made up my mind to be a doctor at that moment. My father was not pleased with the idea, as he thought it was too hard a life for a woman. He himself was an altogether remarkable man. He was the orthopedic specialist at the Children's Hospital and the ear, nose, and throat surgeon at the Melbourne Hospital.

I entered Ruyton School in Kew at ten years of age and finished there at fourteen. I was always the youngest in the class and won many prizes. I sat for the senior public examination and in my finals got first class honors in English and history, finishing third in the state. I was given second class honors in physiology and botany but topped the state. As my mother was suffering from tuberculosis in 1912 and was sent to a sanatorium, I stayed at home to look after the family, with the aid of domestic help, for a whole year.

Mother then insisted on coming home, so I was able to start medicine at Melbourne University in 1913, and lived in residence at Janet Clarke Hall. I found physics and chemistry very difficult, as such subjects were not taught at girls' schools. After getting some tutoring in chemistry, I discovered that it was an easy subject. I took honors in physiology and anatomy in my third year.

World War I broke out during my second year, and I had to go out of residence and help at home with the five younger members of the family. We had a very disturbed time at the university, as at first all medical students except those in their final year, were allowed to go to the war. In the dissecting room we never knew what students or instructors would be there. All students except those in their first year were gradually recalled to continue their courses. There were three other women in my class. We were envied by the lads in the dissection room, as we had a whole cadaver to ourselves, while sixteen or more men had only one among them. It was not considered suitable for women and men to dissect together. The other women did not like touching dead bodies, so I myself completely dissected two.

I did my clinical work at the Melbourne and the Children's hospitals. My father went off to the war. He came home during my fourth year and took my mother to England to see if the queen's surgeon, who was an Australian, could cure her hiatus hernia, which was causing constant vomiting. Dr. Dunhill would not operate, as she was riddled with tuberculosis. She died soon after returning to Australia. My first younger brother was at the war, and my second brother and sisters were sent to boarding schools. I was then doing fourth-year medicine.

During my fifth year another student and I ran the outpatient department at the Children's Hospital for a month. We had a fine time being unsupervised and did numerous minor operations, set fractures, and so on—and luckily did not kill any children.

Meanwhile I had married Paul Loubet, a Frenchman I met at the Children's Hospital. He was not yet fully qualified but was acting as assistant to a Dr. Lane. Everyone who had any medical training was employed in those hectic days, when physicians were scarce and those who did not go to the war were overworked.

The women doctors of Melbourne were very good to me. My husband died three months after we were married, and I stayed at home until my son was born. When he was six weeks old my colleagues Margaret McLorinan and Margaret Robertson got me a position as house doctor at the Queen Victoria Hospital, where I stayed for a month. They also found a young girl to look after my baby, and she used to wheel him from East Melbourne to the hospital for his breast-feeding. Incidentally, she stayed with me for fifty-four years and died only recently.

The Queen Victoria Hospital was small, and it was situated in the slums. It had been founded by women doctors when they were not welcome at the big hospitals in Melbourne, in the early years of this century.

One day I saw an advertisement for a resident at the Hospital for Sick Children in Brisbane at a salary of fifty pounds a year. My father wanted to adopt my son when I accepted the position, and father and I had a first-class row when I refused to give up my son. It was twelve years before the breach was healed.

The Brisbane hospital had 300 inpatients and a huge outpatient department. There was no superintendent or registrar, and there were very few honoraries until they began to dribble back from the war. The honoraries were very good to me, especially Graham Brown, the ear, nose, and throat man who taught me to be quite skillful with the guillotine. I had a junior resident, a woman, Dr. Dillon, for a few months. We used to start working on outpatients at 6:45 a.m.

My baby lived at the residents' quarters, and my nurse came daily to look after him. When I arrived at the hospital, the members of the women's committee met me and were rather taken aback when they found I had a baby. They asked me what he was fed on, and I told them, "nature's fount." They asked, "How will you have time to do it?" I replied that, if male doctors could spare time to have meals, surely I could have ten minutes to feed my baby and that my nurse would come every day to look after him.

We had a dreadful time when the influenza struck. We were reduced to twenty-eight nurses, but the Red Cross women who came to help were wonderful. I was forbidden to admit influenza cases but had to do so. A mother would go shopping with her child, who would suddenly collapse and become cyanotic. These children were rushed to the hospital, and some died within a few hours.

The Brisbane Exhibition Building was opened as an influenza hospital and accommodated 2000 patients. My second husband told me later on that, when the troop ships were returning from Europe, they were pushing dead men overboard every day. It was so sad that they should die of influenza after surviving four years of war and that they should bring the dread disease to their native cities.

I had a delicate man as assistant resident at that time, but the doctors at Ipswich begged me to let him go there, as nearly all the Ipswich staff had influenza. I held out for six weeks and then awoke with the most dreadful pains and knew that I was in for it. My nurse, who roomed near the hospital, was allowed to come in and look after David. I called Ipswich to ask the hospital to let my junior resident return. I was told that he was on his way back, and I was thankful, but it turned out that he was coming in an ambulance, very ill with influenza.

I was put in the nurses' section at the Brisbane Exhibition Building, where the wards were separated only by sacking. I shall never forget the cries of the dying reverberating through the building. Two days after I was admitted, I saw my nurse being brought in. Carrie Shields of Melbourne, who was one of the two women ahead of me when I was a student, was a doctor at this influenza hospital. I asked her to find out what had happened to my baby. She found him crying in his crib, so she took him to friends. The hospital authorities had forgotten about him. My nurse and I had to convalesce for a fortnight at Redcliffe, a seaside suburb of Brisbane. I was too hard up to afford a taxi, so we pushed the pram alternately until we reached the hotel.

Then I was offered a locum tenens at Mitchell, 400 miles west of Brisbane, so off we went. It was in the middle of the disastrous drought of 1919 through 1921. There was no other doctor for 250 miles north and south, 120 miles west, and 60 miles east, and there were only two trains a week. I shall always remember that train journey through miles of desert country and then miles of brown pastures with thickets of prickly pear.

When I arrived at Mitchell, Dr. Clarkson, who was leaving to fetch his wife in England, told me I would have to drive his car, a World War I Hupmobile, which had to be cranked. I just could not do it; so he said he would get me a pony and sulky, and I traveled many a mile that way. I had never driven a pony but Dr. Clarkson told me I had to learn. When we returned home with "Dicky" and the sulky, we did not know how to unharness him, so Nanny and I just undid every buckle in sight. The next morning we could not harness him properly. Nanny very gingerly put the crupper over (instead of under) his tail, and we had the shafts knocking around his hocks. We then led him carefully around to his previous owner. It happened to be mail day, and the whole population of the little town was assembled at the post office. Dicky was very fat and slow, and as I whipped him down the one and only street, a gay young man yelled out to me, "Hit him on the hoofs, Missus" and then shouted with laughter as I leaned out of the sulky to do this. As I told the cheeky young man afterward, it hurts if one is hit across the nails, so I thought a pony's hooves must be sensitive, too. Dicky developed a very sore back from my inexpert harnessing, and I asked the young man what to do for it. He decided that attention every evening was the proper treatment. His name was Garde Wilson, and he was just back from the war. My little son called him Budgerigar, and I did not know why people laughed when I told them. I did not know a budgerigar was a lovebird.

Anyway, Garde and I got married. He was eight years older than me, and he died just after our fiftieth wedding anniversary. We had four children, and I worked each time until my baby was born, then took off a month afterward. None of my children nor any of my fifteen grandchildren every showed any desire to become a doctor. I always did a great deal of obstetrics and was often out at night, so I suppose that is why they chose other careers. Both my sons went to World War II. The elder one is now executive secretary of the Combined Chambers of Commerce at Kuala Lumpur, and the other son lives in Armidale and carries on his father's real-estate business. Two of my daughters are nurses, and one, a clever woman fluent in French and German, lives in England and is employed by the Pergamon Press at Oxford.

I had worked full time in general practice until my doctor made me retire at the age of seventy-nine. I am now eighty-one. I practiced for seven years at Kingaroy in Queensland, after which we moved to Armidale to educate the children. I was an honorary at Kingaroy Hospital and also at the Armidale Hospital. In the country in Australia all doctors in the town are on the local hospital staff.

Armidale, which is about halfway between Sydney and Brisbane, had a population of only 4500 in 1928 but was the center of a large fruit-growing and grazing district. In 1975 there were 20,000 people and a university with about 5000 students. There were twenty-two doctors, three women full-time practitioners, and two women doctors doing part-time work, as they have children. Also, there were often Australian, Indian, and Sinhalese women residents at the hospital.

I have never found that being a woman had the slightest adverse effect on my practice. When I went to Kingaroy, a pleasant country town 250 miles west of Brisbane, there was only one doctor there and he literally welcomed me with open arms. I worked in Armidale in partnership with Roger Mallan for thirty years, until he had to retire because of ill health. We did a lot of surgery, as well as internal medicine and obstetrics. We gave each other's anesthetics with the "rag and bottle"—that is, first chloroform and then ether. When Pentothal was introduced, we used that drug. We gave it intravenously and made the patient count. As soon as the patient stopped counting, we proceeded with ether. Over the thirty years we did all ordinary surgery and never lost a case under an anesthetic.

Over the years I have written many articles on various subjects for the *Medical Journal of Australia*. In one national open competition on the role of the general practitioner in the prevention of disease I won the second prize and my essay was printed in full in the journal.

Since my retirement I have been having quite an interesting time. Several years ago I had cataracts, which were operated on successfully. I now find housekeeping much more difficult than medical work. I have two young men as boarders and the help of a maid until after lunch. I also have a little dachshund called Sally, who follows me everywhere, even appearing on television with me.

I have been made a freeman of the city for my civic work after being a member of the town council for thirty-one years and a deputy mayor for a couple of years. I am the ninth freeman in the 150 years of Armidale's existence; the other eight are all men. The honor was bestowed on me by the mayor in his scarlet robe, and I wore my fellowship gown.

I have also been on the cathedral council for forty years and have now been made a life member, with a plaque in the cathedral.

I was awarded the M.B.E. (Member of the British Empire) for community service, especially to the aboriginal children. In our state there are 40,000 aborigines, of whom only about 150 are of unmixed blood. Some 200 live around Armidale, and their children are continually in and out of the hospital. I succeeded in getting adequate housing for them and the Save the Children Fund built and staffed a fine kindergarten.

If I had to make my career decision again, I would still study medicine. I have never desired to take up any other type of work. I also wanted to get married and have a family. I would never have been able to have five children and run a full-time practice if I had not been blessed with a capable and faithful nurse-housekeeper and another maid as well. If a woman doctor wants to marry and have a family and carry on a practice, she must employ good household help.

My husband was very cooperative, and I always spent the weekends with my children unless I had urgent cases to attend to. I had nearly as many male patients as female, especially older and mentally disturbed men and those with domestic problems.

During the last twenty years I am sure the general public has considered women and men doctors equally efficient. I have been told that a third of the medical students at present attending New South Wales University are women, and they are also employed in the public service and the health department.

I think that, as a rule, women doctors are better accepted by the general public in country towns than they are in the big cities. There seem to be very few women surgeons on the honorary staffs of big city hospitals, except in the field of obstetrics and gynecology.

Grete Albrecht
b. August 17, 1893

I was the youngest of three children, and when I was a child, I paid exact attention to discussions at home about professions, especially about the future careers of my older brothers. Both wanted to become sales managers rather than to study. Whenever I asked, "What shall I become?" my father said, "Girls marry or become teachers." The idea of becoming a teacher frightened me, and at that time I had no high opinion of marriage.

When I was around twelve years old, I informed my parents that I wanted to study medicine. What gave me the idea, I can no longer say. I did not know much more about it than anyone else, but I had a decided feeling that I must study medicine and become a doctor. My father called my plans a bad mood and said "Girls cannot become doctors; it is impossible." He died when I was fifteen.

My mother, after considerable pressure from me, finally agreed to register me at a girls' gymnasium. At that time state institutions of higher education for girls did not exist, so I went to a private school founded by an association for girls' and women's education, Verein für Mädchenbildung und Frauenstudium.

The instruction was somewhat troublesome, since our makeshift school was an adapted old house and had no rooms for chemistry or physics laboratories. We had to walk long distances to boys' schools, where classrooms were finally available to us between 2:00 and 3:00 in the afternoon. Sports were not on the curriculum. The only exercise was a walk during the breakfast break around the lawn of the small back garden.

We took the *Abitur* (matriculation) as visiting students at a boys' gymnasium. We were, in 1913, the third girls' class in Hamburg allowed to take this examination. I did not do particularly well except for a little special achievement in biology when I was asked about the nervous system of insects and happened to be very well informed, having read something about it the day before!

My mother, alarmed by my stubbornness about my career wishes, talked to our old family doctor. He ordered me to his office and said, "Your mother has told me about your crazy ideas. Is it really true that you want to study medicine?" Without waiting for an answer, he came directly to the point:

"That's silly. A girl like you gets married." Then he sent me out to the waiting room to think the matter over and finally he called me back. "Well, did you think about it?" he demanded. "What are you going to do?" "Study medicine," I replied. Before I could dodge, he struck me sharply on the ear. "Silly brat," he muttered to himself.

For the first semester I went to Munich and lived in the home of an elderly cousin because I was not allowed to live on my own in a strange city. There were few women students. Our classmates at first treated us in a generally friendly and polite way but with a certain reserve. Their caution, however, soon disappeared, and I found myself in a group of young people with whom I had discussions, took trips into the mountains, and went out in the evenings.

During the second semester, in Freiburg, I became a member of a traveling student theater. We gave performances for a socialist workers' group and drove into the Black Forest villages with our skis, stage properties, and costumes strapped to our backs. We performed Hans Sachs' plays, and Hofmannthal's *Everyman*, with Friedrich Sieburg, who later became a well-known journalist, in the leading role. I had the part of Love, with a curtain as the train of my dress. Our goal was to meet people whom we could not have met ordinarily. This was only partly fulfilled. Nevertheless, I gathered experience and was introduced to life styles that had been unknown to me. I had won a prize for tango dancing, an honor that I was of course very proud of but that, like the skiing trips, was among the distractions that were not necessarily beneficial for my studies. So I decided to transfer to a different university.

In the summer of 1914 I started at Kiel and devoted nearly all my time to my studies, except for occasional sailing or dancing. This industrious and carefree time ended abruptly with the outbreak of World War I on August 1, 1914.

Because assistants were needed, I registered at the University Surgical Clinic. I was put to work in the laboratory, and I quickly learned how to make and analyze frozen sections. I had, however, to continue attending lectures and to prepare for the *Physikum* (basic sciences examination). As a result, I had no spare time.

In the fall of 1915, after passing the *Physikum*, I started my first clinical semester in Berlin, where I lived in a newly built girls' dormitory, the Viktoria Study House. My room, unlike most dormitory rooms at that time, was very lovely, with every modern convenience. Because doctors were scarce, I applied to the University Surgical Clinic and was taken on as a medical assistant in the outpatient department, where I received good training in minor surgery.

During the last two clinical semesters, I worked as an assistant in a Berlin hospital. I continued going to lectures and prepared for the state licensing examination, which I took in 1918. I did my internship in the same hospital. By then I knew why I had wanted so desperately to study medicine. After I started the clinical work and came into contact with patients, my aspirations were finally fulfilled. During my years of study I had had my doubts, for example when I had to identify plants or attend zoology lectures, which I found boring.

When a general practitioner who was at that time stationed at the front asked me if I would take over his practice during his absence, I accepted with some hesitation. However, work in such a large practice, located in a working-class neighborhood, with fifty to sixty patients in an afternoon, was new and exciting. For the first time I was solely responsible for everything I did or did not do. Even today I remember with a certain anguish how I had to perform a curettage on a hemorrhaging young woman on the kitchen table of her worker's apartment while her husband lit the scene with a kerosene lamp. At that time there was no other way. Doctors and hospital beds were scarce. I learned a lot, although often with fear and a pounding heart.

At the end of my internship I married and continued working at the hospital. In 1920, after the birth of my first child, we moved to Hamburg, where my second son was born. Two years later I took on counseling twice a week at a baby and infant-welfare service.

Gradually the desire to be involved in medicine again and to be better trained became stronger. I therefore started in a Hamburg hospital as a volunteer and worked for two years in internal medicine and for several months in the ward for skin and venereal diseases.

During this time I came to realize that I had a special interest in mental and neurological illnesses. For this reason I trained in 1928 and 1929 at the University Clinic in Marburg under Professor Kretschmer, who earned his reputation through *Physique and Character, Geniuses*, and other books. As I was not taken on as an assistant, I stayed there for two years as a volunteer and received training in clinical and outpatient work, as well as in neurology, psychiatry, and psychotherapy.

At the end of 1929 I returned to Hamburg with the children and completed my specialist training under Professor Nonne at the neurological department of the University Clinic in Eppendorf.

In 1931 I established myself in Hamburg as a neurologist. From the very beginning I had a lot to do. After I received permission to be compensated through the national health insurance system, the number of my patients grew to the point that the work, in addition to family and household, was difficult to manage. The adoption of the "double-earners' law" ended this situation, since its effect during the national socialists' period was to forbid women doctors to practice under the health-insurance plan as long as their husbands earned money.

After the end of World War II I moved my practice into my own apartment, where I still work. A few years ago I gave up using the national health insurance system, and I now have private patients and do psychotherapy for only a certain category of persons covered by the health insurance plan.

In addition to my medical work, I have since the end of the war, in 1945, helped to reestablish the Hamburg Medical Board. I have served on the directorate for seventeen years. I have also participated in the formation of the German Medical Women's Association, of which I was chairperson for many years.

During the years 1958 through 1963, as a vice-president of the Medical Women's International Association, I had to travel often to meetings and conventions. Despite the effort that these trips cost me, I was always happy to see women colleagues from other countries and to discuss with them, officially and privately, things that are so surprisingly similar all over the world.

When one of my granddaughters talks about her life and her future plans, she always emphasizes how important her own freedom is and how terrible it would be for her to work as much as I do. I can barely understand this attitude. I have never felt my occupation to be a restriction of my freedom. I have always worked gladly and voluntarily, and I do so even today. I could, if I wished, stop at any time, but my work has become part of my life over the decades—and I do not want to miss it.

Lady Phyllis Cilento
b. March 13, 1894

I am a third-generation Australian. All my grandparents came from England in the 1850s, and both my parents were born in New South Wales in Australia. My father's parents were of Welsh and Scottish descent and my mother's were of English and Danish extraction. My paternal great-grandfather Davis was a printer and compositor for the *Sydney Morning Herald*. His son became editor, and his daughter Eleanor, my grandmother, was a milliner. My grandfather McGlew was a miner and prospector who discovered tin in Australia in 1871. He was sent out here by his father's wool-brokerage firm to learn wool classing, but was soon attracted to the new goldfields that had just been discovered in New Zealand and Australia. He abandoned his wool-classing career and for the rest of his life was a prospector and goldminer.

My mother's grandfather Captain James Henry Walker was a sea captain. He brought many shiploads of convicts and free settlers to the colonies but left the sea after a disastrous wreck off the Queensland coast in which many of the crew were murdered by hostile aborigines. He escaped and made his way down the coast, enduring great privation for a whole month. He then set up business in Sydney as a ship's chandler and in 1855 brought out his wife and six children, among them my grandfather Henry James Walker, then aged ten, to live in Sydney. Henry James Walker was a bank manager and had 13 children, of whom my mother was the third. My mother's mother, Susan Bond, was the daughter of a seedsman and horticulturist who inherited his trade from his family in England.

My mother Alice Walker was educated in Sydney and, greatly to her father's shame, was earning her living by teaching music when the bank crash in Australia in 1885 ruined many families. She and my father Charles Thomas McGlew were married in 1893 on his princely salary of $150 a year before he started his own business. I was born in 1894 in a seaside suburb of Sydney, the first and only child of my parents. We lived in Sydney until I was five, when father's business as a grain merchant and salt refiner took the family to South Australia.

Some of my earliest memories—apart from my first whipping for disobedience—are of sitting on the cliffs overlooking the sea at Edithburg, a small grain-

and salt-shipping port in Spencer's Gulf. I was about five and a half—mother was teaching me to read—but in those days I was far more interested in playing with my dachshund puppy and learning to swim than in my letters.

Eventually we settled in Adelaide, where I attended a dame's school until, at the age of seven, I became a pupil of Tormore House, then the most up-to-date girls' school in Adelaide. Our headmistress Caroline Jacob, a martinet, was the first to introduce school uniforms into girls' schools in South Australia and to import qualified physical-education teachers.

Father, who always wanted a boy, was keen for me to learn all the "manly" arts, so he taught me to swim at five years, to row, to play cricket, to shoot, and to ride. In addition to school physical education, I attended a city gymnasium once a week. I also learned singing and voice production, not because of any musical talent, but because I could not sing or keep time. However, this training stood me in very good stead for broadcasting and public speaking, which were regular activities throughout my professional life. I had weekly lessons in drawing and painting from the age of eight until I became a medical student, at nineteen.

As a child, I was always considered a "tomboy." I liked to climb trees and used to groom my own horse and look after the bulldogs in our stud. I did well at sports and later captained the university tennis team for three years and won my blue at that sport. The university Sports Committee was composed entirely of men until another woman and I were grudgingly admitted in my second university year. We were tolerated, but there was an element of die-hard conservatism that definitely resented our presence and tried—unsuccessfully—to make us feel our inferiority as females.

I was a student at the Adelaide University for seven years and during that time saw the attitude toward women change. We were finally accepted and regarded simply as students rather than mere females, and we took part in every aspect of university life without arousing comment and feeling the self-consciousness that had prevailed earlier. As I had shown some talent in drawing and painting as a child, it was decided that I should study art, first in Adelaide and then overseas. My father, however, believed that every woman should have a good general education, as well; so I took a three-year scholarship to the university and embarked on an arts course, spending one day a week at art school. About that time I came to realize that I would never be more than a mediocre artist and that, as such, I would have little to contribute to society. Physiology and biology had always intrigued me. I had won honors in physiology examinations at school, so I decided, after much thought and family consultation, to embark on the six-year medical course. Although somewhat daunted by the prospect of six years' hard work, I bolstered my purpose with a philosophy that I still hold: "Whatever you do, you have to work hard at it; so you might as well work at something that will do some good in the world and get you somewhere."

As a student, I was deeply involved in the Student Christian Movement, and I entered medicine with the idea of social service among children and women living in slums. I had never seen a slum in my life and had no experience of poverty, but I had read about the university centers in London's East End and was imbued with what we would now call socialist ideas about the equality of human beings and equal opportunities for all.

Adelaide University was still small. The few women students all knew one another, and the ties of friendship were close. Some of my friends applauded the unusual step I was taking, while others strongly disapproved of such an "unmaidenly" occupation. This did not worry me at all, and I fear that I rather took delight in shocking my conservative friends by studying a human skull in their presence.

I was the only woman student in my year. There were two other women in the whole medical school; one was just completing her course, and the other "fell by the wayside" after her third year. So I was alone until two friends, already university graduates, entered the class in the following year. Thereafter, two, then three, then even more women took up medical studies each year; the number of female medical students has continued to increase to a point where women now constitute 30 percent of the medical students in Australian universities.

There were twenty-one men in my year. They tolerated me quite well— especially as I had a car and no one else did—but it was difficult to find a "partner" to work with in the early years. Later I found myself always in the same group as our top student, Raphael West Cilento, to whom I became engaged in my fifth year and whom I eventually married.

World War I was raging throughout nearly all of our medical course, and we graduated just before peace was declared. My fiancé was then in the army in New Guinea, an experience that set him on the road to specializing in tropical medicine. After working as a house surgeon at Adelaide Hospital, I went to England, doing postgraduate work in London at Great Ormond Street Hospital for Sick Children, as clinical clerk to Sir Frederick Still and Robert Hutchinson. I also worked in mothercraft with Dr. Eric Prichard at the Marylebone General Dispensary and, in addition, dabbled in the new speciality of psychoanalysis.

Postgraduate courses were not organized at that time, and no definite diplomas were obtainable. However, the work I did in England guided my future interest and studies, standing me in good stead in general practice, as well as in the career of homemaker and mother, which I undertook when I married in Adelaide immediately on my return from England.

Returning filled with high and mighty ideas of personal freedom and a career in medicine, I had decided not to marry, at least not for a long time. However, the persuasion of my fiancé and family soon overcame my resistance and I married Raphael Cilento in March of 1920. It was the "rightest" thing I ever did, for although I had six children and worked and lived in various countries, my husband always encouraged me to continue my medical work and never hampered my career in any way.

After a brief period in private practice with me in an Adelaide suburb, Raphael, who was imbued with an interest in tropical medicine, accepted a position in the colonial service in the Federated Malay States.

We left Australia in November 1920. By then I was five months pregnant, and I had my first baby in the little town of Telok Anson on the Perak River, where Raphael was stationed as medical officer for the district of Lower Perak. We had engaged an Australian nurse for the event, but flooding and Chinese bandits delayed her arrival from Kedah, so Raphael had to confine me himself, with my mother holding the chloroform mask while he delivered the baby boy.

I had engaged a Chinese amah, or nurse, for the baby and, despite all my London lectures on child care, I learned a great deal of practical experience from her.

Before I was out of bed, other mothers from the European colony were bringing in their babies for me to see, and soon I was gazetted as "lady medical officer, Lower Perak." I attended women and children in the government hospital, of which Raphael was superintendent, thus becoming the first medical woman in the Colonial Medical Service in the Malay States.

At the end of a year, however, the Australian government invited Raphael to study tropical diseases in other countries and to take his diplomas in England, with a view to directing the Tropical Institute in Townsville, North Queensland. So I returned to Sydney with our year-old son—still breast-feeding.

During that time of waiting I started on the diploma course in public health, but it was not fully organized, and although I attended lectures and did practical work at Sydney University, it was impossible to finish the course.

It was then that I first became interested in nutrition, and before going to live in Townsville, I wrote what I now see as a most elementary article on the subject of food values for the government health magazine.

After some time as director of the Institute of Tropical Medicine, Raphael was sent to the territory of New Guinea to establish a comprehensive medical service, as Australia took over the government of this island territory after the Germans were expropriated.

Our second child was born just before I followed Raphael to Rabual. The conditions in the territory in 1924 were far more primitive than they are today, and I relied on native foods as much as possible rather than on tinned foods and "freezer" cargo, which many Australian families used. There was no fresh milk, so we had to use condensed milk for ourselves and the children.

Although the management of the house and the care of two children (and later one more) took up much of my time, I had, like all Europeans, a staff of native help and also a half-caste nurse for the children. I found the social life and bridge-playing quite unsatisfying, so I started private practice in Rabaul and attended not only Europeans but Chinese, Malays, and people of other nationalities, the native people all being under the care of the government medical service.

My husband, as director general of health in the territory, was concerned not only with the health but with the diet and nutrition of the native peoples, especially the indentured laborers, many of whom, on a plantation diet of polished rice and tinned meat and fish, were showing deficiency diseases, such as beriberi, and lack of resistance to ulcers and infections. He managed to institute legislation to enforce the addition of fresh foods to the diets of all indentured laborers, and he planned many diets for the whole territory. He continued this interest after he returned to Queensland as Commonwealth tropical health officer. His work on the health and nutrition of native peoples in the South Pacific, reported to the League of Nations, won him a knighthood, bestowed in the New Year's honors of 1935.

We settled in Brisbane, and in 1929, a year after the birth of our fourth child, I started a limited private practice in a suburb. Domestic help was easily available in those days, and as I always had my consulting rooms in the house, I could manage a small practice without being away from home much.

With my previous experience and my preoccupation with my own babies and children, my interest in mothercraft and nutrition naturally grew. My practice became centered around maternity cases, babies, and growing families, and in 1932 I was instrumental in the inauguration of the Queensland Mothercraft Association for the education of girls and women in mothercraft and in the care of young children and the training of home assistants to help mothers.

For years the association worked closely with the government Baby Health Centers, initiating many projects, such as the teaching of mothercraft in schools, a hostel for expecting mothers, care of babies and young children, and difficult feeding cases, using the hostel meanwhile as a training center for home assistants. A bureau for the employment of these trained women was also established, filling a long-felt need in country and city.

During the war the Queensland Mothercraft Association fulfilled many roles as the need arose—from caring for wives and families of servicemen to supplying cheap meals for Air Force trainees to training women in the emergency care of evacuated children in face of the threatened Japanese invasion of Australia.

I was president of the Australian Federation of Medical Women from 1939 to 1948, when I went to the United States to join Raphael, who had been there since the inauguration of the United Nations, following his work with a United Nations relief program in Germany after 1945.

It was not until World War II took so many doctors overseas that the demands of general practice necessitated my full-time care. The children were then all in school or at the university, so I could devote more time to medical work.

Ever since 1929 I had conducted a weekly radio session on mothercraft and family problems, written articles for a woman's magazine, and had a weekly press column. This also entailed a medical correspondence service extending to every corner of Australia, and I still meet many elderly women who brought up their children following my mothercraft systems and advice. When television was started in Queensland, I also had a weekly television program on family problems. I still continue regular writing on mothercraft and medical subjects for newspapers and magazines. I have also written several books on mothercraft and other medical subjects. From 1930 to 1934 I was an honorary physician at the Brisbane Hospital for Sick Children and the first lecturer in mothercraft to the medical students.

Following postgraduate work on "natural childbirth" in the United States,

England, and Paris with Dr. Grantley Dick Reed, I carried out the methods in my own maternity practice. I introduced prenatal and postnatal physiotherapy into the Royal Brisbane Women's Hospital, at first in the face of disbelief and definite opposition. Later, however, the principles of educated childbirth became accepted by the profession and I lectured to the physiotherapy students on obstetrical physiotherapy for a number of years. There is now a flourishing Australia-wide Association for Educated Childbirth, following the methods of so-called psychoprophylaxis, introduced by Dr. Lamaze in Paris. I have been a member of the advisory panel since its inception and still lecture to groups of expectant mothers for the society.

For many years I have been interested in early childhood education and have lectured and served on committees and the board of management for the Crèche and Kindergarten Association of Queensland, which conducts and supervises kindergartens throughout the state and trains kindergarten teachers.

Sir Raphael and I had six children, three sons and three daughters, spaced out over fifteen years. All were normal pregnancies and births, and I rather took a pride in maintaining a certain amount of my medical work throughout—"taking the children in my stride," so to speak. All were breast-fed for eight to nine months and were healthy children. All three boys and one daughter studied medicine. One is a neurosurgeon, two are general practitioners, and the daughter is a psychiatrist. This daughter is also a sculptor and has written books, stories, and plays in her spare time. Our eldest daughter is an artist, having studied in the United States, Paris, and London. Our third daughter has attained international fame as an actress in films and on the legitimate stage. All six of our children are married, and we now have twenty-six healthy grandchildren and so far six great-grandchildren.

During the fifty-seven years since my graduation I have maintained my interest in medical practice and in all matters, both medical and social, pertaining to women and children, mothers, and babies. Except for minor ailments my own health has always been good. I carried on a limited practice while the children were small but always in special rooms in our own home until the time when all the family were in school or at the university.

In 1964, when I was seventy, both Raphael and I retired from the general practice in which we had worked together for several years since his retirement from the United Nations, and we passed the practice on to our second son. However, I continued broadcasting and then had more time for writing and lecturing. I still contribute regular weekly columns to two newspapers and various magazines. My interest has recently centered on the newer knowledge of nutrition, which I believe to be the specialty of the future and one of the most important avenues of preventive medicine.

I have never regretted taking up medicine as a career but have many times blessed the day I made that decision at the age of eighteen. Indeed, I believe that all children should be trained in human physiology and nutrition as part of their basic education; girls and boys should also study the rudiments of mothercraft and family relations.

I have never found my sex a handicap in the medical world, but rather an asset. I always emphasized the women's point of view and the interests of women and children. I believe that women have a great part to play in medicine—in all branches. They naturally gravitate to matters pertaining to their own sex and to children because they have greater understanding of their specific problems and their maternal instinct attracts them to the care of babies and children. Also, these studies are of tremendous value in marriage and in the rearing of their own families. I consider medicine, nursing, and teaching to be eminently suitable professions for women, all of which may be called "nurturing" professions. In addition, medicine affords a woman an opportunity for service to the community and an independent and satisfying career.

Florence McConney

b. September 20, 1894

I was born in Lindsay, Ontario, Canada, a town of ten thousand inhabitants. My father was Edwin Austin Hardy, B.A. and doctor of pedagogy, head of the English department in the Collegiate Institute. He had a very distinguished academic career and after moving to Toronto became president of the Toronto Teachers' Council, president of the Ontario Federation of Teachers, president of the Canadian Federation of Teachers, and treasurer of the World Federation of Teachers. After retiring, he was elected to the Toronto Board of Education and became its chairman.

My mother Annie Florence Everett was also a teacher. She graduated from Moulton Ladies' College and the teachers' normal school. As a consequence, I did not go to school until I was seven, as mother had taught me to read and write. I was the older of two children.

There was a long line of teachers behind me, and my only sister eventually received one M.A. from the University of Toronto and another from Oxford and became a professor of English at McMaster University.

Naturally, my family was amazed when I announced that I was going to be a doctor. I was very young at the time, and they could not understand it, but the reason was clear to me. My mother used to suffer attacks of what at that time was called "neuralgia" and would roll in agony on the bed. This distressed me so much that I made a firm resolve at the age of seven to be a doctor and find out how to do something about it. I never regretted this decision because I like people, am interested in their problems, and have been glad to help with my medical knowledge.

We moved to Toronto when I was nine, and after I finished primary school, I went to Moulton Ladies' College. I graduated from there at fifteen with junior matriculation. At that time the University of Toronto did not admit students until they were eighteen, so I spent three years at Jarvis Collegiate, graduating from there with senior matriculation.

In the fall of 1913 I entered University College, of the University of Toronto, taking biological and physical sciences, which included two years of premedical studies. We were three men and one woman in that course and three men and one woman in the companion course of physiological and biochemical sciences. As we took many of our lectures and labs together we eight became great friends. For larger parties we joined the honors-household science students. In 1914 World War I started, and as Canadians volunteered, the men in the courses disappeared. It was a very shrunken class that graduated in arts in 1917. By this time I was engaged to be married to Garnet McConney, and as he was in the army and had his orders to go overseas, I married before I graduated. In the fall of 1917 I entered medical school while Garnet was away. He was anxious for me to finish my education, so when he came out of the army, we continued to live with my family until I graduated, in 1920.

The next six months I spent in St. Michael's Hospital, Toronto, as an intern. In the spring of 1921 we went on a trip to Barbados, which had been Garnet's home. His ancestors were Jacobite rebels who had been exiled to the West Indies and had a sugar plantation there. However, he had decided to come to Canada to live. In the fall of 1921 we moved into our own home, which we had built with an office in it for me. At that time it was not the custom for doctors to cluster in high-rise office buildings, as it is now.

I joined the staff of the Women's College Hospital, at first just taking a clinic once a week. The hospital was small, not the large modern complex of today. It was built by devoted friends to give women doctors a hospital in which they could attend their patients and where women who so wished could be cared for by women doctors. Here I want to pause to pay a tribute to that hospital. In the fifty years that I have been associated with it, I have never heard an argument nor a sneer about race or religion, and on the staff are Jews, Gentiles, Protestants, Roman Catholics, Hindus, Anglo-Saxons, Chinese, Japanese, Africans, Yugoslavians, Latvians, Estonians, Czechs, and other Eastern Europeans. We have had occasional strife but never the bitter quarreling and intrigue that occur on so many hospital staffs. It has been a great pleasure and honor to work there.

My elder son was born in August of 1921; two years later I had a daughter, then another son, and finally, another daughter. Someone once asked me how I managed to have a boy and a girl, then a boy and a girl. I answered, "There are some advantages to being a doctor," to which she replied, "Oh! I never thought of that."

I was most fortunate in that Garnet was sympathetic toward my work, encouraging me to take extra courses and never minding if I was called out in the night or away from a party. As he was a gregarious person and a very charming one, we entertained a great deal.

The American College of Physicians offered many postgraduate courses, which I joined. I took one in electrocardiography from Louis Katz in Chicago; one in internal medicine in Ann Arbor, Michigan; one in blood diseases under Doan in Columbus, Ohio; one on medical management of malignant diseases in New York; and one on heart diseases in Boston under the famous Dr. Paul White. In addition, I went to many of the group's conventions from New York to as far west as Denver, Colorado. I admired the American ability to run a convention extremely well. I attained my fellowship in the American College of physicians in 1950, my thesis being on chronic mercurial poisoning from diuretics. I received my certification as a specialist in internal medicine from the Royal College of Physicians and Surgeons of Canada in 1944 and also from the Ontario College of Physicians in 1945.

I have been in private practice in internal medicine for fifty years and have loved it, even though it means getting as many as three calls in one night. At the hospital I advanced from associate chief to be chief in medicine in fifteen years. At that time one had to retire as chief at fifty-five to give others a chance. I started and was director for ten years of the Cancer Detection Clinic, which we modeled after the Strang Memorial Clinic in New York.

My children are all married. The three eldest ones are graduates of the University of Toronto and are teachers. My younger daughter is a graduate of McGill University in household economics and has been a dietitian in hospitals in Canada, England, and the United States. I have eleven grandchildren, three of them of university age. My husband died of a heart attack in 1948.

Many years ago I joined the Medico-Legal Society of Toronto, which I find most fascinating. We have three dinner meetings a year, at which we discuss the current medicolegal problems. Two other organizations to which I belong are the North Toronto Medical Association, a voluntary group of doctors that meets to hear a speaker once a month, and the Toronto Academy of Medicine. The latter is housed in its own building in the center of the city and has the largest and finest medical library in Canada. It brings distinguished speakers from all over the world once a month and in addition has many sectional meetings, with discussions by local doctors. Its standard of scholarship is very high. I was honored by being made a life member last year. I also belong to the Soroptomist Club, and at their conventions I have met doctors from all over the world.

I have encountered little or no prejudice against women physicians in my work. I have had many men patients in my practice, some of them for many years.

I still carry on a limited practice, with no night calls, and go on ward rounds at the hospital once a week in an endeavor to keep up with the rapidly changing scene in medicine. I thank God many times that I have been privileged to be a doctor.

Gladys Story Cunningham
b. May 24, 1895

I was born in Wawanesa, Manitoba, Canada, the third of five children of John James Story, general merchant, and Hannah Story (née Avison). My mother's ancestors were Scottish on her father's side and English from Yorkshire on her mother's side. In 1910, the Story family moved from Wawanesa to Vancouver, British Columbia.

I took my matriculation in Vancouver in June of 1911. In the autumn of that year I became a freshman in the liberal-arts course in McGill College. This was a subsidiary in Vancouver, run and staffed by McGill University of Montreal, with the same examinations as in Montreal. After two years I went to Montreal to continue my studies and graduated in liberal arts in 1915.

Since early childhood I wanted to be a doctor. My parents thought that I could satisfy my desire to be in the healing profession by becoming a nurse. Although I did not agree, I followed their wishes, and in the autumn of 1917 I became a probationer nurse in the Vancouver General Hospital. In the spring of 1918 I had my "cap." But I was confirmed in my desire to be a doctor, so I left the hospital and took a summer job teaching in a country school in southern Alberta to earn some money.

In the autumn of 1918 I registered as a medical student at McGill University, Montreal, with my parents' consent. That was the year of the great influenza epidemic. The medical school was closed, and the students were sent to do voluntary work in various hospitals. I began work in the hospital for infectious diseases. It was filled with very sick people, and unfortunately, I was soon a patient myself. The mother of a very good friend, a medical student, took me to her home. There, under the care of the family doctor, I gradually recovered but was not able to do any more nursing. In the spring of 1919 I took second place in my class in the first-year examinations in medicine.

Here I would like to interpolate a few facts about women as medical students at McGill. Women had not been admitted to the medical school as recognized students, but at the urging of Professor Ruttan, three female arts graduates of 1915 were allowed to enter, although not as recognized, legitimate students. However, one of these women, Jessie Boyd, took first place in her class the next spring. The authorities agreed to recognize the female students and in future to admit women on the same grounds as men. Jessie Boyd was the first woman to graduate in medicine from McGill. She later married her arts classmate Dr. Walter Scriver, and became a professor of pediatrics and the professor of internal medicine at McGill.

My younger brother wanted to enter the university as a medical student, too. Father said that he could not finance two of us at McGill but that if I would switch to Manitoba, where fees and traveling expenses were lower, he could handle it. Sadly I transferred. For the next three years my brother and I kept house together in Winnipeg, and then I spent the fourth year as an intern. Several scholarships and some summer jobs helped to finance us. On graduation in 1923, I was the first woman to win the prize in surgery.

At no time during my medical studies at either McGill or Manitoba did I experience any discrimination on the basis of my sex. Indeed, at McGill the men students complained that the technician in charge of the specimens for dissection favored the women students. In Manitoba it was said that the professor of anatomy paid more attention to the women. Although the class began with ten women, for one reason or another most of them dropped out, due to failure, disenchantment, or marriage. Marie Cameron and I were the only ones left. We were both given internships in the Winnipeg General Hospital—without question. Marie has spent her life in medical work in Costa Rica.

Attending the opening student dance with my brother in the autumn of 1919, I met Edison Rainey Cunningham. I had heard the other girls talk about him as an outstanding athlete—hockey, football, and track captain. He was a Winnipeg man in fourth-year medicine, and that year he had returned to college a little late from a summer job. I went with him to a hockey match the next week, and in 1921 we became engaged to be married. Ed had already decided to go as a medical missionary to western China, where his mother's sister Anna Henry was a doctor. After a year of postgraduate work he went in 1922 to western China under the auspices of the Methodist Church. I wished to have my degree before marrying. In the fall of 1923 I followed him.

The day I arrived in Chungking, Szechwan province, where Ed met me, we were married by the Reverend George Sparling of the Methodist Mission. At that time there was a war in and around Chungking, between a warlord from Yünnan, a province to the south, and a local warlord. The Yangtze River is very wide at Chungking, and during the fighting the only craft that could move on the river was an American gunboat stationed there to protect American commercial interests. The hospital, doctor, and most of the mission were in the main city. Across the river was a large boys' school and also a school for occidental children. Parents were apprehensive because these children were cut off from medical care, so the mission arranged for the Cunninghams to go across the river and stay there, studying the language and being available in case any of the children became ill. Two days after we were married, we crossed the river in the American gunboat—an odd honeymoon—and lived there with a Canadian family until the next summer. Our language tutor was a Chinese scholar of the old school. He taught us not only the language but also the history and customs. In the late afternoon we young Canadians, along with another couple, walked about the surrounding country and sometimes climbed the Chungking Hills, which are almost mountains.

In the early summer of 1924, with our tutor we went upriver and across a valley to a summer resort where missionaries spent holidays to escape the hot, humid summer weeks. This place was on one of the lesser mountains below the 12,000-foot Golden Summit of Mount Omei, which is one of China's five holy Buddhist mountains. In October we took a four-day journey by sedan chair to the city of Tseliutsing, where Ed had been appointed to work in the mission hospital. In January of 1925 the mission council met, and Ed was moved to the city of Chengtu, the provincial capital and the site of the West China Union University, where we worked in clinical medicine and teaching until we left China, in 1951.

There were three hospitals in which the medical students of the West China Union University were taught—the men's hospital of the Canadian Methodist Church, the women's hospital of the Methodist Women's Missionary Society, and the Ear, Eye, Nose, and Throat Hospital of the American Methodist Church. These hospitals and the West China Union University were partially staffed and financed through the United Board for Christian Colleges in China, which had its headquarters in New York. Thus, personnel of several nationalities and a variety of denominations worked together in a very healthy manner.

In 1927 the first Communist rumblings hit Chengtu. The antiforeign feeling was fairly bitter, and most of the missionaries were directed to leave, as the presence of so many occidentals was an irritant. After a short stop in Shanghai and then in Korea we went to Peking, where we worked and studied in the Peking Union Medical College, a Rockefeller-supported institution, where some of the finest teachers in the world taught in rotation. Ed worked in eye, ear, nose, and throat. I worked and studied in the Department of Obstetrics-Gynecology under Professor Maxwell of England.

On returning to Chengtu in the spring of 1928 I was obliged to take over obstetrics-gynecology in the women's hospital, as the doctor who had been in charge did not return. This involved teaching medical students and nurses. I was also forced into advanced surgery and difficult abnormal obstetrics.

In 1929 we returned to Canada for our first furlough. Ed went to England to study and acquire his diploma in ophthalmological surgery. I stayed in Vancouver and worked in the Salvation Army Hospital for Obstetrics-Gynecology and then in the Vancouver General Hospital. There I learned to do direct blood transfusion. Later I gave the first such transfusion in Chengtu.

From 1930 to 1937 we spent our second term in China; we continued to teach in the Medical-Dental Faculty of West China Union University. During the 1937 through 1938 furlough I spent some time studying at Johns Hopkins Medical School, then went to London, registered in the Postgraduate School of Medicine, wrote my examinations, and obtained my membership in the Royal College of Obstetrics and Gynecology.

Our return to Chengtu for the stint from 1938 through 1945 threw us into war times. There was a large American airfield a few miles from the campus. The war planes came over the mountains from India, refueled, and proceeded from there to bomb the Japanese in eastern China. In retaliation the Japanese bombed Szechwan regularly. Since eastern China was overrun by the Japanese, whole universities moved with students, faculty, and equipment into west China. There were five universities operating on the West China Union University campus. Many thousands of civilians also came west. The capital was moved to Chung-king, about 300 miles southeast of Chengtu.

In 1945, just shortly before the war ended, with other Canadian and American families, we flew "over the hump" into India, from where we hoped to get a ship to Canada and the United States. Because of a lack of ships free to carry civilians, we were delayed in India from January to July. Then the governments arranged for the large numbers of civilians waiting in India to be taken to New York by the Red Cross Swedish ship *Griesholm*.

Ed and I spent this furlough in Canada. The return to teaching in China in 1946 took us into an atmosphere of threat by the Communists, who had made their "Long March" and were established in Yenan, to the northwest. In 1949 the Communists took over the country, and on December 31, they marched into Chengtu. Within a few days they had taken over the West China Union University. Together with a few other occidental families, we stayed on to see whether we could work usefully under the new regime. It was an interesting and informative experience. However, it became apparent that we were an embarrassment to our Chinese colleagues, students, and friends. We left Chengtu on December 31, 1950, reached Hong Kong in March, and proceeded via Europe to Canada.

Training Chinese doctors not only to practice but to teach and to administer hospitals had been the West China Union University's policy. By this time the deans of medicine and dentistry, the university hospital superintendent, and the superintendent of the outpatient department, as well as the heads of the various departments of the faculty, were almost all Chinese. They were men and women who had done postgraduate work in Canada, Britain, or the United States. The woman who took over obstetrics-gynecology sent a verbal message five years later, saying, "Tell Dr. Cunningham that we are carrying on the work she entrusted to us."

In October of 1951 my husband and I set up our private practices in Vancouver, each having accreditation as a specialist. We enjoyed this period very much and were able to save a few dollars against an old age that is not too well cared for by the church for which we worked. (Wives with the United Church missions, no matter what their work, get no salary.) At the end of June of 1962 we passed our records over to other doctors and retired. Since then we have traveled a little and engaged in other activities for which we did not have time before. I am fully occupied (aside from my role as homemaker) with my church, the YWCA, the University Women's Club, family planning, the Soroptimist Club, and general social and family activities. There is time to read and to enjoy the beauties of Vancouver.

It has not yet been possible for us to have any contacts with former Chinese students and colleagues in mainland China. There are a number of them in Canada and the United States, but they do not have much direct contact with China, either. We hope that now, in autumn of 1971, since Canada and mainland China have diplomatic exchange and mainland China has been recognized as "China" in the United Nations, these restrictions may be eased. Then perhaps it may become possible for us to be in touch again with the people and places where our hearts are.

Lore Antoine
b. July 31, 1895

In 1895, when I was born in a mountain village in a beautiful part of Austria-Hungary, life looked safe and quiet and nobody could imagine all the ups and downs that fate had in store for us. Iron ore had been mined in the mountains for hundreds of years, and there were furnaces and hammers in the valley.

My mother came from a well-known family of Ljubljana, in what is now Yugoslavia. My grandfather was a banker involved in the iron industry. My father, who was an engineer, and my mother met, became engaged, and very soon after, married. In 1895 I was born, rather a disappointment because everybody had hoped for a boy. Anyway, there I was, determined to stay and grow. I had a Slovenian nurse, originally my wet nurse, from the most lonely valley in the mountains. She could hardly read or write but was very intelligent and learned these skills in no time. Although coming from a very simple background, she was proud and free and refined. I loved her from the bottom of my heart. Of course my parents also took care of me, but my mother was rather delicate and often ill and my father was occupied with the factory. My languages were German and Slovene.

We had a big house, surrounded by a natural park, a flower garden, an orchard, and a vegetable garden—all cared for by gardeners. We had horses, a coachman, and a farmyard with cows and poultry. Several hunting lodges were at our disposal. When I was four years old, my sister was born.

When I was six, a teacher from the Slovenian school came to instruct me, and when I was seven, my first governess arrived from Munich. Poor thing, she was eighteen, did not know much herself, had no experience, and had a very hard life with me. When I didn't feel like lessons, she had to look for me up in a tree or in a neighbor's home. However, I always passed my final examinations with high grades; I took the tests in a German school in Ljubljana. When I was nine, I read a story in a girls' magazine entitled, "Fräulein Doktor." From that moment on, it was my greatest dream to become a doctor, and I implored my parents to provide the necessary education for me.

Every two years we were taken to my paternal grandparents in Honnef, where there was much to discover in their beautiful old garden. My grandmother was descended from old German aristocracy. There was a stone bench in the garden where Alexander von Humboldt used to sit when he came to visit the family. Of course, I listened eagerly to the grownups' stories about the Humboldt family and Alexander's discoveries. I still have his book *Cosmos*, with his dedication and signature. Sometimes my grandfather told me about the time he was called to Russia to plan the steelworks there. It was interesting to us children to hear how a special train was waiting for him at the frontier and how in the winter he continued in a troika to his destination. My aunt living in Honnef was married to an Englishman born in India. I thus learned a lot about India and saw lovely tapestry, silverware, and other Indian objects. From Honnef we went to Cologne to see the zoo. In Frankfurt we visited the *Palmengarten* with its wonderful display of plants from all over the world.

By the time I was ten, we children were inspired to organize our own zoo, when the greenhouse was evacuated in the summer months. My milk brother Janez, my sister, and I owned as many as 100 different animals, at times several kinds of mice, dormice, hedgehogs, turtles, harmless snakes, bats, butterflies, silkworms, and so on. We made various experiments. We had a female hedgehog with a litter, and one day a big male hedgehog was given to us. We imagined how pleased the hedgehog mother would be to get a father for her young. The next day the "father" had eaten all the young ones and only their skulls were left. Once my sister caught a fat dormouse by covering it with her skirt, kneeling down and pulling it out from her bodice. Next day the "fat" dormouse had nine babies. Great was our surprise and joy!

The country was famous for its flora, and we had guests from all over Europe to collect plants. So we developed a botanical garden of our own. I had books to study scientific work with plants, and I was always full of ideas for experiments. Sports were not neglected, either. I was very good at gymnastics, skating, tobogganing, swimming, tennis, and mountaineering. I had the first pair of skis in that part of the country.

The iron plant of the company was growing, but there was no longer enough ore or coal to be found nearby; so the next plant and furnaces were built in Trieste. Ore arrived there by boat from Asia Minor and coal from England. On visits to Trieste it was very inspiring to see the boats coming from all over the world into the port and to watch them unload all the various types of cargo. I picked up some Italian, and I found the climate very agreeable.

A few weeks at the seaside in the autumn were also considered very good for our health and education, so we used to go to Venice. The mornings were spent in the picture galleries and the afternoons on the beach of the Lido. In 1908 our neighbor at the beach cottage was Thomas Mann, author of *Death in Venice*. The sickness he referred to in his book was cholera. We learned about the epidemic only when we returned home and had to report to the doctor every day for a week. We had moved freely around in Venice all the time we were there and had bought plenty of fresh fruit in the market every day.

This lovely life ended when I was fourteen. All my begging for a school that would prepare me for the university was in vain. Why should a girl study to become a "bluestocking"? I was sent to a boarding school run by Catholic nuns in Lindau on Lake Constance. My mother and some aunts had been educated there, and the nuns greeted me with open arms. To make the coming incarceration more palatable to me, we first made a lovely journey via Bozen, Lake Garda, Milan, and on to Como.

My childhood paradise ended when I entered this convent. The nuns were charming, but it was a different world. I slept in a room with five other girls. We were up at 6:00 a.m. and had to keep silent until we had breakfast after mass in the chapel. Except for a few breaks, we had to continue to observe silence. The food was simple, but I did not mind that. I hated to drink beer at meals and also at the mid-morning break. With the help of a doctor's certificate, I fought for milk.

We were always in uniforms made of a dark blue woollen material, one for weekdays and another for Sunday. In the summer we wore dark-blue-and-white-checked cotton blouses and dark blue woollen skirts. On Sundays we had woollen dresses with bright-blue-and-white checks. Our underwear was changed only once a week, and we were permitted one bath every two weeks—and that in a shirt.

Much was done for our souls. The routine was one prayer in the morning, one at bedtime, at least two services daily in the chapel, one prayer before and after every meal, and one before and after every lesson. Quite naturally, we were the happiest creatures when we were allowed to go home for Christmas and Easter.

I did not finish my first term. Toward the end of May a comet was expected. There was much talk about the end of the world, and we were ordered to pass that night praying in the chapel. Not so Lore, who was always a naughty girl. I had found out where the key to the attic was kept, and I waited for the right moment to get it. I sat up there on a wonderful starlit night and looked out over Lake Constance. I did not see the comet, and the world continued to exist. When morning came, with the mist over the lake and the snow-covered Swiss mountains in the background, it was a sight of unforgettable beauty.

My great sin was discovered, a telegram was dispatched to my parents to fetch me at once, and I was separated from my classmates and not even allowed to say good-bye to them. In my reports there were only top marks for my studies but the very worst marks for conduct. My mother was wonderful. She was modern, read a good deal, had more or less expected some disaster in the convent, and arrived scolding. She had found another school to prepare me for the university.

My new private school in Vienna was directed by Dr. Schwarzwald, a very clever and outstanding woman. She had studied and held a Ph.D. from Zurich University. She was extravagant, wore her hair short, and had her dresses styled for her by artists. For her school she had assembled the best teachers in Vienna. I entered a class where we were to be prepared in four years for the final high-school examination. Only girls with top marks in other schools were accepted in this special class, and there my problems started. I had no solid ground to build on, never having heard of grammar or mathematics; I began to learn grammar by studying Latin. Mathematics were on a higher level. After six weeks the teachers concluded that it was useless for me to continue, and my mother was again called in. At this point Dr. Schwarzwald proved to be splendid. She advised my teachers not to examine me, just to let me go on, to listen and try. On Sundays she invited me for lunch in her own home, where I met many interesting people, among them the Swedish author Selma Lagerlöf, the poet Peter Altenberg, the three "dancing sisters" Wiesenthal, the architect Adolf Loos, and the painter Oskar Kokoschka. The Danish novelist Karin Michaelis also helped me once. When my mother again was desperate because I did not want to give up, Michaelis said, "A girl is called obstinate, while an adult is said to have character."

In the boardinghouse for girls recommended by Dr. Schwarzwald were young women from many nations. Our headmistress was a cousin of the composer Gustav Mahler and the divorced wife of a painter. We prepared the special diet for Mahler and took it to the hospital before he died. Besides living in this world of artists, we read a great deal and went to all the museums, exhibitions, and theaters.

Two happy years followed. I was convinced that our culture was so far advanced that no war could ever disturb our peace. In my third year I moved in with a widow, who took me as a paying guest. I studied under the portrait of Hebra, one of the fathers of dermatology. He was the father of my hostess, and her sister was married to Professor Kaposi, Hebra's successor to the chair of dermatology. I had not the faintest idea how prominent these men had been, and I still dreamed of becoming a botanist.

My father wanted to retire in 1915, and we looked for a country house where we could settle for good. It was understood that this would be our permanent home but that we would spend one winter in Egypt and the next in Paris, the summer in Switzerland, and so on. On Sunday, June 28, 1914, we came back from a very isolated town in Croatia where we had been looking for our future home. On our return we discovered black flags everywhere and were soon informed of the murder of the successor to the throne and his wife in Sarajevo. A few days later in Trieste we watched by night a black-draped man-of-war move slowly into the port. It was all lighted up by innumerable torches and carried the coffins of the assassinated couple.

Everybody was nervous, and rumors of coming war were circulating. Three weeks later we were staying at our hunting lodge in the mountains. Sitting in a meadowful of beautiful flowers, with a unique view of high mountains in front of us, we heard the sound a bells down in the valley. This was the signal for mobilization and the beginning of World War I.

Returning home, we found everyone desperate; men were packing to leave, families were in tears, and there was great fear about the future. The charming life, with tennis, excursions, and parties, was over. We started to work. My mother was made president of welfare activities. By the end of July many workers' families had no money to buy the most essential food. With our own money we bought all the things in the cooperative, and my sister and I, with a few other women, went from home to home to find out how many people were in need. We then distributed the food accordingly. It took weeks before the state organized official help.

One day my mother sent me to Ljubljana to buy sheets for soldiers' beds. There I heard that Red Cross courses for nurses had been started. A telegram was sent home that I wanted to stay with my grandmother and start learning to nurse. The courses were most primitive, and my family tried everything to dissuade me, but I continued. This was my first attempt to enter medicine.

Very little had been done to prepare for war. In a short time eight women in our group were ordered to transform a theater into a hospital of 100 beds, which we received from the army, but we had to beg from house to house for mattresses and all other necessities. One week later we were confronted with 100 soldiers, luckily not seriously wounded, and we started nursing. Once we were also called to evacuate a trainful of soldiers from the Serbian battlefields. They came in freight cars, with straw on the floor and no facilities. The soldiers had been provisionally bandaged days before. Some also had typhoid fever, and some had dysentery. Town practitioners came in the morning to tend to the patients. We ran this so-called hospital for seven months. Better hospitals were built later. The war with Italy began soon afterward, and we were quite near the frontier. My next job was to help in the railway station and to accompany Red Cross transports quite close to the frontier. These were my last days in my beloved mother country. Just then a dear aunt died of a ruptured appendix. After her interment we came home a last time, all in black. My parents had their silver wedding anniversary in a very sad atmosphere, and then we departed. I imagined that my heart would break when we left. I could not even shed tears. To make things easier, we went to my father's old home in Honnef. Three weeks later we traveled via Vienna to Klagenfurt, where my father had rented a flat.

After a prolonged illness because of a ruptured appendix, I started to consider the future. I was too weak to take up nursing again, so I applied to the authorities for permission to join the highest class of a secondary school for boys in Klagenfurt and to take my final high-school examinations. There had been a break of three years. I got out my books and started to study. I was given permission to audit in the finishing class under the condition that I must pass examinations in all subjects of the seven preceding classes. Everyone thought I was crazy, but I insisted. Usually, the final exams were taken in July, but in April, twenty-eight of my fellow students had already been called to join the army. The rest of us, two boys and two girls, had to finish at the end of May. I had to pass the written and oral exams of all eight classes. On the last day of the ordeal I had my certificate in my hand, and the road to the university was clear.

I had intended to study medicine in Vienna, but when my father developed cancer and was in a nursing home in Graz, we hurriedly moved there and I enrolled in the local university. The term had started six weeks earlier, but since it had been impossible for me to enroll then, I was admitted. I had had no preparatory lectures, and it was all rather difficult.

When I had finished my first term it was decided that my father should have an operation. The last evening I spoke to him, he asked, "Do you really want to continue this nonsense about medicine? I have provided for you and the family." The next day the operation took place, and my father died the day after.

I spent the following term in Graz, and at the end I passed biology, physics, and chemistry with the highest possible marks. My chemistry professor was Fritz Pregl, later a winner of the Nobel Prize, and his lectures were so interesting that I always loved chemistry.

Although women were seldom admitted, I petitioned the University of Vienna to let me continue my education there in October of 1918. Soon afterward the Austro-Hungarian Empire and Germany lost the war, and there was chaos everywhere. When the black-and-yellow flag of the Hapsburgs came down and the new red-white-red flag of the republic went up in front of the House of Parliament, I was standing there, watching.

In December of 1918 I made an adventurous trip home. We were preparing our Christmas tree when a former officer who lived near us asked us to cover all our windows, as our house stood on a hill and could be seen from a distance. The Yugoslavs wanted to occupy this part of Austria, and the troops were close. Shooting could start at any moment. We could hear the artillery not too far away, but it was quiet where we were.

Back in Vienna after Christmas, I observed an unknown young man near the professor, and I liked him at first sight. In the dissecting room we were always in a group of six, sitting around one cadaver. Strangely enough, the student opposite me was the one I had discovered that morning. His name was Tassilo Antoine. He was Viennese and very popular. We worked together, and after some time our mutual affection grew.

The political situation in my home province of Carinthia gradually stabilized. I continued my studies and married my student friend Tassilo. By the time my daughter was born, in 1921, my inheritance in both Austria and Germany had disappeared with inflation. I nursed my child for five months and then left her with my mother in Carinthia, where she lived in better conditions than she would have in Vienna. Every free moment I went home to see her and to help on the farm. I did not lose a single term, and I passed my examinations at the earliest possible date. In June of 1923 I became a doctor of medicine.

I had seen women doctors working at the hospital and had promises of a job. However, when I wanted to start work, there were many male medical refugees from all over the old Austrian Empire, as well as returned soldiers, all of whom came first. For a year I had to be grateful to work in internal medicine as a "guest doctor," doing a full job with all the usual responsibility but without pay. I was then promised a salaried position in a town hospital. After fifteen months in surgery on full duty I was finally transferred to gynecology, chiefly to give anesthetics. After five months there, still without pay, I resigned and went to a university hospital to specialize in dermatology. At one time I had intended to become a gynecologist, but since Tassilo had taken up gynecology, I decided on dermatology, as it would give me more time for my family. I preferred to be on my own rather than to become my husband's assistant. Again I worked as a guest doctor only because I did not want to spoil Tassilo's career. Quite naturally, he had more chances than a woman.

In 1927 I went to Paris to work in the St. Louis Hospital, especially with Dr. Sabouraud, a man, and with the plastic surgeon Dr. Noel, a woman. On my return to Vienna I had to borrow money from a kind cousin in order to buy an apartment there, and it has been our home ever since. In Vienna I started to work as a dermatologist in order to earn at least a little. In addition, I took either British or French paying guests, so that we could get practice in languages.

In 1930 I became assistant to Professor Riehl in a private hospital. We were six assistants and ten to twelve guest doctors in our department, which was well regarded but run by voluntary workers only. None of us were paid, but we could live on what we earned in private practice.

After graduating I became a member of the International Association of University Women, and as chairperson of international relations, I attended meetings in Wellesley, Massachusetts, in 1931 and the conference in Edinburgh in 1932. It was wonderful to see New York, New Haven, Boston, Washington, and Baltimore, where for the first time I saw skin diseases in the black population. I made many American and international friends and at the same time tried to improve my medical education. In Vienna we led a peaceful and interesting but frugal life, with many international contacts, until March of 1938, when the Nazis occupied Austria. When we heard the news on the radio, a French woman and I sat there in tears. I had many international friends, and many were Jewish. In our department all but my chief and I were Jewish. I was ordered to distribute registration papers. My colleagues had to leave as soon as possible.

My colleagues in the Austrian Medical Women's Association, which I had joined in 1924, all had connections in other countries. We made use of all our acquaintances to help Jewish friends and patients. My London friend helped with Quaker funds to rescue Professor Freud, among others. All this had to be done with great caution and secrecy during the first years of the occupation.

Tassilo became professor of gynecology in Innsbruck, where he stayed from 1940 to 1943, and my daughter had to join the labor service. I was more than busy with many patients of my own, and as my colleagues were in the army, I was often called to substitute for them in different clinics.

In 1940 I was nominated to teach hygiene (a compendium of medicine and first aid) to young women in a university institute for domestic science. This subject was quite new, and I had to find my own way to teach it. I enjoyed the contact with the young women and went on teaching in the institute for twenty-five years. The first air raids began in July of 1943, and I was "promoted" to air-raid physician for the university ten minutes from my home. When the siren sounded, I had to run to my station there. More and more bombs fell at the end of 1944 and still more in 1945. But after twenty-one bombs had hit the university, fewer and fewer people came into our shelter.

We knew that the Russians were coming closer, and we were ordered to destroy all equipment—X-ray, short-wave, and so on—and to leave Vienna to go west. However, my husband and I decided to remain, believing that doctors should stay with the people. My daughter was able to stay with Swiss friends in the Tyrol. Increasing numbers of troops passed through Vienna. We heard the artillery, and we saw fires in the east. When, on the night before Easter, we went to the cathedral, there was a strange feeling in the air. Everyone was silent, many were in tears, and only the beautiful organ broke the silence.

One or two days later I was sitting in my office when I heard by telephone that the Russians were only three streetcar stops away. I took a few belongings, left my home without looking back, and went to the hospital to join my husband. Doctors, nurses, and patients all went underground. We had practically no food and no light. On the next day the Russians occupied the hospital grounds. Fortunately, the director of part of the university hospital and my husband were able to persuade the Russian commander to spare the hospital grounds. The next day I sneaked under cover the two blocks to my home. The streets were in a terrible state, covered with corpses and war materiel, as well as ruins, broken windows, and rubble. Then I saw our house—still standing. Artillery had damaged the roof, and there was a big bazooka hole in the floor below mine, but I found everything in the apartment untouched. All doctors still residing in Vienna had to report, and soon our names were listed on street corners. The Russians also became my patients. We were very hungry during the following months, and we worked extremely hard. Many of our patients were infected with venereal disease, and medications were in short supply. We still had no penicillin.

One day in August when we were looking out of the window, we saw American soldiers coming in. We knew then that we would not be left to the Russians, and we were happy. Afterward British and French soldiers moved in.

Later that year while there was still no regular mail, I received a letter from a group of my friends in England, asking me to find university women ready to reorganize the Austrian affiliate. When I was taking care of this, other international organizations came to my mind and we refounded the Austrian Medical Women's Association. I worked for the League of United Nations Associations and the Soroptimists. One day I was even called to the prime minister and asked to inform Mrs. John Foster Dulles about women's organizations in Austria. In 1947 Dr. Hitzenberger and I went to Amsterdam for reaffiliation with the Medical Women's International Association (MWIA). It was a great experience to get out into a free country for the first time. In July of the same year I went to Toronto to reaffiliate the Austrian University Women to the international association. A few weeks later I also represented the Austrian Council of Women as an observer at the first postwar conference, in Philadelphia.

Everywhere I tried to meet medical women, and with their help, I was able to get into many hospitals to learn as much as possible about dermatology. I represented Austrian women's organizations at all sorts of conferences, took part in medical meetings all over Europe, and was fortunate enough to make many prominent and interesting friends.

In 1952 I was the first woman doctor to preside over the medical association in Vienna, which until then had been exclusively male territory. I spoke at many meetings of the German and the Austrian dermatology associations. In 1954 Tassilo was asked to give a paper at a conference in Caracas, Venezuela, and then in Bogotá, Colombia, and I accompanied him. During the following years I attended congresses in my specialty and in Tassilo's all over the world.

In London in 1958 the MWIA elected me one of their vice-presidents. Thus I came to know Dr. Esther Pohl Lovejoy, who was the founder of the MWIA and a very interesting personality. We had been in correspondence since 1956, when she was president of the American Women's Hospitals Service and had sent money to the medical women in Austria, enabling us to help Hungarian refugees after the revolution.

Tassilo was elected rector of the University of Vienna in 1959. For two years we had to live like diplomats. For me this meant office work in the morning, lunches with diplomats and ministers of state, office work again, and then cocktails and dinner with official people. In 1963 Tassilo was president of the International Gynecological Congress in Vienna, and I helped to organize this convention of about 3000 people. More and more international patients came to see me from all over the world. In addition to very ordinary people, I saw prominent patients, including diplomats, actors, and singers, which was and still is extremely interesting. It was a special pleasure to see the Hebras and former teachers with their families.

A great experience was my visit to Asia when I went to Manila for the MWIA Congress in 1962. In the following years Tassilo and I worked very hard but were able to travel often, so that I came to know almost every corner of the world. From 1966 to 1968 I served as president of the MWIA. Working for the MWIA, as well as other women's organizations, helped to enlarge my perspective. The golden jubilee in Melbourne in 1970 was a highlight and a good moment to retire from intensive work for medical women.

Summing up, I must say that my life as a doctor was difficult to start, sometimes very hard to keep up, but always inspiring. At no time was it a normal career. I had the privilege of taking care of about 25,000 private patients. It was my good fortune to meet many interesting people from all over the world, to see many different countries, and to study nature, as well as customs and cultures. I was happiest when I was able to work and serve. At times I felt selfish because all altruistic deeds were rewarded sooner or later. I was gratified to read recently in an article about the Nobel Laureate Hans Selye that his guideline for successful living is altruistic selfishness.

Nora Wundt
b. September 13, 1895

My parents were, in their way, rather remarkable people. My father, who was an infantry officer, came from a military family, while my mother's ancestors were chiefly lawyers. She was British born and a very charming woman. Both parents were well-known mountaineers in their time. In 1894 they went to Zermatt on their honeymoon, with the Matterhorn as their chief objective. During that trip they also climbed many of the other mountains around Zermatt, each one of which was over 4000 meters high.

I was their firstborn, and as a child was called Matter, in recollection of the Matterhorn. After me came two brothers, the elder of whom was killed in World War I at the age of eighteen. The second, who was much younger, emigrated to the United States with his family after World War II because he was in danger of being kidnapped by the Russians in postwar Berlin. Up to the age of twelve I played active games with my first brother and his friends, as there did not seem to be any interesting girls about. I did not have any girl playmates or friends until I was about thirteen years old.

In 1914, at the age of nineteen, I joined the Red Cross and served as an auxiliary nurse in a military hospital for several months. I found, however, that I was much more interested in the medical than in the nursing aspects of the work, so I soon decided to give up nursing and study medicine instead. This won the approval and support of my parents from the very beginning.

At that point I discovered a major difficulty: I had had only an ordinary girls'-school education, and I was not adequately prepared for university studies. As our father had been transferred to a different garrison every three or four years, we children had had to adapt ourselves to a number of different schools. This was not at all easy, as these various institutions had different curricula and were not at all in tune with one another. I must also confess that I was not a very enthusiastic pupil! In order to enter a German university, it was necessary to take the *Abitur*. To prepare for this, I had to attend private preparatory courses for girls in Munich, where we lived at that time. I had to take the examination as an extern at one of the Bavarian boys' schools. After two years I passed the examination and was able to enter the university.

I spent my entire course of theoretical and practical training in Munich. All other universities were out of the question at that time because of the difficulties during the war and the inflation in the postwar period. However, I was none the worse for this education because almost all the teachers were people of outstanding capability. There was a true *embarras de richesse* both in the medical field and in other branches of knowledge, and our parents always showed full understanding for our wishes and inclinations concerning our various avenues of study, for instance, the history of art in my case. Despite all this, it was not always easy to manage in those times. More than once an English pound note had to tide us over our financial difficulties. During vacations I worked in hospitals in order to gain practical and technical knowledge. After the revolution, in the winter of 1918 through 1919, when the university was closed, I worked as a nurse in a hospital for infants and gained practical experience that was of great value to me later. In 1922 I passed the final examination, and about a year later I was awarded my doctorate in medicine.

From 1924 to 1925 I held an appointment as an assistant in a hospital for infants in Stuttgart. I earned the magnificent salary of sixty marks per month, plus free board and lodging. In 1925 I returned to Munich to do voluntary work in the clinic of Dr. von Pfaundler, who was an inspiring pediatrician and an altogether fascinating personality. He had an amazing, magic influence on children. I never heard a child cry in his presence. On the contrary, all children, even the most troublesome, always came as close to him as possible, as they felt safe and secure with him! There was no end to what I could learn from him, so it was natural that I should decide to specialize in pediatrics.

From the end of 1926 to 1930 I held a position in the children's hospital in Greifswald. This was a busy time, with a great deal of independence in the medical field. In other ways, too, I found Greifswald interesting, as it was a town in a specifically north-German environment and quite new to me coming from the south of the country. Together with my colleagues, I explored Ruegen and the coast from Hamburg to Memel in my free time.

In 1930 I established myself in practice as a children's specialist in Feuerbach, a highly industrialized part of Stuttgart, where I lived for forty years, changing gradually from a young *Tante Doktor* into an old *Oma Doktor*. When I started, it often happened that my little patients were brought to me by their fathers, who were veterans of World War I and had served under my father in France. Knowing that I was the daughter of their general, they liked to visit me and to tell me anecdotes about my father, who was an original character and very popular with his soldiers.

In the first year of my practice I joined the German Women's Medical Association (GWMA) and my first visit to a congress was to Berlin in the Olympics year of 1936. I well remember the reception given to us on our arrival and the charming way in which our Berlin colleagues befriended us. Especially interesting was the visit to the Olympic Village, which had two kitchens, one for the north and one for the south Germans, and a sauna at the lake for the Finns. We were also shown around the Kaiser Wilhelm Institute by a woman colleague who reported on her scientific work. I remember well some of the prominent members of that period. Since then, right up to 1970, I attended almost all the national and international medical women's conventions held in Europe, seeing many interesting places and becoming acquainted with many worthwhile people. Among these was Dr. Esther Pohl Lovejoy, founder of the Medical Women's International Association (MWIA), who was the senior American woman at the meeting in London in 1958. Among her many other activities, she was the author of the book *Women Doctors of the World*. The scientific level of these congresses was always remarkably high, and the meetings were enriching in every respect. It was a great loss to us when the German association was excluded from the MWIA for almost the entire duration of the Hitler regime.

During the first part of the war, from 1939 to 1940, my work reached its highest peak. There was a lack of doctors, and I was obliged to do the work of a general practitioner. In the third year, air raids became so frequent, ours being an industrial area, that a great number of the women and children had to be evacuated. My office was damaged five times to such a degree that we were wading ankle-deep in rubble. There were no windows and no doors, and part of the ceiling was hanging down. The apartments in which my mother and I lived were totally destroyed. It was all I could do to keep up the semblance of an office in the less damaged part of the apartment, which also had to serve as living quarters. If I had not been given preferential treatment by the workmen doing repairs, I would have been at a loss as to how to continue.

Eventually the air raids stopped, but for another three years it was hardly possible to buy anything, as our money was worthless. Barter and the black market flourished. No real change was possible until the conversion of money came in 1948. This meant that each person received eighty German marks cash for a start, while savings were reduced to a fraction of their original value. I remember that my first undertaking was to get the brakes of my car into working order. This was a Mercedes mother and I owned jointly. I had been driving at a snail's pace for the past few years, with only a weak hand brake to stop the car.

Everything became easier, and it was possible to start life again. The patients reappeared, and my practice returned to normal. The joys of life also returned. I succeeded in getting a garden in a beautiful location, in which I built a small cottage, and this compensated for my not being able to live in a home high above Stuttgart, as we had before. It was nice to be able to work in the garden and not to have to stay in the stench and noise of a big city all the time. It also became possible to travel and meet our English relatives again. We were able to revisit our beloved mountains and go on mountaineering expeditions and walking tours, as we had been accustomed to doing from childhood.

In the early fifties the GWMA was revived, and it was welcomed by a great many colleagues. At the end of 1953 I was elected chairperson of the Baden-Württemberg section, an office I held until 1967. I belonged to the board of the German affiliate for many years and was always glad to be able to cooperate on questions concerning medical women.

At the end of 1969 I moved closer to the outskirts of Stuttgart and retired from the greater part of my work, retaining only a small visiting practice. Patients are often appreciative of this, as house calls to sick people seem to be out of fashion. In addition, I sometimes act as locum tenens for other colleagues.

Considering that I have had the experience of living through more than half a century of medical development, with the metamorphosis in many an illness, due to dramatic developments in therapeutics and research in so many and such varied fields, I must admit that mine has been a life worth living even if it was by no means a spectacular one.

Jeanne Lampl-de Groot
b. October 16, 1895

I was born in the small town of Schiedam, near Rotterdam, the Netherlands. My father was the middle child of thirteen siblings in a Roman Catholic family. My paternal grandfather was a businessman. Two of his older sons were already at the university when my father took his matriculation, intending to study engineering or architecture at Delft University. However, just at this moment my grandfather's business went bankrupt. My father therefore felt it his duty to try to save the business and to keep his older brothers in school, as well as to provide for the younger siblings. After many years of serious economic difficulties, he succeeded in reestablishing the business on a sound basis. Later on, he became well-to-do and finally "rich." However, he hated business life and was always much interested in social problems. Thus, in his free time he established a number of cooperative concerns where the workers shared the profits and finally became the owners. In this way he founded a printing office that still functions, a bakery, and a basket factory. Father left the Catholic Church, which was a courageous move in a small town at the turn of the century. In politics he moved toward the left.

My maternal grandfather was a general practitioner in Rotterdam. He was a very able man, interested in science and especially fascinated by the discoveries of Koch, which revealed bacteria to be the cause of a number of diseases. I never knew him, as he died before I was born. However, the stories my mother told about him filled me with great admiration. This may have been one of the motives for my choice of medicine as a career, although I was unconscious of it at the time I made my decision. Both my parents were free thinkers, which was unusual in Holland around 1900. They had nevertheless very high ethical standards.

I am the third of four children. When I was just six years old, I became the youngest sibling, as my little sister died of meningitis. On the day of her death I remember my father crying, something that had never occurred before. Some time later I timidly asked my mother, "If you are dead, do you stay dead forever?" It was at that moment that I began to realize what death meant and that it was irreversible. My own mourning for my sister then began. I had already overcome my original jealousy by mothering her, she being three and a half years my junior. Perhaps my unconscious wish to have been able to save my little sister was another motive for my later choice of medicine as a profession.

In elementary school I was a quiet and not very happy child. My memories of high school are much more pleasant. I was a lively, "naughty" child, who learned easily, without much work, and who was more interested in amusing herself. However, I was very popular with the principal, and I reciprocated the affection. The only time I really took schoolwork seriously was a few months before the matriculation examination. I was terribly nervous, although I knew I could not fail. The principal was our German teacher, and he wanted me to continue my education in his field. He was very disappointed when I revealed my intention to study medicine. I had, however, definitely decided to do this, although I had no idea of any hidden motives at that time.

I entered Leiden University at sixteen years of age in 1912. I joined the girl students' club as their "baby." However, I was not very happy and often felt quite homesick. I was not interested in the other girls' adolescent activities. I made a few real friends, but on the whole, I was a rather lonely youngster.

The outbreak of World War I was a terrifying event, although finally the Netherlands were not invaded. I worked very hard when the million Belgian refugees fled to Holland after the bombing of Antwerp. The Dutch were isolated from the rest of the world, and I felt in some way as if I were in a cage. Leiden was and still is a small town where students are privileged people. I did not like this atmosphere and decided to go to Amsterdam to take my final examinations. Neither did I really like medicine. I was happier in the wonderful museums than in the lecture rooms.

I had been playing the piano from early childhood and, like my mother, was very interested in music. In Amsterdam I became acquainted with a young man who lived in the same house and who played the violin. Our landlady reported to me that he would like to play sonatas with me. I was enthusiastic, and we had frequent and regular musical hours together.

In February of 1921, I finally became a doctor. By this time I had become disillusioned by the often inhumane professional attitude of many of the doctors and professors. I wondered what I should do. Now that World War I was over, I longed to see something of other countries. Fortunately, my very liberal parents allowed me to travel, so I set off for Paris, where I stayed for four months. My original intention to spend the time in a clinic for internal medicine soon evaporated. Instead I visited the wonderful museums and spent whole days in the Louvre and the Luxembourg, as well as at exhibitions of modern paintings. I went to concerts and to the opera and saw many plays. In between these activities I played the piano and studied French.

By chance at the age of eighteen I had come across Sigmund Freud's *The Interpretation of Dreams*, which quite fascinated me. I realized, however, that I must first finish my medical studies. In retrospect I now understand that my unconscious decision had already been made at that time. While in Paris this decision became conscious and clear. So in the summer of 1921 I wrote to Freud, asking him whether I could come to him to learn psychoanalysis. I added that I first planned to take a lengthy trip through Italy. Freud's answer was of course very nice. I would be welcome, and as he would have no free time for the next few months, it was most suitable that I take the Italian trip.

In Holland I was regarded as an eccentric young woman, for at that time most people considered psychoanalysis a dangerous field. A professor of internal medicine went so far as to beg me not to do such a terrible thing as go to Freud. I was astonished. He apparently thought analysis would ruin my morals. However, his pleading did not influence my decision.

I traveled everywhere in Italy and Sicily with a woman friend. We spent four weeks in Florence and six weeks in Rome. It was altogether a marvelous time, filled with art, painting, sculpture, architecture, and the beautiful landscape of Italy. We had merry adventures and enjoyed endless wonderful experiences.

Finally in April of 1922, I started my study of analysis with Freud. Again a new and entirely different world opened for me. Apart from the removal of my personal inhibitions and neurotic conflicts, I learned the attitude the analyst has to acquire, that of an empathic, flexible, and very human person. Of course I had difficult times in overcoming my resistances, but on the whole it was an extremely pleasant experience, which I described briefly in my Baltimore lecture in April of 1975. I started to analyze patients, and in addition, I attended courses and seminars of the Vienna Society with Anna Freud, among others. I also worked in the Psychiatric Clinic of Wagner von Jauregg in order to get to be a psychiatrist, as well.

I was planning to establish an analytic practice in Holland. However, Freud recommended that I first go to Berlin to work at the Berlin Institute for one or two years. That institute was the very best at that time, and the Berlin society had a number of gifted older and younger members. So early in 1925 I moved to Berlin, where I was received by a colleague, Dr. Hans Lampl, a Viennese and a family friend of the Freuds. He had trained as an analyst in Berlin. We became friends and soon decided to get married. This event determined my destiny. I did not return to Holland but stayed on in Berlin, where my two daughters were born. It was a most fascinating and stimulating atmosphere in regard to psychoanalysis, as well as in a general cultural sense. Berlin was at that time the freest city in the Western World. For instance, plays and movies from Russia, which were prohibited in Paris, London, and New York, were shown in Berlin.

In the very early thirties, when the National Socialist party began to become important, the atmosphere in Berlin became strained, and in 1933, when Hitler came into power, we knew we would have to move. At that time we could have chosen Holland or the United States or any other country. However, we both preferred to move to Vienna, where the psychoanalytical society had been rejuvenated and analysis was flourishing. It was only my elder daughter, six years of age, who was unhappy.

A younger generation of analysts were working in Vienna with great success. Moreover, Anna Freud had developed child analytic treatment and training. I was interested in child analysis, as I had been a consultant psychiatrist-analyst in a child-guidance clinic in Berlin. This I had done on the recommendation of Dr. Bernfeld, a close friend and colleague, who collaborated with social workers and educators and whose workshops I had attended for several years.

In the summer of 1933 we moved to Vienna, where we stayed until 1938. In the meantime I had become a training and supervising analyst. Hans and I were both soon admitted to the "inner circle" of analysts, and several real friendships were the outcome.

During our stay in Vienna we became very close to the Freud family. I visited Freud often as a friend, and we discussed many current problems from psychoanalysis to art and politics. Sometimes his antique dealer would happen to be there to show Freud some of his treasures, and then I was often asked for my opinion on a piece of sculpture or other work of art. I was more pessimistic than Freud about the fate of Austria. He always hoped that the "front" under Chancellor Kurt von Schuschnigg would hold. In 1938, however, we all had to emigrate, much to the distress of my children, who loved Vienna. We went to Holland, my native land, and after a few difficulties we settled in Amsterdam.

Hans and I then started a training scheme for analysts, as there were only about ten practicing analysts in the country. During World War II we gave courses and seminars "underground." After the war we founded the Dutch Psychoanalytic Institute and established a formal training procedure. At present the Dutch Society is among the largest in Europe. We have more candidates in training than we have members. It is, however, difficult to decide whether this situation is beneficial to psychoanalysis as a science and a form of psychotherapy.

Today I am still working with patients, candidates, and supervisors. In 1956 my collected papers were published in a book entitled *The Development of the Mind*. Subsequent articles have appeared in the *Psychoanalytic Study of the Child* and the *International Journal of Psychoanalysis*.

I have been honorary vice-president of the International Psychoanalytical Association since 1963. In 1970 I was made an honorary Doctor of Medicine by the University of Amsterdam. Then, in 1971, I became an honorary member of the Dutch Society of Psychiatry and Neurology.

A few afterthoughts that seem important to me come to my mind. My mother was an intelligent, artistic, warm person, although she suffered from mild depressions. This was especially noticeable after the death of my younger sister and then again when my eldest sibling died in 1918 and I was twenty-two years of age. I think my own tendency toward mild depression had to do with an identification with my mother. As far as I can see, this was removed and solved in my own analysis.

I loved and admired my father, although I always had the feeling that he worked too much and I did not see enough of him. There are three "father figures" who were very important in my development. The first was the principal of my high school. The second was an elderly painter whom I met during my university years. He taught me how to look at and enjoy great paintings. I remember clearly the time we gazed at Rembrandt's "Jewish Bride." The third father figure was Sigmund Freud. It was not until my stay in Vienna in 1922, when I was twenty-six, that I came to realize that all three of these men were Jewish. Much later I remembered that one of my father's most intimate friends was Jewish. I will always thank my parents for their unprejudiced attitude.

Elisabeth Larsson
b. November 5, 1895

I am an obstetrician and gynecologist in Los Angeles, California, although I am writing this in Sweden, where I am vacationing.

I was born on a farm on November 5, 1895, in the village of Grönviken, Bräcke, in northern Sweden. Our farm has belonged to our family for about 300 years. Three generations on my father's side were born here, in a house constructed in 1707. The house has since been rebuilt and modernized in 1798, 1845, 1902, and finally, by me in 1959, when I purchased the property from the rest of my relatives.

Our mother Erika was born on a farm in the same village. She and father were married in 1891 and blessed with twelve children. Two of these died in infancy before I was born, and one died in 1902 at the age of one year. I was seven years old then. I remember how sad we were, particularly mother, who wept bitterly. One brother died at the age of twenty during the influenza epidemic in 1918. I had a deep longing to help him. One sister died at the age of six in 1918 during the polio epidemic. She had blond, curly hair and was sweet and pretty. Our grief was deep.

I was the fourth child and the first girl. Although we experienced many tragedies in our family, I have very pleasant memories of my childhood. We all worked together on the farm and enjoyed it. At mealtime we all sat around a big table, except mother who was too busy feeding her family to sit down herself.

When father, at the age of twelve, was confirmed in the Lutheran Church, the pastor observed his high intelligence and urged grandfather to allow father to continue studying. Father would have liked to do so, but he was an only son and grandfather needed his help to run the farm. Thus, from love and loyalty to his father he stayed on the farm all his life. I remember father saying that, if any of his children wanted to study, he hoped they would be able to do so. Both father and mother went through six grades in the one-room village school. Mother was also a good student. They both loved to read as much as time would allow, with all the work on the farm. Mother read the Bible from cover to cover and could quote much of it. She was a very kind woman. When strangers came to the door, she would treat them well. She would tell us the story in Genesis about Abraham's hospitality to strangers when he did not know that they were angels. Mother knew of the work of Mme. Marie Curie. On one occasion when someone complimented mother on my accomplishments, she replied, "Oh yes, Elisabeth has done quite well, but she has not received the Nobel Prize, as Mme. Marie Curie did twice." Mother loved music. While working, she would hum the songs of Lina Sandell, who was to Sweden what Fanny Crosby was to America. I am very thankful to father for helping me get over the habit of reading cheap novels. He explained to me that they were not true stories, that they were invented or imagined rather than genuine. He helped me to see that reading such material would keep me from appreciating more worthwhile literature, such as the Swedish classics, and from obtaining an education.

In 1902, at the age of seven, I started in the one-room village school, which had only one teacher for all of us. Grandfather had already taught me the alphabet.

One of my schoolteachers was very stimulating and really knew how to motivate her pupils. She would say, "You are doing well in school. If you study diligently, you can be anything you want to be." She did not suggest medicine or any other profession, but she inspired me to want to continue studying.

After my confirmation in 1910, I asked father if I could go to high school. I loved to study and was delighted when I was given a dictionary of my own. Father said that I would have to wait until my twin sisters were a little older. I was the oldest girl and was needed on the farm, especially as mother was not in robust health.

Father died in 1914, when I was eighteen, and further studies were then out of the question. This was a trying time for our family. I had loved my father and revered him, and I missed him very much. Mother's sorrow and grief after father's death were deep, and that affected me also. Mother prayed for strength to continue running the farm and to take care of us children. I could see that mother's strength was her faith in God, and this led me to be interested in religion.

While on the farm after father's death, I was able to take German from a private teacher and to do some work by correspondence. In 1917 I began my studies at the Adventist Academy at Nyhyttan, Järnboås, finishing there in the spring of 1920. During those three years I became interested in studying medicine. Some of the students who were taking premedical classes inspired me in this direction. One day the science teacher called me to his office and said, "You ought to study medicine. You would make a good doctor." I had a lot of faith in his judgment, and his advice made a profound impression on me. In fact, on that day I made up my mind to study medicine. I decided to go to America to study.

I set out for the United States, traveling by train to Göteborg in southern Sweden and then boarding a small ship for Southhampton, England. From there I continued on the Cunard Line steamer *Mauritania* to New York. The North Sea was rough, and I was very seasick; I felt sure I would die. I arrived in 1920 at

Broadview College, ten miles west of Chicago, in LaGrange, Illinois. I had studied English for three years in Sweden, so I had very little difficulty with the language. I attended Broadview College for six years, finishing my high-school, college, and premedical subjects. I had enough money for tuition and books but not to live in the dormitory. However, I was fortunate enough to get room and board with a family in exchange for household duties two hours a day. My employers were both college teachers, and it was a rewarding experience to live in their home.

In the fall of 1926 I was accepted at the College of Medical Evangelists (now Loma Linda University) in Loma Linda, California. However, I felt so lonesome for my family in Sweden that I went home that year and did not start my medical studies until 1927. I graduated in 1931. The four years in medicine were very exhilarating. I was thrilled to have nothing to do but study. I will never forget the first day in anatomy, when we learned about the clavicle. There were eighty-three students who graduated in my class, and when we marched in for graduation in our caps and gowns, I felt as if I were in the seventh heaven. It was so wonderful.

I interned at the Los Angeles County General Hospital. At that time we could not take the state board examinations until we had finished one year of internship. I took the California boards in 1932. It was marvelous to be a licensed physician who could write prescriptions without a medical cosignature.

While interning, I decided that I liked obstetrics and gynecology, but it was difficult at that time for a woman to get a residency—particularly if the specialist training included surgery. Fortunately, the chief of obstetrics and gynecology, Dr. Lyle McNeile, liked my work as an intern and offered me a three-year residency. I remember how thrilled I was the day when my status at the hospital was changed from intern to resident. The work was hard but very rewarding. I was for a time the only woman working with several men residents. I never felt any discrimination against me, either from the chiefs or the fellow residents. I finished my residency training on December 31, 1936, and opened my private office in Los Angeles in 1937.

From 1935 I advanced to clinical professor of obstetrics and gynecology, a position I held at the Loma Linda University from 1952 to 1963, when I became professor emeritus.

I passed the boards in obstetrics and gynecology in 1940 and became a fellow of the American College of Surgeons in 1942 and fellow of the American College of Obstetricians and Gynecologists in 1955. In 1958 I became an honorary member of the Swedish Medical Society and in 1965 an honorary member of the Swedish Gynecological Society.

In my private practice in obstetrics and gynecology I delivered over 6000 babies, and while teaching medical students, interns, and residents, about 10,000 more. I did my last delivery on January 29, 1971. I had delivered that baby's father and mother, as well as the doctor who gave the anesthetic. I was then seventy-five years and three months old. Besides my private practice I enjoyed teaching medical students and writing medical articles.

My scientific papers have been in the field of my specialty and have dealt chiefly with the prevention of cancer of the cervix by yearly examinations, saving the premature baby, and the need for more women doctors.

Between January of 1971 and April of 1975 I did only office gynecology. On November 5, 1975, on my eightieth birthday, I started a new job. Dr. Pilar Centeno, director of public health in East Los Angeles, had persuaded me to help her at one of the county clinics. I had charge of the gynecology department in the Senior Citizen's Clinic until I left for Sweden.

Am I glad that I studied medicine? It scares me to think that I might not have done so.

Anita Angst-Horridge
b. August 1, 1897

My father was the only one of seven children to survive. His father was an English country squire, who was the owner of cotton mills in Lancashire, and father's mother was an Irishwoman, the daughter of the lord mayor of Dublin. He lost both parents at an early age and was then sent to a public school (Winchester) where he must have been an excellent pupil, judging by the numerous prizes he won. At the age of twenty-one he was heir to a sufficiently large fortune to live comfortably without having to earn his living. His taste for new environments and an egocentric character led to much travel and frequent changes of domicile. After visits to South Africa and Canada, where he shared the rough life of cowboys on a ranch. he took up journalism in Paris. During this time he met a young French girl, full of charm, gentleness, and devotion, who became his wife when she was barely eighteen years of age. She had been brought up in Germany, where her widowed mother taught French in Hanover. After traveling on the continent, my parents settled in England.

I was born six years after my brother in a country house near London. At the time of my birth my father had taken up medical studies and was working at St. Bartholomew's Hospital in London. Ostensibly for reasons of health he broke off his studies shortly before his finals; he then devoted himself entirely to literary work, for which he was decidedly gifted, but kept up his interest in biology.

At home we always spoke English, so I suppose I can call it my native tongue, although I never went to school in England and learned to speak French at a very early age, having had a French-Swiss governess. When I was four years old, my father, disliking the English climate, decided that henceforth we should live on the Continent.

We happened to be in Strasbourg—then under German rule—when I was seven years old and ready to start school. In the meantime I had picked up sufficient German to follow classes in that language. The following year we were in another German town, Cassel, where I was admitted to the second class in the state school.

Nowadays parents try whenever possible to avoid changes of school for their children, as it is supposed to create many difficulties for young people. My own experience was not at all negative as far as learning was concerned, but I disliked being "uprooted" and cut off from the friendships I had formed. I never had to repeat a class, however, and I went to school with great pleasure. Learning, except for arithmetic, was and always has been an exciting adventure for me. I was not gifted in arithmetic and must admit that I took very little trouble to become good at it.

After a year in Cassel I had to switch from German to French, as we moved to Brussels, where for the next five years I attended a very good school run by the municipality. We were taught human anatomy, including the names of bones and muscles, which interested me greatly. At that time, when I was about ten years old, we once spent our holidays in a boardinghouse where the son of the landlady was a medical student. In his room I happened to see an atlas of anatomy and—behind a curtain—a skeleton. This fascinated me to such a degree that, overcoming my awe, I would tiptoe to his room when I saw him leave the house so that I could take a good look at the illustrations in his books and a peep behind the curtain. I kept this interest to myself but must have somewhat surprised my parents by the following wishes for the next Christmas—a skeleton, a baby sister, and a dog. Not surprisingly, only the last wish was gratified. With my innate love for all living creatures—and in particular for dogs—my joy at having a puppy to play with and care for was great.

Some years later my mother unexpectedly had to undergo a serious operation entailing a long convalescence, so I was sent to my grandmother's in Hanover, where my brother had completed his schooling. He was then studying music, for which he had shown a very marked talent in his early years, although he was also gifted in drawing, philosophy, and technical fields. Later on, he became a distinguished musician.

I was sent to the girls' state school, the *Lyzeum*, and was found capable of joining a class of girls my own age. For a time I had to have private lessons in mathematics in order to catch up with the others. I look back on these school years as happy ones. I was treated by my teachers with much sympathy and appreciation. When my best friend and I talked about our plans for the future, the idea of university studies would crop up—and for me the course would be medicine. But to be frank, I believe that many romantic ideas about "old Heidelberg" were mingled with this wishful thinking. Besides, I doubted that I would have the brains for it, despite my teachers' expectations. Our school gave only a final diploma that did not lead to university matriculation, as we had no Latin and the standard was slightly inferior to that of the boys' grammar school.

In the spring of 1914 I finished my schooling and returned to my parents, who had settled in Switzerland, having bought a large and lovely property in Lausanne. Without any special aim but out of sheer interest, I went to lectures on the history of art and literature and considered eventually going in for the arts.

Germany's declaration of war in August of 1914 struck us like a flash of lightning. My brother left immediately for England to enlist in the army as a volunteer, my father went to the British Embassy in Berne, and my mother joined a women's league to help the refugees passing through Switzerland and to make parcels for the British and French prisoners of war. Despite the fact that I had just had my seventeenth birthday I made a firm resolution to go to France to nurse the wounded soldiers. I took a course in first aid, and without letting my numerous vain attempts to be admitted to a hospital discourage me, I succeeded at last in getting a position as *infirmière à pansements*, or "bandage nurse," (the so-called *infirmières de salle*, or "room nurses," had to do the menial work) at the military hospital of the Sixteenth Army Corps at Narbonne, a small town in the south of France. There was one condition: that I would not reveal my real age, which only the chief surgeon knew, but would pass for twenty. My parents were willing to let me go, for they had decided that exceptional times permitted exceptional measures and they knew they could trust me in every respect.

In November of 1914 I started work at the hospital. At first it took a great effort of will to bear the sight of the horrible, stinking wounds of the soldiers, who came mostly from the battle of the Marne and who, because of incompetent organization, had been on the way for days before reaching Narbonne. The dressing of wounds demanded of me things that at first sight I thought impossible, but my wish to help was so great that I soon could see and do everything that was required of me, including assisting in the operating theater. At first a medical student worked with me, but he soon had to leave for the front and was not replaced, so I remained alone in charge of four wards with all in all forty-eight patients. In retrospect, I think that only my idealism and my lack of theoretical knowledge relating to all the dangers and complications that might turn up enabled me to do this work. My reward was the gratitude of the soldiers, who were always respectful and who liked to have their wounds dressed by "Mlle Miss," as they called me.

This most satisfying and interesting experience came to an end after six months, when I fell ill with scarlet fever and nephritis. I followed my mother's advice to come home after my recovery and took a certificate of merit back with me.

My work as a ward nurse led to the crystallization of my life's aim. I made up my mind to study medicine, to take up a profession that interested me and would enable me to help my fellow creatures. Before I could enter a university, there was yet another obstacle to overcome—the matriculation examination. After a year of hard work, into which time I had to cram all the Latin that the others had had for eight years, I was able to pass the federal matriculation. As a rule, foreigners went in for an easier examination reserved for them, but only the federal matriculation gave the right to pass all federal examinations and to practice in Switzerland, which was my aim.

I entered the Medical Faculty of the University of Lausanne in 1917. After the first year of science I passed the first preliminary examination in second place. When I was twenty-one, I was preparing for the second examination when a great upheaval in my family confronted me. There were many problems to be solved. I had to carry great responsibility and face serious economic difficulties. Swiss universities charge foreigners double the fee for all examinations, and from one term to another I never knew whether I would be able to make ends meet or would be obliged to give up my studies. Only a very few of my closest friends ever knew what stress I was submitted to. Nevertheless, I passed my second preliminary examination, not quite as brilliantly as the first but still quite satisfactorily. I was able to carry on by giving lessons outside my studies, taking on jobs during the holidays, and spending three terms at the University of Strasbourg—then again French—where the exchange was very much in our favor and I had a very stimulating time.

To pass my final examinations, I returned to Lausanne, where I graduated in 1923. The medical faculty there had very high standards, and we had widely known teachers: Professor Arthus for physiology, Phénemène d'Artus for anaphylaxis, Professor Gonin for ophthalmology (the first to perform the coagulation of the torn retina), and last but not least, the famous surgeon Professor César Roux. Professor Roux was short of stature but great as a surgeon and an individual. Sometimes he had very rough manners, but he was so kind, so human, and a wonderful example to his students, over whom he had much influence. I had the highest marks in surgery, and I knew that Professor Roux appreciated me, so for a short while I contemplated choosing surgery as a specialty. Finally, however, I chose gynecology, as it seemed more appropriate for a woman. My thesis was "Obstetrical Complications Caused by Ovarian Tumors." Although known for his dislike of female medical students, the professor who sponsored it had 150 additional copies printed at his own expense and for his private use.

As a newly fledged M.D., I went to Paris, once more for economic reasons, where I worked as an *externe* in Lariboisière Hospital under Professor Loeper and in the Hopital de la Pitié under Professor Pasteur-Valléry Radot, grandson of Louis Pasteur. Quite unexpectedly, my father died from double pneumonia in Bath at the age of sixty. The executor of his will told us that it might be at least six months before anything could be paid out to us. So for the time being, we were practically without any means whatever. By doing remunerated laboratory work for Dr. Pasteur-Valléry Radot's private patients, as well as translating and summarizing articles for medical journals, I managed to scrape through. Without a French medical degree I could not be given any paid post in France, and resident posts in Switzerland were very difficult to obtain at that time, having to be applied for years in advance. My hardships came to an end when I was offered a well-paid position as assistant doctor in a tuberculosis sanatorium at Davos, and I worked there for eighteen months. Soon my mother and I received a good allowance from my father's estate, and all our economic difficulties came to an end.

I got my gynecological training at the University Maternity Hospital in Basel, where the work gave me great satisfaction. Thinking it might prove useful to obtain an English degree as well, I went to the Royal Free Hospital in London. Unfortunately, the cold, foggy winter weather brought on severe bronchitis and asthma, so I was sent to the Isle of Wight, with its milder climate, to recuperate. It was there that I had my first private patient, an old lady in the hotel whose inguinal hernia threatened to strangulate in the middle of the night. Happily, I was able to put it back in place again without difficulty. After one more unsuccessful try to face the London climate and badly heated rooms, I returned to Switzerland without a British degree and took a voluntary post for six months at the Institute of Pathology in Zurich, with the intention of returning later on to the maternity hospital in Basel, where Professor Labhardt was expecting me. Fate willed differently. I married a colleague at the institute in 1928 and have lived in Zurich ever since.

Honesty obliges me to admit that for the first time in the course of my life I found it difficult to get accustomed to the character and way of life of the people in a new area. The language in Zurich, *Schweizerdeutsch*—a dialect spoken by all classes of the population, despite the fact that German is the official written language—constitutes almost a *conditio sine qua non* for being accepted, and this was also a hindrance for me. All in all, I felt very lonely and forlorn in Zurich in the beginning, and this made me wish to have a home of my own and led me to accept my colleague's proposal of marriage after having refused several others in former years.

My husband and I started our practice in a quarter of this town where he was born and brought up. He was known as an intelligent, hardworking, and conscientious young man, which gave us a good start. He worked as a general practitioner, and I took on the gynecological and obstetrical cases. When I became pregnant, I wished to give up my practice to raise my child, at least during his or her early childhood. My husband would not hear of it, and my mother too urged me to continue my work as long as possible and only interrupt it during childbirth. She volunteered to take over the care of our child. The baby was a boy, born in 1929. My mother nursed him with great devotion and rendered us an inestimable service, but I could not help feeling frustrated and was torn between my wish to have more time for my child and my duties toward my patients, with the result that I felt inadequate in both situations.

Unhappiness in marriage, the impossibility of establishing a warm, harmonious human relationship between us, as well as emotional stress, impaired my health and led to various illnesses, of which the worst to bear was uterine hemorrhage. The bleeding set in shortly after an operation performed under very bad conditions. I had had a twisted ovarian cyst, a result of a skiing accident. The hemorrhaging went on for six years and remained uninfluenced by appropriate therapy. Thanks to my great constitutional power of recuperation I was able to carry on my work but on a reduced scale. When World War II broke out, forcing me to face new obligations, I decided to undergo a hysterectomy. After seventeen years of marriage I divorced my husband and was again on my own. My hitherto chronic insomnia was cured, my general health and self-confidence improved greatly, and I was able to carry on my practice under good conditions for another eighteen years.

Altogether I practiced for thirty-four years. I had patients from many different countries besides Switzerland—Italy, Spain, Austria, England, Germany, Turkey, Greece, Egypt, and Finland. An important factory entrusted me with the complete check-ups of all their women workers before insuring them for medical care. Lack of personal ambition, physical handicaps, and other factors prevented me from achieving any outstanding work in the medical field. My foremost aim was always to do my very best for my patients in a medical and in a human way. Patience and understanding based on personal experience and a serene attitude in face of adverse circumstances can provide a helpful example to those who suffer.

I am inclined to think that the affection, confidence, and faithfulness of my patients proved that I had been doing good, useful work. And yet, if I had to choose today, I think I would not follow exactly the same course. Medicine has developed to such an extent, with extreme specialization and greater application of technique, that I think psychology and psychotherapy would appeal to me more today.

In 1964 I gave over my practice to a younger medical woman who had been my locum. Two years later I was working again in the medical field, organizing and running a family planning clinic at the Maternity Hospital of the University of Zurich, a scheme I had already broached eleven years before without response. Things often take a long time to mature on this soil. I worked there successfully and with pleasure for five years, until 1972, supported later by two colleagues who are continuing the work.

My only son, whose education was anything but easy under adverse circumstances, did not take up medicine. More practical, he successfully went into business after studying law for three years. He has three intelligent and lovely children and a charming French-Swiss wife. Having given up my professional work, I have more time now for my family, my friends, and various other interests.

My autobiographical notes would not be complete if I omitted to mention our Swiss Medical Women's Association, with which my life has been linked for more than forty-five years. I was on the board for eighteen years (secretary, vice-president, president ad interim). I have always followed the activities of the Medical Women's International Association, and I have excellent memories of the congresses I attended. In 1955 our esteemed president Dr. Walthard-Schätti asked me to go as observer to a conference of the International Planned Parenthood Federation in Stockholm. It was a great experience, especially as Margaret Sanger was present, which led me later to increased activity in family planning and to my taking over the above-mentioned clinic.

When I gave my demission as vice-president and was named member of honor in 1970, I thought I would henceforth be able to rest on my laurels. However, at our general assembly in 1972, when the board was reconstituted, no one could be found to act as national corresponding secretary. So—*nolens, volens*—I consented to fill the gap, and I do not regret it, despite my age, for I find the work interesting and stimulating to this very day.

Karoline Mathisen
b. January 5, 1898

I was born far north of the Arctic Circle in Troms, the capital of North Norway, which at that time had a population of about 6000. Troms was then, as now, a characteristic school town and the administrative center of the whole long and geographically impossibly shaped district of North Norway.

I was the eleventh of twelve children in a family of modest income. My father, who was a teacher and later a banker, died when I was about thirteen years old. My parents, who were both of North Norwegian stock, were interested in reading and in the education of their many children. I remember that in my youth father used a quarter of his salary on school fees. We led a simple, yet pleasant, harmonious life. Everyone knew everyone else in our town, which had long traditions of interest in music and culture.

As a child, like other children, I displayed a great deal of imagination in devising games and activities without much material help. One of my interests was gardening. We laid out a garden in the yard behind our house, carried soil, and tended our plants with pride and pleasure. My family soon became acquainted with doctors and hospitals. My sister who was two years older lost a leg and had to manage with a very primitive artificial limb. We also went through epidemics of diphtheria and scarlet fever. It is possible that these events awakened my interest in medicine.

When I entered the secondary school, the sciences—especially mathematics—were my great interest, and I achieved good results in the university entrance examination. Then arose the difficult question as to what future to choose. I had no financial resources, and there was no arrangement in those days for grants or loans of any kind for studies at what was Norway's only university, in Oslo. I chose to go in for pharmacy because I had a brother-in-law who was a pharmacist in Hammerfest and this would enable me to train as a pharmacist without cost. I passed the final examination in 1919, and that same autumn I decided to study medicine while working in a pharmacy.

Throughout my youth I had wanted to study people, and I can safely say that my medical studies have given me every facility for this and for human contact—in addition to many pleasures! Naturally, my years as a student in Oslo were a heavy strain. This was after World War I. Housing conditions were difficult, and food was scarce, as of course was money. The burden of loans increased with startling rapidity because of high rates of interest. In the second part of my studies I was offered a job as assistant physician at the surgical department in Stavanger. I was there for three different periods and gained a great deal of experience that was extremely useful to me later when, in 1925, as a medical graduate, I plunged into life as locum tenens for a district physician in a large area of 6000 inhabitants who had to be visited by boat, by horse and trap, or to a limited extent, by car. The district comprised two long fjords and eight valleys. It was extremely difficult to have a patient accepted at the hospital in Troms because all the local councils were so heavily in debt that patients were only accepted in an extreme emergency. My training as a pharmacist was very useful to me in situations where I had to act completely independently and without help in the face of the most serious problems. There was no electric light in Lyngen. There was no X-ray apparatus, and on one occasion I had to reposition the dislocated hip of an eleven-year-old boy who had been injured in ski jumping—fortunately with good results. On another occasion I had to perform a hernia operation on a seventy-eight-year-old woman lying on three margarine boxes in a tiny cottage; she lived for many years afterward. Action was essential, and there is no doubt that I developed my independence during those years.

Later I was appointed locum tenens for the district physician in one of our most weather-beaten coastal districts, where all travel was by boat on the open sea. There were many serious situations there. Tuberculosis was rife, and there was not much to be done with the explosive infection within certain families. Some of my visits involved ten-hour voyages on the open sea, and my sheepskin traveling coat was essential.

I should add that tooth extraction, with which I had no experience, was a very frequent and necessary operation, and I soon gained a certain amount of practice! My predecessor had left in the office a whole box of terrible examples of extracted molars, which were enough to frighten anyone!

I applied next for a position near the quieter waters of the Oslo Fjord, in a little town in Vestfold with a general practice and a well-equipped tuberculosis sanatorium. I became interested in thoracoplasty, then a new method, and witnessed these operations for about a month at Veilefjord Sanatorium, where Dr. Gravesen carried them out, with the patient under an anesthetic, in twenty to thirty minutes. I went to Paris and visited health centers for children threatened by tuberculosis. I had not yet chosen any special field, but I was attracted by psychiatry and spent a year as assistant physician to Professor Vogt at the psychiatric clinic. I then realized that it was too much of a strain on me to work with all those unhappy people. I decided to become a general practitioner for women, men, children, and the elderly. And this is what I have continued to do in my home town. Even now I work four or five hours a day by appointment, and it gives me great satisfaction as long as my strength holds out.

During World War II Troms was in the firing line, surrendering after two months of fighting and occupied for five years. This was an extremely dark and stressful time, perhaps especially so for the few doctors who avoided deportation. The evacuation of the whole of Finmark and northern Troms was an unbelievable experience. Red flames flickered on every headland as the Germans withdrew, burning everything as they retreated. But even that time passed. People grew closer together, masks fell, and we experienced helpfulness and kindliness such as we never see in normal times.

The privilege of having had a meaningful life as a doctor is a gift for which I can never be sufficiently thankful.

Lena Ohnesorge
b. June 17, 1898

I felt both honored and somewhat embarrassed at the request by Leone Hellstedt of Stockholm that I write my autobiography, since it was clear to me that she did not want a mere list of accomplishments. I have two explanations for my objection to writing a life history in the form of memoirs. First, I feel that at present too many memoirs are published, leading inevitably to some kind of self-importance. Second, I have lived my life, which began in 1898, in an epoch of German history that has greatly influenced my personal feelings and attitudes. Any attempt to write about this entire period would amount to an almost classical nonfiction historical novel, which might be interesting for educational purposes but not otherwise. I will, however, try modestly to present a more or less comprehensive story of my life.

I was born, the second of five children, in Prenzlau, in the province of Brandenburg, which may be called the heart of the Prussian kingdom. My parents were influenced by a strong belief in progress and in the spirit of enterprise in the years following the foundation of the empire, yet were deeply rooted in Prussian principles. They were absolutely convinced that wealth is a social obligation and that a sound education and profession were self-evident for their daughters. My father wanted me to become a national economist, whereas my mother saw me as a future doctor, so these were the early roots of my future life. Both parents were actively engaged in community politics, my father until his too-early death in 1912. My mother worked in local and regional government after the establishment of the franchise for women in 1919. Thus my childhood and early youth were greatly influenced by the three-class suffrage in Prussia until the establishment of the Weimar Republic.

During the course of World War I, I was educated at the teachers' seminary in Prenzlau. At the end of the war my only and beloved seventeen-year-old brother was shot in the Kap riot while defending the municipal supply depot. I was later admitted to my medical studies in Berlin, and accommodated in the social women's residence of the Countess of Schulenberg. In the revolutionary winter of 1918 through 1919 I experienced some rather wild meetings of anarchists and communists, as well as political riots, and this really developed my political instincts and increased my desire to render social aid. I took care of students who were blinded during the war and was engaged in juvenile court aid. During the influenza epidemic I cared for many other students and neighbors and, for the first time in my life, was confronted with severe illness and death.

During the first postwar term at the university we heard the call "Women out," but this lasted only a few weeks, since the low percentage of female students and the generally distressed conditions of the inflationary postwar years tended to result in lasting friendships and an enormous mutual helpfulness among students. After ten terms I was able to do well in the final examination, and I received my doctorate at the University of Kiel in 1923. For me this was a period of a tremendous desire to learn, and I included marginal studies of social economy, social hygiene, and history of the fine arts and literature at the universities of Berlin, Marburg, Mürzburg, Innsbruck, Greifswald, Berlin, and Kiel again. I had actually planned to devote myself to hygiene and bacteriology when I met my future husband and fell in love with him. I sacrificed my personal scientific ambitions willingly, and following a period of clinical work in Prenzlau, we were married and I established my own medical practice.

I had four children, a large house, and a rapidly growing practice, primarily pediatric. In 1928 I was charged with the medical responsibility for a social-welfare institution, caring for about 200 young females, most of whom were either pregnant or suffering from venereal disease. For me this was indeed a very busy and fulfilling life. I also became aware of the social underground. I met with new experiences nearly every day. Even in 1934 through 1935, when the young inmates were transferred into the Hitler Youth for their improvement and education and in their place some 300 tired women were admitted to the institution, I gained considerable social, medical, and human experience.

In 1939 we saw the first shadows fall on our happy and prosperous life. My husband was drafted as a medical officer, as were many of his colleagues. Two very prominent and popular Jewish colleagues, one a physician and the other a dentist, put an end to their lives. Some Jewish patients had left the city under the most piteous circumstances, and others were even deported. Where did they go? Into the unknown, and their sorrows, their grief, and their distress were shared by the doctors who had had their confidence. To render practical aid was almost impossible, since deportations would be carried out suddenly and without warning in the early hours of the morning. More and more people simply vanished, primarily the sick patients. There was perhaps a rumor, but who dared to follow it up? During the war we were at first stunned by the news of victory, but the almost superhuman amount of work we had to do prevented us from being carried away by depression.

In the years to come the final catastrophe became more and more evident. And what a fall it was to be! From January of 1945 on, we saw the desolate columns of despair coming from the eastern provinces. They passed through the streets of our town day and night, many of them walking, some of them riding on and in the most hazardous vehicles, with babies and old people, sometimes with the bodies of those who had frozen to death. Those last four months were a nightmare of horrifying news, cold nights, general distress, fires along the horizon, and air-raid warnings. We had the alarms from Berlin, Stettin (in Poland), and Peenemünde, but we did not face direct air raids. I was personally grateful that my children tolerated this terrible period well. My fifth child, however, died in an air raid immediately after its birth in the gynecological clinic in Stettin.

I was asked by the NSV (the welfare organization of the Nazis, who, it must be admitted, really provided the greatest possible degree of organized help) to visit the emergency camps of the refugees as soon as darkness arrived, in order to provide medical aid to the best of my ability. Since then I have known what it means to be in flight for weeks during an extremely cold winter. Many of the refugees were dead or dying. We tried to arrange for pregnant women and sick people to get emergency beds in provisional hospitals. I learned about the despair and the uncertainty that prevailed when children or relatives were lost in all the confusion. The fact that such misery still occurs as a consequence of wars calls for a total condemnation of all masculine power politics. I have become a determined opponent of war.

On April 19, 1945, my family and the entire city met our destiny. The first Russian bombs fell at the very moment when the public loudspeakers, which for weeks had been the only communication with the outside world, roared, "Fight until final victory!"—part of Goebbels's speech on the occasion of Hitler's birthday. I found my children crying in the house, which was, fortunately, only slightly damaged by the bombs. I seized the suitcases that had already been packed and evacuated the children to my sister's home in the countryside. Two days later, after an extensive struggle with the Nazi officials, I received permission to take them across the border to the adjacent region of Mecklenburg. I was allowed to have two cars of my own on account of my medical practice, but gasoline was strictly rationed. Unauthorized leave from one region to another was prohibited at that time and was punishable with immediate hanging. I was to return within three days, but by then the city was already in flames. The first Russian troops had entered, and we were overtaken by chaos in Mecklenburg. In the middle of June we finally arrived in Lübeck, passing numerous intermediate stations and some dangerous incidents. We had saved but little of our original property, and I had lost the two cars. Lübeck itself was overcrowded with refugees. There were about 150,000 inhabitants and almost as many refugees. Apart from that, the city had been partially destroyed in an air raid in 1943.

Beginning a new life was hard, but there was a lot of work to be done, and with the help of some colleagues, we managed to get what was most urgently needed. I got into contact with the international women's leagues of Sweden and the United States, and they helped, thus giving me the chance to help others. I soon gained a reputation among the refugees, so that in 1950 I was chosen as a member of parliament by the Refugee party in the first election for a regional parliament in Kiel. I searched and finally succeeded in finding my husband, my son, my foster son, and my mother, and they all came to Lübeck. My husband's state of health was poor, and so was that of my elderly mother, and they died in 1951 and 1953 respectively. I was alone with a rapidly growing medical practice, and apart from that, I had parliamentary work to do. On account of this work, I was appointed minister of labor, social work, and refugees in Schleswig-Holstein in 1957. This meant that I had to give up my medical practice. I was by then fifty-nine years old, and I had gained vast experience during many difficult years and was thoroughly trained to work. I remained in this official position for almost ten years and was involved in many interesting tasks.

There were the victims of the war, the survivors of the war, and the uprooted juveniles who were desperately looking for jobs to build up a new existence. There was the social care of sick, elderly, and handicapped people to be provided for. The refugee camps had to be cleared, and an extensive program of resettlement was initiated. Another project was established for the provision of housing. These years were indeed most worthwhile.

It has always been my endeavor to encourage women to participate in social and public life, in women's organizations such as the International League for Peace and Freedom and the International Federation of Business and Professional Women. I worked in the Landesfrauenrat (Regional Women's Council) and in the Deutscher Frauenrat (Federal Women's Council) from the beginning, and I have been a member of the presidency in the Kuratorium Unteilbares Deutschland (Trusteeship Indivisible Germany), as well as of the German Medical Association. Fortunately, the long years of starvation did not affect my health, and I am full of gratitude for my five children and thirteen grandchildren. I do, however, suffer from the division of my country, which has brought us a number of serious problems.

Now, since I have given up most of my public tasks, I am able to devote myself to my family and my personal and social interests.

A. Charlotte Ruys
b. December 21, 1898

The family into which I was born lived in a small village, Dedemsvaart, in the eastern part of the Netherlands. I was the second child and eldest daughter in a family of eight. Our father had a large nursery of herbaceous plants, trees, shrubs, and rosebushes. He had many international contacts, spoke seven foreign languages, and exported all over Europe and North America. Before her marriage our mother, who was very active, had earned her own living as an employee in the Dedemsvaart Post Office. Two of her sisters were teachers, and the brothers of both our parents had university degrees.

We were educated in the Protestant faith and went to church every Sunday. In primary school I was the only one in my class from an intellectual family, all the others being the children of farmers. As a result, I had no friends, and my brothers and sisters were my only playmates. We had every facility in our own home, which included gardens, barns, workshops, horses, and cows. Each child had his or her own small garden. Our youth was filled with music, as my father was an excellent pianist. My mother was very active in the village, as well as in the household. With the help of a few other women she organized the first district nursing service and was thus the first person to do social work in the area.

On Sundays, sitting in church next to my mother, I often asked myself what my future would be. Our parents had taught us girls, as well as the boys, that we would have to become self-supporting. I felt the need to help other people. I had a profound admiration for my uncle, who was an excellent physician in the village. I was also impressed by the work of the district nurse. After considering various possibilities, I decided that I wished to become a doctor in order to discover the causes of illness. At the age of twelve I told my father of my desire to study medicine. He did not approve, as he considered this too heavy a task for a woman. His reply was, "If you are intelligent enough you should study mathematics or astronomy. In any case, I will do everything in my power to make you change your mind."

After two years at the secondary school in the village, I attended the high school in Zwolle, a small town thirty kilometers away. Because of the difficulty of transportation my eldest brother and I had to stay in Zwolle during the week and could only be at home during the weekends. We boarded with a local family, who took no notice of us. In school I became friendly with several of the girls. We went swimming and rowing and playing tennis and hockey, but nevertheless, I felt extremely lonely because children from the country were not invited to the homes of the local families. Only one family, that of a doctor, allowed me to visit their daughter. I thought it was necessary to learn to be alone, so I never complained to my parents. I had no special hobbies and did not read many books, as the more religious ones did not interest me.

At the gymnasium I had an easy time because I had already been taught so much in the village school. Usually I was able to finish my homework in a quarter of an hour. My real interest was biology, which I could study only during school hours.

In 1917, when I was eighteen, I passed the university entrance examination. When I told my father again that I wished to study medicine, he agreed to this proposal and promised to help me. His only condition was that I should go to a university in the western part of the country, as he believed that this was the cultural center. I chose Utrecht because Leiden was too official and I was afraid of the big city of Amsterdam. My mother wished me to learn how to keep house, as well, so during the holidays I was instructed at home in all different aspects of housekeeping for a large family.

In my first year at the university I was introduced to chemistry, physics, and biology. I was fascinated with all aspects of biology and found it a pleasure to attend lectures and follow the practical courses. Our class consisted of fifty students, of whom five were girls.

On entering the university, I became a member of the Utrecht Women Students' Association. There I had the opportunity to meet girls with interests in all fields of science, and I made friends with students of medicine, law, history, and literature. I shall never forget the impressions the books of Zola, Shaw, Galsworthy, and others made on me. One of the most important aspects of student life was the opportunity to discuss all sorts of questions with people of different interests. At this time I left the Protestant church, which grieved my parents. I became interested in politics, attended a number of meetings, but never became a member of any party.

In my fourth and fifth years, when I came into contact with sick people, I delved more and more into pathology. I felt that I needed a more exact knowledge of the causes of the various diseases. At that time neuropathology was especially fascinating to me. Microbiology had not yet attracted my interest, although this subject later became my speciality. The clinical work gave me great satisfaction, but I changed from Utrecht to Groningen in my last year because the professors of surgery and gynecology at Utrecht were discriminating against women students. I did not wish to fight, so I left with five others and graduated in Groningen in 1924.

I then had to find a place to work. For weeks I tried in vain until a friend told me about Professor Paul Schüffer, who had recently returned from Sumatra and was working at the Department of Tropical Hygiene in the Colonial Institute in Amsterdam. Schüffer was a clinician, hygienist, epidemiologist, and micro-biologist. He was an ideal teacher, and I was fortunate enough to be allowed to work in his laboratory. After four months training I chose rat-bite fever as the subject for my thesis. We received large numbers of wild rats from the *Leptospira* research group in the institute, and I tested them for the presence of rat-bite fever. Out of 350 rats I found three carrying this microorganism in their blood but not in their saliva. With a new staining technique I showed that the disease was a spirillum and not a spirochete. In July of 1925, on presentation of my thesis, I became a doctor of medicine.

I was accepted as an assistant in the Department of Hygiene, where I was trained by Professor Johannes van Loghem in bacteriology and hygiene. I helped with the practical courses for the students and organized the first training course in hygiene for doctors in our country. In 1926 I received the first official diploma as hygienist cum laude. During this time I did basic research in bacteriology and practical work in the field of hygiene.

In 1928 I became a lecturer at the University of Amsterdam and was appointed head of the laboratories at the Municipal Public Health Service, despite the fact that I was the youngest applicant and the only woman among the eight who applied for the position and that I had no practical training.

It was wonderful to be able to combine practice and research. My first real success was when I was able to demonstrate that microscopic examination of specimens from children with vulvovaginitis often led to a false diagnosis of gonorrhea. In studying typhoid fever, we found that contaminated water was frequently the source of infection. The new methods of typing bacteria made possible a more thorough study of the epidemiology of many infectious diseases. In the 1930s I gave courses of lectures on food hygiene to girls studying at a school of social science.

I greatly enjoyed the city of Amsterdam. I met a few artists and also made friends in the medical world, but I spent most of my free time working and reading. My best friend was playwright-psychoanalyst August (Guus) Defresne. I learned a lot from him, and our friendship gradually deepened.

In April of 1940 I was appointed professor extraordinarius at the University of Amsterdam, but I was able to continue my work at the Public Health Service.

A few days later war broke out, and on May 15 the Dutch army surrendered to the Germans. At first we could continue our work without too many difficulties. However, there were severe epidemics of infectious diseases and gradually our stock of laboratory materials ran short. My personal problem was whether I should work for the Germans, but I concluded that it was my moral duty to work as hard for them as for the Dutch patients.

My relationship with Guus had grown much closer, but when we decided that we wanted to marry, an existing law made it very difficult for me because, as a government employee, I would lose my job. He and I were both active in the resistance movement, and although we did not have fixed ideas, we followed our consciences. In 1942, when Guus refused to become a member of the Kultur-kammer, the Germans tried to arrest him, but fortunately, he had already left his house. We decided that he should live in my home, which he did until February of 1945, when I was taken prisoner.

My greatest problems were at the university. In February of 1943 I refused to continue teaching because the male students were arrested and sent to a concentration camp. After their release, conditions were so difficult that I still refused, with the result that I was dishonorably discharged from the university.

In September of 1944, when the western part of the country was cut off from all imports, there were serious shortages of fuel and food, and as a result, many people died of starvation. We were saved because my father was living in the country, where they still had enough to eat, and my sister managed to send us the family's food coupons and later, with the help of a kind German officer, quite a lot of food.

In February of 1945 I was arrested because I was in contact with a radio transmitter for the Allies. A colleague bacteriologist and three others who were also arrested were shot a few days later. As I was a woman, I had to be shot in Germany. I was in prison with two other women condemned on the same charge. We were not moved, as transport to Germany was impossible; the Allies had blocked all the roads. The day after the German surrender, we were set free.

A new life began again. Six weeks later, when I had more or less recovered from the famine, I married my friend Guus Defresne. We had a most ideal life together, and although we had very different backgrounds, we could discuss and criticize each other's work. As he was very intelligent, I could explain all my experiments to him. We were in love with each other until his death in 1961.

During the first months after the liberation it was still impossible to buy the necessary laboratory materials, and in addition, we were out of touch with new discoveries in other parts of the world, although I had heard a rumor about penicillin. I wrote to Dr. A. Cohn, bacteriologist of the city of New York, whom I knew. He published my letter in *Science*, and a few weeks later I received a flood of literature and new materials for our work. Within a few months our laboratory was functioning again at an international level. This help was very important, as we were still suffering from terrible epidemics of infectious diseases.

In 1946 I was invited by the British council to visit London with Guus to see a play of his that was running there. Later that same year the Rockefeller Foundation invited me for a three-month tour of the United States and Canada. It was wonderful to see these countries and to discuss our problems with so many experts. I was impressed by the fact that in the United States many bacteriologists did not have medical degrees but were doctors of philosophy only. I felt grateful that, as a medical graduate, I could often understand problems better. This trip enabled me to thank personally all those who had helped me.

The Netherlands Medical Women's Association was founded in 1933 by Elise Sanders and Rosalie Wijnberg, both gynecologists. I became a member but was not very active, as I was too busy in my own field of work and had never suffered any discrimination as a woman. The first postwar meeting of the Medical Women's International Association (MWIA) took place in Amsterdam in 1947. At this meeting I was happy to be able to discuss our problems with people from other countries. I was elected president of the MWIA and served from 1947 through 1950. At the 1950 MWIA congress in Philadelphia I proposed the reacceptance of our German colleagues.

In 1948 I became professor ordinarius in bacteriology, epidemiology, and immunology at the University of Amsterdam. I was the second woman in our country to be appointed as a professor, the first having been Cornelia de Lange, who became professor in the medical faculty in Amsterdam in 1927.

From 1945 to 1948 I was a member of the editorial staff of the *Netherlands Journal of Medicine*, and from 1949 to 1953 I was dean of the Faculty of Medicine. I was also involved in the work of the government organization on pure and applied research.

Guus then convinced me that I could not continue with this workload. I made my choice and gave up all outside appointments except membership in the Government Advisory Commission for Health, a position that I held from 1950 to 1966. One of the reasons for this decision was that my health was not good. Since the war I had suffered from severe osteoporosis. In 1950 I fractured the neck of my left femur. It healed well, but a year later the head of the femur became necrotic, and since then I have been able to walk outside the house only with the aid of crutches.

During the years many physicians have come to our laboratory to be trained as bacteriologists, while others came in order to do research for their theses. I myself became more and more interested in mycoplasma. I withdrew gradually from the field of immunology, as this became an entirely new speciality, while epidemiology remained one of my main interests.

In 1969 I resigned from the university at the age of seventy. My youngest sister, who is a landscape architect, came to live with me. She is a great help in all respects. I have put all my husband's papers in order, and I try to keep in contact with former co-workers, with friends, and with the younger generation.

Inger Alida Haldorsen
b. May 19, 1899

None of those present when I was born could have dreamed that I would become a doctor, later a gynecologist, practicing in Norway. I arrived on Bømlo, an island off the west coast of Norway, with islets all around it. The fishing banks off its coast provided good catches, while some of the land was cultivated, so the population lived from their fishing and their farming and the big herring catches in the spring supplied the necessary cash for trading.

There were few roads for horse-drawn vehicles—only walking and rowing were possible—so on that day in May, with hailstorms and a heavy gale blowing, the midwife was unable to get through. There was nothing for it but to manage without help, and it was my father who delivered me. He had plenty of experience, for he had been a widower with seven children. His first wife had died in childbirth, but this time all went well. I was mother's third child, and she later had four more. It was a large family to grow up in.

My mother's people, who came from the center of the island, were farmers. On my father's side there was a German skipper who had settled in Norway. This German came to be so respected that his name is still used in the family, and it is from him that my father is thought to have inherited the talent that enabled him to become an inventor with a knowledge of mechanics far ahead of his time.

My mother worked as a tailor before her marriage. Like most girls of the period, she received little schooling, but she retained all she heard and was eager to learn more.

My father started manufacturing coach wheels and agricultural machinery. Since steamships were the only means of communication and there were long distances between ports of call, his eldest son designed and built a ship's engine.

As soon as we children were old enough, we were taken into the firm. We learned what it meant to build up a business, with no money apart from what we earned.

In those days there was a natural and clear division between men's and women's work, and the women carried an especially heavy load, for they had to see to the provision of food and accommodation for laborers, other employees, visiting customers, and business representatives.

My father was kindly and humorous and took an interest in his children. My mother wanted the girls brought up to be good homemakers, able to card, spin, weave, and make at least their own clothes. The boys were taken into the business, and young as they were, they had to work. It was a large gathering that sat down at mealtimes, and father used to entertain us with stories from the countryside.

I had seven years of primary education, going to school every other day by a dangerous road passing over soft swampland and across a rocky slope that was subject to landslides in the spring. I was four when my older sister learned to read, and I learned, too. By the time I reached school age, I had so many interests that school almost got in the way. I did, however, read everything I could lay my hands on. As there was no secondary school, I spent an eighth year in the primary school.

I developed in other directions, too. With the business attracting young people from all over, there were youth clubs and choirs, as well as athletic clubs, which were mainly for the boys. There was also a handwritten newspaper, which gave me the chance to try my writing skill. Taking part in a debate for the first time was quite an experience. Our home was used as a meeting place for men, and when they were discussing trade, religion, politics, and other social questions, I was all ears and used to slip away from the housework to listen in.

Like all the others, I was to have a place in the business as a clerk. The idea did not appeal to me, and I was allowed to go to a six-month boarding school for young people from the country. There I acquired a tremendous thirst for knowledge and ventured to write to my father for permission to go to grammar school. As a man trained to work with his hands, my father was not particularly impressed by theoretical training, but he found my request interesting. He explained to me that grammar school meant study for the university, and he asked me if I had law in mind. I did not. The feminist movement had reached Norway but met with opposition, and a battle was being fought for higher education for women, as well as for men. A story circulated about a woman doctor who wanted to become a gynecologist but could not get the necessary hospital appointments because the consultants refused to admit women to these posts. This story acted as an incentive for me; opposition has always increased my determination. I did realize, though, that in my situation I might as well have wanted to go to the moon!

Competition in the entrance examination was stiff, but I was successful. This was during World War I, and there was a shortage of food throughout the country, but my mother was able to send me food from the farm. I read everything I could get hold of and did well in my examinations.

Paying for studies was no easy matter in those days, especially for a woman. It was at this point that mother intervened, quoting another mother who had said, "Even if my last garment is in tatters, my son shall be allowed to study."

Every month my mother sent me something from the housekeeping money, just enough to keep body and soul together. This meant that she had to deny herself much because the other children also had to be educated.

Students flocked to the country's only university in Oslo after World War I. There was quite a stir when 300 students (13 of them women) applied to study medicine, and they just barely got in. Oslo was not prepared for such an influx, and food and lodgings were something of a problem, but the situation gradually improved, as students were ready to make do with whatever they could get. Clothes had to be homemade. I had to wear a winter coat handed down from an aunt, then turn it and wear it again. I spent summer vacations at home on the farm. My friends and companions felt that my studies were taking a long time. And what was in it for a woman, anyway?

There was not room in the hospital wards for all the students who wanted to continue, so an examination was held. Of my group of fifty students only two were women, and we both passed the examination and were accepted. At the end of the seven years came the finals. A woman had to fight her own battles in those days, as there were no colleagues to encourage or support her.

It was surely a desire to see the country that prompted me to apply for a post as a district doctor. It was a time of depression, when there was little money to spare. In those days most confinements took place in the home, with a midwife in attendance, the doctor being called only if there were complications. I soon became aware that my knowledge in this field was inadequate, and this renewed my determination to become a gynecologist. People were not too skeptical about a woman as a doctor, but when it came to driving a horse and sledge on snowy roads—well, that was definitely not a job for a woman. All the same, I had to do it if I was to get to my patients in winter.

Specialization meant hospital training, and at that time openings were few, for state hospitals had to be run as cheaply as possible. Most consultants preferred men for these posts, but a male colleague happened to withdraw and I was given a position. It was particularly difficult to be appointed to a gynecological ward because they were few and far between.

My next appointment was at the State School for Midwives in Bergen. I was now recognized as a gynecologist. Something else had happened, too. In 1934 I had joined the Norwegian Medical Women's Association and become its secretary. As part of the preparations for an international congress in Edinburgh on "Cancer in Women" and "Maternal Mortality and Abortion" I had to read my way through health reports from 1898 to 1920. There was still a high percentage of deaths in childbirth in Norway, and there were still many cases of puerperal fever, hemorrhage, and blood poisoning. Criminal abortion had also become quite a problem in my country.

I went to Edinburgh not particularly well prepared, as I had little practice in languages, but my stay there proved a very enjoyable experience and meant the fulfilment of my ambition to travel and to increase my knowledge abroad. In the winter of 1937 through 1938 I also attended an international course in Paris and enjoyed meeting members of the Medical Women's International Association

(MWIA) from Asia, South America, and Europe, all of whom were very kind to me.

Working as a senior registrar gave me the chance to practice surgery, which was what I wanted most. The hospital in Bergen was also the center for Norwegian midwives, and so I gained experience in drawing up plans for their education. My ideas did not always meet with the approval of the old senior consultant, but I was a born fighter and there was many a battle between us.

With World War II came the German occupation of Norway, a circumstance for which the population was quite unprepared. However, Norwegian history had engendered in our people a great desire for freedom, and as in other countries, there sprang up a resistance movement. I joined, and my job was to help those who were on the run from the Gestapo. My large flat was used as a hideout for a number of refugees, who often used my birthplace as the starting point for their flight to the west. Once there was a very intensive search for one of them. Then at six o'clock one morning three men arrived to take me away. I was charged with espionage and brought before the Gestapo. There was a "day of reckoning" that day, and many arrests were made.

For once it was an advantage to be a woman, for so far, at any rate, the occupation forces in Norway had never shot a woman. Three weeks solitary confinement was not an altogether pleasant experience. However, the young guards were quite thrilled at having a female prisoner, especially one who could speak to them. The period of solitary confinement was followed by more than a year in an ordinary prison. During this time the Gestapo kept saying that I would be set free if I told them all I knew, but that was of course utterly impossible. I always tried to behave with dignity when I was being interrogated.

Time passed slowly in prison, but I made good use of the resources of the library and friends sent me pieces of needlework. Previous experience had taught me that work could offer an outlet for pent-up energy and that it is always a means of retaining human dignity. Dumbbells were sent in to keep me physically fit, and I was given permission to use them in the exercise yard. The Gestapo warder did not like me. I was a dangerous woman, he told me. From this spell in prison I learned a great deal about the human mind and how people handle and react to a dangerous situation—and I learned a great deal about myself.

Perhaps because of a shortage of accommodations in the prison I was suddenly released while the war was still on, but I was kept under observation. I had no job, nowhere to practice, and nowhere to stay. Relatives helped me to find a place that served as a dwelling and office. My health was not as good as it might have been. It was no simple matter to start up a practice again after an absence like that.

There was still a shortage of women specializing in obstetrics and gynecology, and there was also the problem of equipment and instruments. The greatest difficulty was getting patients admitted to hospital. An emergency hospital was the first solution, then a private hospital for performing operations. There was a shortage of cars and petrol, so I bicycled to the hospital in the beginning. The war clouds were still dark, but I maintained a spirit of optimism.

The end of the war brought a tremendous feeling of relief, and my thoughts turned to other things, such as what could be done to remedy all that had been neglected for five long years. One of the first tasks was to assist those who had suffered most from the effects of the war. I helped to establish a political-prisoners' association and became a member of the local committee.

Now that the war was over, an appeal was made to put society in order. My name was put on the list at the first municipal election, and I made political speeches. There were many aspects of political activity with which I was of course not familiar, but my past development influenced me toward the center. So many people turned up to hear my first speech that I had difficulty getting into the hall. I polled the largest number of votes in my party and continued in local politics for twenty-two years. The basic idea behind all the causes to which I lent support was help for the neglected in the community. Since it was only natural that women should look after the social needs in the community, I became a member of the Children's Home and Day Nursery Committee and was involved in the planning of old-people's homes and hospitals.

I was asked to let my name be put up as a candidate for Parliament, but election would have meant being away from my practice for much of the year. Medicine had been my whole life, and I wanted to go on being a doctor.

During this period I gave a series of talks to women's organizations, taking as my theme the rebuilding of the country. There was no doubt that homemakers were worn out, and one of the first issues I became involved in was finding helpers for homemakers who were ill and exhausted. The first course in home-help service was planned along the lines of courses in neighboring countries, and I was one of the instructors.

I had planned to continue my education abroad, but war had intervened. It was a marvelous experience, therefore, to meet members of the MWIA at a council meeting in London in 1946. The following year there was an international congress in Amsterdam and two years later another council meeting, in Finland. At all these meetings I learned a great deal and made many friends. At the 1950 congress in Philadelphia I was elected to the executive committee of the MWIA, an office I held for eight years.

The MWIA congress in Manila gave me the chance to widen my knowledge of the different nations of the world, for it introduced me to the Third World. Later I saw how people lived in other countries, where the woman's special function of giving birth to children was performed under very different conditions. In their fight for women's rights, women in the highly developed countries of the West have to bear in mind these women in other lands, for solidarity with them is essential. This is a field in which an international organization of women doctors has particular responsibilities.

During the war some members of the resistance movement had felt the need to produce a daily paper to provide absolutely objective information and comment on social conditions, and I was invited to become a member of the board. It was a new experience for me to see my thoughts in print. I was filled with an intense desire to help right wrongs in the life of the community. I published a series of articles in which the dominant theme was the family, the position of women, questions of health, and women's responsibilities in these matters.

After a time the field of local government became too narrow, for so many of the important decisions were made in Parliament. A great deal was done after the war to right the wrongs in society, and in this work I was not involved. Finally I was elected a deputy in Parliament. In the course of a discussion in the Parliamentary Finance Committee on amendments to the law of taxation I proposed that homemakers who had paid employment outside the home be entitled to tax deduction for the domestic help they required. The majority of the committee were men, and there was strong reaction among them, not because of the loss in taxation, but because of their traditional attitude toward the idea of working wives.

As a member of the board of the Norwegian Women's National Council, I set up a committee to work out a standard method of theoretical and practical training in child care. For twenty-three years I was medical superintendent of a children's home and was responsible for the teaching given there.

One of the areas Norwegian society wanted to improve after the war was that of public health, and a scheme was set up to finance this. It was called the National Social Insurance Scheme, and from 1956 everyone was required to join it.

A Hospitals Act was passed, but implementing it was another matter. The private hospitals were included in the program, but the financing body, the National Social Insurance Scheme, was not able to do all that was expected of it.

My next appointment was as a member of the Committee of the Norwegian Medical Depot, a government monopoly for the import and export of medicines. Most of the time I was the only woman on the committee, but it was my medical knowledge that was the important thing. I continued to serve on this committee up to the age limit. A small country like Norway did not have the resources to undertake research in this sector of public health, but it was important that doctors be kept abreast of the tremendous advances in the field, and I supported the chairman's proposal that particular attention be given to this matter.

Norway had previously operated a system of state-appointed midwives, who attended home confinements until the extensive developments in medicine brought a desire for special maternity wards. Because of the increase in the birth rate, there were not enough hospital beds in the country to cope with all the maternity cases. Reductions were made in the length of time before maternity cases were admitted and in the length of time they were allowed to remain on the ward. This resulted in a considerable increase in the number of babies born on the way to the hospital, a factor that statistics showed to be somewhat dangerous for the babies. This state of affairs was an immense challenge for a gynecologist. My particular field was ante-natal care, obstetrics and gynecological surgery, which I carried on in a private hospital. When the adviser to the hospital board died, I was given his position, which I held from the age of sixty until retirement.

Shortly after the war I was invited to assist in the work of a family planning clinic. I agreed to do so for a year but I have stayed on to take care of this aspect of women's welfare.

I was close to retirement age when I became president of the Norwegian Midwives' Association, where I continued for six years. The midwives were my closest colleagues, and at an early stage, they had asked me to help them to obtain better training. What I really wanted was independent, comprehensive training; what I achieved was a combination of a slightly shortened nursing training followed by a course in midwifery. There was a drop in the number of applicants, and during a brief visit to Parliament in January 1962, I asked for reconsideration of the matter. As a result, the finances of the student midwives were improved and they were granted an extra year's training.

It was very difficult for me to stir up public opinion in my own country, and without the help of a large organization like the Norwegian Women's Institute, it would probably have taken a long time for people to realize that the status of midwives had to be improved. I presided over three annual meetings of the Norwegian Midwives' Association, and on each occasion resolutions were sent to local authorities, the Ministry of Social Affairs, Parliament, and the chief administrative officer of each county. The general disparagement of midwifery seemed to come from the fact that it was work done by women and ought not to cost anything.

My work as a doctor also brought me into contact with young wives and mothers. It did not take me long to realize that mothers of small children were overworked, and I wanted them to have domestic help so that they could have one free day a week. The coming of the modern industrial society had put an end to the old contact between the generations, and these young mothers were often left to cope with all the work alone. Fortunately, there was more and more encouragement for fathers to share in the care of their children, and I often used to say to an expectant mother, "Let your husband help with the baby. It will make him see the child in an entirely new light." I noticed that many women described themselves as being "just a housewife," but the homemaker and mother are essential to society, and their job is not an inferior one, although professional training is a good thing for a woman to have.

At an international level I became well known in the organizations of which I was a member—namely, the MWIA, the International Council of Women, and the International Confederation of Midwives—and my name was included in the Dictionary of Scandinavian Biography.

As time went on, I saw a change in the women's movement. New groups of women made new demands. The expression *equal footing* was not much to my liking. I felt that *equal worth* and *equal rights* were more in keeping with nature. The female's set of chromosomes may be different from the male's, but that does not make her less intelligent. What is required to bring about improvement in women's status is a new evaluation of the role of women and of the qualities and characteristics with which nature has endowed them.

My birthplace, Bømlo, with its islets, is still there off the west coast of

Norway, although there have been many changes. My thoughts go back with happiness and gratitude to my father and mother, who had the courage to make personal sacrifices for the sake of the future of their children. My wide range of interests often seem to me to resemble a dandelion, with its seeds that scatter with the wind and are not always welcome where they fall. All my activities have been rooted in my interest in the profession I chose in my youth. My achievements have been rewarded by the King's Gold Medal of Merit.

I found my "way to the moon." Was that simply the aspiration of a human being to perform some great feat, or was it something of benefit to the human race? Do women perhaps have a far greater task to perform in fostering new values and working for peaceful coexistence? These are questions that we may ponder.

Edmea Pirami
b. June 27, 1899

I was born at Ascoli Piceno, Italy. My father, from Pescia, was a teacher of arts, and my mother, from Lugo di Romagna, was a homemaker. We were five sisters, I being the fourth. Ester, the eldest, graduated in medicine in 1914; the second child became a drawing teacher, the third died of whooping cough at nine months of age, and the fifth took a degree in chemistry.

In my early childhood we lived in the little town of Ascoli Piceno, and then we moved to Livorno, where I attended kindergarten. When I was six years of age, we were transferred to Bologna, where I started to go to school. My earliest recollections are of a lower-middle-class milieu. I recall the evenings with the family around the dining room table or in the warm kitchen, all of us doing our homework. My father sat with us, meticulously preparing his lessons or correcting his pupils' exercises. Such was the patriarchal atmosphere of that day. Our mother was a highly intelligent woman and a strict disciplinarian.

In my early school years I was usually the youngest in the class, and I was not very industrious, but in the gymnasium in Bologna I began to take my studies seriously. I thereby obtained my teachers' love and esteem and even won exemption from school fees by merit. Philosophy and natural sciences were my chief interests. I took my matriculation at seventeen, specializing in classical subjects.

In November of 1916 I entered the Bologna University Faculty of Medicine and Surgery. Why did I turn to medicine? My sister Ester had earned her M.D. in 1914 with high honors. She had been given the position of medical assistant in Pescia, where all our relatives lived and where our father came from. When World War I broke out, Ester and a surgeon had to run the hospital, and they were able to care for the civilians, as well as the wounded from the battle front.

Overwhelmed by admiration for Ester's tireless activity and skill, I began at the age of sixteen to visit the Instituto Rizzoli of Bologna, where the wounded were hospitalized. There I learned simple treatments and dressings. The next summer I spent all my holidays in Pescia and devoted my time to the surgical department under my sister's direction. It was just my sister's noble example and my early training that matured my true inclination to become a doctor. In addition, my love of science enhanced my humanitarian tendencies to give patients spiritual aid in tragic times.

In 1915 and 1916 two tragedies occurred in our family. A cousin of fifteen years died of tubercular meningitis, and another young relative succumbed to scarlet fever. These events deeply affected me, increasing my desire to devote my life to suffering human beings.

In 1922, at the age of twenty-three, I graduated in medicine with flying colors. My thesis was on celiac disease in infants and children. During my fourth year I had been fascinated by Professor Carlo Francioni's lectures. He was a renowned authority on pediatrics. On the very day of my graduation I consented to take the position of assistant professor at his institute, which was offered as a reward for my acknowledged interest and appraised skillfulness. I thus joined the physicians of the Pediatric Clinic in Bologna.

In 1927 I took my examination in pediatrics and passed with the highest marks and honors. The following year I completed with honors a course in child welfare. I remained at the institute until 1933, when I left with the title of second professor of hospitals. Since that time I have devoted myself entirely to private practice. Without hospital responsibility I could experience the deep joy of fulfilling in a better way the requirements of my work. During my years at the clinic and in my private practice, my chief aim has been to alleviate the physical and mental difficulties of young children. Research problems have retained my interest and have been a means to better fulfill my goals.

At the age of thirty-three, I married a physician, a specialist in internal medicine. For many years my husband was chief physician of the Ospedale Maggiore of Bologna, later becoming director. We have one daughter, Alberta, who has a degree in law and has also studied psychology. Alberta practices in Bologna.

When World War II broke out and bombing began, people started to evacuate the city and went to the country. I also left to live in a small house five kilometers from Bologna. There I was able to devote myself to many patients, but soon my house was occupied by the troops and I was compelled to carry on my medical activities in a small space in the kitchen. Very often my work was interrupted by sirens and bombings. I had to rush out day and night to the air-raid shelters, where I had been appointed to assess the needs of the poeple. I worked hard, was exposed to many dangers, and was always worried about my little daughter and my husband, who was serving in the army.

In the meantime my family had become larger, as I had given six Jewish children a home. They were sons of friends and had been entrusted to me. When my home was requisitioned by the troops, I succeeded in placing these children in a religious institution where they would be cared for.

During these times I never lost heart, for fortune was on my side. Divine providence clearly watched over my activities. It was in this peculiar period that I was assisted by my little daughter, who acted as an interpreter, as she had already learned German and English in school. When it became safe enough, we returned to Bologna. My car had been seized, but I could make my calls by using a bicycle or walking.

After World War II my husband was able to organize the reconstruction of the bombed-out Ospedale Maggiore and is now regarded as its father. During the terrible floods of 1968 we two were able to help medically, as well as to provide food and clothing for the suffering. As a reward, we were honored with the Premio della Bontà ("Prize of Goodness").

My scientific papers have dealt chiefly with celiac disease in children and historical studies on medical women.

I was the first woman to be elected councillor of the Order of Physicians of Bologna. The Medical Women's Association of Bologna was founded in 1946, and I was its president for several terms. I was also president of the Italian Medical Women's Association. I have attended all the congresses of the Medical Women's International Association and in Manila in 1962 I became vice-president for southern Europe. In addition, I am one of the founding members of the Soroptimists of Bologna and have been the group's president for two terms.

I am still practicing actively and with joy as a consultant in pediatrics. I have two consulting rooms, one for spastics and the other for child welfare, for children of mothers who have no national insurance.

Finally, in 1972, after fifty years of medical service, I was awarded the Order of Physicians, along with a gold medal for the work I have carried out with great love and self-sacrifice.

I am as enthusiastic today as I ever was about my choice of profession. I have experienced no discrimination because of my sex. In the university sphere until a few years ago, men were preferred and women regarded as subordinate persons. Today, common sense has overcome such an opinion.

Estrid Guldberg
b. July 6, 1899

I was born in Göttingen, Germany. My mother Elisabeth Dalhoff was Danish, and my father Alf Guldberg was Norwegian. My paternal grandfather was Axel Sophus Guldberg, a doctor of philosophy in mathematics, with the calculation of probabilities as his specialty. He was the second of nine brothers, all of whom were university graduates in mathematics or medicine. One of his sisters Cathinka was the first nurse in Norway and the founder of the Deaconess Institution, which celebrated its hundredth anniversary in 1966, when a sculpture of her was unveiled. My maternal grandfather, who was a clergyman, built a cottage named Björnlia up in the mountains in 1882. It is situated 1000 meters above sea level beside an idyllic lake that abounds in trout. This cottage still belongs to the family and is eagerly used by the new generations. In the beginning it took three days by boat, by train, by carriage, and on foot to reach Björnlia. My mother was visiting girl friends in the cottage when my father came for hunting. They soon became engaged and were married by my grandfather in the chapel of the Deaconess Institution.

My father had just earned his doctorate in mathematics and a scholarship when he and mother proceeded to Paris and Göttingen, the centers for such studies at that time. In this way I came to the world in Göttingen. Father was a little afraid that babies could be mixed up in the women's clinic, but he was contented when told that I was *die einzige Helle.*

Eventually father and mother moved to Oslo, where father was appointed lecturer and, from 1916, professor of insurance mathematics at the university. I remember many things from that time. I recall how I insisted on bobbing my hair as my younger sister had done. She had thin hair, and mine was thick; when I came home and saw the result, I wept bitter tears. My only consolation was a wig for my doll made out of my hair. My family also says that I never passed an open garden gate without closing it. Once I was going for a walk with my mother, and she wanted to hold my hand. I refused, and during the whole walk I kept my hand stiff.

A new period in our life began when we moved to our own house, named

Villa Spes. It was built on Nordre Skøyen. My grandfather had bought the estate in 1884. Spes was about an hour's walk from the university. I was the first of seven children. After my only sister Rigmor came five boys, the eldest of whom died when he was only six months old. I was twenty years older than my youngest brother.

I spent all the time I could possibly spare at Spes. There were five horses, thirty cows, fowl, and as many pigs as a child's heart could desire. I went to the cow barn and learned to milk. I fed the fowl and collected eggs, which could be found everywhere. But I liked the stables best; that was where my horse Svarten was. I always said that I loved horses more than I did human beings. We were allowed to ride when the horses were free from work. I say "We" because my best girl friend Margit and I always did everything together. I also took part in the outdoor work on the estate. The manager would ask, "Is Estrid coming?" when he needed someone to drive the haycutter.

I had close contact with my mother's Danish family. All her brothers and sisters had married, and we had many cousins. We went to Denmark to see them, and they came to see us. It was always pleasant and exciting, and this contact meant a great deal to us. Mother was a frequent and fine letter writer. Her correspondence with grandmother has been kept and collected by one of her brothers, and the letters are now in the collection of the Royal Library in Copenhagen.

These happy days came to an end when grandfather died in 1913. My parents were unable to take over the estate, which was sold. I wept bitterly when the horses were taken away. Grandmother remained the center of the family. As I was her first grandchild, I was a little spoiled and I called myself her favorite. This was accepted without special objection. Grandfather had been more solemn regarding children. We always had to go to church every Sunday. It appears that one of the children once said, "I can't stand hearing grandfather preach."

When Skøyen was sold, father's sister Sia had an addition built to Spes and it was named Fidep. She lived with us as a member of the family and was always very pleasant and good to everybody. We had dinner at 3:00 o'clock, when father came home from the university and the children from school. There were eleven persons at the table—father, mother, Aunt Sia, six children, and two servants. The meals were usually gay, and we all debated the happenings of the day. On occasion, however, father was very tense and tired and needed tranquility. Mother had made an arrangement with us children; if she put a china lion, which father didn't see, on the table, it meant "Be quiet."

A lot of father's foreign and Norwegian friends, most of them mathematicians, were guests in our home. Father would call mother and inform her that he had invited Mr. So and So, and mother was always ready to welcome him. The most famous was professor Albert Einstein, with his daughter. I remember them sitting by the open fire with the family. Mother was a good singer and liked singing, and her friends were fond of making music. We spent very pleasant times with them, too.

Father and mother participated in many mathematics congresses abroad;

they enjoyed these very much and spoke about them with great enthusiasm. Their recital of all the wonderful things they had seen and taken part in may have helped to make me congress-minded.

Mother was a fine wife and was supportive of father. On their daily walks he could talk to her about all his problems. Although mother was no mathematician, she was a good listener and she never asked stupid questions. She translated father's essays and papers into French and German. On their walks they also spoke about their many problems with us children.

As a rule, we had two students, often Danish girls, later on Norwegian girls, as housekeepers. Mother wrote a cook book called *Food for Two*. We children were allowed to have our boy friends and girl friends visit us. We had a good and harmonious home, with a healthy mode of living.

In summertime Aunt Sigrid taught us swimming. We had to walk forty-five minutes to reach the sea, very often in hot weather. In winter we went sleighing and skiing. We enjoyed especially going skiing with father, for he was as steady as a mountain and we could follow him. During the summers of 1915 and 1917 we all spent our vacations together in the Björnlia cottage, where father and mother had met years before.

Mother has been of the greatest importance to me during my whole life. She was always calm, and I went to her with my pains and joys. She understood and comforted me. We resembled each other. I respected father and was fond of him, but I was unable to talk with him as I did with mother. My brothers were on better speaking terms with him, especially as they grew up and were interested in mathematics.

We lived a healthy life. Father and mother taught us morning gymnastics, and I believe this contributed to keeping me in good form throughout my life. We had to learn parsimony, but we never suffered want. We inherited clothes that were in good condition but not always in accordance with our taste. We learned obedience, and sometimes we were birched. We talked little about religion. We went to church, not regularly, but when it suited us. I still do so and feel stronger and more able to meet the adversities of life. We were all confirmed and married in church. Sex education was unheard of. Mother told me about menstruation, but neither in school nor in my medical studies was sexual information mentioned.

When I reached school age, mother was my teacher during the first four years. From the fifth grade on, I attended a girls' school and then spent three years in Halling Gymnasium where I matriculated in 1918. Owing to the milieu in which I grew up, it was taken for granted that I would pursue studies at the university.

In a large family there will always be children's diseases, and we had most of them. Scarlatina with otitis, which I contracted when I was about fourteen years old, was the worst for me; I was isolated at home for six weeks. The disease began with a migraine attack. I have had migraines all my life, always as a result of overworking. Because of this problem I have been obliged to change or to give up many plans. Now I may have a one-sided headache and nausea for several days, which makes it impossible for me to work. The severe attacks are rarer.

After my matriculation in 1918, I considered several lines of study, among others chemistry. Father decided for me, saying that I should choose medicine, as there would always be a need for medical women. Before I made the final decision, I consulted Dr. Louise Isaksen, mother's doctor, who was one of the founders of Medical Women's International Association (MWIA). She gave me wise and encouraging advice. Before I commenced my medical studies, however, my sister and I worked in our home for one year, as mother had the idea that women should learn housework as a sort of liability to serve. The housekeeper was dismissed.

Falling in love is of course also a part of life. When we were quite young, we were enthusiastic admirers of nice and good teachers. Later on, we had young boyfriends, but it was quite innocent and mostly at a distance. When I was eighteen, I met Sigurd in his royal guard uniform. He was a young, newly fledged architect, and I fell in love in a new way. I remember the first kiss and his proposal of marriage. In spite of being in love, I hesitated. I was young, and I intended to study medicine. We never dreamed of combining matrimony and studies, and so we drifted away from each other.

I began my studies at Oslo University, which was the only medical school in Norway at that time. The studies were free and open equally to males and females. There were eight to ten women in the first year. Those who finished their studies have been good friends ever since. The comradeship between males and females was a little more serious. I lived at home, and father paid my expenses, for which I am very grateful. Some of my comrades' lives were more difficult, as they had to earn the money to study. One of the male students in my class lived not far from my home, and we walked together to and from the university and fell in love. He was a nice, clever, and charming young man, but I later discovered that he was overambitious and also very jealous. The cards announcing our engagement had already been printed when I got a letter from him informing me that an engagement might tie him hand and foot and prevent him from pursuing his career. I was terribly unhappy. My parents kindly arranged for me to study at the state hospital in Copenhagen, and there I stayed for six months. After the six months, I had to continue in Oslo, as the training in Copenhagen would not be credited. We hoped the situation had become better, but it had not.

Anatomy and physiology were the main subjects in the first years. We had to work hard to meet the requirements, and we were obliged to learn other methods of study than those we had used in high school. The examinations were most exacting. If we succeeded with the first tests, we could count on passing later examinations. We needed six years of hard work to get the final university degree in medicine. In the course of the following years we were allowed to help in the various medical departments in the hospital. On the whole it was very interesting. We appreciated the instructions given by capable and intelligent professors who taught us how to utilize all our senses. I feared examinations, and I was very happy in the summer of 1926, when I passed the finals in medicine. I had reached my goal. The time for practical work had come. I went to a hospital in Kristiansand in the south of Norway. There were both medical and surgical departments, with a chief in each. I had to work with both. My pay amounted to 150.00 kroner a month, plus board and lodging. I liked the work at once. Both surgeons were amiable and kind. I was very proud when the chief surgeon asked me to assist him privately at an operation, for we had had very little practical training during our studies. I had never used a syringe or taken a blood test. I shall never forget the first time in my life that I counted blood corpuscles. I also made visits to sick people. The first one I went to see was a man of about thirty who had an attack of abdominal pain. The symptoms did not correspond exactly with the textbook description of a wood-hard abdomen. Fortunately, I took him to the hospital, where he was operated on for a perforated duodenal ulcer, and he recovered. I stayed in Kristiansand for six months.

I then discussed with the chief surgeon, Dr. Kristen Andersen, my plans for the future, and I decided to choose women's diseases. I went to Paris and stayed there for three months at the Clinique Tarnier, where I met physicians from many countries. From a medical point of view, I did not learn much, as I was shy and my French was poor.

To get certification as a specialist in gynecology in those days, one needed a year of general practice, hospital experience, and gynecological training in a women's clinic. There were always many applicants, and there were only three women's clinics in Norway. To make matters worse, the chief surgeons were generally elderly men who did not appreciate medical women. It was rather difficult.

In order to get experience in general practice, I took posts as deputy medical officer in different parts of the country. It was a new experience for me to assume responsibility and to make decisions far from a hospital. I had to travel by boat, by rail, on horseback, and on foot when the car could go no farther. I learned a lot and came to admire the district medical officers in our extensive country. I got my specialist education at the women's clinic in Bergen under Dr. Severin Petersen, who received me kindly and took an interest in my education. He also encouraged me to write and publish things, as he believed that everyone who intended to have further hospital education ought to write. I contributed a short paper about the quantity of calcium in the blood of a pregnant woman. The question was, does the calcium level influence postpartum bleeding? Together with J. Lvset, we published "Technical Methods in Placental Extraction and Effects on Convalescence." After six months as a young physician, I continued at the women's clinic in order to be approved as a specialist, and for three months I worked at the Radium Hospital. In September of 1933 I was certified as a specialist in obstetrics.

I liked hospital work, with the interesting cases and the cooperation with colleagues. Nevertheless, I decided to open my own practice. It was natural for me to begin in Oslo, as I had my family and my friends there. I moved back to my parents' home and got an office in the center of town. I had to start from the bottom, without means, for it was rare that an old doctor sold his practice. New doctors had to build up their own practices. I had office hours mornings and afternoons during the whole week and also served at the first-aid station. I went to see sick people day and night and was also on duty on Sundays. In the summertime I worked as a deputy officer in the Bredvedt women's prison, which gave me a lot of new experiences. The practice increased gradually, and I acquired an office nurse to handle my appointments. My patients were mainly pregnant women. For about twenty years I cooperated with private maternity clinics where my patients could be hospitalized and where I could be called in for a delivery. These small maternity hospitals became too expensive and were gradually abolished. Nearly all pregnant women are now delivered in large free hospitals with doctors on duty day and night. The pregnant women I delivered came back to me as patients. Their sisters and friends followed, and now their children also come when they need help. I know the families, their condition of life, and their heredity, and we have become friends. They can speak openly to me about their troubles, and this is often what they need! Thus private practice is of great importance; I hope that there will always be room for it. Large polyclinics with new ever-changing medical officers are not always the best solution for patients. However, private practice is strenuous, as there are no set hours. Our compensation is the gratitude of our patients and their welfare.

Father died in 1936. War came to Norway in April of 1940. Mother; Aunt Sigrid; my sister Rigmor, who was a nurse and physiotherapist; my youngest brother Per; and I lived in our house during the war. I was twice thrown out of my office by the enemy. They took the wheels off our cars and confiscated our radio sets. Food and goods disappeared. We had to queue everywhere to get something to eat. However, the psychic stress was worse than the physical hardship. Despite the suffering, we had the hope that one day we would be free, and that day came in May of 1945. We who experienced the war can never forget what it meant to live without freedom.

I have been a physician for nearly fifty years, and in the course of this period, most important events have occurred. Who even dared to dream that a man could walk on the moon? Progress has been enormous in the medical field, too. Incredible operations have been done, and new remedies have saved numerous human lives.

The Medical Society in Oslo has meetings every second Wednesday, with lectures in all kinds of medical specialties. I have always been a faithful member, and I have always learned new and important things. The Gynecologist's Association meets once a month at the maternal and child health center, in which I worked for some time. The importance of preventive health work is generally acknowledged. I have supported courses of instruction for pregnant women for years. The opposition they were met with in the beginning has been overcome, as the women know that the courses have helped them. They have learned how to handle the various phases of their pregnancy. Very often the husbands are present at the delivery, and they tell me that they would not have missed it. Furthermore, their presence helps and comforts their wives. It is real progress when contraceptive advice is given to married and single women.

I have also participated in various other associations, especially the Norwegian Medical Women's Association, of which I was secretary before the war; the Professional Women's Club; and the Women's League for Peace and Liberty. In this way I met many skillful women from various fields of activity. After the war, as chairperson of the Norwegian Women's Medical Association, I attended the first meeting in London after international relations were resumed. We were happy because the war was over, and we were all very enthusiastic. Since then I have taken part in all MWIA congresses, and I have always enjoyed them. It was marvelous to meet the Far East at the congress in Manila and during the round trip to Japan, India, Thailand, and Hong Kong. For the congress in Gardone in 1954 on the menopause, Dr. Herdis Lund and I set up a questionnaire that was answered by 900 women in Norway. The material was worked on by the National Bureau of Statistics. When we returned to Norway, we were requested by a publisher to write a book on the subject. *Woman's Menopause—To Be Awaited with Calm* was published by Herdis Lund. I have also written other popular papers on pregnancy.

There may be a certain risk in living only for one's profession. I have always tried to keep in contact with the friends of my childhood and youth. My best contacts have been in Björnlia.

Sigurd Sigmundsen, born in 1893, was one of my best friends when I was young. He married and in 1930 became a widower with three daughters. We had many common interests so we married in August of 1956. His home was about half an hour's walk from mine, but all the same, the moving involved great changes in my life. I continued my practice. My husband was an architect and had his office at home. Two of his daughters were married and lived in other towns. One was a single schoolteacher who lived in Oslo. We were all always very good friends. Sigurd died in 1964 at seventy-one years of age. He had been ill for some time but died suddenly. Perhaps it was for the best. Mother died in 1967 at nearly ninety. She was sound of mind until the end. I am glad I lived with her during her last years and was able to help her. My sister Rigmor had been in the hospital since 1965 with a fracture of the femur. She died some months after mother. Thus I lost those who had been nearest and dearest to me.

Again there was a new situation to face. I had to get a new house, as Spes and my husband's house were too large for me. Despite many warnings I built a small, modern house in the old garden of Spes and moved in on New Year's Day of 1970. I was then seventy years of age. I have never regretted that I built my new home. When I retired from the center of town in 1972, I moved my office to my own house. I reduced my practice and was glad not to be obliged to go into town every day. I was pleased that my patients found their way to me in my new location. Old people often complain that they are lonesome. I have no reason to do so. Two brothers live on the same grounds, one brother having taken over Spes. I am busy all day. In addition to my practice, I take care of my house and garden, as servants no longer exist, and I like this life.

Fortunately, technical progress has made housework much easier. I have never had time for hobbies.

When I look back on the fifty years that have passed since I graduated from the university in medicine, it seems to me that the new generation has climbed higher than we pioneers did. A medical woman is at present a Cabinet minister. As a whole modern women have more self-confidence than we had and assume greater responsibility on an equal footing with men. On their part the men consider the women as equals at work, on the job, and at home with the children. I hope that this is the best way to proceed toward a happier future for all people. Let us trust that International Women's Year has contributed to directing us on the right pathway.

Grace Johnston Cuthbert-Browne
b. January 2, 1900

I was born the second day of this century, the fifth and youngest child of Captain and Mrs. John Cuthbert. My mother gave birth to me in our family home, far up a steep hill known as Barr's Brae, in Port Glasgow, Scotland.

My father, a merchant sailor, was the youngest captain in the Shire Line when he was given his first command on the S.S. *Elderslie*. This was the first ship especially built for the frozen mutton trade between England and New Zealand. In 1901 he took up an appointment as chief marine surveyor for a group of insurance companies in Sydney, where he gained an outstanding reputation in shipping circles for competent assessment.

My mother trained as a teacher at Moray House College in Edinburgh. Before her marriage she was headmistress of the primary section of the largest school in the west of Scotland. She was an excellent raconteur. Her handwriting was copperplate, and she maintained a weekly correspondence with her family and my father's. These letters were circulated among the relatives in Scotland, and thus we always felt very close to them all. This routine correspondence was continued until her death in 1937. During World War I my brothers and their friends found many members of my parents' families ready to welcome them to their homes in Scotland and England. This association has been closely maintained throughout the years.

My parents, my three brothers, and I, came to Sydney on the S.S. *Oruba* in 1901 so that my father could take up his appointment as chief surveyor of the Sydney Marine Underwriters. The first-born of the family, Mary Niven, had died in London of whooping cough when she was three. John Ross, the second child, became a marine engineer and served in World War I. He later became proprietor of a highly specialized marine engineering business, and he died in Sydney in 1968. Niven, the third child, was a chemist with the Colonial Sugar Refining Company. He was wounded in France in 1916 and died in Amiens. Noel Millar, the fourth child, studied one year of science at the university in Sydney, and then served nobly in the war and was awarded many honors. On return to civilian life he reentered the University of Sydney and took up medical studies. I was Grace Johnston, the fifth and youngest child.

I first remember my Aunt Jenny's home and garden in Launceston. She had come with her family to Tasmania many years before we did. She and my mother had been to school together in Scotland, and they remained closer than sisters all their lives. Aunt Jenny, the headmistress of a girls' school, invited my family to spend the summer holidays with her.

I remember vividly returning home from Tasmania to a house on the highest point of Kirribilli Point in Sydney. My first school at Kirribilli Point was Miss Taylor's kindergarten.

When I was six we moved from Kirribilli Point to Lindfield, where I attended Lindfield College. My memories of the next four years are of the freedom of the north-shore landscape, where there were endless acres of bushland for us to explore and no built-up areas. The boys cleared an area for a cricket pitch and for a tennis court. Being a strong Presbyterian family, we attended the local church on Sundays; father was an elder, as my eldest brother Ross was later.

Lindfield College was quite close to my home. It was a school that added much to my general knowledge and to my interest in history and literature. It was here, too, that I became attracted to geography and decided that some day I must visit Lake Baikal near Irkutz, which I did in 1965.

Both my parents were fully involved in our education, encouraging us in every way and expecting application in our studies. Father was always interested in my future career and insisted that mother leave me plenty of time to study. Fortunately, she was always fully in accord with the idea of a professional career.

When I was ten, my parents decided that I should be sent to a larger school where competition would be keen and where planning was slanted toward pursuing studies of a kind to qualify for public examinations. I was strongly influenced by my parents and by the Church, and it was at this time that I decided to be a medical missionary. My parents showed no adverse reaction to this idea nor offered any discouragement.

These years were very happy in our family, and we had many friends in the district. We were encouraged to play tennis and cricket. My brothers were proceeding with their careers and training.

The outbreak of World War I in 1914 changed our happy family life. By early 1915 two of my brothers had left Australia with the Australian International Force, and my eldest brother had joined the British navy. With the theater of war 13,000 miles away and communications very difficult, slow, and uncertain, our home was entirely war-centered and there was worry concerning the fate of my brothers and the course of the war. The loss of my nineteen-year-old brother Niven in 1916 was a grievous event. I was due to take my matriculation in that year, but at my father's request, I came home to be with my mother.

The next year I returned to school, completed the examination, and passed sufficiently well to obtain a student allowance for the faculty of medicine. In those days there were only 200 such allowances given annually on the results of the final examination—for all candidates for all faculties. I began my medical training at the University of Sydney in March of 1918, the fateful year in which the war ended and my two surviving brothers were repatriated.

Thus the influences that inspired me to choose medicine as a career can be summed up in terms of the accepted principle in Scottish homes that one should have a good education and a university education. In addition, my two paternal granduncles were medical graduates, as were some of my cousins. My desire to be a medical missionary changed with the outbreak of war, but I did not lose my interest in medicine. My brother Noel had begun his courses, and I always maintained an attitude that I should be able to do whatever my brothers could. A strong influence, too, was that Harriet Biffin had been our family doctor ever since 1907, when we moved to Lindfield, and it was accepted that there was a place in medicine for women.

In my second year in medicine at the University of Sydney about 100 of the ex-servicemen, including my brother Noel, joined us. We had outstanding teachers, many whose names today are famous in medical history.

After graduation the problem of hospital appointments was, of course, a troublesome one. I was fortunate to become junior assistant at the Royal Prince Alfred Hospital in the pathology department. This was an important step in my medical career because from that I was able to get a position in the pathology department at the Royal North Shore Hospital. Later I was appointed to the senior staff, and I thereby gained splendid experience. In those days you were trained to be general practitioners because a young doctor was expected to go into general practice before specializing.

My objective was to get a practice in the country so as to have a full range of responsibilities. A small practice on the south coast at Pambula came onto the market, and my father very nobly decided he would assist me with the financing despite vociferous protests from some of his friends, who felt that this would be very unwise. In this practice I had an extraordinarily interesting and varied life. I had a district hospital and also a small obstetric hospital. Pambula was a farming community in the beautiful countryside, with very wild territory beyond it. We had all manner of difficulties, such as floods, droughts, and bushfires. I was fortunate in having the interest, encouragement, and cooperation of my neighboring colleagues.

A small practice in Eden became vacant, and Marian Fox, with whom I had worked as a resident at Royal North Shore, joined me. She lived in Eden, and I remained in Pambula, and we ran this joint practice for some years. When I returned to the city, I took up what had been Margaret Harper's practice. It was here that I became absorbed in the question of antenatal care for mothers. During the years in general practice I was the Royal Society honorary medical officer for the Welfare of Mothers and Babies (Tressilian) and was also on the honorary staff of the Rachel Forster Hospital. I was intensely interested in obstetrics and in the care of the newborn and the young child.

In 1937 I was appointed director of maternal and baby welfare in the Department of Health of New South Wales, where I remained until my retirement in 1965. This was a rewarding period, for there was tremendous improvement in medical practice, great advancement in research, and a great increase in knowledge. We struggled hard to reduce the maternal and infant mortality rates. Before I became a medical student, in 1918, there had been 58 babies lost for every 1000 born in New South Wales. When I joined the department in 1937, it was 41 per 1000. The Baby Health Centers, which were greatly expanded during the period while I was director of maternal and baby welfare, made a great contribution to the battle for the reduction of maternal and infant mortality, as did our antenatal clinics and our close association with the obstetric hospitals. Not the least important work done was that of the Special Medical Committee Investigating Maternal Mortality, which was established shortly before my appointment to the Department of Health.

Two years after my appointment I went to study in Britain, the Netherlands, and Denmark. In 1950 I was awarded a traveling fellowship by the World Health Organization (WHO). This fellowship took me to the United States and Canada for five months and then on to Britain and the Scandinavian countries for another six months.

In 1935, while I was still in general practice, a book on antenatal care was published in London, the author being Professor F. J. Browne of University College Hospital. This book fulfilled all my requirements for up-to-date guidance in the antenatal supervision of my patients. Later, as director of maternal and baby welfare in the health department, I continued to study each edition of this textbook as it was published. The book retained its vital importance to me in the promotion of high-standard antenatal care, in planning for the integration of the departmental antenatal clinics with the obstetric hospitals, and in obtaining the cooperation of medical practitioners and obstetric hospitals in the work of the Division of Maternal and Baby Welfare in New South Wales.

In 1950 Professor F. J. Browne was invited by the King George & Queen Mary Foundation for Mothers and Babies and the New South Wales government to lecture in Australia and New Zealand. It was then that I met Professor Browne in Sydney. Later that year I traveled overseas to North America, Scandinavia, France, and Britain, and I saw him again in London. In February of 1951 we were married in the Crown Court National Church of Scotland in London.

We returned to Sydney later in the year, on the completion of my WHO fellowship. I resumed my work with the Department of Health. Soon three obstetric hospitals invited my husband to join their consulting staff, and so he quickly settled down to life in Australia. He continued to write the new editions of his two textbooks. His son Professor J. McClure Browne had worked with him in each edition of *Post Graduate Obstetrics & Gynaecology* and from 1960 with the editions of *Antenatal Care*. He now publishes the new editions of both books.

It is impossible to assess the extent of his enormous influence on my work during the thirteen years of our marriage. He was the greatest inspiration to me, as he praised most highly the work done by the department in the field of mothers and babies and he gave every encouragement to me and to the staff of the division. On countless occasions his expert advice was available to me and to my colleagues. As a member of the Special Medical Committee Investigating Maternal Mortality, he made an outstanding contribution to its deliberations. Throughout those years our common interest in the expectant mother, the unborn baby, and the newborn created a deep and abiding bond between us, strengthening my purpose in medical work and providing a wonderful partnership for our life together.

In 1963 my husband died at our home in Sydney and left me with a burden of grief that I found desperately hard to bear. The awareness of his wonderful life, his great intellectual attainments, and his gentle, loving kindness to me quickly brought me to the realization that he would have expected me to use my medical skills to the fullest extent.

Thus I continued my work as director of Maternal and Baby Welfare until retirement two years later. I followed this with medical administrative work in the field of the handicapped child for a further five years.

In addition to my professional work and associations I have always participated in community organizations and societies. From 1966 I was honorary coorganizer and founder of a program on preparation for womanhood in independent girls' schools. In 1972, the Australian Medical Association admitted me to its Roll of Fellows.

Finally, my experience is that my sex has not been a handicap in my career. In the environment of my family and friends the prejudice against women in medicine was minimal. When I entered the medical faculty, the contribution women could make to medicine was recognized, and during my years in medical school I was unaware of any animosity. I entered my medical course with confidence that there was an important place for women in this field. After graduation I found no antipathy during my years as a resident medical officer in the hospital nor later in private practice. In my work in maternal and child health the question was not of sex but of the standard of work.

Throughout my career I have found that women have successfully fulfilled their role in medicine. Ever since women succeeded in obtaining the right to study medicine, they have made an outstanding contribution in innumerable fields. Many distinguished and brilliant women have received acclaim in their own right, and I am certain that they will continue to do so.

Yes, if I had to make the decision again, I would still choose to enter medicine.

Caroline Stenhouse

b. January 14, 1900

In the early days of this century a group of little girls four and five years old might have been seen playing together in a pleasant garden in a country town in Otago, New Zealand. Tired of chasing one another around the shady paths, they gathered in the corner of a verandah in the shade of a flowering shrub—they called it love-in-a-mist—to decide what the next game would be, and they fell to talking among themselves about what they would do when they were grown up. Some had roseate visions of managing a home and children of their own, one would be a nurse, another a teacher, and so on, but one of them hesitated. This was something she had never thought about before, but to her own surprise, she heard herself saying, "Well, I'm going to be a doctor," and even as she spoke, she knew that she had made an assignment with destiny. That little girl was myself. At that moment my career had been decided, and even now, so many years later, when I see that lovely shrub in flower and catch its faint fragrance, my thoughts fly back to that group of chattering little girls and I hear a small voice saying, "I'm going to be a doctor."

Certainly, this was not such an unexpected choice as one might suppose, for I was the eldest of three daughters of a country doctor. My mother had been a trained nurse before her marriage, and from infancy I had been surrounded by all the trappings of a busy country doctor's life. I absorbed the medical talk. There were the perpetual telephone messages, the coming and going of patients to and from the house, and the urgent calls, often to sudden illnesses or accidents on distant farms. And at night in those horse-and-buggy days this meant that the groom had to be wakened, the horses fed and harnessed, and the travelers fortified with hot drinks before they set out on what was often a long, cold journey over incredibly bad roads. But it had its compensations too for us children, for on a fine day we sometimes accompanied father on his rounds—and then what joy it was for us to go spanking along the country roads! From the high carriage we could see everything that passed, and there were moments of bliss when Jim, the groom, even allowed us to take the reins and drive the horses.

But as I grew older, I gradually began to appreciate the motives that lay behind this busy life. I realized that, for both my parents, the welfare of patients was paramount. However tired they might have been and however much it might have conflicted with their personal arrangements, no call was ever ignored or refused, and I never saw even an unreasonable request ruffle father's equanimity. A country doctor's wife was an integral part of the practice, and both were on duty for twenty-four hours of every day and for 365 days each year. Mother had to know the individual patients and be familiar with the geography of the practice, so that if necessary father could be intercepted at some strategic point. Many a country housewife in those days would send a farm lad out to waylay the doctor at the roadside and possibly bring him in for a meal before directing him on to another patient. Although financial success was modest, the reward came from the trust and loyalty of the patients, for whom the doctor was not only a medical adviser but someone they could turn to for counsel and help on anything from personal problems to careers for their children. It was in this atmosphere of dedicated service that my childhood was spent.

Both my parents came from Scottish stock. Mother's people were high-landers, and father's were yeoman farmers from the lowlands. Both families arrived in New Zealand with the conviction that hard work and thrift, together with initiative, offered a better chance of a good life for themselves and their children than they could have hoped for in overcrowded Britain. Both families played a full part in the life of the small colonial communities to which they came. Both had that respect for education so typical of the Scots. Mother's family played a prominent part in the development of education in Southland, and Grandfather Stenhouse, before his early death in a farm accident, was a progressive farmer, using modern mechanical devices well before the turn of the century.

In due course I found myself a pupil at the local school, with the wish to be a doctor foremost in my mind. Mother, realizing that life in a small country township had little to offer to an intelligent young woman, wisely insisted that each of her daughters should be educated for a profession that would give her independence, although each child was free to make her own choice. One sister chose an arts degree and teaching, the other one dentistry, and father was delighted when I elected to follow in his footsteps.

I look back on my school days with undiluted pleasure. Learning came easily to me, and I absorbed everything that came my way. The first sentence in our infant primer read, "Lo, I am on an ox" and was accompanied by a picture of a fat child, sitting on an equally fat bullock—not a method of travel that I fancied. From the time I mastered this gem of literature, the printed word has been a source of delight to me. I count it an advantage too that I spent my formative school years in the country. Our small township had excellent primary and secondary schools, and there all the children of the district—the families of farmers, professionals, artisans, and laborers—mingled on equal terms. It was a closely knit, solidly conservative community. No one was very rich, but neither was there any great poverty; and although no doubt this sometimes produced parochial attitudes, it also gave us a sense of stability, security, and mutual respect that had nothing to do with distinctions of money or class. Life was fun for us children. We were free to roam as we fancied around the town and the neighboring areas. Only the river was forbidden territory. The river was wide and deep and swift, with cold snow-fed water that occasionally claimed a victim, so it was not particularly inviting for the girls, although it was whispered that some of the more adventurous older boys sometimes dared to swim across it.

The years of my high-school life were overshadowed by World War I, and although I had no brothers fighting overseas to worry about, the war brought an element of tension and uncertainty to our hitherto carefree existence. I ended my school days as first in my school, with a record of being a thoughtful and conscientious pupil.

The great day dawned in 1918 when father escorted me to Dunedin to enroll me at the Otago Medical School as a first-year student. I look back at my eighteen-year-old self with astonishment; I was incredibly naive and unsophisticated, blissfully unaware that difficulties and pitfalls might lie ahead, but full of enthusiasm and eager to begin. All the women medical students whom I joined were in much the same state as I. As a generation, we had been brought up with the prevalent Victorian idea that higher education and a professional career were options for a few women only, combined with the comfortable belief that when the war ended everything would naturally "go back to normal." Alas, "normal" seems still as far off as ever.

Our first shock came when we found that our schooling, especially in mathematics, had been woefully inadequate for the preliminary science subjects that we had to tackle, but once this hurdle was behind us, we settled down with zest to the routine courses of physiology and anatomy, followed by medical and surgical lectures and ward rounds. Medical science and the medical curriculum itself have undergone such rapid changes that it is difficult to compare modern teaching with that which prevailed fifty-five years ago. When I look back on my student days, there are several points that stand out clearly. The first is the caliber of our professors, many of whom were of international standing, including some who were splendid teachers. The Otago Medical School, although expanding rapidly, was still small enough for the professorial staff to know each student individually. They took a personal interest in our welfare. Many students, both men and women, were painfully shy and lacking in social graces, but our teachers were unbelievably kind in inviting us en masse to their homes, and long after we had passed through their hands, they were still interested in us and delighted to hear of any success that had come our way.

During my career both as student and graduate I have never personally encountered any hostility to or prejudice against women as doctors. As students, we were simply accepted as part of the student body, and those of us who showed signs of exceptional brilliance, such as Muriel Bell, who gained an international reputation for her work on nutrition, or Alice Rose, who was awarded the coveted traveling scholarship, received just as much encouragement and help as their male counterparts. I suppose I myself would have been classified as an average student—not brilliant enough to be remarkable and not dull enough to be written off as hopeless.

I have in my possession an old photograph of the Otago medical students of 1896, when the Otago school was a mere twenty years old. Out of a total of thirty-four students no fewer than six were women—an astonishingly high proportion of women for the time. This was probably because the egalitarian pattern of New Zealand society was already apparent by then. At the turn of the century New Zealand had become a laboratory for imaginative and advanced social legislation. Women here had been given the vote long in advance of those in Western countries; so it is not surprising that in this liberal atmosphere women should be invading the professions, and medicine in particular must have had a special appeal for them. Later the percentage of women passing through the school dwindled to an occasional one or two students until World War I brought an increasing inflow, which has persisted until, at the present time, women form an appreciable proportion of the medical student body.

As students, we all worked very hard. There was little option, for attendance at lectures was compulsory and heads were counted at each session, but we had plenty of fun, too. None of us came from wealthy homes, and we all had to count our pennies very carefully, but our moments of relaxation were spontaneous, and certainly none of us ever suffered from boredom.

It was during my student years that the first New Zealand branch of the Medical Women's International Association was formed in Dunedin, and as senior students and prospective doctors, we were present at the inaugural meeting. As I remember, our aims were rather vaguely stated as "to further the interests of women in medicine"—but I do not think we had any specific projects in mind at the time.

After we graduated, the medical school washed its hands of us. We were thrown out into a hard, cold postwar world equipped with a medical education that was largely theoretical, since little opportunity had been given us for practical clinical work. For women graduating, as I did, in about 1923 or 1924, there was the added difficulty of men students' returning to medical studies after active service in World War I, which had swollen the numbers graduating to two or three times the usual figure. In consequence, hospitals throughout the country were not prepared to cope with this sudden increase in the number of available junior house officers. It was not unexpected, therefore, that the lay boards responsible for such appointments gave scant consideration to women applicants. In all fairness, I must add that I think this was often a result less of prejudice than of the stark economic fact that governments of the day were short of money. Every hospital department had to stretch as little money as possible as far as it would go, and the simplest way out for a board was simply to say it had no accommodation for women and leave it at that. But none of us fell by the wayside. Some married and were lost to medicine either temporarily or permanently, and some were absorbed by the School Medical Service or other state services. More than a few tackled general practice at a time when this demanded not only physical stamina but enough initiative to cope single-handedly with emergencies—medical, surgical, or obstetrical.

But at this crucial stage in my career I encountered an obstacle that is still with me. My mother had become deaf with otosclerosis, and when I started doing medical rounds, it was discovered that I had inherited this condition. The prospect of progressively increasing deafness, at that time untreatable, immediately put medical specialties such as pediatrics beyond my reach forever. I could hear practically nothing with a stethoscope, at that time the physician's chief implement and the very symbol of a doctor. I would have to choose a branch of medicine where hearing was not essential—but which one? And then two trivial little memories that had been lying dormant sprang to the surface and my course was decided. In my preschool years I had spent a good deal of time with my grandmother, a Presbyterian and a strict Sabbatarian but underneath the Calvinistic exterior a very warm personality. She firmly believed in teaching children the scriptures at the earliest possible age, and at bedtime she used to read me a Bible story. The one she chose was the healing of the man blind from birth. We read the same story over and over, until the idea of blindness and the idea of healing came to be associated in my infant mind. Later on my mother, who during her nursing career had been theater sister for Sir Lindo Ferguson, then New Zealand's first and only eye specialist, had often fascinated me with descriptions of his skill in extracting cataracts. Here was the answer—ophthalmology. And so, after a very profitable year as house surgeon in Invercargill Hospital, where I learned a great deal in the hard school of practical experience, I set out for London and Moorsfields Hospital—a milestone in my life.

In the old Moorsfields—it has been twice rebuilt since then—there was a delightfully informal atmosphere. Eminent consultants rubbed shoulders with junior staff, research workers, and students. There were the latest developments in ophthalmology to be debated; there were distinguished visitors from abroad, each with a special field of knowledge to stimulate us; and all the gossip of the ophthalmic world was ours for the gleaning. I can still remember vividly the excitement caused by Professor Ida Mann's appointment to the consulting staff; she was the first woman to hold such a position and one of the world's most distinguished ophthalmologists. At Moorsfields I made friends with a doctor who was on leave from India, doing a refresher course in eyes, and who persuaded me that India was just the place for anyone interested in ophthalmology. So to India I went, and for three or four years I worked in a variety of hospitals in the Punjab, including a year as relieving professor of ophthalmology at the Lady Hardinge College for Women in Delhi. If India did not teach me as much about eyes as I had hoped—for the common eye diseases of a poverty-stricken tropical country are not those that one meets in prosperous New Zealand—it opened my eyes to the problems of the underprivileged world, a valuable corrective lesson for one brought up in the relative affluence and security of New Zealand. Finally, before I had quite decided to remain permanently in India, family reasons called me back to New Zealand.

In Christchurch I unexpectedly found that there was a vacancy for an eye specialist on the hospital staff. My application for the post was accepted, and in no time I found myself sharing an office with one of the city's senior eye specialists, to whose practice I ultimately succeeded, and there I have remained ever since. The depression years were not an ideal moment for an unknown woman specialist to start in practice, but once I had weathered the initial period, I found my senior colleague on the hospital staff an invaluable friend, and I shall always be grateful for his advice and encouragement.

And then World War II started, and there was little time to think of anything but work and yet more work, as the junior medical staff melted away to join the armed services and a depleted senior staff was left to carry an ever increasing work load.

If it was hard to get extra staff, it was completely impossible to get new equipment. At one stage new batteries became almost nonexistent, and we were reduced to one ophthalmoscope, which we kept for ward rounds and which was referred to as *the* ophthalmoscope. For the rest of the time we relied on some cheap, old ones, which were dug out of some bottom drawer in the dispensary and rigged up by the electrician to transformers anchored to the darkroom wall. I felt in imminent danger of being electrocuted whenever I used them.

By the end of the war there were sufficient women doctors in Christchurch to form a local branch of the New Zealand Medical Women's Association. At our first meetings we did little more than meet and discover mutual fields of interest, but now our attention is focused much less on ourselves and much more on the problems of the community. We feel that we have valuable advice to offer on a host of questions—child welfare and education, women at home and at work, and family planning. Our branch president Dr. Margaret Smith is also this year's president of the National Council of Women, a body that many women's organizations are affiliated with and that now commands sufficient standing to confront Parliament if necessary.

When I started my medical career, over fifty-five years ago, women still occupied a debatable fringe on the medical scene, but now they are accepted by the profession and public alike, as an integral and important part of our health services. Although they have been slow in obtaining the highest administrative offices, their ability in administration is no longer in doubt, and it could well be that a time will come when there are more women than men in the medical profession in New Zealand.

As for myself, my medical career has given me all that I ever hoped for—and more. It was often hard work, and my personal life had sometimes to be sacrificed, but I know that I am still held in affectionate regard by former patients and by my medical colleagues. What more could one wish? In spite of the fact that there are now so many fascinating careers open to women, I believe medicine would still be the career of my choice. To younger women now about to enter the medical profession I would say, "Aim high, and nothing can stop you."

It is of course an inescapable fact that for the young graduates who marry, the child-bearing age comes at a time when they would otherwise concentrate on establishing themselves professionally. Not all maternal responsibilities can be delegated, and there may be moments when young women have to choose between family and professional loyalties. Being unmarried, I have never had to face that dilemma, but there are now so many interesting subspecialties that, with a little forethought, it should be possible for a young graduate to choose one that will give her a reasonable amount of time for family life.

Finally, I should like to pay my tribute to those women who in the last century ventured into uncharted seas, and despite opposition, obtained a medical education. They are the true pioneers, and without them we should not stand where we are today.

Leone McGregor Hellstedt
b. January 19, 1900

My mother's paternal grandparents William and Elisabeth Roadhouse emigrated from Yorkshire, England, with their nine children on the sailing ship *Evergreen*. Landing in New York in 1819, they traveled on by wagon to upper Canada. A grandson Robert Roadhouse married Ann Taylor, a woman of Irish-English descent, and their first child Mary became my mother.

Mama's school life was very happy. She matriculated at sixteen, taught at a country school for six months, saved her money, and went off to Toronto to the Teachers' Training School. A few years later she and two girl friends decided on a great adventure and applied for schools in the Northwest Territories. All three were accepted in districts near Arcola, now in Saskatchewan. Mama taught twenty children in all classes in a one-room log schoolhouse, and boarded with the Taylor family from Ontario. A theology student from Manitoba University also boarded at the Taylor's. The name of this divinity student was Matthew McGregor. He and my mother fell in love and married in Carnduff a year later.

My father's paternal grandparents, born in Ireland of Scottish parents, also settled in Ontario. A son Thomas married Sara Ann Teskey, of Huguenot descent, and in 1889 they moved from Ontario to Carnduff in the Northwest Territories. Their fourth son Matthew, who became my father, was eighteen and had just matriculated.

My father had wanted to be a missionary in China, so he entered Wesley College in Winnipeg to study for the ministry. But before my parents were married, father had first to promise mother to give up the ministry, as she did not wish to be the wife of a clergyman.

I was born on a farm just outside Carnduff. There was a terrible winter storm, and I arrived before Dr. Lockhart could get there. I was a wanted baby, and Mama always told me that she taught me all she knew before I was two years old. By this time she was expecting a new baby. My first memory of my sister Phyllis is of both of us feeding little yellow chicks. A third baby Robert arrived a year later. Mama's best friend from her youth, a graduate nurse in Ontario, had come west to take care of her. On this important day the nurse was dressed in a white, starched uniform and had ordered me to keep Phyllis and myself away from the house. When Dr. Lockhart drove up in his buggy, with two black horses and a black bag, two little girls were sitting on the back porch, feeling very neglected. Soon, however, we were invited in to see the little baby boy lying beside our mother, who looked very happy and told us to pat his head. Then came the tragedy of all our lives. The baby developed acute dysentery and died at six weeks of age.

When I was five, there was a diphtheria epidemic, and as Phyllis and I had positive throat swabs, we were given antitoxin and were quarantined with Mama for six weeks. Later that year Dr. Lockhart decided that my tonsils should be removed. As Carnduff was a town of 500 inhabitants and there was no hospital, the operation was done on the table in our large kitchen. A nurse gave me chloroform, and Dr. Lockhart and Mama tried to hold me still. It was the most terrifying experience of my life.

When Phyllis was about three, she was in bed for a couple of weeks with a high fever and a great deal of pain in her left arm. Dr. Lockhart could not diagnose her illness. Mama was very worried and from then on was always particularly protective toward Phyllis, who has suffered daily all her life from momentary acute pain in that arm. She has never been able to touch anything cold with that hand without inducing these terrible pains. This worried us all a great deal and undoubtedly from my early years on drew my attention to unsolved medical conditions.

At six I began school with a splendid teacher. As I could already read and write, I was given extra tasks. I liked all the subjects in school except listening to the reading of sagas. In my second school year some boys in the classes above me went swimming in a creek outside the town on a summer Sunday. Two of them developed infantile paralysis. One recovered completely, but the other remained very lame. Many people, although not my parents, seemed to believe this illness was caused by swimming on a Sunday. I wondered a great deal about it all.

When I was eight, my father bought a hardware business in Tilston, Manitoba. We drove there in sleighs through deep snow. The one-room school in the new town held all classes. One day while in school my sister put a pussy willow up her nose, and to her dismay, it disappeared. She began to cry, the teacher became alarmed, and I was told to take her home to Mama. On the way she sneezed out the pussy willow. Mama then gave me my first lesson in anatomy and showed me pictures of the air passages.

When I was nine, we moved again, as Papa had bought a rather large general store, post office, and telephone central in a very new town in Alberta. For the first months there was no school, so Mama taught me at home. I was able, however, to observe and take part in the building up of a town. A new teacher then arrived. She had an M.S. in mathematics, and within a very short time she had chased me through all the requirements for four years of high school. I was fascinated and realized that a new world had opened up to me. When I was twelve years of age we moved to Calgary, where I entered the tenth grade in a large high school with 500 pupils, 48 in my class. I loved every day in high school, every subject, and almost all my teachers, unbeknown to them. All but one were men.

When I think of my childhood home life, I remember chiefly the quiet evenings with Mama and Papa reading the books they had fetched from the public library. I look back with great pleasure on the peaceful atmosphere, and I was always very proud of both my parents' great knowledge. I could consult my father about world affairs and politics and my mother about literature and other cultural subjects.

Shortly after I arrived in Calgary, I heard of and saw my first two women doctors. Rosamund Leacock and Evelyn Windsor had come out from the east to practice medicine. They were friends and shared an apartment and office, two black horses, and an elegant black buggy. They wore large hats and long dresses and each carried a black doctor's bag. I saw them pass one day and was terribly excited. A grandaunt had engaged them to take care of her children, and when my granduncle fell ill, he too insisted on having one of these physicians. From that moment on, I knew it was possible to be a young, beautiful, and clever woman and even to have men patients. My grandaunt happened also to have a young Englishwoman visiting her that summer. This girl was planning to begin medicine in England that fall, and she had with her a microscope for preparatory studies. She showed me this with great pride, and I was duly impressed.

At tennis I met Mary Simons, just home from Queens University in the east. She was studying philosophy and lent me Freud's *Interpretation of Dreams*. This was my first introduction to psychology, and another new world opened up for me, the world of the unconscious. This was only 1914, and I did not know that psychoanalysis could be a profession or that the famous analyst Ernest Jones was practicing in Toronto. The book, however, gave me so many ideas that it entirely changed my life.

I passed my senior matriculation at fifteen. Only two of the boys in the class of twenty-four students had not yet gone off to the war. We girls all intended to go on for university studies. Most of us intended to go to the teachers' training school. The entrance age was eighteen, so I was refused and was heartbroken. Four months later I plucked up my courage and demanded an interview with the principal, who accepted me this time. I graduated at the top of the class.

My parents still regarded me as the child I really was and were wondering how to keep me busy until I would be old enough to enter the university. My friend Mary had applied for a country school and had been accepted, so without telling Mama or Papa, I did the same. In a week or so I departed to teach a country school about sixty miles away.

In the summer of 1919 (at nineteen years of age) I sent for the university of Alberta catalog and studied the contents, looking for the professions where excellence in mathematics would be a help. Only medicine and architecture seemed suitable. I did not know of any woman architect, and as I quite clearly wanted a profession where I could earn my living all my life, I came to the conclusion that I definitely should choose medicine. I filled out two application forms, one for architecture and one for medicine, and after two weeks of hesitation sent off the latter.

We were 125 students in the first year in medicine, all but 3 being returned soldiers, who were four or five years older and far more mature than we 3 girls. From the first day, I decided to work very hard. There were dances on Saturday evenings and now and then a real formal. Between times there were walks on the campus and along the river. Despite all the romance, I concentrated so seriously that, to my utter surprise, when the Christmas term marks came out in the newspapers I had the highest marks in every subject.

Our teachers were phenomenal. Dr. Egerton Pope, the professor of internal medicine, was my ideal as a person, a doctor, and a chief. The teacher in abnormal psychology, Mr. McPhee, gave brilliant lectures. The anatomy courses were also a joy for me, partly because of my ability to reproduce in drawing anything I saw.

Finally when we graduated, in 1925, my mother and Dr. Pope were in the audience. I had won the Gold Medal for the highest average percentage in all subjects during the six years, as well as the fellowship in anatomy and the fellowship in internal medicine.

Actually, my only difficulty in my medical-school years was earning enough money to pay the high tuition and my room and board. There existed no monetary scholarships or fellowships. We always had a three-month summer holiday, and fortunately, I got a job every summer as a director with the Dominion Chautauqua Company at a very high salary.

About one month before graduation we were told that there were no internships available anywhere in Canada. The professor of pathology, however, offered me a position that I accepted, and I thus learned the basics of practical medicine that year.

The depression was on its way in Canada, and I did not know what to do. A surprise came from heaven in the form of a telegram from the professor of pathology at the University of Minnesota in the United States, Dr. Elexis Bell, who offered me a three-year fellowship to work for my Ph.D. Although I would never have chosen pathology, I was definitely more interested in research than in taking care of patients. The next three years were infinitely enriching for me. I worked very hard, teaching microscopic pathology, studying the required hematology and colloid chemistry courses, doing my experimental research on producing high blood pressure in rabbits and monkeys, and finally, writing my thesis. I earned my Ph.D. in 1929 and was almost immediately awarded a National Research Council Fellowship at Harvard under Professor Frank Mallory.

I found myself in equally good but very different conditions, with excellent guidance. I continued my kidney research, and at the end of the year Dr. Mallory recommended me as an assistant to Dr. Simon Flexner at the Rockefeller Foundation. When Dr. Flexner interviewed me, I told him how much I wanted to see Europe before settling down. He advised me to work first for a year with Professor Theodore Fahr in Hamburg and then to come back and see him. My fellowship was renewed, and I left for Eppendorfer Krankenhaus.

Hamburg was quite unlike anything I had expected—and far more beautiful and wonderful in every way. I found a nice room in a private home. I took a bus early every morning to the hospital, put on my white coat, and marched in with the other "fellows" (all Germans) behind Professor Theodore Fahr to listen to his lecture. Dr. Fahr was at this time one of the two foremost experts in Europe on kidney disease. The professor of surgery asked me to assist him in his research, and we worked out a program that was of great value for me.

At a party in the home of the Canadian trade commissioner I met the man whom I married eight months later. Folke Hellstedt was an economist and the director of the Bergendörfer Eisenwerk, a large Swedish factory located outside Hamburg. He was a Swede, nine years older than I, and he had lived all over the world as an industrial expert. He was a very broad-minded man who understood my ambitions and wanted me to have a professional life. We married at the end of my fellowship year, and I moved into his beautiful, large flat. Four months later he was made vice-president of Alfa Laval, and we moved to Stockholm, where his head office was. This was 1932.

The depression was in full swing in Sweden. There were too many doctors. Only one foreigner before me had ever been given permission to practice. All foreign medical education was regarded as far inferior to Swedish training. No one could understand that a foreign doctor with a husband in a top position, a beautiful home, and an excellent housekeeper could possibly want to work. Clinical pathology did not exist, and research in pathology had no standing. My training was actually of little use in this situation.

I decided to try to see Sweden in perspective, so I invited two Canadian women friends to travel with me for three months. In my La Salle cabriolet we drove down through Europe to Sicily, over to Tunis, across North Africa, and back through Spain, France, and Germany to Sweden. It was a wonderful journey, and when I got home, I told Folke that I would have to change my speciality. He was willing to help me in every possible way. I had decided that I would train to be a psychoanalyst, and as this was not possible in Sweden—there was not even a professor of psychology in the country—I arranged to work at the Neurology Clinic in Zurich, to start my training analysis with Professor Gustav Bally, to observe at Burgholzli, to take part in child psychiatric seminars at the university, and to take Carl Jung's and Pulver's lecture courses.

These were fascinating months. I was in the medical field I would have chosen from the beginning. The analysis fascinated me. I decided while there to submit once again to a licensing examination, and on my return to Sweden, I applied to the authorities for permission to qualify. After due consideration I was granted a Swedish matriculation in exchange for my Ph.D. and could thus enter the medical school. In exchange for my M.D. I was allowed a Swedish candidate examination, which credited me with the equivalent of the two years of basic sciences in Canada. I was also permitted to repeat the two last years of medicine. This was the first and only injustice I suffered in my entire medical life. I did not want to leave my husband, but there seemed no other way out. I got my license in 1937. Only two foreign physicians before me had ever applied for legitimation in Sweden.

About five months after I got my Swedish medical license in 1937, my planned little daughter Monica was born, followed two years later by my son Donald. I had a cook, a housekeeper and an excellent registered German children's nurse; I was actually living in luxury. The war broke out, and as a result, Swedish training analysts returned to Sweden, the Swedish Psychoanalytical Association was founded, and I was able to continue my education in this field. I gradually became an analyst and was admitted to membership in the International Association of Psychoanalysts. I soon had a full-time practice. I became vice-president of the Swedish Psychoanalytical Association, and during this period the international congress was held in Stockholm.

When I qualified for my M.D. in Canada in 1925, I did not know that the Canadian Medical Women's Association had just been founded the year before. There were at that time only about 280 medical women in Canada. In 1934, when the Medical Women's International Association (MWIA) met in congress in Stockholm, I attended and joined but did not interest myself in the local organization. However, in 1958 I drove with a friend to the MWIA congress in Baden Baden, which I enjoyed so much that I decided to attend the next meeting in Manila in 1962. That congress was a revelation for me. It was the first international medical congress of any sort in Asia. I can never forget seeing the women of all nations standing in their costumes before their flags and listening to their national anthems. The organization that the Philippine women had carried out under Fe del Mundo will never be surpassed. Esther Pohl Lovejoy, the founder of the MWIA in 1919, was present. We were invited to private homes. Everything was perfect. We had toured Thailand before the congress, and we traveled in Japan and India afterward. We were welcomed everywhere by our medical sisters.

Since the Manila congress my hobby has been the MWIA. It was therefore very gratifying for me to become president-elect in Vienna in 1968 and president in Melbourne in 1970. I served in this capacity until 1972.

In 1969 my husband died of cancer, and two months later I was operated on for a hip arthrosis. Two more operations completely cured the arthrosis, but nothing can replace a life companion, especially one who was in complete sympathy with all my medical interests and aspirations, as well as with all matters pertaining to the further development of women in general.

After the thirteenth MWIA congress in Paris I became past president and chairperson of the Scientific Project Committee. In the latter capacity I developed the idea for this book.

My life at seventy-five is still very busy, varied, and interesting. I see my psychoanalytical patients from 7:00 to 10:00 a.m. My children are happy and successful in their chosen careers. My son is in business administration, and my daughter in pediatrics. My five grandchildren are thriving. I correspond with my friends all over the world, and we often exchange visits. I can still travel comfortably and look forward to being at our MWIA congresses. I have indeed been fortunate with my parents, my husband, my children, my schoolteachers and professors, my medical chiefs, my many men and women friends, and finally, in having been able to study medicine!

Now, near the end of my life, there has come a delightful and quite unexpected surprise. On May 28, 1977, I was awarded the honorary degree of Doctor of Science by the University of Alberta in Edmonton, Canada, in recognition not only of my career in medicine and research but of my many contributions to the cause of professional women.

Lola Vilar
b. May 4, 1900

Recently I received an invitation to write a short history of my life, which actually has been easy and agreeable, although I cannot tell of great accomplishments. I begin writing here in Cullera, on the terrace flooded with sunlight, with the tranquil blue sea in the background. There my grandchildren swim and make "invulnerable" sand castles, which the waves destroy bit by bit.

I was born in Castellón, the first daughter of a happily married couple. My mother was very simple. Her beauty reminded one of the eternal lines of a Greek statue. She was hard-working and possessed a lot of common sense, being good at budgeting the small salary of my father, who was very intelligent and loved his profession as a teacher.

My first memories of childhood are of a garden in Alicante, where my sister Carmencita and I played among the graceful palm trees. When I was seven years old, I started school close to our home. There were a few upper-class girls, but most of the pupils were the daughters of fishermen. Our teacher Doña Regina filled the classroom with her personality and talent, as the room contained beautiful paintings she had done herself, as well as copies of Greek sculpture and plants that we cared for ourselves.

Papa was the headmaster of the boys' school on the floor below ours. He had traveled abroad on a scholarship to study pedagogy and had chosen the best from each country to establish a model school of international fame. Besides giving the boys an excellent education, Papa taught them a profound respect for moral values and for nature. He never struck a student. His punishment was to exclude the boy from the class the next day. The punished student would cry bitterly, as all the boys adored and respected my father. After class hours Papa was always surrounded by books and reading. Goethe and Shakespeare often accompanied us on long walks during vacations. Papa read slowly, giving life to what he read. He had a serene character, and I never saw him angry or desperate.

When my little sister Carmencita died of meningitis at the age of six, my home, once happy and bright, turned dark. Papa became sad and never spoke. Mother, half out of her mind, did not eat. The atmosphere was depressed and silent while we vegetated in a gray world, without color or happiness. The abandoned toys reminded everyone of their little owner.

A year later my sister Guillermina was born. When I arrived home, Papa's face was young and full of happiness, and soon after, I saw mother smile again, when she bathed the baby. Light returned to our home. What power there was in such a small creature!

We spent our holidays in Ribersalbes, the small town where Papa was born. We waited all year for those happy days, which meant that I could play with my cousins, swim in the river, pick fresh fruit, and go to my uncle's earthenware factory, a special treat. I loved to watch the potter moving the wheel with his feet while his hands were molding marvelous things. It was great fun to go down to the kiln where they baked the ceramics. People came down from the mountain with burros laden with wonderful odoriferous wood. The insatiable mouth of the kiln devoured this quickly, and big tongues of fire shot out as if asking for more food, which was served by half-naked men with pitchforks. It was like a small and agreeable hell.

My grandfather had been an expert at the famous ceramics factory in Alcora, where my father spent his childhood. My grandmother was a good organizer. I remember her as strong and agile, right up to her old age. I adored her and once drew a portrait of her in charcoal. This and a clay statue of Minerva, which I made when I was thirteen, have been my only artistic undertakings. At that time I told Papa that I wanted to be a piano teacher, as I loved music. "You would die of hunger" was his reply.

I finished my general studies with the highest award in the final examinations. Schoolwork was always simple for me, and I leaned toward science, especially chemistry. During the first courses in the university I decided to become a physician, much to the joy of my parents. My medical studies were exciting, and the professors excellent. Concha Criado and I were the only girls in the class, and our classmates liked and respected us. Their jokes and sense of humor amused us, and we built friendships based on respect and affection. On graduation I was valedictorian.

I studied for my doctorate and specialization in pediatrics in Madrid. I lived in a women's residence run by Maria de Maeztu, who was an exceptional woman, guiding us on the best paths in our work, stressing discipline and responsibility. Every Saturday there was a conference or a concert. Many great personalities, including the novelist-poet Gabriela Mistral, visited the residence. There were many foreign women in residence, studying Spanish. Our group of Valencians felt nostalgic for our local festival, the *Fallas de San José*, so we decided to improvise a holiday with a *barraca*, which was a typical old farmhouse of Valencia, plus songs and dances. Everything turned out beautifully.

Madrid contributed a great deal to my human and social development. I loved the museums, and on Sundays we went on excursions to Toledo, the Escorial, and Aranjuez.

The following year I went to Paris to finish my pediatrics specialty. On Sundays I went to the Louvre, where the Greek and Egyptian sculptures were my favorites. Two years later I returned to Paris to learn about the battle against tuberculosis in children. In Valencia I worked as a pediatrician in the anti-tuberculosis clinic run by Professor Luis de Velasco, of international fame in phthisis.

My personal clientele began to increase. With God's help and without antibiotics the most serious cases improved. I cannot now comprehend how it was possible to practice medicine in those days.

My marriage was something providential. Among the boys who were classmates none had ever interested me romantically. One day a young engineer came to consult me in Valencia, bringing his small, motherless nephew, whom he had taken charge of. I was strongly attracted by his nobility, his natural distinction, his healthy appearance, and his education. Time passed, and one day I asked his sister about him. "He has a girl friend in Madrid, and he very seldom comes to us," she answered. I felt very empty inside. A year later the little boy was very ill, and I went to see him in Cullera, where he lived. Gerardo was there. Returning to Valencia in the car he told me of his disillusionment with the girls he had met in Madrid. We were married the next year, not in his luxurious engineer's uniform but in street clothes, in a very intimate atmosphere. We both felt that loud ceremonies destroy the solemnity of those moments in which two people are united in love. My uncle Julio married us, and only our immediate families attended.

A few months later Gerardo and I went to Germany to visit the children's tuberculosis centers and sanatoriums. Everyone greeted us with "Heil Hitler" and a raised arm. In Babiera they told us, "Communism now rules in Spain." The month we returned to Spain the Marxist revolution broke out. My uncle Julio was martyred in Alcora, the last priest killed in the town. He was a saint and a friend of the poor and the unfortunate. People from another town came and killed him. The motto was, "We must finish with religion." Uncle Julio died forgiving them. His last words were, "You know not what you do."

Gerardo and I lived in Valencia. The criminal war went on. One night a bomb landed close to our house. With the jolt I felt something move within me. It was my son. Gerardo sent me to the country with my parents. When Ricardo was born, the fratricidal war was still on. When Franco's army arrived, it found only desolation and destruction. During the war, houses were ransacked and in the night anyone was liable to be shot. That is how four of our cousins—a doctor, two farmers, and a laborer—died.

Franco later reconstructed our destroyed, desolate Spain. It was a profoundly human and religious strategy that he used, for he was not a dictator, as so many foreigners said, but a father. He saved Europe from a grave danger. His meeting at the border with a conquering Hitler was very decisive. Franco managed to convince Hitler that it would be to his advantage not to have Spain enter World War II. "I would rather have someone yank out a tooth," said Hitler, terribly angry after the frustrating interview.

When the war ended, Ricardo was almost two years old. He was tall for his age, pale and a poor eater, and we longed for life in the country. With a loan we bought a house surrounded by beautiful pine woods, and this is today our weekend paradise. We lived there until Ricardo was eight. Out in the country the boy grew strong and happy and developed the equilibrium and optimism that are so much a part of him. His studies proved easy, and his grades were excellent. We had, however, doubts about his vocation because he always said, "I will be an engineer in the mornings and a doctor in the afternoons." His intuition for mechanics and electronics has always astounded us. Fortunately, he decided on pediatrics as a profession, with mechanics and electronics as a hobby.

The number of patients increased continuously. Guillermina, my sister, finished her education brilliantly and we worked together in my office. In 1960 Ricardo concluded his studies, and Gerardo insisted that Ricardo and I should go to Germany. We stopped in Zurich to visit the Kinder Spital. In the consultation office of Fanconi I heard a voice speaking to me in Spanish. It was Dr. Carmelita Belmonte of the Philippines. "Why don't you go to Baden-Baden to the congress of the Medical Women's International Association (MWIA)?" she asked me. I did not listen, but on arriving in Germany, in Siemens, which was paradise for Ricardo's electronics hobby, it occurred to me to ask the date of the congress. Out of curiosity, we decided to get off the train at Baden-Baden for a few hours to see what the women doctors were doing. To my great surprise, I found a remarkable group of women who were studying current human problems of the "older woman," with Janet Aitken presiding. Carmelita and a group of Philippine colleagues were there. When leaving the congress, I counted the flags of twenty-nine nations. Their colors flew in the breeze, but Spain's was missing, and this left a painful impression on me.

One day Vera Peterson, the honorary secretary of the MWIA, wrote to me, saying, "If you could manage to organize a Spanish association of women doctors, Spain could enter the MWIA at the coming congress in Oslo." On the initiative of Professor Boix Barrios, president of the Pediatrics Society in Valencia, I formed the feminine group of this society. Then on the suggestion of Dr. Monforte, we founded the Spanish Medical Women's Association. At the congress in Oslo in 1964, Spain entered the MWIA. I will never forget the moment when our statutes were unanimously approved and it was announced that Spain was a member of the MWIA. If the congress in Baden-Baden had helped me to see the potential of women because of the profoundness of the themes, the congress in Oslo revealed to me the possibilities of the MWIA, which unites colleagues from all over the world. This congress was also an opportunity to see the beautiful Scandinavian countries, with their national customs and their exceptional cultures.

The congress in Rochester, presided over by Fe del Mundo, permitted us to learn a little about North America. At the first scientific meeting we observed that the flag of Spain was missing. We had not known that each country should bring its own. Since there was no way of finding a Spanish flag in the city, Ricardo, his wife Pilar, and I decided to make one. We worked until dawn, and the next day the red and yellow colors of Spain shone among the others. I spent the last night in Rochester finishing my chronicle for the *Tribune Medica*.

Without considering race or color, we women had interchanged ideas and scientific knowledge. I then wrote the message "Woman and Doctor," which I sent to my MWIA colleagues at Christmas.

At the Vienna congress in 1968, the theme was "The Hungry Millions." As we had been advised in time that our flag was not of the right size, the mayor of Valencia gave us a beautiful flag, this time of true Valencian skill. Lore Antoine presided over this congress. Between our discussions we had time off in which we enjoyed a marvelous excursion down the Danube. We wandered around Vienna, a city where street corners are filled with flowers and girls wearing national costumes. The Spanish Riding School, with its horses of Andalusian origin, gave us a delightful performance.

The next congress, in Melbourne, provided an opportunity to take a fabulous trip. How otherwise could we have visited India and the countries of the Far East?

The golden anniversary of the MWIA was celebrated at the congress in Australia, with homage paid to Esther Pohl Lovejoy, the founder and first president of the association. The ceremony of the jubilee, which had been conceived and planned by the current president Lorna Green, was very moving. The thirty-five national secretaries filed onto stage with the flags of their countries, while pictures of the first women medical graduates in the affiliated countries were projected onto the screen. The history of the faith, work, and struggles of those first women doctors was most inspiring. We have an unforgettable memory of Australia, with its wonderful flora and fauna and its very kind people.

The Paris congress, presided over with distinction and dignity by Leone McGregor Hellstedt, was a demonstration of the heights to which women doctors have arrived, so that they now equal their male colleagues in the field of research, as well as clinical practice. The beauty and eternal charm of Paris and the interesting excursions left us with happy memories.

We had not planned to go to the Brazil congress, but at the last minute we decided that we would like to. It is a country overflowing with life and beauty and has the largest river in the world, the Amazon. This congress, presided over by Alma Dea Morani, was concerned with the largest problem that threatens the world today—that of pollution.

I give thanks to God that He led my steps toward the MWIA. Its congresses have made possible a contact with women doctors from all over the world, and my spirit has been enriched. It has opened my eyes to humanity, to the future, to the Third World, which is dying of physical hunger, and to the so-called civilized world, which suffers from spiritual hunger. In the presidency and on the executive board of the MWIA many exceptional women with great qualities of leadership and extraordinary value have filed past. The congresses have also provided a motive to see the beauties of the world, each country's art, way of life, and folkloric spirit. We have become citizens of the world.

At home in Valencia I work in the clinic with my pediatrician son, my sister, and other colleagues. We are all dedicated to our aims and filled with extraordinary patience with children.

My medical practice as a pediatrician has undergone various changes. At the beginning I followed the feeding and medication techniques I had been taught, but later I became interested in the methods of alimentation of Bircher in Switzerland. For some years now, my sister Guillermina, my son Ricardo, and I have tried to attain what is called "positive health" in our small patients. Our aim is to make possible for each child the following advantages: a nonexcessive adipose panniculus, perfect ossification, good muscular development, minimal infectious pathology, and a low proportion of digestive disorders—all leading to the development of good scholars, tranquil and happy.

Now, in the light of raised feminist consciousness, it is perhaps an opportune time for women to participate more in social problems, health, education, and moral development instead of copying the vices and defects of men, problems that will never be resolved by men alone because their ambition, their unlimited love of riches and power and vice, often cloud their minds and blunt their feelings. Women, the nuclei of affection in the family, transmit the moral and religious values of real love. Only a stable home founded on love and education can produce well-balanced, responsible, and happy children. The home of today, which is less and less stable, has as a consequence an increase in divorce, abortion, battering of children, dissatisfaction of youth, drug addiction, delinquency, and suicide. In all these fields the woman doctor has a great opportunity to use her influence.

At the end of my story I see my life in the same way that one who climbs to the mountaintop stops to contemplate the path she has taken. It has been an easy climb for me because my work has been pleasure. People have been generous. They have taught me and guided me with goodwill. Life has been beautiful. Why can we not teach people how to be happy? When I was young, I loved taking walks barefoot on the seashore, dancing to all kinds of music, especially Spanish folk music, and becoming intoxicated by the beauties of an art museum. Not long ago I was asked in an interview about my hobbies. They are studying, reading, dancing, writing, gardening, taking walks in the country, listening to classical music, and playing with my five grandchildren, Pilar, Ricardo, Lola, Gerardo, and Guillermo—all healthy, beautiful, and intelligent. With them everything is possible—to be a princess, a fierce wolf, Little Red Riding Hood, or an Indian. A child is an enchanting and passionate projection of a human being, dressed in grace and beauty. When I see the sad eyes of the children in the Third World, I always wonder if we are really Christians.

With age one returns in memory to the first period of marriage. The best formula for happy matrimony, as expressed by a missionary friend, Father Abad, is to love the other more than oneself. Arriving at the end of the road, I think of my exceptional husband, who has thought of me, of my career, and my happiness more than of himself, forgetting the long list of his valuable works as an engineer to support and inspire me in my work and my profession.

I believe that the true triumph in life is not having earned a name, honors, or riches; it is simply having had a family united by love.

Tamara Laouri
b. May 20, 1900

I was born in Iran to the noble family of Melik-Shahnazar, the title given to my ancestors by the Persian Imperial Court. There are over 600 years of historical data on this family.

I can remember many details from my third year of life. I was the eldest of three children. Up to the age of fourteen my life flowed on as in a fairy tale. I lived in a large, extravagantly decorated house and had all sorts of privileges, including private education and trips to European and other countries. It was a comfortable life, full of joy and under the protection of loving parents. However, it was during this carefree period that I was deeply affected by the death of my sister from diarrhea at one year of age. The loss of my sister was one of the tragedies of my life. Perhaps it was then that for the first time I realized and accepted the fact that medicine could help human beings to survive. At the age of five I was sent to an exclusive kindergarten and later to a private gymnasium for girls. I was a clever and alert student and usually received good grades.

While constantly wondering about medicine and my sister's death, I was suddenly shocked by the fact that in a society of three million people, there were only eight or ten women doctors. They were regarded as heroic because not many women wanted to do this work. However, while attending the gymnasium and after realizing the need for women doctors, I decided to take up the study of medicine to serve humanity and to help women achieve equal rights.

My decision was well accepted by my father, and I had his full support in entering the Faculty of Medicine. At first my mother was more concerned with my musical education in the conservatory, where I was in my last two years of piano training. However, nothing could change my decision, and I was accepted in the medical school of Azarbaijan Bakou University without any problems. Hard work and love of my chosen profession made my studies very easy. In a short time I became an outstanding student, loved and respected by my classmates, as well as by my teachers. I met my husband-to-be while I was in my third year of medicine. He was an electrical engineer and eleven years older than I. We understood each other perfectly and agreed that I would finish my studies and continue in medical work. We were married in 1920, and I graduated in 1924. My only child, a healthy and strong boy, was born in 1925. He is now director of external broadcasting in the National Iranian Radio and Television.

In 1933 we returned to Iran to serve our country. As a woman doctor, I was accepted in the community from the first years of my career, and I held very good positions in the hospitals and clinics. I was head of the maternity ward, assistant to the professor of the Venereal-Dermatological Section of the Faculty of Medicine, and director of physiotherapy. In the meantime, while working full time in hospitals, I also had my private practice and was participating in different women's activities.

I was one of the founders of the Women's Association of Tehran. I was also on the medical commission of the women's organizations. This commission was established by the Ministry of Labor and Social Affairs to protect working women and their children. I was further involved in all activities to achieve equal rights for women. I was one of the founders of the Iranian Women's Medical Society and of the Family Planning Center in Iran. I was also assigned to the Ministry of Labor and Social Affairs with a group of educated women to visit factories and to organize classes in reading, handicrafts, and housekeeping. Meanwhile we were distributing powdered milk to the workers' children. This had been donated by the United Nations International Children's Emergency Fund (UNICEF).

In the twelve years that have passed since the White Revolution, the condition of women in Iran has changed. We are now far more effective and are involved in service to our people. During these evolutionary years I have participated in numerous congresses in Iran and abroad. As a member of charity organizations, I have devoted my free time to orphanages, mental clinics, and housing for the poor and the aged.

Looking back over the years, I feel that I have not wasted my knowledge and my time. Every hour and day of my life has been filled with positive activities directed toward building up a better future and a healthier nation. Thanks to the wise leadership of our country, I am proud to say that, in the long years of service and hardship, I have seen a great number of obstacles overcome. I have been accepted and respected, and this has made my social and professional work not only easy but pleasant.

Remembering days and nights in hospitals, living through difficult hours with patients and at other times sharing their happiness, I sometimes wonder how many lives I have shared and whether I have been able to live my own life. Nevertheless, medicine was my choice. I wanted to help people and to see them happy and healthy. I do not think any other profession can give such satisfaction.

Ruth Lundeen Memmler
b. August 26, 1900

My mother's parents migrated from Norway to the state of Iowa in the late 1870s. My mother obtained her teaching credentials when she was eighteen years old and taught in a small rural school in North Dakota. My father was born in southern Sweden. He and two of his brothers migrated to the United States in 1889 when my father was nineteen years old.

In 1899 my father met my mother, and after a whirlwind courtship, they married and moved to their home on a prairie wheat ranch. I was born in their one-room house and was the eldest in a family of six children. In later years my father reminisced about the difficulties in obtaining a doctor at the time of my imminent birth. It seems the only available doctor was an alcoholic. Despite the great hardships of the prairie and the difficulties encountered in growing so many acres of wheat, over the years the house was greatly enlarged and the family grew also. My mother would pack huge lunches for the men at harvest time. Now that I think back, I wonder how she could do so much and maintain that marvelous cheerfulness so characteristic of her usual disposition.

The very cold winters, the primitive conditions and the lack of adequate medical personnel led to severe illnesses and deaths, some of which made a profound impression on me at a very early age. A young mother and her newborn baby both died, and their funeral made an indelible mark on my mind. The white coffin was placed in a hall so that people there could file by and look into it. I was too small to see, but my uncle lifted me and held me long enough so that I had a good look. The mother and child were dressed in white, their faces still and very beautiful, and I thought they must surely be angels.

At the age of six, I began my first love affair with school and the books that were there. There were only seven or eight other children in the one-room rural school. Father became eager to join his brother, so in 1907 he sold the homestead and we packed our belongings to start our train ride to California. By then there were five small children in the family. The first part of our train ride was uneventful, but as we came to the mountains of southern Oregon, the train came to a stop. We were finally told that there had been a cave-in in one of the tunnels, and we were asked to leave the train, taking our luggage with us, as we had to catch another train on the other side of the tunnel. To get there we were all required to walk along a muddy, irregular pathway. Mother carried my baby brother while father carried as much of the luggage as he could manage.

The ranch we moved to included a peach orchard, a vineyard, and an area for grazing our dairy cattle. The tank house had provisions for the itinerant farm workers. These men read magazines of doubtful value, but any time when they became available to me, I tried to read them, too. More appropriate reading material came from a country library that sent trucks of books around to the farm families. I borrowed as many of these books as were allowed to me.

With eighty acres of land and the variety of crops that we produced, father worked from sunup to sundown. Mother's tasks were just as strenuous. My brother and I helped in a variety of ways even when we were only seven to eleven years of age. I was the larger and more precocious, so I was entrusted with milking two or more cows each evening. During the summer the farm was a beehive of activity. The peaches were picked and brought to a shed, where mother and I cut each one in half and laid it on a wooden tray. The trays were taken to a sunny area where the peaches dried. In the late summer and early fall we all picked grapes, which were also placed on wooden trays to dry. Delicious raisins and dried peaches were soon ready for the market.

Our school was three miles from our home, so my brother and I walked that distance back and forth each day. Then my six-year-old sister joined us. At this time my father purchased a pony and small buggy that provided transportation for the three of us. The pony was a spirited animal, and each evening as we neared our driveway, he put on a burst of speed. I well remember how hard I had to tug on the reins to prevent the possible upsetting of the buggy. But I was in charge and learned to feel that I was a second mother to my brothers and my sister.

Shortly after my elementary education was completed, father exchanged our ranch for an orange grove in Southern California. High-school days there were full of study and assorted activities. Physical energy was consumed in playing basketball. During the last two years of high school several teachers encouraged me and served as an inspiration. The school principal taught advanced algebra. There were three girls whose names all began with the letter L. He often referred to us as his three L's. We competed with one another but remained fast friends until the early tragic deaths of the other two. It seemed to me that these deaths could have been avoided, and prevention of illnesses and early death still is an important objective in my lecturing and particularly in the writing I do.

During my teens the effects of environment were strangely revealed to me in the shape of two young women neighbors. One lived with her widowed mother and learned to repair farm machinery and to assist her mother in doing the ranchwork. They were self-sufficient, hard working, and capable people. The other young neighbor lived with her wealthy aunt, who showered her with clothes and jewelry, including a beautiful ring. I remember mother's comment to me: "She will have nothing to look forward to, no thrill from an engagement ring, no excitement about a new blouse, nothing. You have much to enjoy in the future. She doesn't."

Mother was a very practical person, and early in my high school days she urged me to take a course in sewing and one in cooking, in addition to my academic program. A few weeks before my graduation from high school my youngest sister was born. The summer following my graduation was filled with helping mother to care for the new baby amid talk about going on to college. There was very little money, and at that time scholarships were not available. My uncle assisted with finding an inexpensive place to live near a teachers' college in Los Angeles. Father provided me with vegetables from his garden, and I particularly remember the large pink beans that were to form an important part of my diet for a year.

The theory classes in the teacher-training program were easy, but the practice was another matter. I was assigned classes of eighth-graders, many of whom were taller than I was and some of whom appeared older. Discipline proved difficult for me, and frequent nightmares were upsetting. Nevertheless, I completed the program, and following graduation, I obtained a position teaching in a small country school near my family's home. For that year I remained at home and saved nearly all the small salary paid to me. The children, aged nine and ten, were active and restless. I played ball with them at recess and provided activities in the classroom that kept them interested. Discipline was no longer a problem, and so there were no nightmares.

During this year my oldest brother was seriously injured, being struck by a car while riding his bicycle. He was unconscious and bleeding profusely from his nose and from his right ear. The doctor whose office was nearby took him to a hospital, where a diagnosis of a fractured skull was made. My parents endured days of anguished waiting for him to regain consciousness, which he finally did, and after several weeks of convalescence, he recovered all his faculties except for the hearing in his right ear. The idea of becoming a doctor interested me more than ever then but seemed to be an unattainable goal, especially for a woman with such limited funds.

My own ambitions and my mother's encouragement led me to seek admission to the University of California at Berkeley. I sought the help of the dean of women, from whom I obtained a list of approved homes in which a young woman could live with a minimum of expense. I selected a three-story home for students. My sleeping and study room was on the third floor, while the small cubicles allotted each pair of young women for cooking and eating purposes were in the basement. To further extend my limited resources, I obtained a part-time job, replacing books on the shelves at the university library.

In order to stretch my clothes budget, I would dye my summer clothes darker colors so that they would be suitable for fall and winter wear. My first objective at the university was to obtain a B.A. and general secondary credentials. The remuneration for a teacher in high school was considerably more than that for an elementary teacher. Also, the sciences of zoology and chemistry would meet some of the requirements for admission to medical school. On graduation and the receipt of my new teaching credentials I sought help from the University Employment Center and received an offer of a job teaching chemistry and biology in a small school in the northern part of the central valley. On arriving, I was told that the man who had planned on taking a leave of absence for a year had decided to postpone his leave. Would I be kind enough to take a combination of English and domestic-science classes? Positions did not grow on every bush, so I accepted the offer.

That first year of high-school teaching proved to be more exhausting than all my previous years of work combined. In addition to the difficult (for me) schedule of teaching English, plus a class in cooking and one in sewing, areas in which my college education was seriously lacking, I was also asked to coach the basketball team and the senior play. I lost weight, and during the summer mother worried about me, but a few weeks on the orange grove restored my health. The second year the science teacher did take his leave of absence, and I felt far more at home with classes in chemistry and biology.

The two years of teaching provided enough money to enable me to start medical school. The university had upgraded the entrance requirements for medical school, so it was necessary for me to return for an entire year of premedical studies before admission to the College of Medicine. I was able to tutor high-school students in order to augment my funds.

The first year of medicine included a class in physiology, in which the professor delighted in embarrassing me. In a biochemistry class I often completed all the problems only to have requests from others in the class for a look at them. The men who copied my work would receive A's, while my grade would be a B. One professor called me into his office to ask me why I wanted to invade a man's world and study medicine. I was attractive enough, he said, to find a desirable husband and then play the role women should play.

The second year of medical school found three of us living in an apartment near the San Francisco branch of the university. The two women students who lived with me had no financial problems, but for me it was a continuous concern. Expenses were mounting, and my savings were nearly depleted. In order to complete the year, I obtained a weekend tutoring position at a private school several miles away.

Medical school was fascinating, and I so wanted to continue, but there simply were no more funds available to me, so again I sought and obtained a teaching position. This time I taught biology and physiology to high-school students in Pasadena, California. There I met a quiet young teacher of graphic arts. We fell in love and were married a few days after the end of our second year in this school, in 1929. My husband continued his teaching career, while I sought to complete my medical studies. In order to remain near him, I transferred to the College of Medical Evangelists (now Loma Linda University). For the first time in my life, I used part of my savings, which had been intended for medical school, for an extravagance. I purchased a Model A Ford car. This made it possible for me to go to clinics and hospitals with ease and also enabled me to help other medical students get around. The new friends in the medical college, my happy marriage, and the relative freedom from financial worries combined to make these years ones of contentment and supreme satisfaction with life.

My internship at the Los Angeles County Hospital involved spending long hours away from our home. My husband often joined me in the intern's dining room for dinner in order that we might spend a little time together. There even were evenings when he helped me on the wards with some of the very sick patients who were brought in during the evening and night. My schedule most of the time included duty an entire day, a night, and then a second day. The night involved taking calls for another intern; sometimes there would be very few and I could get a little sleep, and other times there would be frequent calls all night. For this work of thirty-six hours on and twelve hours off, we received thirty dollars a month. I have been told that our present-day interns are unhappy about amounts of over $3000 a month. While I was an intern, I asked for as much experience in dealing with children as possible. Accordingly, I was allowed to work with the children on the pneumonia ward and in the contagious-diseases units, as well as in general medical wards. My aim was to be a pediatrician, and my ideal was to try to prevent illnesses by appropriate care of children. In answer to my application for a residency at the Children's Hospital I was told that preference would be given to male physicians and that they were not planning on accepting any female doctors. I must add that this ruling has long since been abandoned, so that now there are, happily, many women residents in the field of pediatrics.

News of an opening in the life-science department of a Los Angeles college led me to request an interview with the director. He told me that he was looking for male teachers and that he would employ a mediocre man before even a superior woman. More discouragement! But in a few days a contract came in the mail, and soon I was again embarked on a teaching program.

Then came the hysteria that led to depriving married women of jobs unless their husbands were ill or otherwise disabled. The theory was that men who were unemployed were in need of these positions. The problem was that the unemployed men were laborers, truck drivers, and an assortment of relatively unskilled people, who could not replace educators. Consequently, the Board of Education began rehiring all of us the next year. During the interval I worked in clinics and in the offices of a few busy physicians without remuneration. I was indeed glad to return to a paying position, which would augment the salary my husband was able to obtain.

At this time I joined a group called the Los Angeles School Women's Council. The members sought interviews and meetings with members of the Board of Education, calling attention to the frustration of women who were treated as second-class citizens and to the injustices to married women. Later our group joined the National Woman's party, which had been organized in 1913 by an attorney named Alice Paul. She had been an activist in the suffrage movement, and after suffrage became a reality, in 1920, she discovered there were thousands of local, state, and federal laws and regulations that discriminated against women. She wrote the Equal Rights Amendment and sought its adoption by the United States Congress. A long struggle has followed.

While teaching at the Los Angeles City College I organized a club for those interested in nursing and related paramedical fields. I arranged excursions to clinics, hospitals, laboratories, and other health facilities. In this way I hoped to allow students to see the variety of occupations they could choose from. The heavy teaching schedule did not keep me from visiting my parents, both of whom died in 1940. Then in December of 1941 came the Japanese attack on Pearl Harbor and the subsequent change in all our lives.

As a part of the war effort my husband and I both took on extra assignments. He worked as an efficiency expert at Douglas Aircraft during daylight hours and in the evenings in a printing plant doing photographic work for navy manuals. I taught at the Los Angeles County Hospital and then drove about twenty miles to the Douglas Aircraft medical offices, where I examined the women applicants for work in the plant. It was a strenuous life, with late dinners as the only time my husband and I could see each other. During 1944 there was less need for new applicants; so I discontinued the work at Douglas Aircraft, and in January of 1945 our daughter was born. After a short leave of absence I answered a request from the Board of Education to assist in the organization of the East Los Angeles College, where my work included the development of new programs in the health fields.

My interest in preventive medicine caused me to feel that the required courses in health should be taught by registered nurses with special training in teaching. The administration agreed to allow me to select teachers who could do some of the teaching in our nursing programs and also lecture to the large health classes. Thus, in addition to general information about the human body and its care, we were able to present information about venereal diseases and their prevention, respiratory infections and their care, and alcoholism and other drug problems.

The shorter courses for nurses and the other paramedical programs were difficult for instructors because there were really no suitable textbooks. In 1958 I was contacted by the Lippincott Company concerning the possibility of developing a textbook suitable for the various paramedical courses that were now appearing all over the United States. Accordingly, I wrote a few chapters that tried out a new idea or two. I integrated a little elementary anatomy and physiology with some disease discussion, including suggestions for treatment and prevention. The work on the text continued during 1958, along with a full-time schedule at the college. The problem of illustrating this little textbook was solved by my husband's offer to help. We decided on simple line drawings in black and white, and the two of us developed fifty-four illustrations to go into a 345-page paperback book. It was published in 1959, and to the great surprise of the publishers, it was an instant success. In 1962 the book was enlarged and revised. A third edition in 1970 included chapters on matter, elements of chemistry and physics, and more material on causes of disease.

In 1965 I decided to retire from my position as professor of life sciences and coordinator of health and paramedical courses at East Angeles College in order to pursue some projects with my husband. He had also retired from full-time occupational pursuits so that he could develop a library of educational slides in the natural sciences, including agriculture and related fields. The idea he had in mind was to supply high-quality slides for use in the classroom. To obtain suitable material to photograph, we began traveling not only in the United States but in some of the European countries, in Africa, Asia, Australia, and New Zealand. I work with my husband taking notes and writing explanatory scripts that accompany slides. We sell these slides to the university and colleges to help instructional programs. My husband says this project is a substitute for the rocking chair. We have sent slides to nearly every state in the United States, plus countries such as Greece, Turkey, Iran, and Spain.

One chief interest still is the ratification of the Equal Rights Amendment. During the last fifteen years I have served in several official positions in the local branch of the National Women's party. We certainly need more women doctors, more women in politics and in other leadership roles.

Another interest involves the problems of world health and particularly nutrition. The growing of crops that will be valuable for food for tropical and other heavily populated parts of the world is a part of the reason that my husband and I are producing educational materials. We photograph and explain research in agriculture. In the past, foods that were high in protein were often not available in the tropics. Soybeans and other nutritious foods could not be easily grown until recently, when new, hardy varieties became available. Foods high in vitamins are also being hybridized for use in the tropics. There is so much to do—but as long as we live, we will do what we can to spread the story of food for all and of the need for all human beings to use their potential abilities, whether they are males or females.

FINLAND

Saima Tawast Rancken
b. October 9, 1900

My mother Maria Henrika Varis came from the agrarian class in Savolax. My father August Tawast was from an old Danish noble family. I, Saima Hellen Maria, was born in Pieksämäki, the fifth of six children in the family. My home from the year 1907 was in the small town of Mikkeli, where I went to school until I took my matriculation. My parents were peaceful, hard-working people, and my childhood and youth were spent in a harmonious atmosphere. Of particularly strong influence was the fact that my country won its independence while I was in my sensitive youth. The summers we spent out in the country helped me to understand the circumstances involved.

Mikkeli was an ideal school town. There was plenty of opportunity to keep up with the arts, especially music, as many well-known artists performed in Mikkeli on their regular tours. My father died in 1920, one week before my matriculation examination, and my mother passed away in 1922, so from then on I was without a real home.

My choice of a profession was difficult, as I had many talents. My greatest desire, however, was to be a teacher of gymnastics, and this was economically feasible. I began my studies in the Gymnastic Institute of the University of Helsinki in 1920 and graduated in 1923 as a teacher of gymnastics and as a physiotherapist.

The education I received, however, had not completely satisfied me. The teaching had been reliable, but I had not gotten satisfactory answers to my questions regarding the choice of particular movements and their real physiological value. I felt that the exercises were often without a scientific basis. It seemed to me that it would be necessary to study medicine to understand these matters. This was my most important reason for continuing my studies.

Even in medical school I did not get clear answers to my questions, for at that time physiotherapy was not considered necessary and its use in connection with diseases was not described. A special gymnastic aftercure was considered unnecessary, as was the education of physiotherapists. As I became familiar with the anatomy and physiology of different diseases, I began to understand better the importance of movement in physiotherapy, although I had no opportunity to make any experiments.

There was great astonishment in medical circles when I published my graduation thesis and then accepted a very modest position in the surgical department of the university hospital. Since I regarded my studies in physical therapy as very inadequate, my next endeavor was to investigate the status and development of physiotherapy in the other countries in Europe. During this study period, I acquired many good ideas and began to develop and build up my own department.

In 1930 I married my former teacher in physiology, Professor Rancken. Our marriage lasted only five years, for he died in 1935. He had done the greatest part of his scientific work in the field of exercise therapy. He had given me a home and the economic possibility of fulfilling my purpose in life. I had no child of my own, and therefore in 1940 I adopted a war orphan, Risto, the son of a cousin, who was only two days old when he came into my care.

When the war broke out in 1939, the medical planning of physical therapy had been totally forgotten and was believed to be unnecessary. However, alarming information was soon received from the war hospitals that they needed physiotherapists urgently. I gave many refresher courses for physiotherapists in order to improve their knowledge. Many invalids could have been greatly helped if we had only had more and better trained therapists.

The war thus became my best assistant in the development of physical therapy. At last the need for this work was admitted and our help accepted. In 1944 the real education of physiotherapists began again on an absolutely new basis. I was promoted to chief of the department, which was at last given the same status as other departments in the hospital. I became a professor in 1964. The education of medical specialists in this field was started, and a specialist association was founded.

As I had been quite alone in my interest in this field from the beginning, it was I who had to start all this development. A splendid sign of our progress was the building of a new physical-therapy department, where I worked for the last two years before my retirement in 1968. I had long been a special university lecturer for medical students in Helsinki and Turku.

I am very grateful for the fate that led me into this specialty at a time when it was necessary for me to get training, so that I could spread the knowledge I gained to develop the field of physical therapy in Finland.

Ellen C. Blatchford

b. October 17, 1900

I was born in 1900 in Maple Valley, Wisconsin, while my Canadian parents were temporarily living there. They returned to Canada in 1901. We lived in northern Ontario during the days of the mining boom until I was eight years of age. It was a rugged life among miners, prospectors, and settlers. We had a store with living quarters above it, overlooking deep, dark Cobalt Lake, and I can remember vividly seeing a forest fire hop from tree to tree up the hillside. My brother and I learned to duck for safety when we were out of doors and heard the warning shout of "Fire" from the mines. We would stand and watch the rails and rocks heaved into the air by the deafening blast of dynamite. At one time the town was almost completely wrecked by an accidental explosion of tons of dynamite, and my mother fled with us down the railroad track, fearing the ignition of other stockpiles. I always had a protective attitude toward my brother. I remember begging my parents to leave that awful land of fire and dynamite for a somewhat safer spot.

My brother and I went to the public school in the village, walking over two miles each day and taking our lunch. Memories of being drenched by rain, and in winter gingerly sliding along on crusty, snow-covered drifts four to six feet high, are still vivid in my mind. There were occasional rides by buggy, bell-equipped cutter, or sleigh.

We then moved to Aurora, where my second brother was born. There were then four children, of whom I was the oldest. I went to high school in Aurora. At this time an avid reader, I happened to come across a book about a woman doctor, which started my dream of going into medicine. Never thinking it would be possible, I mentioned it to my parents, and much to my surprise, both my father and mother said they could manage it.

While living in Aurora we attended the United church, where there was a very homely and eccentric minister who nevertheless was an honest and extremely dedicated individual. It was while listening to his sermons that I felt the missionary field beckoning. During this period war was declared, and the horror of it haunts me to this day. I knitted socks for soldiers in the winter and helped my father with the harvesting in the fields in the summer. Both my brother and I always helped with the milking of the cows and the feeding of the chickens.

In Richmond Hill, where we moved in 1918, there was a charming, attractive woman doctor named Lilian Langslaff. Her husband was a general practitioner and was our family doctor. These two respected and well-loved souls were an inspiration to me. A woman in medicine was not unheard of in the community, and my desire to emulate "Dr. Lilian" was looked on with pleasure and a certain amount of pride. That I had the ability to succeed was not questioned.

In the spring of 1918 I obtained a syllabus from the University of Toronto. Then with great innocence, supreme courage, and a real desire to be of some service to humanity, I walked with my mother across Queen's Park and I registered in medicine. When the university opened in the fall, there were 33 women in a class of 250. A large number of the men were returned soldiers. The course at that time lasted five years. It was a happy and interesting, though strenuous life and a great privilege for which I have always been most grateful. I made lifelong friends. We were devoted to our teachers and eagerly endeavored to absorb all they tried to teach us.

In 1923 twelve of the original thirty-three women finally graduated. I was twenty-three years old and was able to obtain an internship for fifteen months in the Philadelphia Hospital for Women. It was a wise move. In Philadelphia I met many people who had never even heard of Toronto.

During my last year in medical school, I had met Douglas Blatchford at our mutual boardinghouse. We were married in July of 1925. I could never have worked as I did after my marriage without a tolerant and very understanding husband, who was interested in my work as well as his own.

As a medical student, I had been introduced to the Women's College Hospital, on Rusholme Road. I learned that there was room for an anesthetist there. I had had some training at St. John's Hospital, where I had interned for six months, and I had taken a course in Toledo. I had also spent a year at the Toronto General Hospital, observing and receiving instructions from experts there. The anesthesia department at Women's College Hospital grew rapidly, as Marion Kerr and Marion Hilliard had large, flourishing obstetrical and gynecological practices.

There were hectic and strenuous advisory-board meetings, discussing the separation of surgery from gynecology and obstetrics. Then, through Dr. Stewart, who had great foresight and wisdom, it was decided that we should have a new hospital, with a view to proximity to the university and with the objective of becoming a teaching institution. A campaign was organized in which board and staff really worked hard raising funds, and by 1935, we had our new hospital.

Early in January of 1933, our son Bob arrived on the scene, and in June of the following year our daughter Ann came to live with us. Our family was now complete, and we were exceedingly happy. At present we have six grandchildren, who are a never ending source of wonder and joy.

Early in the 1930s Dr. Evelyn Bateman joined the anesthetic staff, and together we literally worked day and night to provide relief from pain in surgical, gynecological, and obstetric procedures. I know that I could not have managed without Dr. Bateman's loyal and tireless support. In 1937 I received my certification diploma in anesthesia from the College of Physicians and Surgeons.

As we grew, we began adding new members to the anesthesia department of Women's College Hospital, and they have all proved faithful, dedicated anesthetists. We were about the first in the city to organize a group, thus ensuring some definite hours for work and rest and rendering more efficient and careful care of our patients. During these years there was great advancement and development in the various methods, procedures, and drugs used in the art of anesthesia. We kept abreast of the times by attending conventions and by reading our medical magazines while our board supplied the new machines and necessary equipment. I was chief of the department from 1932 through 1955, when I became active consultant. I then kept on working until 1967.

In 1953 Douglas and I had our first trip to Europe, and this gave us a taste and appetite for travel. By 1958 he had retired from the teaching profession; I arranged for a two-month leave of absence in the early part of each year so that we could visit various parts of the world. It was an ideal arrangement, and we were privileged to see a great many countries. Perhaps the grandest sights were the awesome and beautiful animals of Africa. We took many pictures to remind us of the beauty and the wonder of all we saw.

We have a country cottage and spend almost six months each year enjoying it. Retirement has not been difficult for either of us. Being able to read the morning paper is a luxury—and not having to worry about that difficult case the next day is a happy relief. True, I miss seeing my friends and fellow workers at the hospital, but I know they are there if and when I need them, and that is a comforting thought. I have been privileged to be a member of a truly great and noble profession, and I humbly do thank my dear parents for making it possible and also my husband for all his help and understanding.

Kamala Isreal Vytilingam
b. June 28, 1901

I was born to a family in South India (Tamil Nadu, formerly Madras state). My father S. Isreal Pillai was the only Christian in his family; the other members are still Hindus. My paternal grandfather was a landlord with a great wish to educate his three sons. The first, Suminathan, became a surgeon in the general hospital in Madras and died at the age of thirty-five, leaving three children—two girls and a boy. My father, whose name was Mangaan (meaning "never fading Krishna") became a graduate of Tanjore Christian College. He had been baptized as Isreal (the Conqueror). The third son, who became a teacher, died young, leaving three boys. My mother, whose father was also a landlord, hails from the same farming community. Her father was a well-traveled man with coffee and cocoa plantations in Ceylon, but these failed because of some plant disease, so he returned to India to take care of his property there. The first two brothers married two sisters. My maternal grandfather, who was a very powerful man, loved and respected by his clan, was also a lover of knowledge and learning. Hence, the younger girl, who was supposed to be clever, was given as a bride to my father. She in turn demanded that my father educate her at home, which really boosted the pride of the family. This was in about the year 1889. My mother had four children, the first being a son who became a doctor specializing in leprosy and in charge of leprosy sanatorium. I was the second, born in 1901. When I was a little girl my father doted on me because I was smart, keen to learn, and very active.

My parents also wanted to educate my cousins, who had lost their parents and were living in villages, so my four cousins, all boys, were brought to our house. We were all more or less the same age ranging from five to ten years. There was no school for girls at that time, between 1905 and 1910, so I went to the only existing school with all my cousins. As a civil servant my father had the luxury of attendants. The head of these, called the dhabedhar, used to take all five of us for games and walks in the evenings. We used to rag one another, and the boys used to tease me, saying, "After all, you are a girl, meant to wash dishes." One day the dhabedhar asked us what we would like to do when we grew up. One cousin said, "I will be a policeman"; another wanted to be an engineer; and a third planned to be a doctor. Then he asked me what I would do. I said with pride that I would be "a teacher for doctors." At that moment I thought this was the finest thing in the world. In truth, I wanted to be something much greater than all my cousins.

A sad blow came in 1910, when my mother died. She had a difficult childbirth, as she refused to be attended by a male doctor and the woman doctor, Miss Parker, had to be fetched from Madurai, about seventy-five miles away. My mother's last wish was that I be educated to become a doctor so that I could help the women of our country. Those were the days when there were no antibiotics or trained midwives. A handful of women doctors existed in district-headquarters hospitals. All my cousins left our house after my mother's death, and my father was alone with the children. He married again after two years, but he never forgot my mother's request, and he educated me accordingly.

I entered the medical school at Vellore with great difficulty, as my stepmother's family was very much against the education of girls and still more against keen interest in studies. One of the family members went so far as to hide my certificates when I was ready to apply for admission to the medical school at Vellore. The intense desire to go to medical school entered my mind after I saw Dr. Ida Scudder in March of 1919. She visited my school and pleaded for girls to register in medicine. Her personality and her talk attracted and inspired many of us to apply to that medical school in Vellore, which she had founded in 1918. Just then the government was also encouraging women to enter medical schools and colleges and was offering them scholarships. I applied for and got a merit scholarship. This monetary assistance was a great help to me, as my father could ill afford to educate me, particularly as my stepmother was not in favor of it. My parents' relatives were Hindus, and it was not possible for me to get any help from them.

I completed my studies and got my LMP (Licensed Medical Practitioner) in 1923 (Madras University). Soon after, I worked in a small women's hospital. I was the resident doctor, and in November of 1923 there came a flood. The hospital compound was overrun, and water was rising into the wards. There was great panic. With the help of ayahs and peons we evacuated the patients from the maternity and general wards to safer places; I was the last one to leave the hospital compound, and the flood water was up to my neck as I went out. This act of mine as a young doctor attracted the attention of the public and the authorities, and I was given a cash award.

In January of 1924 I was offered the post of demonstrator in anatomy in the Lady Wellington Medical School for Women in Madras, and in 1926 I joined the medical school at Vellore as a tutor in anatomy and as hospital assistant. Here every step in my progress was guided by God through Dr. Ida Scudder, who encouraged me all along. I also gained a great deal of knowledge and experience from the "roadside work," whereby medicines were carried to the poor people of the villages.

I married my cousin, who became a Christian in 1928. He was in the educational service, and he encouraged me to study when he became aware of my great thirst for knowledge. He used to sing a Tamil song saying, "One can control the angry tiger in the forest, quench the hunger of the wild beast, but no one can control the mind of a human being." God endowed me with a very good pictorial memory, which I greatly appreciated while teaching anatomy and certain other subjects.

The urge to specialize and to take up chest diseases in particular came to me in 1940, when I took charge of the medical ward. There I encountered patients with diseases of the chest, such as asthma, cystic lung diseases, and pulmonary edema resulting from heart disease. There was no surgery for them in those days. I was a bit jealous of my surgical colleagues, who could remove tumors and make the patients feel happy. My problems were always shared with Dr. Scudder, who never would allow anyone to be discouraged but instilled confidence by saying, "Try, dear. You will succeed." She encouraged me to study for the M.D. in general medicine in Madras Medical College. Dr. McRoberts, who was then the professor of medicine there, questioned my capacity to earn a M.D. in general medicine. He was of the opinion that women should specialize in gynecology and obstetrics. When Dr. Madhaviamma of Madras, who obtained her M.R.C.P. in England, returned to India, she could specialize in gynecology and obstetrics by studying for an M.D. in those subjects. To the astonishment of Dr. McRoberts, I earned an M.D. in general medicine in 1945. With a pat on my shoulder, he told me, "You were the best of the lot" after the clinical examinations.

As a medical specialist I did not have an easy time in Vellore. Dr. P. Kutumbayya, a great physician and principal of C.M.C. in Vellore, had no place for women teachers or specialists in subjects like neurology or cardiology. Therefore, developing a cardiology department from scratch had its own birth pangs.

To me everything was a miracle, for I never expected to have a responsible position in Vellore. Many men were against women specialists, but Dr. Reeve Betts, the great and devoted thoracic surgeon who also did cardiac surgery, gave me all the help I needed to build the cardiology department. If it had not been for his encouragement, I would have failed. With appreciation I must add that I had the good fortune to have a fine team of workers, who were extremely cooperative. Dr. Helen Taussig of the Johns Hopkins Hospital in Baltimore, Maryland, was very generous and kind to me at her cardiac clinic, where I gained a great deal of experience during my postgraduate studies in 1953 through 1954 and later in 1962 through 1963.

I was very happy that I was invited by the cardiology section of Johns Hopkins Hospital to attend its twenty-fifth anniversary in 1976, as well as the celebration of the 200 years of the existence of the university. There was a reunion of all the fellows who were trained by Helen Taussig at the cardiac clinic. As chairperson of the Twenty-Fifth Anniversary Reunion Committee, she very kindly offered me a grant to cover all my expenses, including the air fare from Madras to Baltimore and back. During this visit I reported the progress made in the Department of Cardiology during the last twenty years at C.M.C. Vellore.

As I look back on the way I have progressed professionally, I recall the development of the Christian Medical College and Hospital in Vellore. It was a medical school for women when I joined its staff. Under the able guidance of Dr. Ida Scudder it has developed into a fine hospital and a coeducational medical college. It serves the medical needs of the poor from the surrounding areas and even the ones from far-off places. Many professional experts from India and abroad have contributed to its growth. Dr. Scudder's devotion and broad vision have guided this development. As each department advanced, it became possible to give many students and doctors their medical education and specialist qualification. Above all, the Christian Medical College and Dr. Scudder's guidance have helped persons like me to develop and to contribute to the institution. I would fail in my duty if I did not mention the new branches in medicine, such as transplantation of kidneys and open-heart surgery, with valve replacements and so on. There are also many other fields in which research is being done.

From my small beginning as a medical woman with four years of training, I was given an opportunity and facilities to undertake postgraduate studies and to specialize in subjects like medicine, chest diseases, and cardiology. I think I would have had a great deal of difficulty if I had not had the encouragement of a person like Dr. Scudder and without the facilities that are provided at Vellore. A woman doctor would not have had these opportunities in any of the other medical institutions, as medical men in those days were opposed to women becoming specialists in areas other than obstetrics and gynecology. Even after I had established a good cardiology department, some men patients, educated and uneducated, looked at me with awe and wonder, questioning the capacity of a woman doctor to do cardiac work and even to be a physician.

I retired from this institution at Vellore in 1967. A colleague Dr. J. L. McPhail, was in charge of the surgical thoracic unit and was asked to write an article on this department. He paid me many compliments and said that a woman, if given proper facilities and opportunities, can rise to a distinguished position in any branch of medicine.

After leaving Vellore, I could not sit still with my daughter and three grandchildren, so I decided to work in Bangalore, where there existed a great need for a medical department. I joined the hospital in 1967 and worked there, developing the medical department and starting some cardiology, as well. Many of my patients from Vellore and other parts of India returned to me for a follow-up. The C.S.I. Hospital was upgraded as a teaching institute in medicine and surgery for the students of St. John's Medical College. It is a great satisfaction for me to be able to work in a hospital and to give comfort and relief to men and women patients. I have been amply rewarded and feel gratified that I have been able to use to the fullest the opportunities God granted me.

I am at present helping a medical friend to look after her patients (mostly gynecological and obstetrical) in her nursing home at Coimbatore. My family would like me to stay at home and relax. I feel that I relax better when I am of some help to others and I will continue to work as long as I am able.

Maria Jolanda Tosoni Dalai
b. October 11, 1901

I was the youngest of a family of nine children, six boys and three girls. When I was born, my older brothers protested because I was one too many and, what was more, a female child. My mother, a gentle industrious woman, who was overtired with bringing up children and working on our large farm, felt sure that her last-born could not inconvenience anyone, as her milk was sufficient for the infant's needs. This lack of welcome lasted almost a year, but gradually my older brothers became devoted to me, and all through my life, I have remained their darling and to some extent their adopted daughter. This situation has given me the feeling of always being young in comparison to them. Their satisfaction in the success I had in my studies and my profession has been a steady spur, encouraging me to do my best so as not to disappoint them.

My father was active, strong-willed, and strict, a real organizer, like a general in command of an army. For me only, he had a special affection, and from my early childhood on, he wanted me as his companion, whether on foot or in his gig, on the rounds he made in the cow sheds, through fields to check the work being done and to observe the growth of his herds, cereals, and vegetables. This relationship lasted until my graduation, which unfortunately coincided with his death. I owe to him my love of the countryside, of botany, zoology, and of nature in general. Even today nothing gives me such a feeling of peace and continuity as does the splendor and fruitfulness of the country district where I was born.

My mother completed my knowledge of nature in her gardening activities and poultry breeding, at both of which she was an expert. I got my first lessons in anatomy from her when she searched through the entrails of animals, looking for edible portions for her large family.

The medical officer of the village was our friend and family doctor. He had studied in Bologna, where Augusto Murri, a clinician of high repute, ruled in the medical faculty. Our doctor was a real gentleman, cultured and keen on music. He played the flute and often came to us.

Together with two of my brothers, who played the violin, my oldest sister and a pianist friend gave operatic and symphonic concerts in the large hall of our home, where a grand piano dominated. During the intervals at these concerts, my mother would question the doctor about university life in Bologna. He always ended by talking about Professor Murri's skill and about the prodigious recoveries of those operated on by him. Our local doctor was called many times to treat me for bronchitis, caused by the absence of heat in our house in winter. Then, at mother's request, his tales of medical matters became frequent and very interesting at my bedside. Thus from early childhood I was exposed to and interested in these tales of medicine. It was during this period that my idea of becoming a doctor was born. This dream never left me throughout my school days, although as my studies progressed, I became interested in many other subjects. I was always the best pupil in my class, which caused envy among my schoolfellows, who were almost all boys. After I had mastered the natural sciences, physics and chemistry opened up new horizons, and I became convinced that only by studying medicine could I advance in different fields of knowledge.

After primary school I was sent for five years to a nuns' boarding school, because the grammar school was some distance away in our town. These sisters also ran an institute for deaf-mute girls, whom they taught to speak, and I must say that they were pioneers in that art. I can verify this, as after some time I was able to converse with the girls by syllabizing slowly, while they answered by following my mouth movements, thus learning to make a few sounds. This work of the sisters also stimulated me to study medicine, as I wished to try to find a way to help the deaf to hear.

In 1915 the thunderbolt of World War I shattered the quiet of our fabulous rural world. My brothers were all called into the army, and the peasants had to leave our large farm, which, because of wartime exigencies, was deprived of horses and cattle, so that field work and harvesting became almost impossible. My two sisters did all they could to help and even learned to use the farm machines. I was at boarding school and therefore unable to help. I thought that, had I already been a doctor, my place would have been in a hospital. We were all distressed about the fate of my brothers. In fact, one died and another was injured. My youngest brother, who was eighteen years old, was sent to the trenches in the front line after the fortunes of war turned against Italy with the defeat at Caporetto.

When the war ended, I was finishing grammar school and was ready to enter the university. It was time for me to communicate to my family my decision to enroll in medicine. I knew that I would encounter some opposition, particularly from my father. I realized that for country people who lived in a narrow and repressive community, as ours was at that time, it would be difficult to let a young girl move into town, away from her family, without any control, and to let her enter medicine, which in 1920 was reserved for men.

Fortunately, my mother consented to my decision and rejoiced as though it had been her own. My brothers, just returned from the war and remembering the good work of the Red Cross nurses in the front line, declared themselves proud of my courage. But as I had expected, my father showed himself astonished and a little grieved, as I had destroyed his hope of a teaching career for me. He pointed out that medicine was a long and difficult course and not suited for a woman. Our society looked suspiciously at a woman doctor, and I would be running the risk of spending my youth studying for a career that might prove impossible. Moreover, I would be forced to live away from my family. Despite his unfaltering and dictatorial character, I think the close bonds that linked us in the love of nature and the peculiar tenderness he had for me were the reasons that finally convinced him to go against my decision. I believe, however, that his justified fears determined my choice of a specialization in pediatrics. What mother would refuse the help of a woman doctor for her child?

The University of Pisa was chosen for my studies. I did not find any hostility either from my colleagues or my teachers. They showed me the highest esteem and cordiality, since I was the only woman among them. I passed all the examinations and graduated with honors. I should have liked to continue with specialist studies in pediatrics, leading to a university career. However, my family called me home as soon as I graduated. They needed me because my father was seriously ill. He had heart trouble, resulting from articular rheumatism from which he had suffered in his youth, and now had severe pulmonary and renal complications. I still feel distressed when I think of the few therapeutic weapons we had then and of the scant relief he was given. His only comfort was my presence and loving help. He died in my arms.

After father's death our large family collapsed, and my plans for further study were upset. A number of my brothers married, and each couple went its own way. I could not return to the University of Pisa, as it was too far away, and I had to assist my mother, as she was alone and recovering from serious peritonitis.

At this point my belief in medicine and in my skill as a newly qualified doctor, already tested by my parents' serious illnesses, were to suffer a further setback. My youngest brother died from tuberculosis, contracted during the war in the mud and snow of the trenches. I realized that doctors did not have the means to ensure cures and were powerless when confronted with serious illness. I wondered if the profession I had chosen with such enthusiasm would cause only sorrow and disillusionment later. Was it worthwhile going on? It was a difficult moment for me. My brother had asked me for a cure, which I could not promise him. He had placed his confidence and hope of recovery in his medical sister, who had always stood by him and never deceived him. But the disease, despite all possible treatment, was inexorable. I have never resigned myself to the fact of his death and the thought that I betrayed him. Only twenty years later, streptomycin, the drug that could have saved him, was discovered.

The person who helped me come out of this state of mistrust for medicine was the director of the pathology department in the hospital at Proscia, where I had done part of my training. He realized my troubles and encouraged me to continue my studies, showing by his example that medicine is not only a science but an art that includes goodness, moral support, sympathy, and love of one's neighbor. I followed his advice and resumed my pediatric studies, a branch in which there was a wide range of work to satisfy my feminine feelings. I chose the University of Milan, as not many universities had training for specialization in pediatrics.

There I met the man who later became my husband. At the time when I met him I was discouraged, felt alone and had many doubts about my profession. He was a noble-minded person, older than I was, with much experience of life, and he gave me the trust I looked for. Giacomo was well educated, having studied chemistry and commercial sciences. During World War I he had managed a pharmaceutical chemistry plant. He came from a teacher's family, his mother and his sister having been real educators and benefactors in their poor rural village. They had contributed a lot to raising the social status of the population. Coming from such a family Giacomo was able to appreciate and approve of my profession. He was always helpful, and to him I owe a great deal of my success. My marriage contributed to making me a more mature woman and doctor. We had four children, in whose up-bringing I was able to apply all the principles that medicine and pediatrics had taught me. This experience later gave me confidence in my work. At that time most women doctors did not marry for two main reasons: first, the attitude of society toward them was hostile, as people had no confidence in women doctors; second, a lot of my colleagues thought that their profession was not compatible with marriage, that marriage would take time and knowledge away from their medical work and at the same time suffer from the demands of the profession. It was considered beneath the dignity of the profession to be interested in clothes and to wear smart gowns; only tailored clothes were approved. In one of our early medical women's congresses I remember the president exhorting her colleagues to wear evening dress for the formal dinner. Unfortunately, only a few had brought such a garment.

The Italian Medical Women's Association (IMWA) was established in 1920 and had about thirty members, presided over by Professor Carcupino. She was a fighter, and she fought for the right of women to take part in hospital competitions for professorships, from which we were excluded at that time. The association aimed at asserting our right to recognition and to working conditions similar to those granted to men. I joined the association in 1932 and was treasurer until 1954.

During the first ten years of my marriage, during which period the four children were born, I spent what free time I had practicing pediatrics in Milan. Every summer we spent three months in the mountains, a thousand meters above sea level. There I worked as the doctor in three summer health resorts for delicate children. I gave free consultations to the local people who otherwise seldom saw a doctor but badly needed one. Many of the men suffered from silicosis, caused by inhaling the dust from the iron mines in which they worked. These mines dated back to the period of the Roman Empire. The families in this isolated area were very poor and ignorant, with low standards of morality and hygiene and with primitive living conditions. The parish priest could not get them to church, and children were kept out of school on the pretext that they were needed to work in the fields and woods.

I took a step that radically changed their way of living. Since it was impossible to work with the adults, it was necessary to start with the children. We had to have a nursery school where these children could stay all day and be cared for, fed, and educated. They could then become the educators of their parents when they went home in the evening. The parish priest was my ally, and he put a building site at my disposal. The school inspector contacted communal and provincial authorities and also the bank that had to supply the money for the building. He showed wonderful initiative in solving all the problems that arose. My husband collaborated with me financially and in other ways. We went from door to door, explaining the project and convincing the mothers that they should send their children to school so that the youngsters would not be left alone and neglected while the parents worked in the mountains and in the mines. They all knew me as a doctor, and this helped to convince them. I was fortunate in finding a teacher who was a hospital nun and who carried out our aims with regard to moral education and hygiene.

Thus started the transformation of the village, which was completed in the postwar period when motor roads were built, linking the village to neighboring towns, thus creating better opportunities for work and increased earning power. This in turn gave the people the means to build proper houses.

As the years passed, the clouds leading to the calamity of World War II were gathering. When war broke out, Giacomo volunteered to join the antiaircraft regiment defending Milan. My children and I left the city and settled in a large country town, where I carried on an active practice for the next five years. The authorities and the townspeople received me with open arms, as I was both a physician and a pediatrician, a little-known speciality. After the local doctors and the hospital surgeon joined the army, I had to care for the whole population. The only other doctors left were two in their eighties, who were retired and still equipped only with the medical knowledge of the previous century. This was the most intensely active and the most important period of my whole professional life. The experience I gained at this time gave me certainty in the years to come.

In therapy I used sulfonamides, which were the most effective drugs available at that time. With them I achieved many recoveries from infectious diseases. Then came the antibiotics, and I experienced the greatest satisfaction a doctor can have in that I never had to issue a death certificate. My transportation was by bicycle or on horseback, which reminded me of my childhood. I braved bombing and strafing to visit secluded farmsteads where some seriously ill patient needed my care. I was obliged to solve all medical problems myself, as there was no colleague whom I could consult. The recovery of my patients gave me great satisfaction, as it verified my diagnoses and the correctness of my therapy. Surgical conditions still remained a problem, but it was resolved when a young assistant of the local hospital returned from the front. He was able to use the knife and radiological equipment to a limited extent. He was full of goodwill and humility, frequently consulting me about diagnoses and wanting me in the operating theater with him. "Do not forsake me, Madam," he would say. "You don't know how much I have learned from you." What an epic time that was, compared to the present; nowadays I notice that a lot of young physicians cannot make a diagnosis without first demanding a series of laboratory and other tests, which are often unnecessary.

After the war ended, I stayed in the same town for five more years, collaborating with other doctors in mutual esteem and friendship and carrying on health education and preventive pediatrics in my consulting rooms.

In 1950 I was obliged to return to Milan so that my children could continue their studies. It was not easy to embark on such a doubtful course, but at that moment my duty as a mother prevailed over my duty as a doctor. I have been compensated for this sacrifice, as my four children have all succeeded in life. One daughter is a psychiatrist; another is professor of art history in Milan; the third studied Italian literature; and my son, who studied law, has continued his father's commercial activity. They are all married, and I have seven grandchildren.

On my return to Milan I got in touch with the IMWA and devoted a great deal of time to it while continuing to practice as a pediatrician. In 1955 I organized the Seventh International Congress of Medical Women at Gardone. There I had the honor of being elected president of the Medical Women's International Association (MWIA), a post that I held for four years, from 1954 through 1958, and that gave me the pleasure of meeting a large number of colleagues from other countries. I finished my term as president at the Eighth International Congress of Medical Women in London. Presiding over the international association was an experience that enlarged my horizons. It involved great responsibility and much work, but I was helped by a very capable secretariat and by the collaboration of my colleagues.

When I gave up my international activity, I had more time for my profession and for study, through which I developed an interest in genetics. I became a genetic adviser to the Institute for Human and Eugenic Genetic Research in the University of Milan, a post that I still hold. The study of genetics augmented my medical knowledge and has given me great satisfaction, as through it we now know the genetic origins of many illnesses and the possibilities of preventing them.

The IMWA supported me in carrying on eugenic propaganda in Italy, culminating in a congress in Milan in 1971, where the theme was "Problems in Eugenics and Eugenic Advice." It has been a just corollary to my fifty years of professional activity that I should devote myself to precautionary measures in the field of hereditary diseases.

If I were just embarking on a career today, would I still choose medicine? My answer is yes, but I have some reservations. The status of the doctor has changed in the last ten years with reforms in the health services that have rightly increased the opportunity for medical and hospital care for all citizens, with the discovery of new drugs and of advanced operating techniques, and with the development of revolutionary research methods. If I were beginning in medicine now, I would have to adapt myself to a different reality from the one I was familiar with in my youth.

I believe that the woman doctor is proving that she can excel in every branch of medicine and that she is even favored by some qualities that are deeply rooted in her nature, such as patience, exactitude, devotion, common sense, and sensitivity. These qualities can be summed up in the Latin motto, conceived by me and adopted by the MWIA, *Matris animo curant.*

Dorothy May Satur
b. May 28, 1902

I am an Indian national, born in Madras. My parents, middle-class Anglo-Indians, were Roman Catholics. My paternal grandfather was of Armenian descent, and his wife was of mixed French-Indian origin. My mother's father was of Portuguese descent, and her mother a Dutch burgher from Kandy, Ceylon (now Sri Lanka).

My mother's father was manager of the accountant general's office of the Madras government. My father was a self-made man, having lost his father at an early age and therefore been obliged to leave school to work. However, he was an intelligent man, and he rose to be the manager and director of a very large coffee and tea plantation syndicate, the Ouchterlony Valley Estates in the Nilgiris. Mother completed high school with the Irish Presentation sisters in Madras and was married to father at the age of seventeen, while he was twenty-one. She had the aptitude and taste for higher studies, but opportunities for these were practically unavailable for women at that time. She had passed the higher local examination of the Trinity College of Music in London, but her performing ability was much above her grade. She was also a good writer (her calligraphy too was excellent), and she had an aptitude for poetry, as well. My father too was fond of music and played the violin and flute and also sang. He was a sports fan. These interests—music, writing, and sports—as well as such values as precision and industry, have been passed on to their children. Father was a man of integrity and morality, although he was not exactly religious. He was charitable, even to the point of improvidence. Mother was very intellectual, with a keen sense of humor, and yet she was simple, patient, and devout. Her fidelity to her marriage vows was admirable. My parents had fifteen children, of whom I was the second, and they considered each child a blessing from God. They had full trust in Him for the rearing of their children. Even had the need arisen, they would never have resorted to the restriction of their family by artificial methods. I recall my father muttering one day when birth control was being discussed (about the early thirties of this century), "Not birth control but self-control is needed." Ten of their children survived infancy and entered various careers, including the Church, medicine, and railway engineering. One of my brothers, who was in the India police force, left it after many years to become a Jesuit priest. Another was principal of a high school in Bangalore. A sister, just next to me, joined a Carmelite convent engaged in education and social service. Two younger sisters are well married. One lives now in England with her British husband (a retired Indian civil servant) and two sons. Although I was the second child of my parents, I was the eldest living one. There have been educators, doctors, technicians, nurses, artists, and musicians among our many relatives.

We were on the whole a fairly healthy family, although not very long-lived. My father contracted diabetes and died of a heart attack in his sixty-third year. My mother died in her seventy-third year of progressive muscular dystrophy. I myself enjoyed fairly good health and strength until my sixty-sixth year, in 1968, but I now am considered to have a possible mild case of Parkinson's disease.

I did not welcome going to school, and I indulged in some childish ruses to escape even home tutoring. I was always a homesick child, of a shy, retiring nature. My father was strict and very ambitious with regard to our education. I was not too interested, but finding my younger sister progressing fast at school, I became motivated to do the same. This sister entered the field of education and became the principal and professor of English of two Carmelite colleges.

At this stage I felt that no one understood my inhibitions, and I longed for encouragement to discover and develop my own potential. This was later given during my high-school years by an Irish-born educator—may her tribe increase—Miss Mary Boardman. Under her I virtually bloomed and blossomed. I became aware of myself and my own gifts, and from that time onward, I faced all challenges in my education and my medical career and never looked back.

From ten to fourteen years of age I was still at school with no opportunity to learn scientific subjects except elements of domestic science and physiology. These attracted me and were probably the beginning of my later avid interest in medicine. I was also good at mathematics, including algebra and geometry. My second language was always Tamil, in which I gained a great deal of proficiency.

Desiring to study medicine later, I went to Queen Mary's College in Madras until I was eighteen, taking as electives chemistry, physics, botany, and zoology. I then earned a B.A. degree, majoring in chemistry, from the Presidency College in Madras. I gained a First Class throughout my school and college career and spared my family much expenditure by winning scholarships. Being an honors university graduate, I had no difficulty in being admitted to the Madras Medical College. No one discouraged and everyone encouraged my keen desire to be a surgeon. There was always a human skeleton, to which all my brothers and sisters became accustomed, hanging on the wall of my study. One little brother would prod me to read a little more of Gray's *Anatomy*. "At least the upper limbs," he would plead before permitting me to take an afternoon doze!

I entered Madras Medical College in 1923 at twenty-one years of age and graduated with M.B., B.S., in 1928. I was hard-working and enthusiastic and won many prizes and certificates of honor. I had a clear and determined aim to succeed as a doctor in the service of my fellow human beings. I therefore took my studies very seriously. I have been able, thank God, to be successful and give maximum service to the medical world and to humanity in my own country.

Marriage was no obsession with me, but neither was I averse to it if the question arose. I well remember that when I was interviewed for incorporation in the Senior Women's Medical Service of India I was informed that, if I married, my service might possibly be terminated. I did not therefore accept appointment at the time (1934) but instead went overseas to specialize in obstetrics in Britain. In 1936, however, I was drafted into the service, where I worked until its dissolution in 1949.

In the Women's Medical Service between 1936 and 1946 I held posts as deputy medical superintendent, then medical superintendent, then professor of obstetrics and gynecology in hospitals in Calcutta, Visakhapatam, Lucknow, New Delhi, and Gaya. After taking the MRCOG in 1947 in the United Kingdom and making a study tour in the United States, I acted as professor of obstetrics and gynecology, in various colleges, including Bangalore, where I settled in 1961. In 1968 I became professor emeritus.

I was a member of various medical societies and on the Advisory Committee for Maternity and Child Welfare of the Indian Council of Medical Research. I was also a member of the committee of the *Journal of Obstetrics and Gynecology of India*, and a fellow of the Royal College of Obstetrics and Gynecology. As a professor of obstetrics and gynecology, I was examiner for many universities in India, both for the M.B., B.S. degree and the postgraduate examination for the M.D. and M.S. degrees. I taught for twelve to thirteen years. It was an experience that I enjoyed, and I was a success at it.

Undoubtedly I would again choose medicine as a profession. I have never found my sex any handicap to my career. Medical women are definitely needed in developing countries like India, especially because of the illiteracy, barriers of caste and creed, and the reluctance of women in general to be under the treatment and care of male doctors.

My country's needs, as I see them, are a poignant theme on which I would like to make some observations. Obviously, our subcontinent of India is in dire need of skilled medical services, particularly in the countless rural areas of which the country is chiefly comprised even today. Ours is still a developing country, despite much advance in industry and technology. Unfortunately, few doctors are imbued with the spirit of sacrifice, to give of their services to the most needy sectors of our population. It must also be said to justify this reluctance to some extent that the conditions in the rural areas are very difficult and can perhaps be faced by only saints and heroes.

There is a further aspect to this problem, namely the high cost of medical education and the unremunerative postmedical-graduate period that face young doctors. This is perhaps a result of the present economic condition of the country.

Finally, as involved citizens of our dear motherland, we are all conscious that we cannot regard with complacency the present conditions in our hospitals and medical colleges, despite signs of awareness, dedication, and hard work everywhere. Nothing but the best is worthy of the medical profession.

Irene Brenk
b. December 2, 1902

I come from a family of businessmen. We lived in Zurich, and so I spent my childhood there and completed all my studies at the University of Zurich. As I was the only child, school was a source of social contacts and change. I learned easily and had no difficulties with the lessons. Music was important in my parents' home, so I was given piano lessons and enthusiastically played in various ensembles. The desire to go to the gymnasium after grammar school was my own idea, perhaps somewhat promoted by older friends who had taken that step. My father, a very open-minded and educated man, wanted a good education for his daughter and supported this endeavor, as well as my later medical studies, in every way.

In the spring of 1918 I entered the girls' gymnasium of Zurich. This school was started 100 years ago as a private foundation. Long before the turn of the century, numerous foreign women students came to Zurich to pursue their studies and earn a doctorate or take a state examination. At that time the girls who profited from the freedom of the Swiss universities and the girls' gymnasium were chiefly German and Russian. The historian Ricarda Huch describes in her memoirs, *Spring in Switzerland*, how she came to Zurich in 1899, earned her *Matura* (matriculation) and subsequently studied history, which at that time was impossible for her to do in Germany because no girls' gymnasium existed. At the beginning of this century there were already women doctors in Zurich, notably, Dr. Heim-Vögtlin, the wife of the well-known scientist Professor Heim. Katja Mann, now over ninety and living in Kilchberg near Zurich, the surviving widow of the famous author Thomas Mann, writes in her memoirs how difficult it was for a girl to be admitted to a high school in German cities at the turn of the century. This was possible in Zurich, and by the time I entered the gymnasium, the pioneer spirit of girls' schooling was no longer noticeable. The *Tochterschule* was a very modern and open-minded institution for its time. In addition to the necessary mathematical and scientific preparation for medical school, we studied modern languages (French, English, and Italian) and naturally Latin and Greek. We read modern literature by such authors as Ibsen, Hauptmann, Wedekind, and Mann. We also went in for sports, which included not only gymnastics but swimming and tennis.

My inclination and talents clearly lay in the direction of the natural sciences, and this facilitated my choice of a profession. Finally, my father suggested that I study medicine. I might have taken it up myself after first getting a degree in biology, which would have been an absolutely unprofitable undertaking. After World War I still more women doctors were practicing in Zurich. There existed also the *Pflegerinnenschule*, which was a general private hospital for training nurses, and it was served mostly by women doctors.

During our final year in the gymnasium, we were oriented toward the different professions accessible to women. A young woman doctor informed us about what we could expect if we studied medicine. We learned that in Swiss clinics only very rarely was a woman allowed to become a chief physician and that the highest positions were almost invariably closed to women. On the other hand, we were told that the road to private practice was open. There was a woman head physician, Dr. Birnstiel, with Professor Naegeli in the medical clinic in Zurich, as well as a woman doctor, Dr. Hedwig Frei, in anatomy. These women who oriented us toward our later profession made a strong impression on me. Their objective calm and superiority impressed me. They inspired me to follow a career such as they described. The hospital work at that time was still closely connected with both the laboratories and the care of the sick, in which one could give help and comfort, and this situation suited my desires and inclinations.

After the matriculation examination five of twenty girls in my class took up medicine. Three out of those five actually finished their state examinations and their dissertations.

While I was still set on preparing for the state licensing, my father fell ill with a serious and at that time hopeless heart ailment. It was a very bitter experience for me to have to live through. I was to lose the only person who had been close to me and who had given me support and security. My parents were separated, and I had no other living relatives, so I was alone in life. Although I was not in dire straits, it was clear that I had to stand on my own feet as soon as possible. My father died in January of 1928, and our family life ended.

The director of the medical polyclinic in Zurich was Professor Loffler, and it was he who had taken care of my father during the worst of his illness. I had just done well in Professor Loffler's examination in internal medicine. At this point he asked me to join his polyclinic and to work half-days there. At the same time I would be able to begin my dissertation on lymphogranulomatosis under his supervision. Thus it became possible for me to work half-days on my dissertation and half-days at the polyclinic. After about four months I had completed most of this study. Having taken an interest in the course of my life, Professor Loffler then suggested that I attend the psychiatric clinic as a volunteer. I would have preferred the children's clinic or a clinic in internal medicine, but positions in the university clinics were rare during that period and I had to be satisfied to get anything. Thus in 1928 I began working as a volunteer in the psychiatric clinic under Professor Maier. In retrospect this step was most decisive for me. I met my husband there, and although my medical background had prepared me for another field, I stayed on in psychiatry for eighteen months and gained certain basics in this field.

In August of 1929 I married Dr. H. Brenk and went with him to Basel, where we both found positions as assistants to Professor Stachelin in the psychiatric clinic. There I completed my specialist training in psychiatry, while my husband, who had already completed his specialist training in neurology, started his own practice in Basel.

Then began another new period in my life. I had to manage a larger household with employees, and what was more important, I gave birth to three children, two girls and a boy, between 1932 and 1940. Pregnancy, childbirth, child care, and household duties occupied me fully during those years. I had neither the time nor the strength left to work in medicine. From 1938 on, the political situation in Europe became graver and graver. When World War II broke out and the German army marched into France, the Swiss called for general mobilization, and all men with military training had to report for duty. All women doctors were likewise mobilized, but in contrast, they had to do civil service in the cities and countryside, taking medical care of the populace. Basel is a border city, and it was thus heavily exposed. Our Alsace and German frontiers were closed and occupied by our militia. The inflow of food, which for ages had come from Alsace, was interrupted, and Basel experienced a state of war that included bombing from both sides (partly because of the confusion of location on the Rhine). During these years I took care of my husband's practice alone, with only short breaks. As a general practitioner I had to do minor surgery and pediatrics, as well as to take emergency cases. In addition, we had bomb-shelter duty, which meant that we women doctors had to set up underground bomb-shelter hospitals and to keep them in a state of readiness in case of bombings. Unexpected flights over Swiss territory and bombing attacks warranted our preparedness throughout the war, and we took care of those wounded in the air raids. It wasn't an easy time for me, expecially because my youngest child was born in 1940 and was in the care of a children's nurse, who least of all wanted to work in a frontier city. The situation improved with the end of the war. My husband returned from military duty with his health impaired. He suffered from stubborn, recurrent bronchitis with high fever, so that he was only able to work from time to time. I remained involved in medical practice for many more years.

Of my three children, my eldest daughter has taken up the study of medicine. Like me, she loves her profession and practices it despite the difficulties. She is married and has two sons and is thereby restricted in her freedom of movement and power to work.

My husband and I gave up our practice in Basel when he was seventy-one years old and I four years younger. Now retired, we live near the Lake of Zurich in the district of our youth. Today, at seventy-three years of age, I would like to say that, looking back over my long life, I still find medicine one of the most rewarding professions for a woman. Never, not even in the most difficult times, have I regretted my choice. Given the opportunity again, I would certainly take up this profession.

Alice Drew Chenoweth
b. February 21, 1903

Perhaps a small town in the U.S. agricultural heartland is an unlikely place for a shy, protected little girl to metamorphose into a doctor of medicine. But Albany, Missouri (always with a population of slightly less than 2000) had a junior college. A high percentage of young people attended college, and a number had master's degrees or Ph.D.s or professional educations. There were also many who furthered their education through travel.

I was born in Albany, delivered at home by the family doctor, and named Alice Drew, for my two grandmothers. My father, second in a family of five sons, had just graduated from high school and was ready to enter college when his father decided that they must move from Greencastle, Indiana, to Missouri to get enough land to pass on to the sons. Grandmother Chenoweth, who was born Elizabeth Drew and was a cousin of the actor John Drew, was a graduate of a "female seminary" and was considered a well-educated woman in this pioneer land at that time. Tall, dignified, and somewhat reserved, she could speak in public and was active in her church and the Women's Christian Temperance Union. She took me to the Methodist Sunday school as soon as I could walk. Grandmother Drew instilled a respect for education in my father, to whom it was a lifelong disappointment that his family's move prevented him from attending DePauw University. About fourteen years later he did work his way through veterinary college in Kansas City. Graduating first in his class in 1901, he was encouraged by his professors to go on to study medicine. Since he was thirty-two, on the verge of being married, and without financial backing, it seemed an impossibility. It was an unfulfilled dream he carried with him all his life. Thus in my home medicine was rated the highest of all the professions. My brother, who was younger and was supposed to be the doctor in the family, became a successful veterinarian.

My maternal grandmother was a "nurse" by nature, the kind of person the neighbors called on to take care of them when they were ill or having a baby. My brother and I always called for grandmother when we did not feel well because she knew how to make us comfortable.

I always loved school and enjoyed studying. Father, particularly, praised each small achievement, and mother was probably just as proud. In my home I was never aware of any difference in the importance of education for me or for my brother. Since I always did well, father willingly supported my continued education. Elementary school was not too memorable, except that I received a silver spoon for winning a spelling bee in the third grade and also won some acclaim for my performance in a ciphering contest in the eighth grade. Like other campfire girls, I designed and made my own headband. I chose as my symbol the owl for wisdom.

I attended junior college in my hometown and was the valedictorian of my class. My chemistry professor at Palmer College advised me to take more chemistry courses at the university. By coincidence, my faculty adviser at Northwestern University was also a professor of chemistry and was delighted to guide me to his department. Chemistry was my undergraduate major. I can still see my professor of physical chemistry shaking his finger at the Ph.D. candidates and saying to them, "Miss Chenoweth got that problem."

In my organic chemistry class there was a woman premedical student. Up to that time I had never known a female physician nor even met a woman who aspired to be one. She was a nice, gentle black woman who had some difficulty learning organic chemistry. Our laboratory desks were side by side. We were usually the last students to finish, which meant that we had time to talk with each other. I have wondered whether it was at this time that I first began to think of medicine as a career. It was not until my senior year at the university that I wrote my parents about my wish to study medicine. Father replied that, had I been a man, nothing would have pleased him more. With that I suspect father thought the matter closed. I am sure that, like all parents, mine expected me to get married. Until I was near graduation from the university I do not recall being seriously concerned about choosing a career. In my day women who went to college became teachers, so there was no decision to make. However, I do remember very vividly one morning—I must have been in my early teens—when I was sweeping the front porch at home and the idea came to me that I would like to be a social worker. I had never to my knowledge met a social worker, but I thought they tried to help people and I knew that was what I wanted to do.

In 1924 at Northwestern University I was elected to Phi Beta Kappa and graduated "with highest distinction" and a B.S. degree. My history professor, who was also the dean of the graduate school, offered me a scholarship in history. Since my way to medical school seemed blocked for the time being, I accepted it and in 1926 received an M.A.

For the next two years I was an instructor in history in a women's college in Montgomery, Alabama. Although seemingly a diversion, I look on those years as important in my development of independence. Incidentally, despite the fact that I was the youngest member of the faculty, the dean of women permitted me to chaperone the girls on dates, which was required at that time in that college. Not all members were given this dubious privilege.

During those two years I allowed myself very little spending money because I knew I was going back to school.

During my spring vacation I stopped in Nashville, Tennessee, to see a cousin and also a former neighbor from Albany who was then the dean of women at Vanderbilt University. The latter asked about my plans for the future. I told her that I was going to study for my Ph.D. in history or go to medical school. Dean Ada Bell Stapleton, Ph.D., from the University of London, advised me to study medicine. Without hesitation she telephoned the dean of the School of Medicine and asked if she could bring me over to see him. Evidently, my interview was satisfactory because it was not long before I received a letter telling me that my application had been accepted.

I wrote to my parents, explaining what had happened, what savings I had and asking, "What shall I do now?" In reply father wrote me the longest letter I had ever received from him, detailing all the hardships and indignities I would suffer, saying he doubted that I was physically strong enough for such an arduous profession. At the very end, however, he added that if I was still determined to go to medical school, he would of course back me, as he always had.

Father's fears that I would be exposed to embarrassment and indignities never materialized. There were a few pranks, such as a raw kidney in my laboratory coat pocket, and some teasing, but it was all in fun. A lot of good comradeship existed between me and my classmates. The only clinic that the five women in my class were excluded from was the genitourinary clinic. I never felt discriminated against on the basis of my sex. I recall one incident at the end of the course in biochemistry. I had consistently earned the highest grades in the class. The professor discussed the situation with me and my male runner-up and said he was inclined to give the latter top rating. My professor was open and fair about it, and I agreed with his decision. I could answer questions and solve problems on an intellectual level, but I knew that my competitor had more practical knowledge of biochemistry.

My memory of the first meeting of our class with the dean is still very vivid. He told us we had been carefully selected in the expectation that we would be good students and good physicians. However, he said, "We may discover that some of you would have made better farmers or teachers than medical doctors." I must confess that I did have a sinking feeling, and it did not give me any more confidence to hear some of my classmates boldly bragging that he was not referring to them.

Vanderbilt had many advantages for me. Our classes were limited to fifty; so we had the opportunity to know our professors well. A substantial infusion of Rockefeller money had made it possible for Vanderbilt to have excellent, full-time faculty. I was able to live within easy walking distance, which saved me energy and time in daily travel. Being able to give full attention to studies paid off because I was in the first group elected to AOA, the medical honor society, at the end of my third year. I received my medical degree in 1932.

In my day internships seemed to be arranged among professors. Through the recommendation of my professor of pediatrics, who took a special interest in me, I was accepted as an intern in pediatrics at Strong Memorial Hospital, the teaching hospital of the University of Rochester in New York State. Strong turned out to be a happy choice both professionally and socially, as this is where I met my future husband. Because of the prestige of the Johns Hopkins Hospital, because one of my assistant residents at Strong spoke so glowingly of his experience there and of Professor Edwards A. Park as a teacher, and possibly also because the first Chenoweths had settled in Baltimore when they arrived in America in colonial times, I chose to go to Johns Hopkins to intern the second year. I have never worked harder in my life, but it was a rewarding year.

Toward the end of the year at Hopkins, one of my assistant residents was appointed chief resident at the Children's Hospital of Philadelphia. This hospital had never had a woman in that position before I arrived. When it came time to appoint a chief resident for the following year, Dr. Joseph Stokes, Jr. discussed his concerns with me regarding disciplinary problems. Since I preferred not to have those "headaches," I stayed on in the second year as assistant chief resident. As the new chief resident lived outside the hospital, I was in fact chief resident for many hours of the day. This was excellent experience for me, and I was glad to make the medical decisions.

I had been doing a little research, and I thought I might like it. In 1937 I was given a research fellowship at the University of Pennsylvania, and while it was a valuable experience, I missed my contact with patients and decided not to accept an appointment at the Child Research Center in Denver the following year. Instead I accepted an offer to join Dr. John Mitchell in his pediatric practice. Because I had not had a rotating internship, as required by Pennsylvania law, I took six weeks of surgery at the University of Pennsylvania Hospital and six weeks of obstetrics at the Lying-In Hospital. I was pleased to return to patient care, and what I enjoyed most was being used as an unofficial consultant to the pediatric house staff of both hospitals.

My four years of private practice with Dr. Mitchell gave me an opportunity to view medicine from a different perspective. He said that our job was to help parents keep children well. Because of the emotional ties I developed with my patients and their parents, it wasn't easy to leave the practice when John Pate and I decided to get married. Nor was a busy practice conducive to courtship. On his last visit before we were married I had made calls every day and evening, for Dr. Mitchell was away on vacation. On the last evening it appeared that all would be quiet and that I could get away for a dinner in Philadelphia. However, I had to make a few telephone calls. Since one little boy had been vomiting, I thought I would stop to see him on our way to dinner. After hearing his history and examining him, I was almost certain that he had an intussusception. So we met the surgeon at the hospital, and we spent our last evening together in the operating theater. I don't remember whether we had any food at all that night.

John and I were married on February 12, in Radnor, Pennsylvania, by a clergyman whose children I had cared for (free of charge) and whose family had given me a lovely trip to Bermuda. I joined my husband in Louisville, Kentucky.

It was early in World War II, and several pediatricians wanted to leave their practices to me. John was working for the state Department of Health, and the state health officer insisted that I take the position of director of maternal and child health. What a strenuous but exciting job it was. In addition to supervising a nutrition staff and a network of clinics for mothers and children, the state Department of Health had just assumed responsibility for a maternity hospital in the mountains of Kentucky, and soon I was administering a wartime program called Emergency Maternity and Infant Care. It was a big leap from private practice to the administration of a medical-care program. Here I learned the value of consultation from the U.S. Children's Bureau in what later became the Department of Health, Education, and Welfare. This experience sparked my interest in the provision of medical care, which has been an absorbing interest of mine ever since.

A further enriching experience of my six and a half years in Kentucky were the visits of physicians from developing countries, who came to do their field training with us. It was in Kentucky that our son and only child was born in October of 1944. I had the good fortune to be living near my office and of having excellent help. I scarcely took any time off (I worked through Friday, had John, Jr. the following Monday, and was back at part-time work in less than a month).

It was my valuable experience in the field of public health that prepared me for the positions I have held in the U.S. Children's Bureau for the remainder of my professional life. When John was moved to Washington, D.C., I accepted a position with the Division of Research in the Children's Bureau, partly because it required less travel than did other programs in the bureau, an important consideration, since John, Jr. was only four years old at the time. Later I moved to the bureau's international division, where I planned educational and observational programs for fellows from abroad, especially pediatricians, obstetricians, and health workers in maternal and child health. John and I still visit and correspond with these foreign friends, all of whom have been guests in our home. Finally I was transferred to the Division of Health Services in the Children's Bureau, where I was a consultant to the kind of state programs I had administered in Kentucky and where I accepted increasingly greater responsibility.

Looking back over the years, I would say that the life of physician, wife, and mother is not an easy one, but it is rewarding, exciting, and altogether satisfying.

IRAN

Safieh Rafatdjah
b. June 26, 1903

I was born in Moscow of Iranian parents. Both my grandfathers were merchants and were distantly related. My paternal grandfather was the patriarch of a large family, living in Alexandria, Egypt. He asked my maternal grandfather to bring his youngest daughter to marry my father, who was his eldest son. At that time most marriages were arranged; so the deal was made, and my mother was taken to Alexandria. She lived with my paternal grandparents for two years before the marriage took place because even for that time she was too young. My parents were married when my father was seventeen and my mother eleven years old.

After graduating from the university in Alexandria, my father started to work. He mastered the Arabic, Persian, Turkish, and French languages perfectly and knew a little English, as well. Not satisfied with his life in Egypt, he left home, with his father's permission, in order to find a place where he would like to live. My mother and her son were left in the care of my grandparents. My father traveled to France and England, trying his luck here and there, and finally went to Russia and settled in Moscow. He started by teaching Persian in the Institute of Eastern Languages and later earned his Ph.D. degree and became a professor. Meanwhile my paternal grandfather left Alexandria for good and returned to his native country Iran to live in Meshed. My mother lived as a grass widow for ten years until finally, when she was thirty and my brother was eleven years old, my uncle took them to Moscow. At that time all Iranian women wore veils, and it was very difficult for my mother to unveil herself. She did not leave the house for the first year in Moscow until I was born. Another boy and two girls were born after me.

I have very happy memories of my early childhood. We were not rich, but we lived a comfortable upper-middle-class life. My father was hard-working, and his aim was to give us all a good education. He was a very intellectual person, and throughout his life I hardly saw him without a book. He worked for thirty years on a Persian-Russian dictionary, which became the handbook of all who studied the Farsi language and is still in use and much appreciated today.

We lived in Moscow and spent the summers in the country at a beautiful place where we had marvelous times. The climate in Moscow was very healthy, very cold in winter and moderately hot in summer. I love snow and cold winters, probably because most of my early life was spent in the north. It was fascinating to drive through the country in a sledge drawn by two or three horses.

I was five years old when I learned to read, and ever since then reading has been my chief recreation. I studied Russian and later French and German. After three years in the kindergarten I went on first to junior and then to secondary school. Our life flowed peacefully and comfortably during my childhood. Three years of World War I passed swiftly, and then, in 1917, we were confronted with the Russian Revolution. I passed my matriculation examination at the age of sixteen, and as soon as I got my certificate, I had to go to work. Our family was large, and my father had trouble providing for us, as life was very difficult and strenuous after the revolution. As the eldest child at home, I had to help, so I worked as a typist for three years, until we moved to Vienna in 1921.

Our new home was in Baden, a small resort town near Vienna. My father could not get work because the Austrians did not give work permits to foreigners, but he was accepted as an honorary professor in the Persian language at the University of Vienna. My brother was sent to Germany to study, while we girls learned German, continued our piano practice, and helped our mother in the house. So time passed until my parents' resources were exhausted. My father would not take us to Iran to be dependent on his youngest brother, so the only solution was for us to return to Moscow, which we did.

As soon as we had settled down, I decided to go to the university to study medicine. First, however, I had to pass the entrance examination. Several years had passed since I had finished my schooling, and everything was vague and shadowy. With the help of two teachers I worked very hard for a year without any recreation. I wrote the examination with a heavy heart, being unsure of myself, and awaited the results with fear. Imagine how happy I was two months later when I received a letter from the university, confirming my acceptance for the medical course. Vigorous and full of energy, I started my first year in the university.

My two sisters and I were brought up in a very old-fashioned manner. We were not allowed to have boyfriends and were made to understand that we were Iranians and Moslems and therefore could never be married to Christians. During my first year at the university I met a Polish boy, who was very fond of me. He was in his last year at an engineering college. After some time he proposed to me, but I could not make up my mind; I had to consider my parents. I knew that, if I married him, I should break with my family for good. I could not bring myself to deal my parents such a blow. I refused my suitor, and they never found out about this event.

My future husband was the vice-consul in Tashkent, one of the southern towns. It seemed to be a good match, and I realized that my parents wanted me to marry him. The only obstacle was my medical course, which I could not abandon. I told him that I would marry him on the condition that he would agree to let me continue my studies at the university. He accepted this, and we were married but lived separately for nearly five years, meeting only in the summer, until I got my degree. My university work occupied all my time, and I found it interesting and fascinating. Although my marriage was not a love match, I lived happily with my husband until the end. He was a good husband and an affectionate father to our children.

During my second year in the medical school I became pregnant. I suffered from morning sickness and felt miserable. Unfortunately, the pregnancy coincided with the time of the examinations. I was so keen on my studies that even the thought that I would not be able to sit for the examinations made me frantic. Abortion was the only solution. I was young and inexperienced and did not know that I might never be able to have a child again. I shall never forget the relief I felt after the operation was performed.

As soon as I graduated from the medical school, I joined my husband, who had been appointed consul in one of the towns in the south of Russia. I managed to get a post in the hospital in that town, and my medical career began. It was wonderful to feel that at last I had reached my goal. I loved the work. Nearly every day we had three or four operations, at which I was usually the only assistant.

Then I became pregnant again. This time I wanted a child, so despite the fact that I had morning sickness, I carried on bravely, not minding the inconvenience. Thus my first child, a girl, was born. When she was five months old, my husband was ordered to close the consulate for good and leave immediately for Tehran. This was a disappointment, as we had only just settled down and I was happy in my work and just ready to start minor surgery on my own. All my hopes vanished.

We decided that I would go to Moscow to live with my parents while my husband went to Tehran, hoping that he would be able to get another position in Russia. As soon as I had settled in with my parents, I lost no time in getting an appointment in a large maternity hospital, where I found the work very satisfying. After a time I received a most disappointing letter from my husband, saying that he could not return to Russia and that I would have to come to Tehran.

In 1932 I left Moscow for good with my daughter. I was going to Iran for the first time, and I knew that in the future it would be my native country. After arriving there, I became pregnant again. My husband decided that I should have another abortion. Although I was against his decision, I had to submit, but fortunately, my mother-in-law came to my rescue and talked him out of his decision. I had the baby, who was a boy.

In Tehran I carried on my practice from my home until my husband got another appointment and we had to leave for Iraq. The same business of packing and moving was once more necessary. After two years in Iraq my husband was recalled to Tehran, but shortly after this he was appointed consul-general in India, where we lived for five years. During all this time, to my great sorrow, my medical career had to be sacrificed. I was a homemaker, and all I could do was read the medical journals.

In India our son contracted cholera and was so ill that for a time we gave up all hope for him. It was a miracle that he survived. Our term of office came to an end in 1939, and we left India to return to Iran at the beginning of World War II.

We were happy to be home again, and as soon as we had settled down, I started thinking about medical practice. For two years I worked in a maternity hospital and also had a private practice. Then I was appointed to a government post in the Ministry of Education, which put me in charge of the medical care of schoolchildren. I was about to start this work at the beginning of the school year when a dreadful blow struck us. Our son fell ill, suffering from a condition called diverticule Meckel. An operation was essential, but unfortunately, it was unsuccessful. In forty-eight hours a healthy, vigorous, clever boy was dead. It is difficult for me to describe the state we were in after this great misfortune. My husband suffered terribly, while it seemed that I, as a woman, was more capable of bearing the grief. From this time on, my husband started slowly to lose his mental faculties, and he was never his old self again.

Fortunately, I had my new appointment, which kept me going. My only daughter married a diplomat, and they left for Paris. Saying good-bye to her was another blow to me. I worked for twenty years in the health department. When the Medical Women's Association was formed in Iran I joined and became their secretary and later their treasurer for several years.

In 1961 my youngest brother died and left some money to be spent for charity. As I was his trustee, I decided to build a clinic and to donate it to our Medical Women's Association. This was accomplished a year later. Dr. Kia, one of our most active and efficient members, worked very hard to get our clinic into running order. I was her assistant and treasurer. Over the years I participated in many medical congresses all over the world.

Gradually I had to abandon my work in the clinic because of eye trouble. I suffered from glaucoma. My left eye was operated on unsuccessfully by a famous eye specialist in Vienna. Then I went to Spain, where both eyes were operated on by Professor Arruga. This time I was fortunate, as my right eye was saved. It was a most anxious time, as I feared that I might be blind for the rest of my life.

Meanwhile my husband was losing his mental faculties and was in poor physical health. He spent the last few years of his life in a wheelchair, which was a great strain and difficult for both of us. My only recreation during this period was studying at the British council library. Since my husband's death, I live in my old house with my housekeeper. My daughter lives most of the time out of Iran because of her husband's diplomatic career. I have two grandchildren, a boy and a girl.

There is a great need for women doctors in our country. Although Iranian women have been unveiled for many years, there are still quite a number, especially in the provinces, who would prefer to be treated by women doctors. I loved my career, but unfortunately, because of the nature of my husband's profession, I was not able to work as I wished in the medical field. Still, if I had to make the choice again, I think that I would once more choose a medical career.

Herdis Gundersen
b. July 3, 1903

All my ancestors were Norwegian farmers, coming from a valley in the southern county of Telemark, now known as the cradle of skiing. After the farm of my maternal great-grandparents burned down, the family moved and bought a new farm in Skien, the largest city in Telemark. In this same town Henrik Ibsen was born and raised. My grandfather was an engineer on a ship, and my grandmother was a very clever and intelligent person. They had five children, the second of whom became my mother. She was very pretty, intelligent, gay, and active.

At fifteen years of age my father was sent to sea on one of my grandfather's ships. He sailed to Australia many times, each trip taking about nine months. My mother was sixteen years old when my parents became engaged, and they married when she was eighteen and my father was twenty-five.

I was born in Skien on July 3, 1903, a premature baby weighing less than three pounds. The midwife had difficulty getting me to breathe and had to give me rather rough treatment before she succeeded. I was fed artificially on cream and water. During my first years I was very delicate and had many colds and even bronchitis.

When I was four, a brother arrived. At seven years of age, I started school, where I had no problems. I learned easily, enjoyed studying, and made many friends.

At that time my family experienced a serious crisis. Steamships began to displace sailing vessels. My grandfather had been advised abroad to change to steam but refused to do so. He had troubles with his ships, and one was destroyed in a hurricane near Savannah. My father by this time was working in my grandfather's office. As a result of serious family problems, as well as the crash in shipping, my mother, brother, and I moved to Oslo to live with my grandmother and three uncles. All three of my uncles were studying pharmacy, and one of them became a professor at the University of Oslo. We rented a large apartment, and both my brother and I were put into good private schools.

At the age of twenty-seven my mother was alone with the responsibility for us two children, so we all stayed with my grandmother until she died at the age of ninety. My mother has devoted her whole life to the welfare of her children, her family, and her home.

At the new school I had no difficulties, and I soon acquired many new friends. I had a good memory and was very fond of reading and needlework. For several years I was among the best in my class, and before I finished high school, I had even skipped one year. I loved to read good literature and was especially fascinated by an old book written by a Danish professor and printed in 1882. It was a health dictionary, and I became very eager to learn as much as possible about different diseases.

In the meantime my grandfather had again built up his business and my father had started in insurance. During World War I they were both rich men. With the improvement in his financial status, my father helped us more and gave us many presents.

In my teens I became lazy and had too many interests outside school. I particularly loved to go dancing, and in this way I met many medical students, whose talk about medical studies always interested me. My mother wanted me to continue my education; so after high school I started in college. A year later my father sent me to a boarding school in Switzerland to learn French. This was a very interesting time, for we were an international group of young girls. We traveled quite a lot, and I matured and became more independent.

After one year I returned home for two more years of college, from which I graduated with poor grades. My mother then stated very firmly, "No courses in cooking or sewing for you. You are going to get an education. You're interested in medicine, so why not study it?" At that time I had also met several women doctors whom I admired.

A friend of mine and I both applied to medical school. We were thin, timid, and shy, and were received by a doctor with the following not-very-encouraging words, "Two sisters, what will become of you? I think you must eat each other." At that time the difficulties for doctors had already started.

I found the courses very difficult. The theoretical part of the studies did not attract me. I was lazy and had too many extramedical interests. My grades were not very good, and as the university then began to restrict admissions, I had to wait one year before I could start the clinical studies. In the meantime I got some practical experience in a medical department. This I enjoyed very much, and I looked forward to my work every day. My enthusiasm in the clinics never abated. I enjoyed learning and working in hospitals. In 1933 I became a doctor, but it was difficult to get jobs, especially for women. I finally found out that the only solution was to start my own practice, and for this I chose a town on the east coast. There were already many well-established doctors there, but three of us had the courage to start out at the same time. It was hard competition, and after six months the two men gave up. I stayed for two and a half years, carrying on a small practice with a small income. I learned to wait for patients and adapted myself to an empty waiting-room.

I finally decided to apply for an internship and was accepted. It was in a hospital with 140 beds in a little town in the middle of Norway. We were three doctors in all. The chief was a well-known surgeon. He was very clever and had the greatest capacity for work I have ever seen. He always did a fine job and devoted himself totally to the patients. He also expected the utmost of his co-workers. I was stimulated by his capacity and really learned to work hard. It was no eight-hour working day; I was free every other afternoon, but otherwise the daily average was sixteen hours of work. That two-year period was very interesting and instructive.

My enthusiasm for surgery was so great that I even took another job in the same kind of hospital in my native town, where I stayed for one year. When World War II started in Europe, I wanted to go back to Oslo, as I thought I would be needed by my family. My brother, who for years had suffered from bad health, became very ill and died in 1942.

When the war reached Norway, it was very difficult to get a job in a hospital, as most doctors preferred to work there. I took many short appointments at the Oslo Municipal Hospital and thus got a taste of different specialties. I happened finally to get a steady job at the bacteriological department in our largest laboratory, the National Institute of Public Health, where I stayed for three years. We had many epidemics, so I chiefly did routine work. We had a great deal of tuberculosis and diphtheria, as well as many intestinal infections. Sometimes I had to travel around in the country on behalf of the chief doctor of the State Department of Epidemic Diseases. After three years of being a microbe-hunter, I found that I liked people better than microbes and that I wanted to become a specialist. I had had a lot of practice in finding gonococci on slides, and thus I considered becoming a specialist in skin diseases. I succeeded again and got my training and qualification at the state hospital in 1946. That same year I was awarded a scholarship from the university to study skin diseases in the United States. I spent six months in Chicago, New York, and Rochester, Minnesota, at the Mayo Clinic. In Chicago I studied at the rapid-treatment centers. Coming back to Norway, I acquired a fine full-time job as an assistant in the dermatology department of the Oslo Municipal Hospital. This appointment ended after three years. I then started private practice in Oslo in 1950 and enjoyed taking care of my own patients, gaining their confidence, and making personal contacts. This mutual understanding means so much to me and helps me to serve.

In 1959 I was given a part-time job in the Oslo Public Health and Venereal Disease Department, where a female doctor was needed for the treatment of women. I kept this job for fourteen years, the last years as assistant to the chief. This position was perhaps the most interesting I have ever held. I had the opportunity to see a small department develop into a large one with all modern facilities and with high international standards. We all participated in ideal teamwork with clever colleagues and nurses, treating the patients in an effective way and trying to inform and help them.

I have also been privileged to be elected chairperson of the Norwegian Women Doctors' Association for the period between 1949 and 1952 and chairperson of the Dermatological Association from 1958 through 1960. I have been on the board of the Oslo Medical Association and a member of the Norwegian Medical Association for several terms. The latter affiliation obliged me to participate in meetings held every other year in different cities. I have also attended several Scandinavian dermatological meetings and two international congresses.

I lectured to medical students for a short time on skin diseases and for a longer period on venereal diseases, and I have published a few papers on the latter subject.

My work in the Oslo Public Health and Venereal Disease Department is now finished. I am retired but still have my private practice. I work six or seven hours a day, as I love to be active and hope to continue for many more years.

If I were to draw any conclusion about myself and my life, it would be the following: I have been blessed with excellent health. If once again I had to select a profession, I would not hesitate. I would choose medicine. I am grateful to many people—but most of all to my mother. Without her I could never have become a doctor. She has given me a splendid home and we live a harmonious life which we both enjoy. She is now ninety-one years old. Thanks to her, I have had a high standard of living and I have been able to devote myself to my profession. I am grateful to my colleagues for all their help and advice.

Soledad Arcega Florendo
b. October 17, 1903

I was born in the Philippines, the fourth of five children. My mother was a homemaker, also engaged in a small retail business. My father was a community leader. He took part in the revolt against Spain and sought political asylum in the Mariana Islands. While in exile, he practiced as sanitary health inspector, having served as a medical aide to Spanish doctors. I had two uncles who held bachelor's degrees in pharmacy.

My husband is Gerardo Florendo, a lawyer and professor of law. We have four children, two boys and two girls: Maria F. Slack, married, with a Master's diploma in piano and a B.A. in psychology; Gerardo, married, a mechanical engineer; Antonio, married, with a bachelor's degree in architecture, and Gloria, single, with a bachelor's degree in business management.

Our family physician was a gentle, soft-spoken, mustachioed, and dignified person, to whom we entrusted all our secrets—physical, financial, emotional, and spiritual. I remember my mother saying that, when any member of the family was sick, there was a feeling of relief and comfort at the sound of the doctor's knock at the door. As a child, I often wondered how the doctor could exercise such power over his patients, and I was greatly impressed with his importance in the life of the community. His only competitor was Dr. X, equally dignified and competent. However, Dr. X was unpopular because he antagonized the families of his patients with his manner. As soon as he entered a patient's house, he would ask for a basin of hot water instead of approaching the patient to ask how he or she felt. This angered the family, and the doctor's reputation in the community suffered accordingly. People ridiculed him and called him Dr. Basin (in Spanish, *el doctor Palangana*). I promised myself there and then that I would never commit the same error if I should ever become a doctor. Fortunately, health education has greatly advanced since then, and without being asked, the family always prepares a basin of hot water—and woe be unto the doctor who does not wash his hands before feeling the patient's pulse!

At that time in the Philippines only three learned professions were regarded as eminent—priesthood in the Roman Catholic church, medicine, and the law.

The family status was determined by the number of sons who became priests, doctors, or lawyers. During the Spanish colonial period the Filipinos were discouraged from taking up the learned professions, but the rich ones managed to send their sons to Europe, particularly to Paris, Madrid, Rome, London, and Brussels. Women were not considered fit for or worthy of such distinction, and therefore they were trained in the "gentle arts" of embroidery, cooking, and praying for the virtue of chastity and for the salvation of the soul in purgatory and hell. Such was the destiny of women: to marry, to bring up children and grandchildren, and to pray.

In 1908 my father died, and my mother struggled to give us five children primary and secondary education. My uncle more or less adopted me so that he could give me a college education. It was quite natural that I should choose medicine for a career, and there were no questions asked. With the victory of the Americans over the Spaniards, the Filipinos received from the Americans four things: the Protestant religion brought by the missionaries, universal public education for girls and boys, the public health system, and the constitutional form of democratic government.

Girls were encouraged to study for careers, and the status of women was raised further through the granting of suffrage and the right to hold public office. At that time four women obtained college degrees and thus earned national distinction. They were Librada Avelino, lawyer, educator, and founder of the first university for women; Josefa Abiertas, lawyer, who founded the House of Friendship, a home for unwed mothers and their children; Honoria Acosta Sison, the first Philippine woman doctor, who graduated from the Woman's Medical College of Pennsylvania and became professor and researcher in obstetrics and gynecology; and Olivia Salamanca, the second woman doctor, who also graduated from the Woman's Medical College of Pennsylvania.

Dr. Salamanca was my cousin, and the family was justifiably proud of her achievements as a specialist in tuberculosis, the number-one killer in the Philippines. She organized, with the help of the leaders of the country, the Philippine Antituberculosis Society, which has established more than forty hospitals and clinics in the country. Unfortunately, she became a victim herself and died after having led the crusade against the white plague for several years. I recall that, as a young girl, I would walk past her house on the beach, where she lived in complete isolation, and I would hear her hacking cough breaking the stillness. I remember her as a small and frail woman, full of enthusiasm despite her lung condition. I was inspired to follow in her footsteps.

My uncle sent me through medical school, and after graduating and passing the state medical boards, I applied for a job as a laboratory physician in the Philippine Tuberculosis Society hospital, the Santol Sanatorium. This was located in the wilderness among the rice fields because tuberculosis was a dreadful illness in those times and people literally believed in the saying *Abandon hope all ye that enter here.* There were no electric lights, and we made our nightly rounds in the *nipa* ("grass") cottages, wearing knee-high boots to protect us from the poisonous snakes that abounded in the rice fields. Like Florence Nightingale, we used a kerosene lamp to light our way. Another woman doctor joined our staff as a radiologist, and people in general, especially our male colleagues, looked with favor and respect on us women doctors.

I was promoted to ward physician, then outpatient doctor, and later to physician-at-large to organize the regional and provincial branches of the tuberculosis society. After several years of clinical work, I was appointed chief of health education and information and assistant editor of the magazine *The Crusade*. Later, when I was acting executive secretary, I participated in the Antituberculosis Educational and Fund Drive, a job that brought me into contact with the mass media; business, banking, and industrial firms; schools and universities; and high government officials. The president of the Philippines was a victim of tuberculosis, and he readily allocated funds for the expansion of services. Doctors were sent abroad to specialize in lung surgery, and I was sent for residency in the National Jewish Hospital in Denver, Colorado, to specialize in medical-social services and rehabilitation of tuberculosis patients. This was the start of my interest in social work. On my return, the home-visitation program was expanded to help patients cope with social, emotional, and financial problems that proved to be obstacles to their recovery. At the golden-jubilee celebration of the Manila Medical Society I received the award for my contribution to medical social service.

In 1956 the United States Agency for International Development granted me a one-year scholarship to study hospital administration. Two male doctors and I were commissioned to get our master's degrees in hospital administration so that we could help upgrade hospital services in the Philippines. It was necessary to convince the medical profession that medical and surgical competency was distinct from administrative skills in organization, management, funding, and public relations. On my return, I was appointed training officer for medical residency and internship programs in the North General Hospital, one of the biggest and most modern hospitals of the Department of Health. I was then promoted to medical superintendent (equivalent to hospital administrator) in the Quezon Institute, the biggest tuberculosis hospital at that time, with a 1600-bed capacity. In the same year I was appointed professorial lecturer in hospital administration at the Institute of Hygiene and Public Health. In 1965 I retired from the hospital and was appointed chairperson of the Department of Social Work in the state university. In January of 1969 the United Nations made me a member of the United Nations Mission for the Evaluation of the Family Planning Program for India. The mission, after five months, proceeded to Geneva to finalize its report and recommendations to the United Nations Population Commission. It was a most rewarding experience, with family planning closely related to maternal and child care. Up to the present, family planning has been one of my concerns, specifically the training of social and community workers for urban and rural areas. Overpopulation is one of the obstacles to our social and economic development, and family planning is one of our top national priorities. We are using the multisectoral approach with a multidisciplinary team concept. Health, education, and social welfare are our main goals.

My desire to serve my country by better delivery of health services in the fields of tuberculosis, family welfare, family planning, and hospital administration has made my life more meaningful. If I had to start my career all over again, I would engage in the same activities.

Fernanda Borsarelli
b. September 28, 1904

I was born in the early years of this century. My home town was Turin, which in those days was just embarking on its career of industrial development. I studied there and have also practiced there. Life then was reasonably smooth and quiet, mainly because of the serious, thoughtful character of the Piedmontese people.

My family belonged to the intellectual bourgeoisie for whom study, hard work, honesty, good manners, warm friendships, and a happy family atmosphere were the most important things in life. My father had a degree in engineering and worked for the provincial government, building roads, bridges, and public works. My mother was a pioneer of classical studies. She had gone to the university on a scholarship and had a degree in literature. This was followed by a degree in philosophy. She then took up teaching literature to prospective primary-school teachers because, being a woman, she was not allowed to teach in the higher schools. In spite of the fact that she married and had four children, she continued working until her retirement in 1933.

My parents were married in 1902, and their first child Paolo Emilio was born in 1903. I followed in 1904; Cesare came along in 1909; and Rosa Maria arrived in 1910. We were brought up in an atmosphere of love and understanding. We were allowed full freedom of choice, and our parents answered all our questions and explained all the most important problems in life to us with a great deal of patience. They also helped us in our studies.

In the autumn of 1909 my grandfather had taught me my ABCs and I had soon become an avid reader. He once confessed to me that he would have liked to be a doctor, like his younger brother. My grandmother was a lively and romantically inclined woman. She was born in the beautiful city of Verona and was herself the daughter of a doctor. Frequently she would recall the days of her youth, her own grandparents, and especially her father, from whom she had inherited a rich library of medical books.

My elder brother had a quick and lively intelligence and showed an inclination for deep thought even when a little boy. A keen and scrupulous observer of nature, it was he who taught me to study and love the world of animals and plants. He was a truly precocious inventor, and as early as 1917, when he was only fourteen years of age, he forecast the use of methane to power automobiles, as well as the invention of the jet engine. He was also very fond of saying that chemistry, which he studied with passion, was the science of the future. However, when he was only twenty-two and just about to get his degree in chemical engineering, he died of pneumonia. His death cast a shadow over the whole of my youth, for he was the closest to me in age, the brother with whom I had grown up. The other children, four and six years younger than I, had begun their education as a game with Paolo Emilio. He taught them history, geography, and natural sciences, while I entertained them by telling fables and stories that I nearly always made up myself and by reading to them the works of various authors, a favorite being Jules Verne. I acted as instructor to my sister for the three years of her elementary education because, having had bronchopneumonia, she was rather prone to illness and was not able to go to school regularly. As time went on, however, her health improved and she later earned her degree in literature. She started on a career in the state archives and rose to the post of superintendent of the archives in Piedmont and the Val d'Aosta. Cesare earned his degree in engineering at the age of twenty-two, and by winning scholarships he was able to continue his studies and specialize in radiotechnology. He later became one of the pioneers of television, and his studies took him for a year to England and then to Harvard University in the United States. In 1938 at the Milan Fair he carried out the first experiments in television in Italy.

When I was seven, I was sent to a private school. I was very tall for my age, and I believe I was also quite advanced mentally. I made friends with girls in the higher classes, and my opinion of the efforts of the nuns and teachers was not always charitable. My first year in junior high school was 1914 through 1915, and I decided to study classics. In August World War I broke out. By that time I was developing very fast, and at ten and a half I was already so tall and well-shaped that people thought I was fourteen or fifteen. My father, who had been an officer in the army, was called up again. I remember reading tales of war and patriotism while my brother discussed the news with my mother. She was profoundly shocked by the war and yearned for peace. In 1895 through 1900 she had founded a women's peace league that gained much support throughout Europe. During the war I went through junior high school and studied the piano at the age of thirteen. I already considered myself a young lady. Perhaps it was the war and all the anguish and heartache it brought that inspired me to consider the profession of medicine. My dream, however, was to cure mental, as well as physical, disorders.

In 1919 I started high school. My father had finally come back from the war, and the family was reunited. Times were bad then, with unemployment, public disorder, factory occupations, and politically inspired strikes. In the area of Turin there were many sad incidents, and all this led to the advent of fascism. On October 28, 1922, Mussolini, in agreement with the monarchy, took power with a coup de main. I have fond, nostalgic memories of the three years I spent in high school, with the excellent teachers I had and the friendships I formed.

It was while I was in high school that the idea of studying medicine really took hold of me. What were the reasons that drove me in this direction? In the whole of Italy there were no more than 200 women doctors, who were pioneers in the field. Some, indeed, were truly first-class physicians. It seems to me that I decided to be a doctor in order to help humanity in an independent way. I earned my high-school diploma with brilliant grades and then informed my parents of the wish that had been growing within me during the previous three years. I think my decision was influenced to a certain extent by a sort of nineteenth-century romanticism. Father was a humanist, a philosopher, and a poet, and he was well aware of sociomedical problems. He was a profoundly religious man. My paternal grandmother also helped to stir my interest in medicine. She was forever praising the goodness, charitable spirit, and professional worth of her own doctor-father and therefore welcomed my decision enthusiastically. Thus the general atmosphere of a family that recognized the moral virtues of the medical profession strengthened my resolve and spurred my parents to grant their consent. They did, however, take pains to point out the difficulties I would meet along my chosen road.

In October of 1922 I enrolled for my first year in the Faculty of Medicine at the University of Turin. I was extremely enthusiastic, and I tackled the very difficult subjects of the first three years of study with dogged determination. At the beginning I found it difficult to get used to sessions in the anatomical laboratory where we dissected corpses. In my first year I attended all non-compulsory lessons and frequented the chemical laboratory. In the second year I was an intern student in the Department of Physiology, where I learned how to carry out experimental work. In my fifth year I prepared my dissertation on the physiology of the eye. Even after I earned my degree, I continued to go to the Department of Physiology both in Turin and in its clinic 3000 meters up in the mountains at the foot of the Mount Rosa Glacier. There we studied fatigue in the formative years and the development of laboratory animals at high altitudes.

In my fourth year I became an intern student in general medicine and learned at first hand about symptomatology, diagnosis, and prognosis. I remember how happy I was when I made a diagnosis on my own and had my conclusions confirmed by X-ray and laboratory tests. In 1928 I received my degree with a dissertation that obtained full marks cum laude.

Believing that for a woman it would be very difficult to make a career in general medicine, I decided to specialize in pediatrics. I started as a voluntary assistant in the pediatric clinic, and this was the gateway to a career as a university lecturer. I then became a school doctor and a member of a team employed by the sanitation department of Turin. Later I became one of the team of doctors working for the Mother and Child Board. After a few years in which I directed consultant pediatrics clinics in the province of Cuneo, I became head of the pediatric department of the Ospedale Mauriziano in Lanzo-Torinese.

During this time I also had a private practice and was consultant pediatric specialist for some sociomedical bodies. In 1970, for health reasons and much against my will, I was obliged to give up my work as a doctor.

My first experimental work was carried out in the Department of Physiology at the university. I did research on the modifications in respiratory turnover resulting from exercise in children in their second year of life. In the pediatric clinic of the university I studied infant tuberculosis and antitubercular vaccination. I also did various studies on the antirickets value of human milk and on other similar subjects. Since I was a doctor for children's holiday villages, I studied heliotherapy, the physiological effect of gymnastic exercises on children and problems of fatigue in children. I was interested in bacteriology and undertook research on behalf of the hygiene department of the university. Further, I carried out experiments on the development of reflexes in newborns and older babies. In 1940 I published a book, *Puericulture and the Spiritual Formation of Babies*, in coauthorship with a philosophy graduate who was a professor in pedagogy and infant psychology. The book constitutes one of the first attempts to throw light on the nature of the individual in the period from birth to adolescence. It was written especially for students in the upper high-school grades and for young mothers, to teach them a more rational way of bringing up children.

In the years following the war I was very busy with my professional and social activities, and yet I found time to present many scientific papers and bulletins in Italy and abroad. Above all, I was interested in the raising of children in their developing years, and I published the results of observations carried out in Mother and Child Medical Board clinics for newborns and in the medical, psychological, and pedagogic center that I directed on behalf of the Organization for the Moral Protection of Children.

By natural inclination I started teaching as soon as I had my degree. I undertook a series of lectures to promote interest in hygiene, puericulture, and pediatric subjects on behalf of the National Union of Women and the Fascist Women's Organization, to which the regime had entrusted certain tasks in social assistance.

After I was appointed lecturer in pediatric medicine, I ran my own free course in normal and pathological mental development during the formative years at the University of Turin. I also held a government appointment to teach puericulture in the Elementary Teacher's Training College and in the Technical College. My task was to instruct future elementary-school teachers and future mothers in infant health. I taught scholastic medicine to sanitation inspectors and professional nurses, scholastic medicine to doctors specializing in pediatrics, and pediatrics and puericulture to the nurses of the Green Cross. On behalf of the Ente di Protezione Morale del Fanciullo ("Body for the Moral Protection of the Child"), I gave lectures in infant health, puericulture, and child rearing to the parents of elementary-school children. I was particularly fond of this job because, while curing the illnesses or setting right imperfections of my young patients, I always made an effort to understand their developmental problems and to advise parents individually, to make them conscious of the importance of their role in the physical and mental development of their children.

I have been a member of the Italian Pediatric Society since 1938, and I have always closely followed its national and international congresses. In the same year I enrolled in the Nepiology Society and afterward in the Health Society, the Society for Social Medicine, the French-speaking Pediatric Association, and the Latin-speaking Pediatric Association. In 1935 I learned of the existence of the Italian Association of Women Doctors, which had been founded in 1920, and I joined that, too. I became its chairperson for Piedmont in 1947, and from 1962 to 1967 I was the national chairperson. On its behalf I organized three congresses of a socioscientific nature. The first was held in 1948, the centennial year of Italian unity, in cooperation with Pro Cultura Femminile, of which I was also a member. The second and third congresses were a part of the Turin International Medical Conferences. These were, strictly speaking, national congresses, but numerous delegates from abroad belonging to the Medical Women's International Association took part.

In 1949 I was appointed by the Home Office to organize the Turin section of a new body set up to integrate into society children who were rejected by it. Some were abandoned war orphans, others were less intelligent than average, some had personality defects, and others were maladjusted because of their environment. This was the Body for the Moral Protection of the Child, and its job was to complement the work of the Mother and Child Board, which was responsible for such children. To make the new body work properly, I sought the cooperation of welfare assistants, elementary-school teachers, people appointed by the ministry, and volunteer workers. In 1950 I founded the Medical, Mental, and Pedagogic Consultant Clinic in cooperation with a psychiatrist, a psychologist, and a welfare worker.

When I started my career, the woman doctor was seen as a pioneer, and her activity was more or less limited to pediatrics, obstetrics, gynecology, and social medicine, whereas today she can engage in all branches of the profession from general practice to any of the specialties. When I was in the Pediatric Clinic I was unable to become a salaried assistant because under Fascist law a woman could only hold a subordinate position. My chief once said to me, "You are much better qualified than the other candidate, but I must select him because he is a man." Even in the service of the town council in Turin a woman could find a secure position only as a typist, certainly not as a doctor. For this I resigned from the city health board, although I had worked there for ten years and had even directed the school health department for a year. None of these services received any form of recognition from the authorities.

Is it better for a woman doctor to be married or single? The obvious answer seems to be that the single woman can devote herself to her mission without any of the restrictions that marriage and motherhood impose on her. Nevertheless, it is my opinion that, because of the experience of life and completion of the personality that married life entails, the married woman is better able to understand the many psychological needs of her patients. As time goes on, the single woman may feel alienated from the lives of those around her. Frequently she lives alone and is obliged to solve by herself all her own problems, as well as those of her patients, who consult her and confide in her with full trust. To reconcile a life of hard work and study, like that of a dedicated doctor, with the pressing needs of a wife and mother, who must devote some of her time to her husband and children, may not be a very easy thing to do, but experience shows that it is possible and indeed desirable.

A doctor must organize her activities extremely carefully. All my colleagues feel the need to have someone near for moral support, and for this reason many get married. Indeed, most doctors' wives feel that they too play an important part in their husband's profession. The married woman doctor, especially if she is married to another doctor, feels that she has the necessary support even if her husband works in quite another branch of medicine. A single woman doctor may feel that the presence of a devoted nurse is a great help to her, but if she lives with a still active mother or a sister, whether or not they know anything at all about medicine, they can help her through periods of discouragement and worry and share with her the moments of joy. In a word, they can create a warm family atmosphere for her.

In my case, I think it was more a question of circumstances than any other consideration. In my university years I had greater contact with women than men colleagues. In those days, although we enjoyed mutual respect for and friendship with members of the opposite sex, men and women treated one another very circumspectly even when they were in contact for purely academic reasons. I was completely dedicated to my studies and my work. I did not go dancing or take trips to the mountains, so I had little opportunity to meet men outside the university. Now that our graduating class has a reunion every five years, I find that we are on much more intimate terms than we were in our school years. When I graduated, a number of problems distracted my thoughts from matrimony, and the premature death of a colleague with whom I had established a certain degree of intimacy completed the process of estranging me from close relationships with men. In 1937 in Rome, during a congress on infant health, I met a foreign doctor who wanted to marry me. He came to Turin with me to meet my family, who were naturally a little chary of allowing me to go to live so far away. Perhaps my excessive reserve and caution at the thought of the unknown dissuaded me from taking the big step immediately. In 1939 I went with my father and sister to visit this man in his own country. As he was accompanying me to the ship that was to take me back to Italy, he told me that he wanted to come on board with me and celebrate the marriage there. I thought his desire to get married on board a ship a little strange and persuaded him to return to land. Shortly afterward World War II broke out, and that ended the matter.

If I could begin again, I would study medicine with the same enthusiasm as before. I would make that decision again despite the difficulties of the job and the inevitable disappointments because I really do believe that I have been in some way useful to my little patients by advising parents not only on how to look after their children's physical development but on how to form their minds and their hearts. However, if I could begin again, I would try to find some way to get more enjoyment from my youth.

Moon Gyung Chang
b. November 30, 1904

I was born in Jinju, Korea. My mother was forty-five years of age, and I was the only child except for my older sister, who was already married.

At that time primary schools had just been set up in our country. People were reluctant to send their children to such institutions, and school officials had a difficult time recruiting pupils. A curious fact is that most of the early pupils were grown-up women, most of them concubines or bar hostesses, who are called *kisaeng*. Although I wanted to go to the primary school, there were two reasons why I could not do so: in the first place, most of the pupils were of the type mentioned above, and second, my father did not allow me to go because he thought education was useless for a girl. However, when I was eight years old, my father died, and the following year I began to beg my more gentle mother to let me go to this desired school. At first mother opposed me, remembering the will of my late father. However, I persisted, and at last I dared to leave home to stay in the teacher's house for a few days in order to show that I could study.

My mother finally gave her approval as a result of the teacher's cordial solicitation and my unwavering persistence. I then returned to my home. I had only five cents in my savings box. With this money I bought a pencil and a slate. I never asked my mother for money to buy notebooks. I was consistently the top student until I graduated from this school. Then I sold my honor student prize to a rich classmate, and with this money I was able to buy the writing paper I really needed.

For a time after graduation I attended a dressmakers' institute without giving up my dream of going to high school. I had many agonizing days because I could not manage this. Finally I fell ill with tuberculosis. At this point my mother decided to sell her house to enable me to go on to high school. She loaned the money to others and with the interest she planned to pay my high-school fees. In the fall, when I was sixteen years of age, I left for Seoul, our capital city. I had already thought of becoming a doctor. Unfortunately, all means of entering the high school were closed to me although I had come with an ardent desire to acquire a higher education. I was told that autumn was not the season for admission and, in addition, that I was too old and did not have sufficient basic knowledge.

I returned home very much disappointed, but a new opportunity soon presented itself. When I recollect this now, I see that it was a reckless adventure for me. At the time I did not feel this way because I was so very eager to acquire an education and I had definitely decided to become a doctor. When I was seventeen, I went alone to Japan with a letter from a relative whose wife was running a boardinghouse in Tokyo to support her son in school there. In order to improve my scholastic knowledge, I first attended a preparatory school for a year, learning mathematics in the daytime and English at night. The following year I decided to enter Jong Wha Girls' High School. I passed the entrance examination with excellent grades, which qualified me to enter in the second year.

As I was always at my desk, studying, my classmates called me Study Bug. During these years in Japan I felt very homesick for my own country, which was a colony of Japan. I also felt sad when I thought of my poor mother, who had sold her house to pay my school expenses. Although I was a Korean, I was awarded scholarship funds, as I was consistently an honor student. However, the school officials decided to place me second at graduation because, according to the rules, they could not place a Korean student first.

The money sent to me by my mother and the scholarship funds were barely enough to get me through high school. Then, without a penny, I took the entrance examinations of two renowned schools, the Imperial Women's Medical College and the Teachers' College. I successfully passed both. I chose to enter the Imperial Women's Medical College in the hope that I would be able to get some financial assistance from my high-school principal, who had shown me much affection and had sympathized with my poverty.

During my five years at the medical college I was always an honor student and thus received more scholarship funds. My fiancé was a student at Meiji University in Tokyo, majoring in law. His parents did not want us to postpone our marriage for three years for the sake of my internship. After obtaining my medical license from the Ministry of Health of the Japanese government, I worked for one year and three months in the obstetrics department of my medical college until my fiancé graduated.

Staring out to the sea from the ferry as I returned to Korea, I made myself two promises: one was that I would devote myself to medical service for women with the utmost enthusiasm and sincerity, the other, that I would help poor students who were unable to get higher education because of a lack of money. When I look back now at the age of seventy and see how well I have kept those two promises, I have a great feeling of satisfaction. I have treated all my patients with my best techniques and greatest devotion throughout the forty years of my medical practice. I am still on very friendly terms with many of them. As a doctor, I have done my best for them, and in return they have respected me and relied on me.

During the ruthless Korean War I lost my husband, who was the chief of the

General Affairs Department of the Police Bureau. Since then I have devoted myself solely to the care of patients. A large portion of my income has been spent for poor students, many of whom have eaten and slept at my house. I have paid tuition and other expenses for dozens of students.

In 1934 I bought a building located at 195 Kwanhun-dong, Chongro-ku, Seoul, at a cost of 5000 won. I opened the Jong Wha Doctor's Clinic in this building. There were so many patients coming to my clinic that I often had to wrap the medicines in newspaper because of the scarcity of wrapping paper. I earned as much as 20,000 won in three years, so I could repay my debts and build a new annex, as well. I helped three students at first by supporting them, giving them board and lodging, and paying their tuition fees and other expenses for their college courses. This was the beginning of my "help-the-poor-project." With the additional rooms I was able to aid five students at a time. So far I have helped more than fifty.

In 1964 I was elected director of the Seoul Medical Association. Since then I have held many positions, such as president of the Seoul Medical Women's Association, vice-president of the Korean Obstetrics Institute, president of the Korean Medical Women's Association, auditor of the Korean Medical Association, vice-president of the Seoul chapter of the Korean Red Cross, vice-president of the Korean Women Bachelor's Association, and president of the Seoul chapter of the Korean Tuberculosis Association. During this period, putting aside my personal affairs, I have devoted myself to the improvement of public health in our community and to the guidance of many younger women doctors. Nowadays I often suffer from a lack of time because of my busy daily schedule with the Korean Tuberculosis Association, the Korean Red Cross, the Medical Women's Association, and the Women Bachelor's Association.

Now that I have kept the promises that I made to myself so many years ago, the only task left for me in the remainder of my life is to set up a foundation. I intend to sell my closed-down hospital building and its site in order to be able to finance poor students. At the closing of my beloved hospital after forty long years of practice I felt a deep sorrow, as if I were cutting off a support on the ladder of my career, but I am already planning to pioneer a new life. Although I have retired from the medical front, I have determined to do my best to help numerous poor people. At present I am planning to set up the Moon Kyong Educational Council, giving it my maiden name. In anticipation of its establishment, I have selected seven directors for the council. I have also made my last will and testament and had it notarized by an attorney. When my hospital building and site are sold, the money will be used for the general funding of my educational council. I intend to deposit the money in a bank, or I may buy certain profitable stocks. With the interest on this money I will help poor college students who are faced with financial difficulties. My final desire is to contribute all my property for social welfare so that I can help many less fortunate people.

My friends say that my busy routine, by not permitting me to rest, keeps me healthy at the age of seventy-one. I am thankful for my splendid health, and I promise to work eagerly until the last day of my life.

Agnes K. Moffat
b. January 11, 1905

I was born in 1905 in the village of Weston, then a suburb of Toronto but quite an independent municipality, politically and socially.

My father Frederick William Moffat with his father Thomas Lang, four brothers and one sister, and mother Elizabeth King emigrated from Scotland to Canada when my father was ten years of age. My grandfather had been a master metal molder in Scotland and on reaching Canada set up his own foundry in Ontario, producing propellers for Great Lakes ships. From this he progressed to the manufacture of wood and coal, then gas, and finally, electric stoves, exporting to all corners of the earth.

My mother Janet Catherine, née McNish, was born in southeastern Ontario. She was one of ten children, and her father was a farmer, second generation in Canada from Britain. She graduated from the local primary and secondary schools and completed her education in Toronto at the School of Pedagogy. Her second teaching position brought her to Weston, where she met my father through their affiliation with the local Presbyterian church. Both of them were dedicated church people.

When I arrived on the scene, I already had two brothers; then, in sixteen months, I had another brother and seven years later my only sister.

Our family life was centered around the home, the church, and the family business. Mine was not a politically or professionally oriented background but one based on hard work and dedication in both business and religion. Family prayers were said three times a day, and Sundays were devoted entirely to church services. Naturally, our outlook on the world was colored by our way of life and interests. The only extraneous insights came from our close association with church missionaries in foreign lands, such as India, China, Africa, and so on.

This autobiography originally appeared in *PORTRAITS * Peterborough Area Women * Past and Present.* Editor: Gail H. Corbett B.A.; Foreword: Flora MacDonald M.P. © Portraits' Group, 1975, Box 1602, Peterborough, Ont. Printed at Homestead Studio.

These men and women were frequent visitors in our home, and they often made use of Moffat holiday cottages on furloughs.

My father was a very moral man with fine principles, a strict Scottish Presbyterian with definite ideas regarding discipline. He was an elder in our church for as long as I can remember and superintendent of the Sunday school for over twenty years.

Although individually and as a group our family spent little time socializing outside the home and church, we were active and industrious within the family group, each doing his or her "thing." Little time was spent lazily relaxing or idly communicating with one another. My father was a most inventive and industrious person. He spent many hours in his workshops at home, creating in metal and wood or in photography or printing. We children learned early to use tools, to repair our own bicycles, to print our own photographs, to set type for our printing press, and so forth. This drive to create and produce has followed me throughout my life, and I think some of the latent drives of my husband were kindled in these directions by contact with me and my father. My husband, like my father, had superabundant energy, and these outlets brought a wonderful balance to his professional life. I have always admired men with great energy, originality, and self-confidence. These I found in my father and later in my husband.

My mother too was interested in church work and was president of the Women's Missionary Society for many years. Her interest in education brought her the distinction of being the first woman on our local Board of Education. She was a fine public speaker and was a great help to my father in many ways. But their strict discipline and seeming intolerance prevented their children from enjoying some of the pleasures of childhood and "growing up" that others seemed to have. My parents restrictions were so severe that my second brother ran away from home at sixteen years of age to join the Royal Canadian Mounted Police, and I at a later age threatened to do the same unless I could go away to a university in some community other than Toronto. Fortunately, with time these differences disappeared and I had the greatest affection and admiration for my parents.

I have few recollections of my preschool and elementary-school years. Of course, there were no nursery schools and kindergartens at that time; one started formal education at seven years of age. My memories are centered around extracurricular activities.

By the time I entered secondary school, my younger brother Fred who had been promoted beyond his class, joined me, so the two of us continued together until the end of high school. These years were mentally stimulating, especially since we were able to skip a year, and the challenge of "keeping up" was good for us. I enjoyed mathematics, ancient history, Latin, and biology most. Our homework hours together were well arranged, and we became fast friends. Social life, apart from that centered around the church, was limited—or prohibited. Social contact with the church missionaries was frequent during this period, especially over the summer holiday months in the lake district. I found one missionary, a medical doctor, particularly interesting. His hospital was in India, and to me he was the kindliest and most human of all the missionaries. He had a natural gift for storytelling. This, combined with his soft, flowing words as he described exciting incidents in medical practice in India among the poor and the maharajahs, had considerable effect on me. What a fascinating life and yet at the same time one that involved helping people! This was my first insight into the satisfaction, fulfillment, and gratification that come with the practice of medicine.

When it came time to apply for university studies, my brother Fred did not hesitate to sign up for medicine at the University of Toronto. I held back a bit because of the length of the course. During this period of indecision some pressure was exerted on me and my parents by friends who felt a diploma course in physical education would be a "fine thing" for someone like me. I had never before seen a real gymnasium with parallel bars, traveling rings, vaulting horses, and so on, but I succumbed to the suggestion and graduated two years later with the General Proficiency Medal. When this training was completed, I felt somewhat stranded in thinking of my future. I asked myself several questions: Is this the end of my formal education, even though my parents can support me financially in any course? Do I want to—and will I be able physically to—teach physical education all my life? Do I still want medicine? What other courses are available to women? What will bring me the greatest gratification and sense of fulfillment of duty? What would satisfy my longing to be part of the world, helping people? What would be most challenging to me, as a woman? So, in spite of having rejected medicine earlier, I ended up in favor of it.

Just at this time my brother Fred (having finished his second year in medicine) was killed in a car accident on his return from a visit to see our mother in the hospital. He had been trying to persuade her to allow me to go away from home for my university training. His death was a tragedy for me, as well as for my parents. He had been my confidant and support in the family. I was devastated, and I couldn't communicate with the rest of the family. Living at home would have been impossible without Fred.

Queen's University in Ontario would not accept women, and there were no medical departments in the newer Ontario universities. So I decided on McGill University in Montreal. I was accepted, and I entered the second premedical year in 1925—one of 2 women in a class of 125. Once I was on my way, the years flew by.

There was little time for social life or school activities at McGill at that time, for long laboratory hours kept us from joining the various groups of women arts students. However, I did manage to play on the hockey team and become a charter member of the Delta Gamma sorority. Through the latter society I met a student of exceptional qualities, and she has been my closest and dearest friend ever since. A busy career and family life do not allow time or opportunity for the cultivation and nurturing of many friends, but throughout these many years this special friendship has given me the greatest comfort and support in times of grief and worry and genuine joy in periods of relaxation.

On graduation from McGill in 1931, I was accepted (as one of two women interns) at the Toronto General Hospital for one year only, on a general rotation service. It was here I met a senior intern, Dr. Magee, whom I married in 1933. I made many lifelong friends at "the General" among the interns, residents, and junior staff. I think it was the happiest year of my life. Of course, I was in love!

At the close of this first year of junior internship I was anxious to get a senior internship in obstetrics. However, senior positions were not handed out to women, so I reluctantly left Toronto for the United States and the Children's Hospital of Michigan in Detroit. A few months before the year was up, I left Detroit and became first resident at St. Joseph's Hospital in Guelph, Ontario. This was an excellent introduction into general practice.

With the permission of the professor of surgery at Toronto General Hospital, Dr. Magee and I were married in September of 1933, although he had one more year to finish his surgical course. In those days there were no living quarters and no salaries for married interns and residents (an honorarium of twenty-five dollars was given each month). However, we managed to find some upstairs rooms near the hospital, and there I set up a part-time office and part-time home for the two of us. I did outpatient work at the Women's College Hospital one afternoon a week, but my major endeavor was at the Banting Institute, where I was working in pathological chemistry toward my M.A. degree.

When the year was up and I had my M.A. and Dr. Magee had finished his surgical course, we went to London, specifically so that my husband could study for his F.R.C.S., there being no such advanced degree in surgery in Canada at that time. I was to do and see what work I could in the various hospitals. We both had dozens of letters of introduction to the English medical and surgical elite, but those from Sir Frederick Banting drew the greatest attention. We both were fortunate that for seven to eight months of the year the hospitals in which we were residents were nearby. Many, many strange and wonderful things happened to us and our Canadian medical friends during those two years.

The socially and medically stimulating highlights while in London included an invitation to the theater from Dr. Maude Abbott and Dr. Paul Dudley White; meeting Dr. Frederick Banting unexpectedly in a bookstore, having dinner with him, and hearing of his recent trip to Russia and his visit with Pavlov; an invitation from my chief Dr. Eric Pritchard to attend a dinner meeting of the Preposterous Club (*pre* for prenatal and *post* for postnatal), which included the highest-ranking obstetricians and pediatricians in London.

Returning to Canada a few months before my husband, I set up an office in Toronto and did outpatient work at the Women's College Hospital. When Dr. Magee returned to Canada with his F.R.C.S., since there were no worthwhile university openings available, we approached the Standard Medical and Surgical Clinic of Peterborough, the first partnership clinic in Canada. After personal interviews with the board of the clinic, Dr. Magee was accepted as a junior surgeon at $1500 a year, and on second consideration they decided that they would take me, too—on approval for one year, at $1000—to help in the pediatric practice and also do some work with women and anesthesia. This delighted both of us tremendously, for we were keen and anxious to work and show our worth to the group.

We were on call twenty-four hours a day. Office hours were six days a week, with a special Saturday-evening period for farmers coming in to shop. On Sunday afternoons each took a turn for two hours, refilling prescriptions and treating emergencies. It was during these hours that I really learned my pharmacology, getting to know the explosive and coagulating mixtures, discovering how to smooth out ointments, and so on. Drugs that were only names to me in medical school, I could now see and handle—and never forget.

When we moved to Peterborough in November of 1936, we went into the first real apartment building in town. Ours was a small one-bedroom apartment (fifty dollars a month), but the Murphy bed in the living room rested many medical confreres, the most illustrious being Dr. Maude Abbott when she came to Peterborough to speak to the first open meeting of our new University Women's Club; her topic: "Sir William Osler."

My husband and I were formally admitted to the staff of both hospitals. I continued to be the only woman in practice in Peterborough until after the war, in 1947, when Dr. Nancy Chenoweth, at the age of seventy, came to Peterborough to practice with her son Dr. Rodger Chenoweth.

The early years of our practice in Peterborough were during the depression. Then World War II followed, so one can imagine the frustrations, work, and worry of those days. I was the only woman among nine men in our group, several of whom were ready to retire. We all worked hard, day and night. There were many house calls, and we looked after many of the minor surgical cases in our own surgery, since no such thing as the modern hospital emergency units existed. There was no telephone answering service, but Dr. Magee and I offered to install a second line in our home, to answer clinic calls on nights and Sundays. These were the days of unsophisticated anesthesia methods: open chloroform, open ether, semiclosed ether, nitrous oxide, and oxygen with an old McKesson machine. Pentothal was not yet generally accepted. Dr. Magee and I had brought the first to be used in Canada. Spinal anesthetics were popular at that time. And in the delivery rooms the anesthetic, usually open-drop ether, was dispensed by the nurse in charge. Imagine the responsibility of those in charge when there was a retained placenta or a premature baby or twins!

Dr. Magee joined the R.C.A.M.C. in 1942, went overseas, and returned in 1946. Those of us at home were truly overworked. I was doing all the pediatrics, all the anesthesia, helping in obstetrics, and carrying on with office gynecology, making four to eight house calls a day and often serving as an ambulance. We had to be courageous, resourceful, and untiring.

Following the war there was an increasing influx of doctors into this locality, and the ratio of women to men increased from 1 woman to 28 men in 1936 to 16 women to 120 men in 1975.

My practice had been so heavy and so diversified for the first ten to fifteen years that, with the return of our medical men from the war, I was glad to hand over my obstetrical cases to Dr. J. C. C. Dawson (who later became president of the Ontario Medical Association and then registrar of the College of Physicians and Surgeons of Ontario) and my pediatric cases to Dr. Ross Matthews (later president of the Ontario Medical Association and Canadian Medical Association). Now I was able to concentrate on anesthesia and continue my office practice, chiefly gynecological, with women.

I had two prewar children (taking four to five weeks off duty for each) and two postwar, adopted children (whom I delivered myself and took into my home without any time off from my practice). The loss of our prewar son at the age of six and a half from cancer was a great tragedy. It was following this that my husband and I became so interested and active in our Canadian Cancer Society and Research Foundation.

When I look back on my forty years of combined practice and marriage, I must confess that in my most romantic imaginings I could never have envisioned a life granting me so much. I had evidently chosen the best profession for personal and career fulfillment and the ideal husband for love, understanding, and companionship. Working side by side with him in our offices, in the operating rooms, sharing our worries and problems, encouraging and inspiring each other, knowing and admiring the other's work, created a bond of unusual strength. Traveling together for pleasure and to congresses, enjoying winter and summer sports alone and with the children, cemented this union.

I was constantly being reminded by my husband that his love for me was enhanced by his admiration of my continuing to practice. This encouragement, support, and closeness formed the greatest driving force outside my inherited love of action and urge to excel.

I practiced full time until 1972, when Dr. Magee's health was failing. After a total gastrectomy in 1969 his health had declined. While in Durban, South Africa, attending an international orthopedic congress, he had developed an intestinal obstruction, and we had flown home to Canada. He died a month later, in November of 1972. I was devastated. In March of 1973, at the age of sixty-eight, I resigned from anesthesia in the two hospitals.

Surfacing after this catastrophe, although I had known it was inevitable, was a long, lonely, and grief-strewn journey. A new life style has had to be created. No part-time anesthesia was available in the hospitals, and my office had been taken over during the last year my husband was alive. My youngest child had left the nest. But I am gradually finding my level and branching out into other fields, some allied to medicine and others to my hobbies. Life memberships in several medical associations provide easy access to medical interests.

I shall always hold my association with medical women at home and abroad close to my heart, and I hope to renew some of those acquaintances in Hamburg in 1978. I hold in great esteem the medical women I have met in my many travels. They have always been an inspiration and a joy to know. So I have no regrets about the profession I chose, which helped fill my life with wonderful memories—and will no doubt create more for the future.

Annaliese Hitzenberger
b. March 30, 1905

When I was born, Austria was ruled by the emperor Franz Josef I, who was a very old man. He held together the ancient Hapsburg Empire, over which at one time "the sun never set." When I was three years old, Vienna shone in all its glory and final magnificence. The sixtieth year of the monarch's reign was being celebrated, and many prominent guests from abroad had been invited to the great *Jagoausstellung*. Kaiser Wilhelm of Germany and Emperor Franz Josef marched side by side along the wide Praterallee, past a rejoicing crowd. I was there, too, a small child, lifted up by my father so that I could see better.

I was born in a suburb of Vienna, in a long, low house overrun by mice. My mother was always beside herself when these small rodents appeared, but I found them amusing. Being an only child, spoiled and protected accordingly, I liked to oppose authority even in early childhood. This rebellious streak probably played a substantial role in my subsequent development.

One evening before I had really fallen asleep, I had a strange vision. A tiny woman was walking across my chest, bearing a yoke with a small bucket fastened to each end, and she balanced the yoke so skillfully that the buckets kept their equilibrium. This dream must have made an enormous impression on me because I can remember it perfectly even after so many years. I have often tried to interpret it, and it seems to me that it pointed to the future development of my life, which has always driven me to strike a balance between profession and avocation.

When I was six, I was not allowed to go to school, as my parents held the unusual opinion that I could be "ruined" by going at such an early age. Consequently, my mother taught me herself for two years, during which she conveyed to me an uncommonly vast amount of knowledge, even though the situation made her life and mine miserable. Finally, at the age of eight, I was allowed to enter the third grade of primary school, where at last I was among other children and was blissfully happy. This happiness lasted one year only. On the day after school closed, my mother and I were sitting in the garden when a stranger appeared and asked to see my father to inform him that Franz

Ferdinand, the heir to the Austrian throne, and his wife Sophie had been assasinated that morning in Sarajevo, Bosnia. After hearing this terrifying news, my mother, who was still very young, could only stammer, "That means a world war." She had always had a prophetic mind and an understanding of history. For me personally the news meant leaving school, leaving Vienna, moving to the western provincial capital Bregenz on Lake Constance, and another year of lessons with my mother. I spent most of the year after that as a "half-boarder" in Marienberg Convent near Bregenz. I have very pleasant memories of this time because I was among children again and because the convent sisters gave me preferential treatment, as I came from the city.

From 1914 to 1918 we were at war. At the age of thirteen I experienced the fall of the Hapsburg Empire quite consciously and with deep consternation. Afterward came hunger, cold, and disease. Somehow we managed to live through this time. School went on much as before. At the end of my fourth year we had to decide whether I should attend the newly founded gymnasium, with eight classes, or the traditional girls' school, with six classes. Both were housed under the same roof. I was one of the few who chose the gymnasium, and many of my classmates dropped out after another two years, so that there were only nine girls in the final year, a situation that gave us many advantages. Then came the crucial decision between two possible careers—the balanced buckets of the childhood vision!—my artistic side leaning toward acting or writing and my professional side toward medicine.

My interest in medicine had started when I was about fifteen years old. I read a touching story about two faithful school friends, one of whom became a doctor. The other married, and they lost touch with each other. One day the child of the young married woman contracted diphtheria. The old doctor in their small town could only look on helplessly. The child was about to suffocate when the school friend appeared, as *dea ex machina*, and saved the child's life at the last minute by a skillful tracheotomy. Nevertheless, at the age of seventeen I was still fairly determined to become an actress.

At that time our teacher of German literature and language started reading Dostoevsky and Tolstoy with us. She herself was a passionate admirer of Tolstoy, and she conveyed her enthusiasm to all of us. An urgent wish grew in me, a wish to imitate the old Russian count and devote my life to the service of the poor and the oppressed. What better way was there than to become a doctor for the poor? At that time I even began to search out the ugliest quarters of beautiful Vienna in order to imagine, with an exaggerated sense of sacrifice, the horrible areas in which I would have my practice later on.

Then came the matriculation examination, and by this time I was determined to study medicine—something more easily said than done! My parents, who had not sent me to primary school for fear that I might be "ruined," shuddered at the thought of seeing me together with men, crossing the threshold of a dissecting room. My father was a relatively high bank official and was very old-fashioned even for those days. Consequently, I was strictly forbidden to study medicine, although curiously enough, my parents would have allowed me to become an actress. My rebellious instincts reached a boiling point, and I was absolutely determined to do exactly what my parents had forbidden me. At first I allowed myself to compromise and registered to study German philology and history at the University of Vienna. I attended the various lectures faithfully, and a semester passed while I continued to hope that my parents would withdraw their veto for the next year. When it eventually became evident, during some heated discussions, that there was no chance of this, I took the reins in my own hands. I registered secretly in medicine for the summer term, meanwhile pretending at home that I was diligently continuing my studies of history and philology. As I would not be of age for five years, I needed to know whether parental permission was required. So I sent three of my friends (a medical student, a law student, and a philosophy student) each to his respective dean's office to inquire about the judicial aspect of the problem. They all returned to reassure me that no one in the office had ever come across this question before.

Thus the summer semester passed, crammed with lectures on medicine and only interrupted occasionally by a lecture on the ancient Romans or Goethe's *Faust*. After all, I had to have something to tell my parents about my studies. When autumn arrived, the situation became critical. The anatomy course was about to begin, and I would scarcely be able to conceal the odor at home. So I took the bull by the horns, and one fine day I explained the true situation to my shocked parents. I told them quite clearly that I intended to earn the money for my medical studies myself. This I did, in fact, by tutoring backward schoolchildren. I also warned my parents that, if they persisted in their veto, I would not lift a finger at home and would only twiddle my thumbs. What could they do but consent? That is how my study of medicine began.

A poor grade in an examination in anatomy cost me a whole year. A number of involved love affairs complicated matters further, so that until the end of my first *Rigorosum* I was not exactly in the best of spirits. However, in the autumn of 1927 a new life began for me in the truest sense of the word. I had decided that no love affairs would deter me from my professional studies, and I began my courses in internal medicine. The chief of the department welcomed me with stern words, the gist of which was that he had had enough trouble with female students and that he categorically forbade any flirting. I was just as annoyed about such unfair and premature reproaches as I was keen to prove them unwarranted, so I pursued my work with enormous diligence and interest. Only a few weeks later the chief Dr. Karl Hitzenberger, who was not so stern after all, invited me to accompany him to a meeting of the medical association. This meeting was to be attended by Professor Wagner von Jauregg, who had just returned from Sweden, where he had received the Nobel Prize. What an experience for a young student! It was only with great difficulty and with influential friends that it was possible to enter the crowded auditorium. The chairman was Professor Eiselsberg, a man with snow-white hair, a pleasant face, and an enchanting manner. After opening the meeting, he announced, "I have the exceptional honor of handing over the chiar to Professor Wagner von

Jauregg." Deafening applause followed, and the Nobel Prize laureate stepped calmly to the chair, continuing the meeting without a change in expression.

Another experience from the time of my first clinical studies has remained clearly in my memory. There was a poor old woman in our ward, deathly pale and almost dead. She had pernicious anemia, and until then no one in Europe had ever succeeded in curing this disease. At this moment the news reached us that two American doctors had fed two similarly terminal patients with liver (raw, cooked, fried, or minced) until they recovered. In a miraculous way the red blood corpuscles had increased from a minimum to a maximum. The head of the department said, "I can't believe it, but of course I will try it out on this poor old woman. Bring the liver and give her as much as possible." Our patient ate liver in every form, and we dutifully and excitedly counted her red blood corpuscles. We saw, at first unbelievingly and then more and more enthusiastically, that the number increased from 1 million to 2, then 3, then 4 million per cubic centimeter. After six weeks she was well! From that time on, I have been a medical optimist, the essence of which is my belief that methods to conquer currently incurable diseases will always be discovered. I had entered the clinic in September. On the day before Christmas, my chief Karl Hitzenberger, who was no longer stern at all, asked me to marry him. As I had foreseen this development, I consented immediately, and we were married on Easter in 1928, at the end of the next semester.

Now a guessing game began among my friends and acquaintances. They laid bets with me on whether I would finish my studies, as I was now married and "taken care of." Most of them were convinced that I would not. My stubborn character came into play again, this time in full force. I had discussed my decision with Karl, and he completely agreed with me. What I had started, I must finish.

My first child, a boy, was born just as I was beginning to prepare for my pathology examination in December of 1929. At the end of the following March I passed the examination with high marks. In June, when I had my pharmacology final, I was pregnant again. The weather was hot, and I was very unwell. The result was a mediocre mark in pharmacology. However, I had cleared this hurdle, and from October to December I took my examinations in internal medicine, pediatrics, psychiatry, skin and venereal diseases, and surgery. Much to the surprise of some of the examiners and students who one month before had not observed my condition, my second child, a girl, was born on January 8.

Because I wanted to prove, just as I had done before, that having children and being a nursing mother did not exclude other activities, I finished the remaining examinations as quickly as possible. It so happened that two of them—medical jurisprudence and hygiene—took place on the same afternoon in two different institutions, which were a long distance apart. During the short pause between the two examinations I went home and breast-fed my daughter. On May 31, 1931, I had won all my bets. On that day I became a doctor of medical science. First I practiced in the clinic, then in the adjacent internal medicine department of the Vienna General Hospital, the least modern of all such institutions. All went well until I was expecting my third child. As I had previously suffered from tubercular pleurisy, I gave up my post at the hospital in the third month of pregnancy and stayed home. My little daughter arrived in 1933.

Conditions in Austria were becoming more and more difficult, and Parliament was dissolved. A type of Fascist government came to power under the leadership of Engelbert Dollfuss. In 1934, only five months after the unsuccessful uprising of the Socialist workers, the putsch by the Austrian Nazis against Dollfuss and his regime took place. The Nazis forced their way into the chancellor's office, shot him down, and entrenched themselves in the government building. At the end of the affair the Nazi ringleaders were hanged and others found their way into Austrian concentration camps, and Kurt Schuschnigg, a former university professor of history who had been minister of education, became the new chancellor. It was to be his privilege to helplessly watch the fall of Austria.

We, at home, still observed these events from the outside. I had begun to do scientific work together with my husband. My father died in 1935, still young. In 1936 my fourth child, a boy, was born. In 1937 Karl was appointed chief medical officer of the Rudolf Hospital. We celebrated New Year's Eve and New Year's Day with good friends in a mood of hectic cheerfulness. What followed was one catastrophe after another.

In February of 1938 Karl was called in to consult the well-known theatrical family Thimig. At the second examination Karl made the surprising diagnosis of psittacosis. The next morning Karl was taken to the Vienna Hospital for Infectious Diseases, where he remained for six weeks in a room next door to that of the celebrated actor Hermann Thimig, who had caught the same disease from his parents. There was no specific treatment. The doctors had to rely on the resistance of the patient's body and restrict themselves to treating the symptoms.

Karl recovered and returned to his hospital and his private practice. As he was an internist of international repute and was popular with the young doctors and nurses, the hostility of the Nazis could be kept within reasonable limits. All the same, we longed to get out of Austria. In March of 1939 we had almost reached our goal. Karl's appointment at the University of California at Los Angeles seemed to be a fact, but the Nazis must have heard of it. An agent of the Gestapo came to demand our passports, and that very day my husband took his bed again with profuse intestinal bleeding, which was the beginning of his fatal disease. Two days after World War II broke out, we got the passports back again—a sheer mockery.

Karl died in September of 1941, at the age of only forty-eight. There I was, left alone with four children between the ages of five and twelve, continually threatened on two sides—the horrors of war and the dictatorship of the Nazis. Even in peacetime the pension for a widow and orphans would not have enabled me to support my children—let alone get them to school and the university, which I finally did. At this point my obstinacy, which people had laughed about earlier, came in handy. At least I had my completed studies to fall back on.

Many doctors had already been called up for military service. Ten days after Karl's death I took over his practice in his former office. At the same time, in order once more to become accustomed to medical work, I ran the outpatient department in the first surgical clinic at the university. I very soon learned more about diagnosis and therapy than I could have done during many years in a hospital in peacetime.

Finally I managed quite successfully. I must add that I could not have done this without the help of my mother—who had at last come to accept my studies—and of very reliable domestic servants. As war slowly approached Vienna, then as bombs dropped and houses went up in flames, and finally as Russian shells blew holes in walls, many patients were grateful that I had not left the distressed city, as had many of my male colleagues. Amid bombs and flames I walked or cycled through the streets to help the sick and injured. Thus my earliest dream of being a doctor for the poor had come true in a different but perhaps more dramatic way. My mother lived in constant fear. Often as I left for a patient's home despite the sirens, she called after me from the window, "Stay here and think of your four children. . . ." In war, however, you have to prove your bravery, especially if you are a woman.

Even in hard times there are always cheerful and happy interludes. My children had inherited my passionate love for the theater, and disregarding air raids and the horrors of war, they turned our large apartment into a theater. During the last days of the war and during the first few years afterward they put on serious and comic plays with the help of a few equally enthusiastic friends. My oldest son was always the producer. He almost went on the stage—and my youngest daughter actually did. After his matriculation, however, he changed his mind and went into medicine. Today he is an established university lecturer, and his son is a student of medicine.

My children's passion for the theater eased for them the horrors of war, which finally came to an end. Among ruins, upset trams, and the dead bodies of men and horses, the first Russian troops marched into Vienna. The occupation began and with it new problems of hunger and privation. Essential materials were almost entirely lacking. In 1945 a dysentery epidemic terrorized the city. I managed to get hold of some precious sulfonamides, which saved the lives of many of my patients. A month before the end of the war my surgery was destroyed by bombs. As soon as the sirens permitted, my patients flocked back in crowds to clear away the rubble. For some time I had to work in my other flat in the same house. But soon all these problems were solved, and in the autumn of that year I moved back into my old office.

I was not yet at peace with myself, for I had come to realize that it was wrong to keep out of politics entirely. The enemy had taken over the populace like a flock of sheep. Why? Because too few well-disposed people had taken an interest in politics and politicians. I did not want to make the same mistake, so I decided to join a party in Austria. The only one I considered right for me was the Socialist party. I had not forgotten Tolstoy or the Austrian doctor Victor Adler, both of whom had seen the misery of the industrial workers at the turn of the century and had become enthusiastic socialists. I have enjoyed working for the Socialist party and have done so for many years in medical and social fields. For twenty-one years I have written weekly medical and social articles for the women's magazine *Die Frau*. In this way my early ambitions in the field of art have also come true.

Meanwhile I did not forget medical politics. For some years I edited the *Vienna Medical Journal*, and I spent many long evenings at the board meetings of the Vienna Board of Medicine. In 1947, as national corresponding secretary in our newly founded Association of Austrian Women Doctors, in company with Lore Antoine, I attended the first postwar congress of the Medical Women's International Association (MWIA) held in the Netherlands. In our position as Austrian doctors it was still rather difficult to get into contact with the MWIA and especially with Dutch colleagues. The prejudice that followed the German occupation was still very strong. However, we finally succeeded in regaining their understanding and friendship.

New problems arose abroad. In 1956 Hungary revolted against the Communist regime. Then the Russian army invaded the country, and the revolt ended in blood and terror. People fled to Austria in large numbers. At that time we women doctors organized Aid to Hungary. We were helped by generous monetary contributions from our American colleagues. At first we offered our help to Hungarian women doctors only, but later we supported their families, as well. We arranged for their accommodations and clothing and helped them until they were able to emigrate to the United States or to settle in Austria. We ourselves looked for appropriate housing, bought clothing and smoothed over difficulties between Hungarian lodgers and Austrian landlords. As I prefer practical tasks to attending theoretical discussions, this work never seemed too much for me. I believe that a great many of these Hungarian refugees will have good memories of Austrian women doctors.

For many years I was vice-president of the Association of Austrian Medical Women. I then succeeded Lore Antoine as president in 1974. I have now dropped all such jobs except for the management of our pensioners' home, which we opened about two years ago. I nevertheless continue with my purely medical work, which I still love in spite of my seventy years.

Helena Sibelius
b. April 24, 1905

My grandfather Ernst Fabritius was a violinist, composer, and farmer. My father Harry Fabritius grew up in a rural environment and is said to have been called on to help when he was a youngster if one of grandfather's tenants was cut or hurt. Father knew early in life that he would become a physician. He eventually held the chair of psychiatry at the University of Helsinki and was also a clever neurologist.

As a young doctor, in the summer of 1903, father was a spa physician in a charming small town on the Gulf of Finland. There he got to know his future wife, an art student, who was spending her summer taking the waters with her parents. My mother's parents came from St. Petersburg (today Leningrad) where my grandfather W. Friedlaender was a stockbroker. The young couple married, and my mother completely adopted Finland as her native land for the rest of her life. I was their first child. When I was two, a little brother arrived but he died the same year. My sister, who was born in 1909, became a botanist.

My father taught me early to know the world of the sick. One of my clearest childhood memories is of a visit with him to the children's department at the surgical hospital of the University of Helsinki. I must have been four years old. I remember well the large, light hospital room and the small patients in their plaster casts.

Around this time one of the first woman physicians in Finland lived in our home. She became our lifelong friend and added to the medical atmosphere. My own dolls were lined up in their beds as in a hospital, and each one was named after a patient or a member of the hospital staff.

In 1910, when I was five, father was granted a scholarship for three years of study abroad. The whole family, along with our Finnish housekeeper, moved to Berlin, where we lived for the next two years. The most important experience in my life at that time was entering a German school. Mother took me to school in the morning and called for me in the afternoon. Her beautiful, large eyes were my security. In 1912 we moved from Berlin to Vienna, where father continued his studies, which included the lectures of Sigmund Freud. I continued my schooling in Vienna.

When we returned to Finland, in 1913, father entered me in a Finnish-language school. We spoke Swedish at home, as mother had learned this language very well. Our country in those days was very definitely bilingual, and a considerable proportion of the educated class spoke Swedish. I remember that father's relatives regarded him as slightly odd for placing me and my sister in a Finnish school. However, it opened up a new world for me.

Father had his reception room at home, and patients were a familiar sight to me. The first Christmas party was at the hospital. Father also took me to see autopsies performed; he wanted us to learn early to view life and death in a natural light. Nevertheless, during these years I did not think about becoming a physician, nor did I have other plans.

By 1923, when I matriculated, I had to decide on a career. It was by then almost self-evident, and I told father of my intention to follow in his footsteps. He was a man with a sense of humor; so he said, "Don't you know that on a woman white is beautiful only as a bridal gown, a nurse's uniform, or a nightie?" He had no objections, however, and I began my medical studies.

My future husband was my classmate Jussi Sibelius. His father Christian Sibelius had held the chair in psychiatry at the University of Helsinki before my father. The composer Jean Sibelius was my husband's uncle. When we began to plan our marriage, during our student years, I decided to give up the exacting profession of a physician. I considered that it would be difficult for me to combine marriage and medicine. So I graduated with a B.S. in 1928, majoring in chemistry, after which I worked in a laboratory for some years. We married in 1929. Later on, we moved to the country, where my husband was manager of the Littala Glass factories.

World War II broke out in 1939. Finland became involved in December of that year and fought what is called the Winter War against Russia. Jussi volunteered for active service. Our war ended on March 13, 1940. A few days later I learned that my husband had fallen on March 9. I shall always remember the night following that day. I was not in the habit of crying. I was proud of the sacrifice my husband had made. But then my thoughts turned to myself. I was the mistress of a large home in a rural district. I did not want to stay there alone. What should I do? I was educated as a chemist and could return to my former profession. It suddenly became clear to me that I would prefer to continue the medical studies I had begun seventeen years earlier.

I moved back to Helsinki to my parents. This time my father was very happy about my choice and followed my studies closely. My parents' home was in the psychiatric hospital, which put me in a position to follow hospital work closely. My fellow students were far younger than I, but we got along well.

I graduated as a physician in 1947, at the age of forty-two, and began my psychiatric specialist studies in the clinic headed by my father. He died in 1948.

As mother and I were very close to each other, we made a new small home. I received my specialist certification in psychiatry in 1950.

I had gradually to obtain a permanent position. Fate again intervened in my life. The post of psychiatric department head was vacant at the National Board of Health. I applied and was appointed in 1952. I was then a medical counselor (civil-service title). A new Mental Diseases Act had been passed in Finland in the same year. My work included its implementation, the development of hospital and noninstitutional therapy, and numerous other tasks of civil-service office in the psychiatric sector, for example, the Abortion Act.

I was then the only woman to hold the post of department chief in the National Board of Health. In my own opinion, I got on well with my male colleagues. There were more difficulties over the fact that psychiatry seventeen years ago was not so highly esteemed a speciality as it now is.

I retired in 1968 after completing my tour of duty. Despite the numerous difficulties, I have often missed the work.

I have never had any really special hobbies. After my retirement I began to take a few private patients. The contrast with administrative work was considerable. Thus, I find myself once again, with a new phase of life ahead of me.

Sellina Gualco
b. May 23, 1905

My father was a Piedmontese from Alessandria, and my mother came from Turin, although she was born in Buenos Aires, where her father was a pharmacist owning seven chemist shops. Father was an engineer. My parents' third and youngest child, I was a precocious youngster. At the age of four I attended the elementary school, where I learned to read and write and do simple arithmetic. At six I often answered the questions the teacher asked the older children. School was a great pleasure for me. In this elementary school I always had high grades and was able to skip several classes, so that at ten I was already in the sixth form. Latin and Greek were my favorite subjects, and I could translate from one into the other without any intermediary language. Much of my success with these classical languages was due to my teacher, the famous Latinist and Hellenist Professor Galante Garrone. My greatest inclination was undoubtedly toward literary and humanistic studies, so much so that at fourteen I was able to take the higher-education certificate and at seventeen the higher-education classics diploma.

At eighteen I began university studies, but instead of enrolling in the Faculty of Literature, as my teachers advised and my father desired, I enrolled in the Faculty of Medicine. My decision to study medicine was not a very difficult one because I already had an intense interest in pharmacy and I liked the idea of following the profession of my grandfather. I had three additional basic reasons for this decision. The first was the influence exerted on me by my high-school professor of natural sciences Rota Rossi, a very cultured man who decreed that my intelligence was essentially "masculine" and my intellectual maturity distinctly scientific. The second reason was the modern and unconventional character of my mother. Her mind was open to all new ideas. She was full of life and in favor of cutting free from traditions, so she very willingly saw a daughter undertake medical studies, which at that time represented a real rebellion against the old belief that the woman should be bound to the study of the arts for the sake of atavism and ancestral obedience. My third reason was the example of one of my high-school companions, who had chosen to study medicine. She was two years older than me, an excellent student, and I was perhaps a bit jealous of her.

Because of all these considerations I enrolled in medicine despite the objections of my father, who thought that I had made the decision too quickly. I remember leaving home, accompanied by my mother, with a stamped piece of paper on which I applied for entry to the University of Genoa, where I was to take my university courses. The paper was still blank; my father had insisted on filling it out for me, as he wrote beautifully, but he had not done so because he still wanted me to enroll in literature. Instead, in the university secretariat, I myself filled in the questionnaire and, with the support of my mother, enrolled in medicine. My father was forced to accept what we had done, and although he never encouraged me very much with my studies because of his antifeminist attitude, he was very proud of my scholastic and career successes. There were some financial problems because my father was always a civil servant, and my parents had to make sacrifices to allow me to complete my studies.

I began my university courses in medicine at the age of eighteen and followed them through with interest and diligence. In 1928, at the age of twenty-three, I obtained my degree in medicine and surgery at the University of Genoa, with the first prize for the best graduate of the year.

My leaning toward the field of endocrinology began in my fourth year in medicine, when I worked in the wards of the Medical Clinic, of Genoa, directed by Professor Nicola Pende, the founder of the Italian school of endocrinology. In the same year I published my first paper on female hormonal anomalies in the field of growth and constitutional illnesses. I have continued to concentrate on these studies throughout my career.

Immediately after graduation I was made an assistant at the Medical Clinic. At the age of thirty I was transferred from Genoa to Rome, having been called to the university professorship by my teacher Professor Pende. I continued my research and as a result was soon teaching special medical pathology, endocrinology, and orthogenesis (the science of curing growth illnesses) at the University of Rome.

In order to obtain qualifications for teaching, I published more than 150 papers, all involving application of the field of endocrinology to the various sectors of human life. I never married, and perhaps for this reason I was always able to work full time and with the greatest dedication. Having acquired my academic titles, I developed my own methods of teaching the university courses for students, doctors, teachers, and directors of didactics.

I always participated in national and international congresses, especially those connected with the national and the international medical women's associations, often in the capacity of official rapporteur. At present I am carrying on intense professional activity as consultant in the area of endocrine diseases.

I can honestly say that I have never encountered any great difficulty in making my career, but I believe this is mostly because I have always tried to obtain advancement after thorough preparation and increased knowledge. My viewpoint regarding women in medicine is slightly skeptical at the moment. I believe that today the women who study medicine rarely have the drive that existed in my epoch. I think, however, that this phenomenon is part of the general frivolity with which the youth of today of both sexes undertake their careers. If I were once again embarking on a career, I would still choose the medical profession, but I do not know if I would be capable, owing to the times in which we now live, of throwing myself into it with the same enthusiasm as I did fifty years ago. My sex has never represented a serious handicap in my career, but I think this is attributable to the seriousness and honesty with which I have always carried out my tasks.

UNITED STATES

Frances H. Gitelson
b. June 19, 1905

I was born in a small suburban community about ten miles from the heart of Chicago. My parents moved to this area when they knew I was on the way. They bought a three-bedroom house near the school that I would be attending, and it was in this house that I arrived. The neighborhood was not densely populated at the time, and it was a typical middle-class, white Protestant community. I was the elder of my parents' two children.

My father was a relatively uneducated man, having quit school at ten years of age, when his own father died. He was clever with his hands; so in order to help support the family, he eventually learned the machinist trade and went to work in the reaper works of the International Harvester Company. He stayed with that company until he retired at sixty-five, having gradually worked his way up until he became foreman of the experimental department. He invented several machine changes, but the patent rights in each case reverted to the company. Thus, despite his promotions, he never earned much. However, through a profit-sharing plan he was able to lay away some money. We were never without food, housing, clothing, and some luxuries, but we always had to be careful.

My mother had finished high school before her marriage, at which time she was working as a deaconess in a Methodist church, having graduated from the Deaconess Seminary Training School, which was then associated with North-western University. The second oldest of five children, she came from a middle-class western background. She was religious and took a very active part in the church activities in the community. She organized Sunday-school classes, missionary societies, and Christmas pageants with enthusiasm. My father sup-ported her in these matters but participated very little. He had been reared a Catholic, and had his father lived, my father would probably have entered the priesthood. However, once his father was gone, he showed little religious interest.

During World War I my mother acted as a substitute teacher in the public schools. That gave her the incentive to teach there on a regular basis, so she went back to her studies for enough semesters to qualify for teaching in Chicago. There she taught until my father's retirement. Her main interest in teaching lay in the fact that she wanted my brother and me to have a college education, and this would not have been possible on my father's income alone.

As for the beginnings of my career, they started early and were very much influenced by my mother. In fact, I have often thought in later years that I was fulfilling one of her ambitions, but at the time of my decision, this was not apparent to me. When I was about twelve, as mother and I were working together one day in the kitchen, she asked me what I would like to do when I grew up. I answered that I was not sure but I thought it might be interesting to be a nurse. I have a vague feeling that I had once heard her say that she would have liked to be a nurse. Anyway, her response to my reply was to say, "Why don't you become a doctor and give the orders instead of receiving them?" From that moment on, there was never a consideration of any other profession on my part. My high-school and college studies were all oriented toward the sciences, which I knew would be required for entrance into medical school. For a while I toyed with the idea of becoming a medical missionary. This was during a short period when I wished to be religious. This idea did not last very long, and ever since then I have been anything but religious. It was as if I accepted my mother's wish regarding medicine but rebelled at identifying with her in religious outlook.

One way of getting into the city was by electric elevated train. The track passed the Cook County Hospital. I recall the many times that I used to say to myself when passing this structure, "Someday I shall intern there." And that is just what I did.

My high-school grades were above average, my college marks a high B plus, and my medical school work was good enough to earn me membership in the medical honorary society, Omega Alpha. I graduated from Northwestern University Medical School in 1932. It was the only medical school to which I had applied, and I was accepted without difficulty in the second class of women to attend that school. We were not very well received at first, as the men thought that our presence would restrict them. It did, of course, but all for the best because there was less wasted time. In addition, it turned out that women students seemed to elevate the general academic level.

Between college and medical school I spent a year working in a hospital emergency room doing X-rays, giving anesthetics for minor troubles, and assisting the doctors who were handling emergencies. This was to make certain that medicine ought to be my career.

My education was financed in part by my parents and in part by my working during the summers and taking out loans, which I paid back later on. I graduated at the end of the depression, when things were tough, but I was able to get by by being careful with my money.

During my eighteen months of internship I began to realize that I did not want to specialize in obstetrics, gynecology, or pediatrics, which were the usual choices for women. After one month in the Psychiatric Hospital, I became truly interested in trying to understand people and their actions, so much so that I exchanged a month in obstetrics for a second month in psychiatry. This was something unheard of, and I enjoyed it tremendously. I then arranged to have my residency in psychiatry at the Institute for Juvenile Research in Chicago. One day when I had time to go to the library, I happened to read an article on sibling rivalry in an early issue of the *International Journal of Psychoanalysis*. It seemed to answer so many questions for me about my difficult relationship with my only sibling that I almost at once decided that this was the field of work where I wanted to be. I had been cast into the role of caretaker very early, and that has been my chief role in life ever since. I started out taking care of my baby brother, then became the neighborhood baby-sitter, and eventually became a psychiatrist. That I had my ambivalences toward this role goes without saying, but for the most part I have found it rewarding and satisfying. Going into psychiatry was a natural development without any of the glamorous, altruistic reasons that seem to have propelled so many others into this field. My parents had little understanding of the specialty of psychiatry. My mother probably understood better than my father, but they allowed me to choose my own path and to develop it as I wished. It soon became clear to me that psychiatry and psychoanalysis would allow me to be a caretaker without the responsibility of having to deal with daily life-and-death decisions. In my own estimation, despite excellent marks, my clinical sense was not of the best, but I did have human consideration for the patient as an individual, which a lot of my colleagues in that large charity hospital lacked.

At the Institute of Juvenile Research, Max Gitelson was a senior member of the staff, and he and I soon became friends and had many discussions about psychoanalysis. While he was in analysis with Franz Alexander, I left for Boston to do my third year of residency at the old Boston Psychiatric Hospital. At the same time I attended all the lectures I could at the Boston Psychoanalytic Institute. Then Max came east, and we married and returned to Chicago. There I went into analysis for four years, at the end of which time I had my only child. Max went into analysis again but with a different analyst, and we both completed our training at the Chicago Institute. From then on, analysis was almost a way of life. Max became a training analyst, and I followed in 1952.

By 1961 he was president of the International Psychoanalytic Association. After he died, in 1965, I attended the Amsterdam congress, and following this I took a trip around the Greek isles and became a close friend of Leo Rangels. Leo was to become president of the international, on which occasion he asked me to be honorary secretary. Apparently, I had been able to prove that I could work and achieve even after my husband's death. Since my term as secretary I have served on a number of important committees in the American Psychoanalytic Association. I owe a great deal to Leo for getting me started once again. It has been a way for me to continue involvement with Max's interests and in a way make them my own. Life has become much more bearable and possible because of this. Max had been a supportive figure always, although, as was the custom in years past, his career came ahead of mine. This went on without rancor or hostility on my part, as I experienced a great deal of satisfaction from his achievements. I hope that I was able to be as supportive to him as he was to me.

On looking back, it seems to me that, being the straightforward, direct sort of person I am, I made a decision early in life and marched on to its completion without any fuss or frills.

Patricia Massey

b. July 5, 1905

Graaff-Reinet, the little Karroo town where I was born, has much to offer and has played an important part in my life. Founded in 1786, it is the fourth oldest town in South Africa. It nestles in a protecting curve of the Sundays River, under the foothills of the Sneeuwberg, the gigantic and vast range of mountains that divides the great Karroo. Graaff-Reinet is the center of the wool industry. The town, tranquil and secure, is known as the Gem of the Karroo.

I remember with nostalgia the days of my very early childhood, when I spent holidays on a typical Karroo sheep farm. We would be awakened at 4:30 a.m. with coffee and rusks and bidden to accompany the farmer on his rounds of the farm. On these rounds he would inspect the fences, looking for holes in them, watch for jackal tracks, check water holes and dams, collect sick lambs, and generally see how things fared. I will never forget the exhilaration of galloping in the early dawn over the wide Karroo and watching the sun rise over the far horizon and mount into the already hot sky. Nor will I forget the pleasure on our return of the enormous breakfast of lamb chops grilled outdoors over wood coals, fried eggs, and rice—all this at about 7:30 a.m. All outdoor work ceased by 10:30 a.m., and all the laborers had to find work that could be done under shelter from the heat of the sun. Not until after 3:30 p.m. did anyone go out into the sunshine again unless it was for a very special reason.

The vast plains, so hot in summer and so bitterly cold in winter, and the steep hills and mountains, rising to the summit of the Sneeuwberg, have given all of us who lived there a sense of the immensity of Africa, its glory and its beauty. Its demand on our lives for service, hard work, and dedication is one of the messages I caught in my youth, and I was quite determined to become a medical doctor. Especially perhaps because there had been so many physicians in my family, I felt that only something as worthwhile as medicine would fit me into the picture of so grand and gigantic a setting. My father was a general practitioner who had come to Graaff-Reinet from Ireland in 1902. His paternal uncle had been a doctor in Eire, and his younger brother became a doctor and joined the colonial service. My mother was born in Graaff-Reinet and was of German descent. One of her brothers became a physician, and an uncle on her mother's side became the first pediatric specialist in South Africa.

I was the eldest of four children. Having decided to study medicine at the age of eight years, I even refused to have music lessons because I maintained that a doctor was too busy to play the piano. I was strong and healthy, active and energetic, and willing to tackle anything. Good at games and sports, I got things done quickly and was always very practical. I loved people and needed them.

My father believed firmly in higher education for women and was always telling us that he would not die a wealthy man but that he would see each of us through a university degree if we so wished and could work hard enough to earn it. On the lonely farms and in the villages and small towns he had met many frustrated, badly educated, dependent maiden aunts and older sisters who had never had any opportunity to get an education nor any hope of independence. As a result, he was instrumental in encouraging and helping many a woman to strike out for herself and go off to a training college, hospital, or even a senior school to better chances in the employment field. He smoothed the way for her, convincing parents, brothers, and even nephews to accept the idea and assist the woman in every way. Thus the incentive in my home as a child was positive. Higher education was considered essential to my future. Medicine was my only aim, but whenever I said I wanted to study medicine, my father would dismiss the thought with, "It is far too hard a life for a woman." However, I managed during the Spanish-influenza epidemic of 1918 to help in a pharmacy to dispense and do other useful jobs for the chemist until I was called home to do duty at the telephone for my father.

Once I had eventually gotten my father's permission, I had no difficulty in gaining admission to medicine. In the classrooms, lecture halls, and laboratories I encountered no problems with regard to my sex, for the University of Cape Town has always been "liberal" and women have constituted 25 percent of each medical class. There were five or six other women in my class, and we mixed freely with our male colleagues. My internship did not present any problems, either, and I enjoyed it all to the fullest. My father then began to encourage me to specialize, but he was rather upset to find that I had chosen obstetrics and gynecology. He said that the work would always be demanding, with long hours and sleepless nights, but this did not deter me in any way, and I cannot say that at any stage I met with any prejudice because of my sex. In fact, to the contrary, I was encouraged because of the speciality I had chosen. It was evidently by then accepted as suitable for women. I never had any difficulty getting the appointments I wanted, either overseas or on my return to South Africa.

I never married. In my day we could scarcely "have our cake and eat it, too." The offers of marriage that I did receive did not fit into my scheme of things. My chosen career at that time was all-important to me. I practiced privately, with part-time consultant appointments at the teaching hospitals and at the university. Since retirement from these I am kept busy with family planning clinics and part-time work at nonteaching hospitals.

I am strongly in favor of women in medicine and have encouraged many who have been keen to study medicine. I shall certainly continue to do so.

Happily, the higher qualifications required for specialist practice are within the grasp of women today, and there are better-paid registrar posts available. Women no longer need to make such great sacrifices to attain higher degrees. Also, today there are many well-paid full-time posts available.

I would most certainly select medicine if I had to make the choice again. I have no regrets and have enjoyed every minute of it all—and I still do so. It has been a very satisfactory and satisfying life, and I am truly grateful that I was allowed to follow so useful and happy a career.

Rosa Lee Nemir
b. July 16, 1905

I was born in Waco, Texas, the second child of David and Emma Nemir. I was welcomed even though I was a girl because my brother had died of diphtheria many months before. Five children were born after me.

My very earliest memories are those of a loving father and mother and of feeling very important to them. I remember singing songs and reciting poems as a young child in the rural town of Clifton, Texas, where we moved because my father found it a good place for his dry-goods store. Often I was featured for my father's special friends; he would lift me up onto the counter, where I sang and was frequently rewarded with a nickel. These coins were spent on my friends who came home from school with me. Soon I had quite a group, requiring more hard candy and cookies. When I ran out of money, I charged these to my father. It was a standing joke in the family that a four-year-old girl would think of such a maneuver, and I remember it all vividly. I was not physically punished, but I soon learned the difference between my rights and those of my parents, as well as the importance of earning my own funds for extravagances. These qualities I have to this day—a desire to give to my friends, independence, and a tendency toward what many would consider extravagance.

The next move, when I was approximately six years old, was to another small rural town. The trip required a change of trains in Dallas, Texas, where my mother had to cope with four young children. I recollect playing on the train with my mother's large pocketbook, which contained her jewelry—a dowry from her parents when she left Lebanon to come with my father to America. In Dallas, where we disembarked to change trains, my mother's jewelry was stolen from the basin beside her when she stooped to wash her children's hands. It was believed that someone who knew of the contents of the pocketbook might have followed her from the previous train. My guilt feelings in this connection are obvious. I well remember mother's consternation and grief and even more vividly my father's attempts to console her: "My darling, you know that I can't replace all those gems right away, but I'll try. Or would you like a piano now and jewelry later, whenever it's possible?" I can never forget their mutual decision to buy a piano so that I could learn music properly.

I recollect entertaining the British minister and his wife at tea. It was a real English afternoon tea, which no one else served and which delighted them. This was possible because my mother had been educated in an English Presbyterian junior college in Beirut. I also recall my school, in which I always did well. This, to my astonishment, made my classmates jealous, a fact that probably had a permanent influence on me, for in all my learning years I never again admitted to high marks or high ranking but quietly concealed such matters. I can recall my father's large rambling store and my frequent visits with him there.

When I was about nine or ten, we lived for one year only in a very small rural district where the farmers had an abundant cotton crop. This was obviously a lucrative area for my father's business while he was deciding on a permanent place to settle and rear his four children. The fifth child Fred was born here. My most vivid memory of this year was a conversation—not meant for my ears—between my parents one night. Father had just returned from a scouting trip to find a permanent place of residence. He told mother that he must decide between two possibilities. One was a thriving, booming town where he would be sure to succeed financially and do well, but he did not consider it a good place to bring up children. The other possibility was Austin, the capital of Texas, where there were good schools and a large university so that they could educate all us children inexpensively but where they would never get rich, just make a comfortable living. I have always remembered their mutual choice: for their children.

When we moved to Austin, there were many more children in the classes, with a great diversity of racial and ethnic background. In many respects, the move to Austin achieved just what my parents had anticipated. It was a fertile field for education, being a university town and dominated by the University of Texas and the state capital. Our teachers were often graduate university students, supplementing their incomes by working in the Austin public schools.

These schools had a farsighted program that included physiology in the sixth grade. This subject captured my imagination and sparked my interest in medicine as a career. In high school, well-organized biology courses further strengthened my professional resolve. The biology teacher Miss Sarah Brooks became a special friend. Years later, when I had entered medical school, she reminded me that I had seriously declared my intentions to study medicine when I was fourteen years old and had said at the time that I meant to go to the Johns Hopkins University medical school.

Another memorable teacher taught eight-grade civics. As part of the course, a court trial was set up for performance in the junior-high-school auditorium, where about 300 to 400 children assembled once daily. I was chosen as one of the lawyers. The logic of the law and the importance of correct use of language and voice had great appeal for me. Temporarily I considered law as a profession, only to discard it quickly, in part because I ascertained that women lawyers were treated almost with contempt and certainly not with fairness. The civics course, however, led to my active participation in high-school public speaking and debate, and I represented Austin High School in the state competition, twice coming up to the semifinals. I learned early the value of clear thinking, of careful organization, of give and take in discussions, and of good public-speaking techniques. These experiences in public speaking have served as an invaluable background for my many years of teaching and numerous public appearances, including those on radio and television.

My childhood in Austin was happy in many ways. I had a close personal relationship with my parents. Being the oldest of six—the youngest was born in Austin when I was thirteen—I was given the responsibility of being the family helper and the pacesetter for the other children. My father found my services in his store on Saturdays very useful. He paid me for this work, as he would have any other person. I was proud to be earning money, and I tried to save it for my advanced education but was often tempted to spend it on my friends for ice creams. When I was about fifteen, during one of the quiet moments in the store, my father asked me, "What will you do when you grow up?" "Oh, Dad," I said, "I have decided to be a doctor." "Good," he replied. "You should be prepared to earn a living in case you become a widow or need to work for other reasons." This mark of his approval gave me comfort, but the die had been cast long before and could never have been changed.

We were all churchgoers, and we attended the First Southern Presbyterian Church. In young-people's groups, such as the Christian Endeavour Society, I was often the leader in various projects, as I was in the choir. The minister, the Reverand John Minter, had a great influence on my spiritual life. He was quiet, loving, and deeply religious. His daughter Catherine, who later became a nurse and went to Johns Hopkins with me, was my closest friend.

My summers were spent in West Texas with my uncle, whose home was in ranching country. I came to enjoy the wide-open spaces of Texas and to love the earth and those who tended it. To this day my garden is a very important part of my life. My uncle and aunt were very influential in my emotional life, for they loved me very much, as I did them. My aunt considered me her daughter and talked to me more intimately than my mother did. My uncle regarded me as a sort of business partner, asking me to compose and type his letters and visit his farms on business errands.

After graduating from Austin High School as valedictorian in 1922, I attended the University of Texas. I enrolled as a premedical student and spent four delightful years at the university, where I received excellent scientific preparation for medical school. I also took economics with Dr. Ruth Allen, my friend and earlier Sunday-school teacher. Probably, in a very quiet way, she strengthened my belief in the importance of women's expressing themselves through their own industry and through utilization of their talents to the fullest. She was one of the earliest feminists I have known.

In the midst of the 1918 influenza epidemic, my youngest sister Aline was born. Both she and my mother almost died from influenza, contracted a few days before the delivery. I remember so well my father's great concern and sorrow, as well as his private talks with me about my mother and her survival and about the little baby who came home ahead of her. We had to feed her with a bottle. On one occasion, while feeding, she became cyanotic, collapsed, and almost died in my arms. However, these near brushes with death were not what motivated me to study medicine; I had already decided two years previously.

College days in my home town at the University of Texas were very happy ones. For my junior and senior years I was a laboratory instructor in first-year chemistry, a privilege I especially appreciated because it provided generous funds to be banked for my medical-school education. The choice of medical school was never a problem. Someone had called Johns Hopkins University and its medical school to my attention. It was known for its liberal and optimistic attitude toward women candidates, and I decided that it was the school for me, although I might easily have obtained a full-tuition scholarship elsewhere.

Leaving for medical school was a great event. It was my first time away from home for such a long period, my first time in the East, and my longest, most expensive undertaking. I had earned enough money for the first half of my first year. My father had a serious talk with me before my departure, encouraging me but reminding me that I was the oldest of six, all of whom should have a college education. He suggested that the three oldest children were secure in his care but asked me to help with the two youngest in return for his assistance with my medical education if anything should happen to him. I happily agreed and felt proud that I was so entrusted. The aid to my brother and sister was never needed.

My departure for medical school—one week in advance of enrollment to permit time for getting acquainted with Baltimore—was an event to remember. There must have been a dozen people or so—friends, my siblings, and my mother—gathered at the train station to see me off. When the train pulled out, I was waving good-bye and looking for my mother, who was nowhere to be seen. Suddenly she emerged from behind a post, where she had been weeping. This was the first time I fully appreciated what my leaving meant to my dear, quiet mother. Her desire that I realize my life goals must have enabled her to contain her feelings until that moment.

Johns Hopkins medical school was always unusual in its approach to medical education. My class was the experimental one for unstructured education. No assignments were given, nor were there any examinations except at the end of the second and the senior years. No monitoring of study nor guidance of any kind was done. Not because of this but rather because I wished to enrich myself in a broader sense, I decided for the first time in my life that I would deliberately not make an effort to excell academically; instead, I would attend all the worthwhile musical and theatrical events in Baltimore—and this I did.

I should mention two obstacles to my progress in medical school, one financial and the other physical. In neither instance did it ever occur to me that I ought to take time out. On returning from my first year in Baltimore, I discovered that my father had suffered serious financial reverses because of the approaching depression. My last check from home had really been loaned to my father by our neighbor, who sensed his difficulty and went to him saying, "We want to educate Rosa Lee in medical school." Thereafter, I signed notes each year, and these amounted to $10,000 at 6 percent interest, by graduation in 1930. I was able to repay all the principal with the interest after many years and was then told that the money lent to me had been a good investment; had it been banked, it would have been lost in the 1932 bank closure.

The second obstacle occurred in the summer after my second year at Hopkins. I was typing a graduate thesis, when suddenly I became aware that I could not see well. Various consultations with ophthalmologists failed to give more than the vague diagnosis: "interstitial keratitis of unknown etiology." At Hopkins I was told the same thing and advised to stay out of medical school for one year because I would need to wear dark glasses for at least six months to protect the dilated right eye, with no assurance that the left would remain unaffected. I requested the chance to try the third year using one eye and was granted permission. For most of this important year I did wear glasses, but I managed very well and was delighted that the left eye was spared.

Internship in the San Francisco University Hospital gave me a view of the West for which I shall be forever grateful. The West had a freshness and an unspoiled and healthy friendliness that I found invigorating.

New York, where I completed my training in 1931 and 1932 as an intern and assistant resident in pediatrics at Bellevue Hospital, had such a different atmosphere. It was a conglomerate of many races and languages and a center for music and theater—and there I acquired a first-hand knowledge of poverty, in part because of the Bellevue patient population and in part because of the depression.

Shortly afterward I met Elias J. Audi, a strong man with faith in himself, a belief in the goodness of humanity, and a clear idea of the sort of woman he wanted to marry. I had no intention of marrying anyone, having decided I could not do justice to both my career and marriage as I conceived of it, with my mother and her devotion to her family for an example. Many an argument ensued between Elias and me until finally he agreed to accept my major premise of never giving up medicine and we both promised to make every effort to achieve a happy home life. This is how it was to be!

My success in combining a medical career with marriage is in part a result of my husband's support and encouragement and in part because of my determination to give generously of myself in building a home and family. I must admit that I gave up fun and personal pleasure for the sake of the family and often for social reasons, such as constant entertaining on a fairly large scale, which was my husband's delight. In time, I was richly rewarded by my husband's friends and social contacts, who gave me love and attention far beyond that received by most spouses.

In all honesty, I must say that I made choices in favor of my family, refusing certain positions because of the possible jeopardy to my personal relations with my husband and children. One example was a top position in the City of New York Health Department, which I won in 1936 through the civil-service examination. Nevertheless, I regret the loss of none of these opportunities and I am grateful for my family life, my husband, children, and grandchildren.

Yes, there was plenty of prejudice against women in medicine. This was obvious in salaries, in positions, in advancements, and even in the original internship, where only two positions were open to women regardless of the worth of the candidates. I rarely protested but determined to perform always in as superior a fashion as possible, in part for the sake of the women who would follow me. In every way I could, I tried to make it easier for my young sisters in medicine. This is how and why I became so active in the American Medical Women's Association and its various collateral and allied associations.

It was a struggle to have children during the war years in the early 1940s. The medical schools required more work from the faculty in this period. It was hard to obtain household help and to travel to and from my home in the country, where the children were comfortable. The rationing of gasoline and the curtailment of vacation time added to the multiple woes for a physician-mother. I believe that at no time did I fail to give a generous measure of service as a faculty member of New York University Medical School. My eight-year-old daughter, so impressed with the importance of my medical contribution, used to urge me to go overseas and take care of the wounded soldiers. I think, as this suggests, that my children were partners in my career and understood my activities in medicine.

Since the war years, I have continued to serve full time as a teacher of pediatrics for all levels from medical students to house staff and research fellows specializing in chest diseases. As a clinician, I have worked on the Children's Chest Service at Bellevue Hospital throughout the years. For ten years I served as director of the two children's tuberculosis laboratories, furnishing the background and guidelines for research in the treatment of tuberculosis during the crucial years of establishing the role of chemotherapy for this disease. Since 1960, as director of the Children's Chest Clinic of Bellevue Hospital, I have enjoyed giving care and guidance to many underprivileged ghetto children and their families. I have derived much satisfaction from watching these young persons grow up into good citizens, with understanding and good management of their various problems.

For a short period of four years the New York Infirmary in New York City, Elisabeth Blackwell's hospital, claimed part of my time and teaching endeavors as director of pediatric education and research. Many of the house staff were foreign doctors, from such places as the Philippines, Korea, India, Pakistan, China, Japan, and South America. My ten years' experience as professor of pediatrics in the graduate school at New York University was most valuable in helping me set up programs useful to these foreigners as they adapted to American medicine.

I must devote a few words concerning my role in the community as a wife and mother. I very soon discovered that the mothers of my children's friends were involved in some sort of community service in Brooklyn Heights, where we lived. I thought I owed it to my children to give them some reason to be proud of me as their mother Mrs. E. J. Audi, not only as a physician Dr. Rosa Lee Nemir. Thus much time and effort went into serving as a member of boards of directors and a committee member for such things as kindergarten societies, settlement-house work, schools, and cultural institutions. In many of these areas I was known only as Mrs. Audi, and many of my fellow workers were unaware that I was a professional woman. I enjoyed the participation and the associations developed in these activities. Indeed, a part of myself was expressed in them. On retirement, I may well intensify my work in this field.

Maria Hallgrimsdottir
b. August 21, 1905

I was born in Iceland in the new house that my parents had just built. My father was one of two sons of a farmer whose wife died in childbirth at the age of twenty-eight. My mother's father was also a farmer and, in addition, a county sheriff and shipowner. He had many employees, all of whom lived most of their lives in his home. Five of his nine children were daughters, of whom my mother was the youngest. Two of her sisters married fishermen who perished at sea, leaving them young widows, and they and their many children lived in my grandfather's home. At the age of nineteen my mother had been engaged to a fisherman whose boat went down before her eyes in a terrible storm. My father, a seminarian and teacher, was one of the people who lived in this household. Here he met my mother, and they married in 1903. Mother had attended primary school, but her main education was in the school of life.

I was their first child and very welcome. As my father was a poet and a writer, he composed "A Hymn of Life" for my first birthday. I was named Maria Vigdis for my mother. In 1906 my father prepared and published a spelling book, and it has been reprinted many times. My mother had six children between 1905 and 1914.

My first real sorrow was the death of my younger brother when we both had measles. I was nearly three years old when he died at the age of nine months. I clearly remember the emptiness in our home after this tragedy. For years I looked in vain in every baby carriage, hoping to find him. Another brother arrived when I was six. He died at the age of four as a result of mumps, and one week later another baby was born, only to die very young from poliomyelitis. The winter of 1914 was very hard, and many children were unable to survive. The deaths of my brothers affected me deeply.

At nine years of age I was no longer a child. The silence of death had come into our home, and the great questions of life whirling around me were the same ones that follow us all our lives. The children whom I saw die suffered so much that I resolved never to have a child and never to have anything to do with men.

Instead, I decided to become a doctor. I prayed to the Almighty to help me to serve others, especially children and exhausted, weeping mothers.

In the meantime I had to go to school to get my education. There is little to tell about this part of my life. In 1945 I was selected to write my memories of grammar school for the hundredth anniversary of the school I had attended. In my opinion, this was rather a waste of time, as a really famous Icelandic author has written a wonderful book, *The Soul in Danger*, about our school.

After I matriculated my father allowed me to teach in my old primary school, where he had taught and had later become headmaster. The class I had to teach consisted of thirty pupils, wide-eyed and brimful of questions. I felt deeply my lack of pedagogic training. In addition, I did not know what marks to give these children. I am not a believer in grading children, as it gives the teacher too much opportunity to favor some pupils and to deprecate others.

It was not until 1925, when I was twenty and had already been accepted by the medical school, that I told anyone of my plan to become a doctor. The medical school had no quarters of its own but was permitted to use three or four rooms in the House of Parliament.

At that period of history the status of women in Iceland was low; all the power and money were in the hands of the men, who tended to disparage and ignore the women. The same conditions persist to some degree up to the present time. I can never forget a twice-widowed woman with only one child, who earned her living as a practical nurse. One day she went to the head physician of the school for midwives to apply for training. He told her that midwifery was indecent and advised her to remarry and have more children, that being her duty as a woman.

In 1931 I took my final examination in medicine. I am very grateful to all those who helped me during my years of study. My teachers in the grammar school and at the university were overloaded with work. None of them had learned how to teach, but some were born pedagogues, while some, I fear, were alcoholics.

At this stage I was longing to come into practical contact with all I had been studying in my large German and English textbooks, which I had difficulty understanding because of the languages. Medical students were expected to spend one month in a tuberculosis sanatorium and one month in a Catholic hospital for medicine and surgery. I tried to get into these hospitals after graduation, but there was no vacancy. The nuns were kind and gentle, but the doctors, who were true Icelanders, told me with boyish smiles that the real duty of women was to have children and to make food for the family. I then applied to the new municipal hospital, which had been built by Icelandic women and then handed over to the state. There was no vacancy, there, either, which turned out to be advantageous to me in the end, as there remained no other solution than to look for training in Denmark, to which Iceland was united at that time. I obtained help from a Danish-Icelandic fund, the condition being that I should first work in the maternity wards in Denmark for one month. I enjoyed Denmark, both the country and the people. I spent nine years there and in Sweden, for the most part in pediatric clinics because I wanted to specialize in pediatrics.

At that time the "political circus" in Iceland included a head physician who was also a member of Parliament. He believed that, as rickets did not occur in Iceland, there was no need for pediatric specialists. Women in his opinion could be delivered at home or even in a cow shed and maternity wards were unnecessary. It was a hopeless task to discuss these matters with this doctor, whose thinking had not advanced beyond the nineteenth century. This same physician in 1936 introduced a law regarding the requirements for a doctor to become a specialist. Unfortunately, this law was made retroactive and prevented me from becoming a specialist because I had not done research, although I had worked in so many hospitals for many years. The hospitals in Iceland at this period were overfilled with medical men.

I was in Denmark when the war broke out and the country was occupied. The Icelanders, however, were generous enough to send a ship, the *Esja*, to take us home to our country. I was one of 258 persons who traveled through Sweden and Finland and up to Petsamo to join the *Esja*.

In my absence there had been some changes in life in Iceland. Women had been given legal rights, at least on paper. In reality they were still poor, looked down on, and worn out from hard work. They did not know how to behave when the soldiers arrived, and the soldiers took advantage of this. The result was that twenty-one percent of the newborn babies were illegitimate. Exaggerated stories were written about "five hundred serving the foreigners," and one of the foreign papers wrote, "Life is much better for the Icelanders since we arrived."

In Iceland it has been the custom for thousands of years for the woman to have one or more children before her wedding and more children thereafter. In my opinion, all these children are legitimate, and the word *illegitimate* should be removed from every language.

At the outbreak of war there were many physicians in the capital who had so much to do in hospital and in private practice that they could scarcely keep up with the work. I did not like practicing in the old-fashioned way, but for ten years I did so, working day and night. It was a very interesting but hard life. I had a good bodyguard, a former policeman, who drove me everywhere, as such protection was necessary.

The municipal hospital was by then far too small. The professor of obstetrics wrote to the papers about this, and so did women throughout the country. I also wrote articles in the newspapers, urging the authorities to establish better health services. My first article was entitled "Only a Birth, Only a Hemorrhage," this being the usual answer from a hospital when a patient required admission. Eventually, in 1949, a new maternity ward was opened, greeted by silence.

By this time I was tired of night work, so I asked a colleague, a good friend who later became the greatest Icelandic authority on obstetrics, to give me the opportunity to learn more in this field and in neonatal care. I began working under him in 1951 and am still in the same clinic. It has been a wonderful, although not financially rewarding, period of work.

People in Iceland today are young and gay. They begin to make love early, and why should they not enter the real school of life and be young with their children? Those people who are old in outlook believe that everything is going to the devil, but I say that each new day is young and interesting, even wonderful, and sometimes rather strange.

E. Elizabeth Cass

b. August 21, 1905

I was born on August 21, 1905, the eldest of three girls. My father's family the Casses were of French Hugenot descent; their ancestors had settled in England in the fifteenth century, having escaped from France in a boat. Many of them were doctors. My great-great-great-grandfather William Eden Cass was a doctor, as were his son and my great-grandfather. My great-grandfather, when he was a medical student at Guy's Hospital in London, made two trips to the Arctic, the first in 1822, as ship's doctor on the expedition with Sir James Ross, and the second in 1824, on a ship named the *Brunswick*, which was captained by the infamous Captain Bligh. I have the diary of this voyage, written in great-grandfather's own handwriting, and the diary of the 1822 voyage is in a museum in Yorkshire. My great-grandfather was a well-known surgeon. When he was eighty-two years of age, he received a message that a man had had his leg caught in a reaper some thirty miles away from Goole, where my great-grandfather was then living. Great-grandfather must have been a very strong man, for despite his eighty-two years, he was not deterred; he rode on his pony thirty miles across the moor, successfully amputated the man's leg by candlelight, and returned on horseback to Goole. Nowadays, I am sure, very few of us could accomplish this at half his age. He had three sons; two became doctors, and both went to Guy's Hospital. Unfortunately, they both died young, one when a plague ship came into Goole and the other of diphtheria.

My father had an elder brother who became a doctor, carrying on the family tradition, and he himself was a classical scholar, earning honors in Hebrew at the university and later becoming a minister.

My mother's family the Armstrongs were originally, I believe, Vikings who settled on the border. Apparently, they fought indiscriminately for the Scots or the English in wars between Scotland and England, but they were not mercenaries. They seem to have fought with a conviction of what was right.

My maternal grandfather was a general in the Indian army, and my mother was born in India. She was sent home from India at the age of three, as was customary in those days, and was brought up in Bruges, Belgium, in the home of her grandmother. My mother therefore spoke French long before she could speak English. She came back to England at the age of eight, and her mother died shortly afterward. Mother was brought up by two devoted servants, my grandmother's lady's maid, who stayed on with the family to help with the children, and the old cook. My mother wanted to become an artist, but my grandfather was adamant. He was completely against any daughter of his having any profession. Mother was very frustrated by this prohibition; she would have been, I believe, quite a good artist, judging by the remarks that art dealers and artists have made about her oil paintings, of which we have a certain number at home. When she married my father, life was very different for her, and she had to buckle down and learn how to do a lot of cooking and housework in the country vicarage.

I was brought up in the country, and the first years of my life were spent with many animals, which I loved dearly, and with a beautiful garden, which produced luxuriant fruit and vegetables. I had two younger sisters, and our education was started by a series of governesses. I know that at the age of five I could read fairly well. Then, when I was seven, my father taught me some Latin, which I continued to learn at school. French, however, although we started it, was rather lacking and was not well taught. We also learned music, as my mother and father were fond of it. They both had good voices, and my mother could play the piano and also the banjo; so we children were brought up hearing the old Negro spirituals, and I was taught piano from the age of six or so. Mother did take up painting again, when I was in my teens and my sisters were growing up.

It seems to me that in England, even in my day, all the school medical officers were women. We had a local general practitioner who was a friend of the family and who delivered us all, but the visiting school doctor was a woman, and I know that my mother liked her, for we used to put her up whenever she came to the little village, which was a mining community.

At the age of three—no one knows why—I was already determined to become a doctor and announced the fact. At five, after I had been taught to read, I started my education on my own in my father's library. He had an immense collection of classics, among which *The Myths of Greece and Rome* was one of my favorite books. There was also a classical dictionary, from which I learned a lot. In addition, we had an Encyclopaedia Britannica, in which I discovered skeletons, and they fascinated me. I decided that I would like to learn the names of the bones from the pictures of skeletons, and so I did. Then I also decided that I should know about animals and that I would like to be able to treat animals, too. So, being a horrible child, I used to bury dead birds, mice, or any other creatures that I could find, then wait patiently until I thought they had become skeletons, and finally dig them up. I used to come out with some astounding information, which rather floored my mother's polite visitors.

England, I think, was relatively broad-minded about medical women, and life was not so difficult for them. They were accepted even in those days, especially for looking after children. The village school was poor, and we did not go to it, but at the age of eleven, my godmother, who had been a doctor before she married, offered to take me to live with her in Nottingham so that I could go to high school. Thus, from the age of eleven to the age of fourteen, I attended Nottingham High School, which was an excellent school for girls. There we were taught Latin and French, so we did have these languages. At the age of fourteen, I attended Cheltenham Ladies' College. At first, I did not like it at all. I much preferred the freedom of the high school, and I did not like living in a boardinghouse with a lot of other girls and with a lot of restrictions. It wasn't until I got to do what they called the Over Seventeen House—that is, when we were doing preuniversity work—that I appreciated Cheltenham. The only thing that interfered with my ambition to become a doctor was music. I was passionately fond of it, and I used to love playing the piano; in fact, I played at many school concerts. We also had visiting pianists in the town of Cheltenham, and I attended all the concerts. Even when I was doing matriculation and first medical, I used to get up early in the morning to go over to practice on the excellent piano we had in the main hall in the school, since the pianos we had in our boardinghouses were awful. And at one time I considered changing to music, but I realized that I would never be good enough to be a concert pianist and that I would only be able to teach. Education at Cheltenham was good, especially in Latin, where we ended up being taught the direct method; all our explanations were in Latin, and we had to speak it, too. I have never regretted this, as I have found Latin a great foundation for many languages, as well as for English grammar. I left school, having finished my premedical studies, and I went to London University, where I was placed in the London School of Medicine, which was for women only, a situation that I did not like at all.

I lived in a women's university hostel, where we did have other people besides medical students, and I decided it had been very constricting to only have medical-student friends. We had students from all fields of study, and we also became friendly with some of the men from the University Hospital. On Sundays we would take to the country, where we took long walks, and we also went to dances.

I managed to enter St. Mary's Hospital, rather than the Royal Free, and there again we were a limited number of women. However, we were, on the whole, treated extremely well. The only people who objected to us were some of the ultramanly rugby players, but in the end they capitulated.

St. Mary's had excellent teachers, and as there were few students, we got wonderful clinical experience. Such famous men as Sir John Broadbent; Sir William Wilcox, the pathologist; Paton and Juler, the ophthalmologists; Sir Zachary Cope, and Professor Pannett, the surgeons; and Alex Bourne, the gynecologist were all wonderful teachers and wonderful men. St. Mary's nurses were always taken to nurse the royal family, and Dr. Juler was the ophthalmologist for the royal household.

Dr. Juler took me to Moorfields, and I obtained a position as outpatient officer. I was also given the senior clinical assistantship in the outpatient department of St. Mary's. With this position came the examination of all the schoolchildren, for which I ran two clinics a week. I also started and had charge of the first orthoptic clinic, with two orthoptists to help me; it ended up as a five-day-a-week session. Moorfield's is one of the biggest eye hospitals in the world, and we used to average about 500 outpatients per morning, having many "firms" of consultant ophthalmologists with assistants. I was extremely lucky and ended up as chief clinical assistant. I did not intend originally to go on with ophthalmology, but it became my first interest.

In 1932 I married a pathologist. I quickly found that he really was a man who should not have married at all but should have simply continued with his work in the Almroth Wright Institute, where he had a position. There were faults, of course, on both sides, but our marriage was just not working out.

It was when I was working in Moorfield's that I realized how appallingly ignorant I was in languages. We used to get so many people who couldn't speak English. I therefore determined to learn Spanish and German, which I did. In 1934, a Spanish woman was sent to learn English, and in 1935 I exchanged and went to Spain, where I not only lived in her household but attended the hospitals and university and acquired many Spanish friends.

In 1935 I was beginning German studies and also collecting German books on strabismus. In fact, I obtained a London University scholarship just for work on this problem. This scholarship was a very coveted one, but alas, it was then 1939 and by then I had been asked by the Spanish and the Brazilian ophthalmologists to lecture on strabismus and orthoptics, until then an unknown field in those countries. It was in June that I sailed for Argentina and Brazil, where I was given diplomatic privileges. I had written a course of seven lectures in Spanish, and I lectured for three months in those countries. The people who had been most desirous of getting me there had been Malbran, the Argentine ophthalmologist, and the late Moacyr Alvaro in Brazil, who was a very well known, kindly, and erudite young man.

When in Brazil and Argentina, I got to know a lot of people, and a funny incident occurred. A young man read my lectures, which I had written in Spanish; wanted to be a doctor but did not have the money for it, so he decided he'd try and learn orthoptics from my lectures, which he did. He presented himself to an ophthalmologist and asked if he'd take him on as an orthoptist. Thus the young man started his professional life as an orthoptist and earned enough money to become a doctor. Years later, he met me in Montreal at a Pan American conference. To this day we are firm friends.

My lecture tour ended just before war was declared, and we left Rio de Janeiro, proceeding without navigation lights. A week later, while we were at sea, war was declared. However, we had been busy preparing, blacking out the portholes and camouflaging the ship by painting it. I then was very active, giving first-aid lectures to the crew and the male passengers. The women were working too, sewing and cutting bandages and making splints.

We took six weeks to get home; as there were submarines off the coast of Brazil, we shot across the Atlantic, ending up in the Azores, where we had to get water. We sailed into port with a blackboard announcing that we were the *Avila*

Star. When we finally did arrive in England, nobody knew we were coming, although all our families had been anxiously inquiring about us. We landed late at night, and to my astonishment, the officials started asking me all sorts of questions. Finally I asked what in the world was happening. I said I had been lecturing in Argentina, and it came out that, because I had diplomatic privileges, the government was rather suspicious of what I had been up to. I then arrived back in London to find that my husband was working and living in his laboratories and that the maids and the cats had also been taken there. The maids and cats were brought back, and we went through the bombardment of London. I joined the emergency medical service. I had volunteered to serve in the army, and in October of 1940 they sent for me for an interview. I had my physical and was told I was accepted, although I had to wait at home until they called me. I was then sent to the Davy Hulme Hospital, a 500-bed military institution just outside Manchester. There I was in charge of "eyes," with 25 eye beds in the officer's wards. We didn't get the heavy air raids, but we used to hear them in the distance in Manchester. I found that the young soldiers had been accustomed to women doctors while in school, and I had no difficulty with them. Some of the older seargeants and officers did look at me askance at first, but I had no real troubles. I did have quite a number of operations to perform—and then of course we had the business of war! The Italian prison camps I used to visit! We worked outside the camp in a reception station examining the eyes, but any cases I wished to treat or operate on had to be taken back to the hospital with me. I knew that the prison-camp doctors had no medical books and were very worried, so I managed to get some of my surgical books passed by the censor and let through to these doctors. I treated almost all nationalities—Italians, German prisoners, English troops, and Spaniards.

In 1943 the Davy Hulme Hospital was disbanded, and I was sent to East Grinstead to find my way into MacIndou's facial maxillary unit, where I learned a lot.

During my years on Gibraltar I had some amazing experiences, treating patients and meeting interesting people. I met most of the American admirals, including Admiral Crewdson, who told me all about the Arctic. Little did I think then that I would ever find myself in the Canadian Arctic! I also got to know the military governor in Algeciras and, at the invitation of the Spaniards, lectured to them, with the consent of the army. Later, as soon as the war ended, I gave a course of lectures in Madrid, again on strabismus, and demonstrated operations in the Madrilenian hospitals.

There were very few women in Gibraltar during the war—and I was the first female army officer the troops had ever seen. It was so different from England. There was no blackout because, with the lights on, Gibraltar was impossible to find, oddly enough. We had a couple of air raids, but the bombs were dropped on La Liwea. We had incidents at the docks when the sticky bombs manufactured by the Italians blew up some of the fleet. I was smuggled on board a destroyer by some very young men during the war when the destroyer went on trials. While we were at sea, these eager young men showed me the Aztec, the radar, and other instruments. I remember saying of the Aztec, "What a pity that we cannot use ultrasound to distinguish foreign bodies in the eye!" And now we can.

I was also taken up flying in a Beauford and, in addition, I was thumbed into the turret of the rear gunner in a Beau fighter. After the war, because Spanish was my second language, I was asked if I would stay on to work for both the military hospital and the colonial hospital in Gibraltar, which I did for a number of years. I also practiced in Tangiers, where I made friends and learned some Arabic. At the end of the war some Russians came down and ran the hotel near Algeciras for the duke of Bailen, and he and his wife became friends of mine. And as for the Russians, they are now like my family. They had one son, and it was impossible for that poor child to learn, as there was only a village school. So Sacha lived with me and was my ward. When I left Gibraltar, I managed to get him to school in England, a Catholic school near one of my sisters. When I came to Canada, he was still at this school, and he later continued at Oxford University. He had a distinguished career, but alas, in 1974 he was hit by a drunken driver and killed. It was a most tragic accident. Sacha was an only son and the last of a dynasty. His great-grandmother was Princess Paley.

My friendship with these Russians proved very helpful because after the war Soviet fishing boats and other ships used to come into Gibraltar and I went on board many of them to treat Soviet patients. In fact, I treated the first Soviet navy man ever left behind in Gibraltar. They all came to check up on me, and they told me they left him with me because I was a woman and thus, they believed, would have maternal feelings and look after their comrade better. I went on board a Russian ship that had come up from the Antarctic in the Geophysical Year, and as the captain had no caviar or vodka to give me, as was the custom, he gave me his beautiful sable cap, which I have to this day and which I wear in the Canadian Arctic. It is a historic item.

When we had political troubles, as we did in the end, I left Gibraltar and went to Geneva, to the World Health Organization. They planned to send me to Amman as an expert on trachoma, as I had seen quite a lot in my work in North Africa. I took a long holiday in Mallorca. Alas, in December there was this revolt in Amman, and the insurgents threw out Glubb Pasha. That was that; no English person would be permitted to work in Amman. So I wandered up to Madrid, where I stayed with friends. I had no idea what I should do next, but my Spanish friends suggested that I contact the Canadians to see if I could go to Canada. I saw the Canadian ambassador in Madrid, and he said, "Certainly. We need ophthalmologists in Canada." He dispatched me to a charming personnel officer, a Frenchman, who looked up an address for me—that of the head of Blindness Control in Ottawa. From there, to my amazement, I suddenly received a letter from the Department of National Health and Welfare, inviting me to come to Canada as an ophthalmologist. After many delays I received a telegram informing me that I had passed the civil-service examination, and finally, the following Christmas, I arrived in Canada. I came over by boat to New York, which I fell in love with, for in those days it was far different from the way it is now. Then, with a stopover in Montreal, I made my way to Ottawa, where I stayed and worked. After four weeks in an office that I loathed, I was sent north among the Crees at Moose Factory. I was promptly adopted as a daughter by a Cree. In fact, the Indians looked after me in a way far better than the strange whites. They told me more and taught me a great deal about their country. To the horror of my dear Cree friend Jimmy, I went up to Fort Albany with him in a snowmobile, not knowing that I was the first white woman to have done it. He was having fits because I knew nothing of the country and had never been on snowshoes, but the young American doctor who accompanied us, was laughing up his sleeve. I enjoyed myself very much, and I came home alone with Jimmy after having walked six miles on snowshoes in one afternoon—my first attempt. I wasn't stiff, as Jimmy thought I would be.

After Moose Factory, I went all along the North Shore and got to know the Ojibways, the Ottawas, and the Algonquins. I have never had any difficulty with or fear of Indians; I've always gotten along with them, and they have been extremely kind and hospitable. Just as I was getting used to going along the North Shore, from North Bay to the Sault, learning about the customs and the life and hearing the stories and legends, to say nothing of treating all the different ocular ailments, the department suddenly decided to sent me to Edmonton despite my objections. However, I didn't stay so long in Edmonton. I managed to get north again, making my first journey in a DC3. It took us from 7:00 a.m. to 7:00 p.m. to arrive at Aklavik. Inuvik had not yet been built then, in 1958; it was known as East 3. We landed at East 3 and had to take our own luggage up a bank. Then we were all piled into a drafty Otter for the trip to Aklavik. This Otter was flown by a character named Pappy Hill.

In Aklavik I worked at the two mission hospitals, and then I started around the delta for three weeks that ended up as nine months. I found so much to do. I came in contact here with all the Eskimos and have many friends in Tuktoyaktuk because I made an Eskimo child breathe! I was informed many years later that, according to Eskimo belief, this child was my son because I had given him life. I still keep in contact with my son and many old friends of mine.

I have traveled to many places in the world on lecture tours, for conferences, and so on, and just before I left the service of the Department of National Health and Welfare, I founded the International Society of Geographical Ophthalmology. The first meeting was held to commemorate the centennial of the Northwest Territories. Everyone said that I could not possibly have an international congress in Yellowknife, but I did—with thirty-two ophthalmologists from thirteen different countries, all of whom I knew intimately. We are holding our fifth congress this year in Cagliari, and the membership reelected me president. We now cover the world.

In 1968 I received the Commissioner's Award for my work and in 1970 the Order of Canada. In 1973 the Spaniards gave me the Order of Cadiz for the work I had done for their poor people during the war.

I still work hard, and I know many Indians and Eskimos and am now treating the third generation.

Rosita Rivera Ramirez
b. May 3, 1906

I was born on Cabangan, Zambales, on the Philippine Islands. My father Don Benito Rivera was mayor, justice of the peace, and a businessman. He was the owner of a general store, a bakery, and extensive farmlands. Unfortunately, my father died when I was four years of age, and our mother became the sole support of her seven children.

My early education in elementary and secondary schools was in Iba. I graduated from the Zambales Provincial Farm School there as valedictorian.

It was during my early years that I saw much sickness and disease with no access to medical care; people died without having seen a doctor. Even in our own home I saw afflictions when there was no way to get a doctor. I recall helping my father to unpack merchandise for the store and to arrange these goods in their proper places. Some canned goods accidentally fell and hit one of my brothers on the head, causing profuse bleeding. There was no doctor to be had. Thanks to my mother's first-aid measures, the wound healed. Another such incident made a profound impression on me. A table was accidentally pushed into my leg and lacerated it, resulting in an infection and an ulcer that took months to heal. My mother taught me to dress the wound, and I learned to care for it myself.

During my high-school days, the sad health conditions of my town and its citizens touched my humanitarian feelings and aroused my compassion. People became ill and died without receiving any help except perhaps that of herbalists or a sanitation inspector. Babies were delivered by the *hilots* (untrained midwives), and the mothers and infants often died. Newborns would frequently die of tetanus. All these conditions motivated me to take up medicine.

But how could I manage to study medicine? Since the death of my father, the store, farms, and bakery were our sole means of support. To study medicine was expensive, and it took seven years. If I did undertake these studies, I might be depriving my brothers of their education. However, before my high-school graduation, my well-to-do, childless paternal uncle came to visit us. He was a godsent savior. Knowing the situation, he voluntarily offered to send me to the University of the Philippines College of Medicine and to shoulder all the expenses.

During my vacations and while awaiting the examination results, I always returned to my hometown to take care of the sick. I made use of the free medical samples from various pharmaceutical houses and did not charge for my services. In return, the patients gave me eggs, bananas, chickens, pigs, and fish, for they were so poor that they could not afford to pay me cash. Despite this, I was happy to be able to make them well.

In 1930, at twenty-six years of age, I received my doctor's degree, and I was one of the top ten in the graduating class. In the latter part of 1930 I was accepted as a resident physician at the St. Teresita Hospital in Manila. There I spent ten years being trained in obstetrics, gynecology, surgery, and medicine. My vacations were spent in my hometown, doing my medical missionary work.

During World War II, while the enemy occupied our country, I was in charge of the hospital and had many responsibilities. In 1942 I married Adolfo Ramirez, a lawyer, pharmaceutical chemist, and USFFE officer. My husband has been my inspiration, moral support, and congenial helper ever since. We had only one child, a son, who died in infancy. We adopted a son Raymond, who went on to study medicine at Santo Tomas College of Medicine and Surgery and is now specializing in radiotherapy and oncology at Wellington Hospital in New Zealand. Our foster daughter Teresita is also a graduate of Santo Tomas and is now practicing at the Nichols Air Force Base Hospital. Another foster daughter, who is also my niece, is married, has four children, and is currently a supervisor in Rideout Hospital in California. In addition, we have had twenty-one wards under our care. These were children left by their parents at our hospital. At present we have only seven still with us.

During the liberation of Manila and the bombing of the war, Santo Tomas University and Hospital were damaged, as was the encampment of the enemy. As a USFFE officer, my husband was wanted by the enemy and therefore had to go into hiding during the occupation.

After the war the owners of the St. Teresita Hospital gave it up. My husband and I purchased it and, in our humble way, established the St. Teresita General Hospital and the School of Nursing and Midwifery in 1948. By 1954 we expanded it into a three-story structure with a maternity department and social-welfare facilities.

In 1958 we constructed a maternity charity branch in Bago-Bantay, a squatter area, in order to serve indigent patients. By 1971 this branch was enlarged with an outpatient department and a family planning clinic.

The St. Teresita School of Nursing was expanded to improve nursing services in 1961. Another three-story building was constructed, and the hospital was reorganized for the training of more nurses. In 1972, to meet advanced medical and surgical demands, a new four-story wing was started.

During its years of service from 1948 to 1974 St. Teresita Hospital had over 61,000 admissions and 72,000 outpatient visits. Free clinics serving thousands of patients were established with the cooperation of the nursing and medical personnel of the hospital and of civic organizations such as the Philippine Medical Women's Association (PMWA), the Quezon City Medical Association, the Capital Medical Practitioners, the Barangay Lions Club, the Jaycees, the Zonta Club, and the Catholic Women's League.

The St. Teresita School of Nursing has had as of 1974 some 666 graduates, all with the very highest marks on board examinations. In the School of Midwifery we have had over 880 graduates since 1949. Some are in government service, while others practice in rural areas. Our institute has also given financial aid to sixteen scholars—graduates in medicine, nursing, and midwifery. In addition, our hospital has sponsored numerous conferences and seminars for many medical and civic societies.

Throughout my professional life, my main concern has been to render full service (medicine, food, and clothing) to the poor, sick, and indigent and to participate in community programs, such as employment development, health-assistance clinics, children's aid, Girl Scouts, and so on. Other projects that have occupied my interest have been the raising of funds to equip children's playgrounds and miniparks, building projects for the Philippine Medical Association, building a vocational center for destitute children, in addition to the usual Red Cross, Catholic endeavors, Community Chest, and so on.

Professional organizations have been of great interest in my life. I was president of the PMWA from 1956 to 1961 and was fortunate enough to be chosen to represent them at the Medical Women's International Association's congresses in Italy and in England. I have also been active in and have served on the boards of the PMA, the Philippine Obstetrical and Gynecology Society, the Philippine Hospital Association, and the Philippine Federal and Private Medical Association.

In 1965 I received a plaque from the Philippine Medical Association as the most outstanding physician in Quezon City. Then, in 1966, the National Radio and Television presented me with a trophy as one of the ten outstanding hospital directors.

Among the treasures in my memory are the honor of being the recipient of the CAWP Presidential Medal of Merit for Community Service, presented by President Ferdinand Marcos, and also the plaque of appreciation as one of the ten outstanding hospital directors of the Philippines, given by the *Philippine Leaders and Progress Journal.*

Hildegard Schmidt-Fischer
b. May 13, 1906

In Danzig in 1914 four boys and three girls of the Plankengasse no longer played robbers and princesses in the casements of the old fort that once defended the Hanseatic town. A war was on. The fathers had gone to the front, and we children also played at war: Germans against Russians! The battle of Tannenberg had been fought; the first wounded soldiers had returned, some with bandaged arms in slings, others walking with difficulty on crutches, and one slender soldier with a black patch over his right eye. Then the castle of the princesses became a hospital. The youngest, eight-year-old Hildegard, borrowed a small officer's uniform from her father, a real one with silver shoulder straps, a cockade on the cap, and a small sabre with a sword knot. Around her sleeve was a white band with a red cross made of hairribbons. The little "doctor" was ready to function. We children had not yet heard anything about women doctors. The two other girls put on white pinafores, nurse's caps, and red crosses on their sleeves. Our hospital was prepared—but where were the wounded soldiers? Here our dearly beloved dolls had to help out. The field-green handkerchiefs belonging to father's dress uniforms were sewn into soldiers' tunics. The cruel enemies cut off the braids of the girl dolls. It was war, and we shed real tears over such military cruelties. We doll mothers also had to make sacrifices. Our soldiers went into action. We hid them behind bushes in the strangely shaped ceramic chimneys—or were they ventilation shafts? Then a signal was given, and we observed the enemies from our hospital castle as they attacked our soldiers with their lances, rifles, and sabers. Woe to the poor soldiers who were found! With our small knives we slit open legs and arms so that the sawdust poured out from the pink fabric covering. Then "blood" from a bottle of red ink was dropped in. We had to search all over the battlefield before we could start the operations in our hospital. The little doctor was in her element, using a fruit knife to cut out all the spots smeared with "blood" while the nurses used their school rulers as splints and bandaged the injured arms and legs. The healing process did not take long, since new soldiers had to go into battle.

After the end of the war, my father finally laid aside his uniform and returned to civilian life. The postwar inflation decimated my parents' capital and shocked them so much that they took me out of school one year before I would have matriculated. My secret ambition to become a doctor was destroyed.

The enchanting meeting with a forester and his two little children led me to an early marriage at the age of nineteen. We had a merry life. Music joined us most of all; the violin, piano, and French horn, plus singing, provided a reliable bridge. I came from a home in which the musical harmony of the violin-and-piano duets had formed our evening pleasure. Radio and television had not yet invaded homes. I read a great deal and at an early age began to write my impressions of various books. This volume became a thick tome, which I finally showed to Mrs. Magnus-Unzer, the head of the Women's Radio in Königsberg (Kaliningrad). She was interested and asked me to read my essays on the radio. In this way I began to broadcast lectures at regular intervals. Such was the origin of my little booklet *The Heart Continues to Beat*, based on the letters of German women. All these activities kept pace with the times until the Third Reich came into being.

My stepchildren Ingeborg and Peter, four and three years old at the time of my marriage, had had a Jewish mother, who died at the premature birth of her third child. When the time came, I invited their grandmother to Ingeborg's confirmation. From then on no one spoke to me, not even the people who had enjoyed my hospitality. They denounced me to the radio station where three of my lectures had been read. I became completely isolated; the children were not admitted to the school nor even to an apprenticeship. They were deprived of the joy of living, and I had to make every possible effort to brace their will. I gave them a guiding principle that Kurt Götz had once written to his wife Valerie von Martens: "Love your fate; it is the way of God with your soul." We three tried to live up to this together, and I think we succeeded.

My former headmaster, a good fatherly friend, visited me and asked whether his daughter could spend her housekeeping year—a custom that was obligatory at that time—in my home. I complied with his request with pleasure. A charming young girl came to us, glad to learn and to help. Her often sorrowful eyes were a mystery to me, but the solution became apparent after some weeks, when her pregnancy could no longer be concealed. Her parents did not know anything about it. "Will you let me stay on in the future, too?" she asked anxiously. "Naturally," I replied. It was my duty to aid this helpless young creature, to encourage her to look forward to the happiness to be expected, and to try to free her from the fear of people condemning her. In addition, I had to accept and combat the obvious envy within me, since my own marriage had remained childless. She was radiant when she called me once into her room to say, "I feel now that something is alive within me. Please, do listen to it, too!" I laid my ear on her body and comprehended the miracle of the new life. This was a maturing experience for both of us. At the pump in the garden where she drew water for the flowerbeds she swung the handle too energetically and an unexpected, excessively quick birth took place. In the advanced training of the Red Cross we had learned what to do in such a situation. The young mother, frightened as well as happy, was taken to the hospital with her little Hildegard, who became my godchild.

My grandmother's widowed sister then came to live with us. This brave old lady of eighty-two kept secret an illness until it could no longer be concealed. Metastases were causing pain that gradually became intolerable, and nursing was very difficult. It was not possible for us to transfer this poor, suffering woman into the anonymity of a hospital, and so we all went through the tormenting cruelty of a death that was helped only for a short time by the morphine prescribed by the sympathetic physician. At this point my father sent for me to help my mother, who had suddenly fallen ill. An apoplectic attack at sixty had left her lying for nine days in a smiling sleep, with no pain and no knowledge of her illness. At last a merciful death took her into the other world.

In 1939 war broke out. Peter my stepson was killed in action outside Moscow. A tragic situation of conflict gave my life a decisive turn. I moved to the home of good friends in Berlin, where there was a possibility of taking the "special matriculation for the talented." Professor Diepgen was the counselor for the medical faculty. I told him of my desire to study medicine and showed him my school records. It seemed to me that at this examination knowledge would not be the only decisive factor. After examining my records, the professor of medicine said, "Now I will give you the title of your thesis: "The Women in the Lives of Famous Physicians."

In Berlin University and its institutes the science of the meaning of life and death was studied in chemistry and in physics. To botany and zoology I brought the knowledge that I had gained from my husband. He had taught me to observe the actions of animals, to draw parallels with the human race, and also to perceive differences. In physiology, biology, and medicine I experienced an unforgettable fascination. To see pulsating life—the flow of blood in the web of a frog extended under the microscope—was fantastic. And then my first entrance into the anatomy theater, with the many human bodies lying there in silence, gave me a feeling of awe and mystery until forceps and scalpel made the first cut. The understanding that death probably begins at birth, as stated by the eminent anatomist Professor Stieve, became clear. It was in the course of the premedical examination that I received the news that my stepson had been killed in action outside Moscow. Berlin was bombed more and more, and we were evacuated. I went to Danzig for the last clinical terms and passed the state examinations. In January of 1945 I stumbled through great heaps of snow the long way to the medical academy to fetch my precious license to practice medicine. My fellow students had fled long before. By remaining, I had missed the sailing of the *Wilhelm Gustloff*, which had been hit by a mine and sunk. On the *Deutschland*, which followed her several days later, I performed my first medical service on a bed in a cabin in which six men were sitting. On the open deck people were shivering in the bitter cold. Children fell ill more quickly than adults and were the first to die.

In Kiel in Schleswig-Holstein it was not possible to get work or to help in a hospital or a practice. So I boarded a car or mounted a horse and tried to do the work of a farmhand on the farm where I was quartered. Kiel and its environs were a continual target for enemy bombers. After many difficulties and petitions I succeeded in being allowed to open my own practice in 1946 in Niedersachsen. My new home was in Lauenstein in the Weserbergland. It was then necessary to put into action what I had learned in the lecture hall and the hospitals. Here in the country the nearest hospital and the nearest specialist were twenty-five kilometers away. There were no head physician and no medical superintendent at my disposal to help in critical situations. Problems ranged from apoplexy to a difficult delivery with violent hemorrhage to a cardiac infarction to an accident in the street or in a factory. The university had not taught the necessity for a deeper understanding of the patient, and yet only with true empathy with the patient is it possible to help.

After ten years of intensive work, in which I was the sole woman doctor in the whole region, I was able to afford to build a house in 1955. I chose a site in the meadows on the slope of the wooded mountain range of the Ith, with a view far over the valley to the foothills of the Harz Mountains. *Amemus—servemus gratias agamus* was inlaid with small mosaic stones in the wall of the hall. This was the rule in my father's life, and I adopted it for my own.

Today in a retrospective view of my thirty years of medical practice, I realize that two parallel functions required both my personal and medical attention: the genesis of the individual, the entry into life, and the passing away, the end of life. Again and again with the mothers in labor I experienced the miracle of creation. When I heard the fetal heartbeat, I often asked myself whether the little creature in its security could hear the cardiac sounds of the mother. Again and again I experienced with my patients the merciless law—the final journey of the aging on the way to certain death. Is it, then, not the duty of the physician to remain with the dying patient until the frontier has been passed? And should we not free patients from their great dread and ameliorate the cruel, excruciating pain? Are not we physicians God's helpers, and should we not fulfill His law?

In addition to my duties, I have also had many hobbies. After the house was built, I was able to realize a dream of many years. I bought a horse. The friend who shares my home is an enthusiastic horsewoman, and we now have two horses and two foals in our stable. Our early-morning rides through the woods are a most beautiful prelude to our day's work.

I have also filmed the Asian and Inca peoples, as well as the birds, animals, trees, and sights of those regions. With the assistance of a woman friend who is a psychotherapist, I have made a film on the psychotherapy of children, showing how neurotic conflicts can be reduced.

Finally, I also have my music. Actually, medicine and music as arts are integrated in my home. Making music with my pianist sister is a curative for the soul. The physician and the musician have in common an intuition that makes it possible for them to free curative impulses for the body, as well as for the soul.

Unfortunately, it is too late in my life to acquire the necessary medical training to integrate both riding and music into therapy with patients, but it would have given me great joy to be able to do so.

The German Medical Women's Association has been of great value to me. The congresses of the Medical Women's International Association have not only acquainted us with the world at large but strengthened the associations of women doctors in all the member countries.

"And has it not all been wonderful?"

Frances Harding
b. June 3, 1906

Motivation is one of life's great intangibles, like love or the Spirit, as described in John 3:8: "The wind blows when it will, and you hear the sound of it, but you do not know whence it came, or whither it goes. So it is with everyone who is born of the Spirit." Motivation is like the wind. You can see what it does, but you cannot know whence it comes or whither it goes.

Statistics show that the two most important determining or motivating influences on a woman's decision to make medicine a career are parents and high-school and college counselors. Parents with limited financial resources are more inclined to spend their educational dollars on sons, who traditionally must be the breadwinners of the next generation, than on daughters, who are expected to marry and be wives and mothers rather than pursue careers. To be sure, this is changing, but the difference between the male and the female role concepts is still dominant. Counselors are still inclined, when a girl indicates that she wants to be a physician, to say, "Wouldn't you rather be a nurse or a teacher or go into one of the allied medical fields? Medicine is long, expensive, and demanding. It will interfere with your marriage and family plans." Fortunately for me, none of these negative attitudes was brought to bear on my decision to be a physician.

I was born in 1906, the only child of parents who were both physicians. They had graduated from the University of Illinois and Jefferson Medical College and had gone to practice medicine in a Seventh Day Adventist hospital in Sydney, Australia, where almost at once mother was told by the British Medical Association that, as a woman and a foreigner, she could not take the New South Wales state board. My father was accepted at once, but he was all for women in medicine and knew that mother would never be happy under such circumstances. This was in 1901.

Fortunately, a member of mother's medical class, Sir Maui Pomari, was a Maori and was minister of health for New Zealand and the Cook Islands. On hearing of her dilemma, he wrote to say that, if my parents wished to come to New Zealand, he would see that mother received equal treatment, and furthermore, she could be the physician to the Maori Royal Family.

My parents practiced medicine for twenty years in New Zealand. I was born at my grandparents' home in Washington state on a trip to America and returned when three months old with my parents to New Zealand. They practiced for five years in the country, at times riding ten to twenty miles on horseback through the bush to make a house call.

After my birth they moved to Auckland, New Zealand's largest city, where I remember accompanying them on house calls, literally in the "surrey with the fringe on top."

My mother had a problem obtaining hospital appointments. She was a surgeon and the only woman doctor in Auckland at that time. All public hospitals were managed by the Hospital and Charitable Aid Board, to which members were chosen in the general elections. She decided to run, or as the British say, "stand for office," and much to the surprise and chagrin of the local British Medical Association, she was elected with 10,000 more votes than the men who were elected. This put her in the position of not only being on hospital staffs but having influence as to who else would be appointed.

I heard discussions at dinner between my parents about the delightful situation, for my father was as pleased with her successes as if they had been his own. She was reelected to this office several times, and I remember my friends at school asking, "Do you think she will make it this time?" My answer was "Of course. She always gets everything she goes for."

We returned every three to four years to visit my grandparents in America, and on one such trip, my mother performed an appendectomy on a passenger at sea because the ship's doctor was not a surgeon. We were six days from the nearest port, and antibiotics were yet to be discovered. The operation was successful; there was great rejoicing on the ship and much favorable publicity when we landed in Vancouver, Canada. All of this added to my feeling that to be a woman doctor was very special.

When I was fourteen, we moved to California, where both my parents joined the faculty of Loma Linda University, mother as chairperson of the Department of Gynecology and my dad as chairperson of obstetrics, positions they held for ten years, until I had graduated in medicine. It was always taken for granted by my parents that I would study medicine, but for a while I had other ideas. I liked history and was not sure whether to take premedicine or major in history. I decided on the former with history electives and summer-school history courses. I entered medical school at the age of eighteen. In those days only two years of premedicine were required. This decision was due to parental pressure, and almost all of my friends were in the same class. During the second half of my freshman year I contracted scarlet fever, which in the days before antibiotics was a serious illness. I did a lot of thinking and suddenly realized that the thing I most wanted in life was to be a doctor.

My husband was a classmate. His grandfather, grandmother, father, older brother, and later a younger brother and sister were all physicians. He was the nephew and namesake of President Warren G. Harding, who had died in office two years before we met. We were married right after he was twenty-one because he had inherited enough money from his uncle to marry, even though our parents thought it unwise; they were sure I would have a child and never finish medicine.

Family planning methods were not as well known or reliable as they are today, and I did have a daughter fifteen months later, which was three months before graduation. I was out of class only one week, which in the late 1920s was unheard of, and this gave me a lifetime interest in planned parenthood. We were friendly with a couple; the husband was a classmate, and his wife was working to put him through medicine. She became pregnant, and in those days employers did not want obviously pregnant secretaries. We rented a house for all of us and paid her the same as her previous employer, as three of us were interns, and she kept house and cared for my baby when we were on duty.

Since my parents had practiced medicine for many years in a British country, they offered to send us to Scotland to the University of Edinburgh to obtain licentiates of the Royal College of Physicians and Surgeons. As soon as our internships were finished, we did this, and then continued residency training in California.

Three years later Warren was invited to sign a five-year contract as surgeon at the same hospital in Sydney, Australia, with which my parents had been briefly connected thirty-three years earlier. He returned to Scotland and became a Fellow of the Royal College of Surgeons, which is necessary to be a surgeon in a British country. We practiced medicine for eight years in Australia. Those were some of the most rewarding years of my life. We set out for Australia in 1933 with our two daughters, then aged five and one. The trip by ship took four weeks, including several ports of call. There was no air mail, only surface mail once a month. It took more adjustment to move halfway around the world than it does today.

The hospital we worked in was operated by the Seventh Day Adventists. Our salaries were very small. My specialty was obstetrics and gynecology, and I also gave some of my husband's anesthetics.

We liked Australia. It was very much like California in climate and natural surroundings. The people are more like western Americans than like those of the British Isles. The Australian continent is as large as the United States, but the total population then was no more than that of the city of New York, with three-quarters of the people living in five cities on the coast. Sydney was the largest, with two million inhabitants.

The majority of my patients came from the city, but some would come long distances from the outback, or country, areas to have surgery or to be delivered in our hospital. There were also wives of missionaries or plantation owners from Fiji, Papua, and the Solomon Islands, as well as engineers' wives from the goldmines of New Guinea and Fiji.

I look back on two medical experiences outside my normal medical practice that made these years very special. I started the first family planning clinic in Australia. In 1934 this was not a popular endeavor anywhere—and certainly not in a country that needed population more than anything else. But the individual woman had the same need and right to decide the size of her family that she has today, and the country woman with five to nine children and no medical help within a hundred miles needed birth-control information desperately. There was no law against giving contraceptive information, but there was one forbidding importation of any contraceptive into Australia. Since it was a primary producing country and the only company manufacturing rubber products was owned by Catholics, we had to manufacture our own condoms and diaphragms and also our own creams and jellies, which we did with great effort. No one made any personal profit from this, but the clinic was financed in this way. There is no space in this short narrative to elaborate on some of the details of the endeavor, but it could fill a book.

The second special reward was due to the fact that our salaries were vary meager and we could not afford interesting vacations. Therefore, each year Warren would sign on as a ship's surgeon for one trip to China, Japan, or the various South Pacific Islands. Wives were not allowed to accompany a ship surgeon, and women physicians were never hired.

The Seventh Day Adventists had several interisland schooners, from thirty-five to forty-eight feet in length, and once a year men from headquarters in Australia went to inspect the mine stations. I was allowed to accompany them, providing I took medical supplies and helped the sick as best I could during their days of inspection.

I spent six weeks on a forty-eight-foot schooner in the Fiji Islands; two weeks in Papua and New Guinea on a forty-two-foot schooner with ten Caucasians, twenty native inhabitants, several chickens, and one dog; and two weeks in the Solomon Islands. We spent a day on Guadalcanal before it became the sands of history. Samoa was included in one of the trips. Many of the missionary wives had been my patients while on furlough in Australia, and this was a meeting of old friends. Much of my work was in small, dirty villages, at times including tooth extractions, which could hardly be considered obstetrics and gynecology! In most of the villages the people never saw a dentist, so I did what I could. It was hard work, but looking back, I believe it was most rewarding. Certainly, these trips were something a tourist dollar could never buy.

We returned to the United States just before Pearl Harbor. Down under, there had already been two years of war. Anzac casualties had been numerous. Warren felt the United States would soon be involved and that we should return home. Our ship stopped at Tahiti and landed the Free French Forces, who in three days took the island from the Vichy French. Our ship waited until the Free French were in control.

Warren was a surgeon in the United States Navy during World War II, stationed in various places. Our family accompanied him when his duty was stateside. During this period I had a son.

After the war we returned to Warren's home in Columbus, Ohio, and we opened offices together. He was in full-time surgical practice, with the rank of clinical professor in the Department of Surgery at the Ohio State University College of Medicine. I was in part-time private practice and worked half-time in the Gynecological Clinic of the Ohio State University Student Health Service, also teaching a course on marriage and the family in the Department of Sociology and lecturing in adjacent educational institutions, such as Otterbein, Oberlin, and Marietta colleges, and Denison, Capital, and Ohio Wesleyan universities. For twenty-five years this has been my professional life style.

Ohio State University now has 47,000 students on the main campus, and 18,000 to 20,000 of them are women. Attitudes about obstetrical and gynecological student problems have changed during this time to an objective, completely permissive stance. Contraceptive advice is now given to all students regardless of age or marital status. Student insurance includes payment for abortions. Last year of 285 known pregnancies, 272 ended in abortion. All students are tested for venereal disease and treated in the health service.

My other voluntary medical interests have been in Planned Parenthood politics. Planned Parenthood of Columbus began in 1933 but became well organized in 1949, when the Academy of Medicine recognized us as an agency they would sponsor. Each year the academy appoints an official medical advisory board. I have served on the staff and as president of the governing board, of which I am a lifetime member. Two years ago we were funded by the Department of Health, Education, and Welfare to establish a family planning nurse-practitioners' school, which has graduated two classes of twelve Latin American students and six classes of registered nurses from Ohio and contiguous states.

At a national level, I have served for six years on the Planned Parenthood World Population Board and have been to India twice and South America once in this capacity. The American Medical Women's Association has been my other national interest. After serving in several national offices, I was president in 1972, which included being on the board of the Woman's Medical College of Pennsylvania.

January 23, 1974, was the one hundred and twenty-fifth anniversary of the graduation of Elizabeth Blackwell, the first woman physician of the Western world. The United States postmaster-general issued a stamp to commemorate the event, and I received the Elizabeth Blackwell Award from her alma mater, Hobart and William Smith Colleges. In June of 1975 I received an honorary doctorate of humane letters from Otterbein College.

In my opinion, my one accomplishment that transcends all others is the fact that all of my three children have been motivated to choose medical careers. The eldest, a daughter, specializes in pediatrics; the second daughter is a dentist specializing in pediadontia; and my son, the youngest, with J.D. and M.D. degrees, specializes in psychiatry. All are married and have children.

Through the years Warren has cooperated in everything in which I have been involved. In fact, I believe this is the most necessary ingredient in the life of a married woman physician—a husband whose ego is not threatened by his wife's successes.

Like the Roman god Janus, who had two faces, I can look backward to my mother and forward through my children, with a view of women in medicine that spans all of the twentieth century.

Reba Willits Schoenfeld
b. June 22, 1906

My parents are counted among the pioneers in Kelowna, British Columbia. My mother Ellen Carrie Bailey came to Kelowna with her family in 1893, when she was a little girl. My father Palmer Brooks Willits came in 1903 and went to work as a clerk in the village's only general store. He was a pharmacist, and a year or so later he went into partnership to establish the drugstore that was named after him.

Father and mother were married in 1905, and I was born the following year. We lived in an apartment over the drugstore until I was three, when we moved to a small farm on the edge of town. Mother and father were farmers at heart, but father continued his profession. It was a lonely life for me, as there were few neighbors and no children of my age nearby.

When I was six, my sister Mary was born. I have always felt a close bond with her and later developed an almost maternal attitude toward her. This interfered with a normal sisterly relationship, and it is only during the past years that I have overcome the tendency to "mother" her. This has resulted in an improvement in our feelings toward one another, and we are now very close.

When I was eight or nine, I became interested in medical things. We lived next door to the small cottage hospital that served Kelowna and the district. Father was on the board of directors and mother on the women's auxiliary. I was frequently allowed to watch the babies being bathed, as even in those days women occasionally went to the hospital for delivery of their babies; but no one thought of the health hazard created by a child in the nursery. My interest was no doubt fanned by father's attitude toward medicine. He would have studied for the profession had it been financially possible.

When I was ten or eleven, I met the girl who became one of my dearest friends—Audrey Knox. She was the eldest daughter of Dr. Benjamin Knox, whom I used to see around the hospital and who was a close friend of my father's. Audrey and I were inseparable companions until her marriage in 1930.

Kelowna's first physician Dr. Boyce had a marked influence on our family. He and my father were very close friends, and he was also our family doctor. All important decisions were discussed with him, and this included my education. When the time came for me to enter high school, there was serious talk about my future. Audrey's father and my father both wanted us to go into medicine. My mother did not approve, and I cannot ever remember being asked what I wanted. It did not occur to me to go against my father's wishes; but I think that, if I had been left to make my own decision, I would probably have studied nursing.

In June of 1922 Audrey and I passed our junior matriculation. We were both sixteen and too young to enter the University of Toronto, which had been picked as the most suitable of those accepting women in the medical course. As chemistry had not been taught in the Kelowna High School, we spent the year attending a private tutor to get a grounding, as we thought, in this subject, but even elementary chemistry without a laboratory is a poor introduction to a subject so vital to the study of medicine.

Then came the great day when I left with my father for Toronto, over 2000 miles away. Never will I forget my complete abandonment to tears as I said good-bye to my mother and sister. However, it didn't take me long to recover, and if ever there was a naive and overprotected first-year student, it was I. We had to enroll in the first year arts course, as we had not been able to take the senior matriculation in Kelowna. This enabled us to live in Queen's Hall, the residence for girls in University College.

When we entered the medical course after obtaining our senior matriculation, we had to leave Queen's Hall and move to Argyll House, the residence for women medical students. Here the women were more serious-minded, and on the whole closer to our financial level. My family made a real sacrifice to send me to college, and most of the women at Argyll House were in the same position.

The course at Toronto that led to the degree of M.D. was six years in length. The first three years dealt primarily with the basic sciences and the last three with clinical subjects, to me the most interesting. In my class there were seven women and ninety men. I do not remember suffering any discrimination, but of course we did a certain amount of complaining. One incident in particular comes to mind. In our final year the women's names were put on the slate for Saturday-evening emergency-ward duty, and we grumbled about the men's unwillingness to give up their fun night. However, we were soon pleased with the arrangement, as the accident cases brought in on this night far outnumbered those on week nights, and the experience we gained was well worth the sacrifice of giving up our Saturday evenings.

I managed to involve myself in some of the social activities on the campus, taking an interest in the Medical Women's Undergraduate Association. I was vice-president in my fifth year and president in my final year.

During my college years I did not return home for Christmases but spent them in the little village of Burford, Ontario, with my father's only sister and her family. The summers I spent at home. After I had started my clinical years, I made rounds with Dr. Boyce, who allowed me to assist with maternity cases and to observe at operations.

In May of 1931, I graduated without Audrey, as she had left college to be married. I shall never forget the thrill I felt the first time I was addressed as "Doctor." It was almost as though I had never believed I would become a qualified M.D., and this convinced me. The highly charged atmosphere of bidding farewell to so many dear friends and college associates, of being the center of attention as the envied graduate, and most of all of starting out on my career at last made graduation an occasion I don't think I will ever forget. I had an appointment at the Vancouver General Hospital for a rotating internship, and the thrill of being in the west again equaled that of starting to work, even in the lowly position of an intern. It was my first taste of having a job with a paycheck.

Although the Vancouver General Hospital was not a teaching hospital, the staff and many of the visiting doctors were most generous in sharing their knowledge and experience with us. There were about thirty interns, and only two of us were women. I enjoyed my two years at the hospital both for the experience and knowledge that I gained and for the social life I enjoyed as part of the large hospital.

I had planned to continue working at the Vancouver for a third year, but Dr. Boyce was anxious for me to come into practice with him, and this was in the middle of the hungry thirties. These things combined to launch me into practice in Kelowna in the spring of 1934. Father built an office at the back of his drugstore. Half the space accommodated Dr. Boyce's office and ophthalmic chair. I had an examining room and a consulting room, and we shared a small laboratory and waiting room. It was with mixed feelings that I undertook practice in my native town and working with the doctor who had delivered me. As it turned out, my practice was a mixture of men and women, children and adults, old friends and new acquaintances. I was the first medical woman most of them had encountered and so was a bit of a novelty; in fact, some of my patients came out of curiosity. However, many of them came because they preferred to attend a woman doctor. Dr. Boyce was endeavoring to confine his practice to ophthalmology, and he referred the other patients to me, but there were some who would have none of that. This was particularly true of people in the older age group and of the Indians. Well do I remember having to deliver an Indian woman of a retained placenta in a dirty home, without any assistance from the disgruntled husband because the "old man" hadn't come.

Dr. Knox and Dr. Boyce would still on occasion take home deliveries. However, I didn't like maternity work at the best of times, so I began to try to educate the women on the advantages of going to the hospital for delivery. Eventually I won out, and even Dr. Boyce was converted.

The night work I found very trying. It was the interference with my sleep that troubled me rather than the unpleasantness of being out alone at night. At first it was a real challenge to get out of the house and away on the call before my mother could get dressed to come with me. Eventually I persuaded her to let me out on my own. I think she always imagined that the call came from a dope addict who was waiting "to do me in." Even in Kelowna, which at that time had a population of about 3000 to 4000, we had transient dope addicts. Twice in the five years I practiced there, my medical kit was stolen from my car. Each time the bag was recovered minus the morphine and heroin. Some of the very early morning calls in the summer provided me with beautiful experiences, reminding me of the early morning horseback rides that Audrey and I used to take when we were at school.

Another aspect of general practice that bothered me was the irregular hours at work and the resultant interference with my private life. In a small town with a central telephone operator it was almost impossible to get away from the telephone. Central, as we called her, knew who my friends were, in many cases knew my patients, and seemed to be able to ferret me out if I had purposely neglected to leave word at home as to where I might be found. General practice was so demanding and so discouraging, for few people could afford medical care, that I looked about for a change.

During this time I had been conducting a "well-baby clinic," which was sponsored by the Women's Institute. Here babies were weighed and measured, health habits were discussed, and mothers were advised about general health. I found this very satisfying and more meaningful than patching up sick children. I had also been appointed to be visiting physician at the small local preventorium. The patients were young children who were malnourished and therefore, in those days, considered to be susceptible to tuberculosis. This work I also found rewarding, and so my interest in preventive medicine began.

At the beginning of World War II I gave up my practice and went back to Toronto to study public health. I was the only woman in the class of about thirty men and had the advantage of having done general practice. I think this gave me a greater appreciation of the value of the preventive side of health care, and I thoroughly enjoyed the course. In May of 1940 I obtained my diploma in public health; I was the first woman in British Columbia to do so.

Most of the men had been granted fellowships through their city or provincial health departments. I had applied for one to the provincial officer of health in British Columbia, but he did not bother to answer my letter. Two young men were granted fellowships, however. With my mother's financial help and all my savings, which at the end of the thirties didn't amount to much, I had scraped through, but again a job was essential. There were two prospects: the first was a National Research Fellowship to work with Dr. Ronald Hare on the War Wound Commission, to study streptococcal infections in war wounds; the other opening was with the Provincial Department of Health in British Columbia. The new provincial health officer Dr. Gregoire Amyot told me he would never employ a woman as a health officer, so that left the War Wound Commission.

The research project under Dr. Hare's guidance proved fascinating and was a year well spent, but I missed working with people and longed for the west; so at the conclusion of the grant I returned to Vancouver.

Dr. Stewart Murray, senior medical health officer of the Metropolitan Health Committee of Vancouver, did not share Dr. Amyot's views on employing women and took me on his staff without hesitation. Nevertheless, the newspapers reported my appointment with the headline "Woman Takes Man's Job." In September of 1941 I started to work in Vancouver as a health-unit director, and so began twenty-three years of satisfying and exciting work. The city and surrounding districts were divided into units, and each had a director, who supervised public health nurses, nursing staff, and clerical workers. The area that I directed was a large working-class district with many health problems. I was responsible for the examination of schoolchildren, and I acted as consultant of well-baby clinics and advised the public health nurses on their work.

In 1942 the director of School Health Services retired, and Dr. Charles Gundry, who was director of mental hygiene, was appointed; in his absence overseas I was made acting director. This meant I had two positions, for as staff was difficult to obtain, no one was available to take over the health unit. The broader scope of the new position added greatly to its interest, even though it meant much extra work. Everyone was working hard during the war years, and the excitement of being on the planning level of so many projects made up for the inconvenience.

When, at the end of the war, Dr. Gundry returned from overseas, he retained his title but did not take any responsibility for its direction. He continued to direct the Division of Mental Health. In recognition of my direction of the service my title was changed to associate director.

After the war years the doctors returned, and I was able to turn over the health unit to its previous director and confine myself entirely to the School Health Service. This afforded the opportunity of coordinating the various aspects of health care with the outpatient department staffs of the Children's Hospital and the Health Center for Children at the Vancouver General Hospital. I also took part in the medical examination of students at the University of British Columbia, where the Metropolitan Health Committee conducted the Student Health Service. The university was booming, as men and women recently returned from the war were taking their reestablishment credits, and we were faced with examining hundreds of new students.

Another very interesting part of my work was the medical supervision of the students of the Provincial School for the Deaf and Blind. There had been very little communication between the medical and educational professions in the field of diagnosing and educating these children, particularly the deaf. When the university established its medical school, around 1950, there was an influx of top-flight doctors and an upswing in new plans for health care of children.

One of the most exciting medical discoveries was the development of the Salk vaccine for protection against acute anterior poliomyelitis. Only someone who has practiced medicine before the day of Salk vaccine can fully appreciate the relief from anxiety that it afforded. In 1955, as soon as the vaccine became available, we held clinics throughout the metropolitan area. The vaccine was in short supply, so we could not immunize all schoolchildren the first year, but in a matter of two or three years the vaccine was available at no charge to all infants, children, and young adults.

About this time, there was a reorganization of the health department; I was transferred from the school-board staff back to the Metropolitan Health Committee, and my title was changed to director of medical services. I was then in charge of child-health conferences, preschool children, school health services, and the preemployment examination of teachers.

With the establishment of the medical school at the University of British Columbia came the involvement with the medical students who attended school health examinations. During these we stressed, as always, the preventive aspects of health care.

Although Dr. Murray did not appear to have any prejudice against employing women on his medical staff, he had certain reservations about giving them much authority. This was brought home to me very forcibly when his assistant was about to retire. My position was next in line, but I did not want the job, as I preferred the work I was doing in the schools. I told Dr. Murray that I was not going to apply. Nevertheless, he advised the Metropolitan Health Committee against employing me on the basis that a woman was not suitable for the position.

In 1964 I retired. I was only fifty-eight, but I felt the pressure of change and was eager to plan my retirement. In 1947 I had bought a lakeshore property in Kelowna for my dream home and was impatient to get on with it and the garden. A most suitable young man with certification in pediatrics, as well as in public health, was found for my replacement. The staff gave me a big farewell party, at which I shed copious tears—tears of sentiment, not sorrow, through which I was able to laugh. It was one of the highlights of my life.

It was again with mixed feelings that I took the next step, that of selling my West Vancouver house, where I had been so happy, and moving away from all the wonderful friends I had made. Mother was living in Kelowna, crippled by a car accident, and there was my beautiful property, so this seemed the wise thing to do. When I finally moved in, there was plenty to be done, especially in the garden.

A retired person in a town like Kelowna need never want for something to do, as there are many agencies that need volunteers. I had worked in Vancouver for the United Way and was soon at it again here. There were other groups that I worked with, and soon I volunteered for the Elizabeth Fry Society and to drive for Meals on Wheels.

Shortly after I moved into my home I joined the Unitarian Fellowship, which had just been organized. There were only about twenty-five of us, and we held meetings every second Sunday evening.

While I was in Vancouver the women in the normal school would ask me how to meet young men who were single. I always advised them to join a church group. One would almost imagine that I was taking my own advice, as it was at the Unitarian Fellowship that I met Henryk Schoenfeld, who was a Polish chemical engineer. It wasn't "love at first sight," but we were certainly attracted to each other from the beginning. Six months later we were married at the Unitarian church in Vancouver. Henryk had been a widower for three years and was lonely, and so was I. We marveled at our good fortune in finding each other and settled happily into the house built for my retirement. We enjoyed our common interests, going to concerts and traveling to Vancouver to hear visiting artists. We enjoyed our friends and took trips back to London, Ontario, to visit Henryk's elderly mother and his old friends there. My mother was still alive and was delighted over our marriage.

It was too good to last. In March of 1970 Henryk was stricken with symptoms of a brain tumor, from which he died in March of 1971. I was shattered. I had waited so long to enjoy the love and close companionship of a respected and highly intelligent man—and to have him snatched away so soon seemed most tragic to me.

However, the passage of time has modified my grief, and my friends have rallied around, so that I once again find life worthwhile as I sit here alone in my lakeside home, writing about the things I have done.

AUSTRALIA

Joan Refshauge
b. December 3, 1906

The eldest of five children, I was born in Australia in the Edwardian era to parents reared in the Victorian age. My mother was eighteen and my father almost forty years of age at my birth. My mother, a Scot, was an only child, raised in a strict Presbyterian atmosphere. My father was the youngest of four sons of an English mother and a Danish father. Both my parents grew up on the land and owned dairy farms in the rich western district of Victoria. My mother was all the ideal mother is said to be; she was gay, brave, deeply understanding, and wise, giving invaluable and correct advice when asked. At the time of his marriage, father was a primary-school teacher, and he was the headmaster of an agricultural high school at his retirement. He knew the effect of chronic illness very early. My grandmother was bedridden following her last childbirth, and her condition was said to be due to a drunken doctor attending the birth. The money for my father to study law went in futile attempts to cure her. When my grandmother died of "Russian flu," my father undertook the care of my grandfather.

There were four young children in my family when my father was medically boarded out of the education department for disseminated sclerosis and was given three to five years to live. My mother spared no effort to get further opinions. Actually, father had had poliomyelitis, and he lived for another sixteen years, finally dying of cardiac failure. Father suffered from "nasal catarrh" and severe headaches. Our whole life revolved around health. No doubt, the family suffered financially and socially, but the brunt fell on mother. Father rarely went out, never at night, and mother's gaiety ceased. We had many visitors, scholars and professional people, as well as others from most walks of life, who enjoyed discussions with father. We children were allowed to go and play away from home. As we grew older, we had parties every weekend, which altered in type as we grew up. Our childhood and youth were very happy, and I feel we were unconsciously taught consideration of others because of father's illness and mother's great love for him and for us.

According to my mother, father's experience had made him cautious, and he would sometimes call the doctor unnecessarily. Doctors became friends and guests, so I have little memory of them as physicians in my early life. I do not remember the school doctor who found that I was almost blind, but I do remember the ophthalmologist who gave me sweets. I have a gross astigmatism. I remember fainting before hepatitis was diagnosed and a little boy's putting a pillow under my head, as I had a severe headache, but I do not remember the doctor who came. I was then about four years old. It is possible that doctors were part of our life and were friends. As far as I know, there was no medical interest on either side of the family. The exception was a cousin, my mother's age, who married a doctor at the end of World War I. Indeed, he was a hero to us; he was in uniform.

We were an allergic family, although that term was not known. We suffered from headaches, hives, skin rashes, bilious attacks (after certain foods), and in addition, we children developed most childhood diseases.

It is hard to be sure what is real memory and what I have been told. When I was four years old I remember a night with noises, voices, and movement. We were hushed and ushered elsewhere to sleep. The next morning we had a new baby sister—the only one born at home. I did connect the unusual night with the unusual event. I remember kicking a doctor when revaccinated at about six years.

Adjacent to the Wangaratt State School was the agricultural high school, of which my father was headmaster. He often came across to see how I was progressing and found me standing on a form outside the door or in a boys' class for talking out of turn. I was also very bad at spelling. Father forgave me for the latter because of my eyes but not for the former. We spent a lot of my playtime together so that I could learn spelling by heart. I am still a bad speller, and I did not like school.

When my father retired, I was about eight years old. We moved to Melbourne from the country, but even this change of environment had no effect on me. Father was still master of the house, and his word was law. If necessary, however, my mother would manipulate a decision in our favor. When father was well, he was great company. He would discuss our problems and tell stories from history, literature, mythology, science, and many other fields.

On medical advice, I was taken from school when twelve years of age to "run wild," because I was too emotional and because the fact that blindness might ensue could not be ignored. The pneumonic influenza hit Melbourne that year. Both mother and I developed it. I remember mother's being taken away and my youngest brother being born shortly afterward. They were in the hospital for three months. In this day and age it seems fantastic to think that I did not know my mother was pregnant or understand what the neighbors were talking about when they discussed her "condition." I had "learned" cooking when I was ten years old and loved it. This was a help to father, as I shared the responsibility of running the family in mother's absence. Because of father's grief and worry over mother and my lack of fun, I was allowed to stay up an hour later than the others. During that time I learned a lot about adult sorrow and worry and about my parents' background in early Australia. I learned what a moral code was and also how the wrongdoing of one member of a family could reflect badly on the whole family—a lesson that guided many of my future actions.

When mother came home, my music lessons recommenced and it was decided that I should sit for the examination held at the university conservatorium. I did well, and the acting professor sought an interview with my mother. She was asked to allow me to be taught at the conservatorium, as I showed promise. It was the only subject I learned while "running wild."

About two years later a friend said to my mother, "Educate Joan. Give her a chance to let her mind grow even if she goes blind; otherwise, she will only be the family slut!" *Slut* caused immediate action. I was sent to a tutoring college to learn the subjects my father could not teach me, and in six months I passed eight subjects in the intermediate certificate, including music, and I had suffered no deterioration emotionally or optically.

I later learned that our parents had discussed our future and decided in favor of leaving us educated rather than leaving us money. About this time I learned of the three noble professions—the clergy, teaching, and medicine—and how fortunate it was that one of these—teaching—was open to women.

The next year I went back to school and continued at the conservatorium. I did well, getting honors in the senior certificate (matriculation). My conservatorium teacher died at the end of that year. My father believed that this had made me unstable and immediately stopped my music lessons; mathematics and science, he said were a stabilizing influence, and in fact, these became my main studies that next year.

At the university I entered a science program, majoring in mathematics and chemistry. I found some girl friends from school doing medicine and loving it. I also heard that "free places" were available for medicine. I approached my father about changing over to medicine and explained that the fees would be paid. The answer was "No." No woman should pursue such a course. In retrospect, I feel he probably reckoned that I would be independent sooner if I took up teaching. I ended up with an M.Sc. in chemistry and started working toward a diploma in education. During this course the medical officer of school health spoke to us. I was fascinated and thought what wonderful work it was. It was then that I was told about the school doctor who had first discovered my disability. Then we were taken to visit various schools for those with differing disabilities. At the school for retarded children I saw a beautiful girl knitting. When she looked up, her eyes were blank. We were told a lot of facts about the pupils, that their parents were former pupils of the school. At about that time I heard about a doctor working among the poor, treating them and giving them medicine, all free. My youthful egotism and idealism were fired by these events, and I decided that, if I could ever get the chance, I would study medicine.

Father wanted me to get my Ph.D. in science in England. He died that year, and mother insisted that I go to England. I did not get there in time to enter the university, and as this was during the depression, there was no work available to keep me going until the next term, so I came home.

At the invitation of the professor, I had been a demonstrator in chemistry from my third year, and I had tutored in various subjects at my old school and had later taught chemistry and math at the university. I arrived home from abroad in time to regain my demonstrating job and was able to teach math and science at several schools and to tutor, as well. Indeed, I was well off. Two years later, after a broken engagement, I went straight into second-year medicine, picking up botany and zoology and carrying on demonstrating, tutoring, and teaching. It was a tight schedule but an enjoyable one. When I had to start hospital clinics, I had to give up all my day work except tutoring. I was fortunate to be appointed to lecture in math to engineering students at the Working Man's College. I quickly found that women were not acceptable, but by explaining that I worked at night and studied during the day, I overcame that opposition, as well as the disciplinary problems.

When I married, my husband insisted that I finish my medical studies, and I agreed, provided I paid my own fees. Once married, I had to resign the lectureship, although I did continue tutoring until my final year. I borrowed from the university to finish that year. I obtained a residency at the Alfred Hospital—a training school—having missed out at the Melbourne Hospital, my student training school. The male graduates objected because I was a woman and the women because I was married. But the unpleasantness passed, and the others were very helpful.

The following year I had to resign from the Queen Victoria Hospital for Women because of morning sickness. When this settled down, I accepted a residency at the Chronic and Incurable Diseases Hospital. Comfort and understanding were as important as treatment, and I enjoyed my time there, only leaving to enter the hospital for the birth of my son.

My husband was in Lae, New Guinea, as a civilian, and there was no word from him after the bombings there. When my son was about three months old, I was informed that my husband was presumed alive and a private A.N.G.A.U. and that monetary adjustment was necessary, backdated to the first bombing of Rabaul. My mother looked after my son, and I became senior medical officer of the Mildura Base Hospital. I spent every weekend off duty in Melbourne. My mother became ill, and I resigned my position only to find I was "man-powered" and had to await approval and replacement. A mothercraft nurse then looked after my son in Melbourne. On my return to Melbourne I was directed immediately to the Royal Women's Hospital.

When my mother's health improved, I enlisted in the Army Medical Corps as women medical officers were urgently needed. I was posted to 2/2 A.O.P.D. (Army Out-Patient Department) and subsequently was responsible for the health of the women in the army and allied services stationed in and around Melbourne.

After demobilization and a holiday with my husband and son, I took a refresher course at the Royal Children's and Queen Victoria hospitals. I was the first woman to be appointed medical officer to the Public Health Department (PHD) in what was then the Territory of Papua and New Guinea, and I joined my husband in Port Moresby, Papua, when I was permitted to enter the country. My work at first was that of a general practitioner, but I eventually pioneered in the Infant, Child and Maternal Health (ICMH) service. This started as a minor branch of a division of the PHD and was a mobile village clinic to bring infant, child, and antenatal care to the villages, although no treatment of any sick people was undertaken. The ICMH service expanded to include school health, preschool activities, and the training of indigenous girls in all facets of the work. The ICMH became a division of the PHD, and I was appointed the first assistant director, with direct access to the director of public health.

I retired from my position in Papua in November of 1963, had a holiday, and joined the Queensland Public Health Department as a medical officer in the Maternal and Child Welfare Service eight months later. Eventually I became deputy director of the service and retired on December 31, 1973, having served for nine years. I have recently completed a refresher course and am never happier than when practicing my profession.

I must say that some of the senior medical women of my acquaintance lost part of their femininity en route. Today, however, I believe that any successful woman has a certain responsible and reliable air, irrespective of her work. The position of women today is entirely different from what it was in my youth. I knew that, although I did better in examinations than some men, they had more and better opportunities open to them. The resentment, however brief, over my appointment to a junior residency at one of the three training schools exemplified this. My forced resignation from the lectureship because I was a *married woman* was just a fact of life. When the public health service was reformed in the Territory of Papua and New Guinea, I was one of the first women to obtain permanency. Imagine how angry I was to find that a woman received only a percentage of a man's wage and that of course my units of superannuation were smaller than those of a man in my position. My joy and pride turned to anger. Apart from this drawback in Australia, women had been "liberated" since before federation. There were certainly women in the medical and legal profession, and I think there were also some architects, with a growing range of choices open to them. In my day at the Melbourne University there were not only women lecturers but associate professors. As to my motives for going into medicine, I am fairly sure my youthful desire was to be like mother—to get married and have a large family. I believe that if I had the opportunity to choose a career today, I would once again go into medicine, but I would choose a different field. I liked government work, for there was no involvement with money from patients. I do object, however, to the fact that, at an age determined by the government, retirement is mandatory, the assumption being of course that senility ensues on that day. In private practice men and women work until death, disease, or some disability prevents them from continuing, and that is far better than forced retirement.

Elisabeth Meyling-Hylkema

b. February 3, 1907

I was born in the Netherlands, and until my eighteenth year I lived in a small village in Friesland, in the north of Holland. The village was mainly inhabited by rich farmers and very poor workmen. My parents, however, belonged to the middle class. My father was a clerk and my mother a qualified midwife. Mother had to practice under the most difficult circumstances; working mostly during the night, she had to walk through a bare, dark countryside and along small roads, canals, and bridges. She was a beloved helper of the poor. My father too was much respected. He was a fervent socialist of the pioneer period. In the part of Friesland where I lived, the general poverty led to the development of socialist and syndicalist movements. I am convinced that these circumstances have been of great importance in my way of living, my choice of work, and my attitude toward my parents, who had three children, of whom I was the second.

When I was thirteen years old, my brother developed multiple sclerosis, which was a heavy blow for the family. This circumstance intensified my childhood wish to become a doctor of medicine. However, at the end of my secondary-school education, it turned out that my brother's illness had jeopardized my chances because my parents had too many expenses. Still, I managed to finish my first year at the university with a minimum of money, and after that I received a scholarship. From 1925 until 1932 I had a wonderful and interesting time at the University of Groningen. The studies went very smoothly, and the eight female students had a sound and pleasant association with the fifty-two male students.

Just before my graduation there was a vacancy at the psychiatric-neurological clinic in Groningen. I was advised to apply for the assistantship, since I had shown great interest in this kind of work. The professor, however, told me, "Of course, you may apply, but I will not appoint you, as I do not want any female assistants." Imagine my surprise when, after I had received the final certificate, the professor suddenly put his hand on my shoulder and said, "Ladies and gentlemen, this doctor will become my first female assistant." But he whispered to me, "And you start tomorrow." This was some kind of revenge, as he did not want to appear weak. Future assistants were always given a two-week holiday before starting work.

My training period lasted for four years. This was a wonderful time. We worked very hard, but a nice friendship developed among the colleagues and we learned a lot from interesting patients and from our severe but human professor. I was allowed to work only in the female wards of psychiatry and neurology. Our professor had introduced active therapy in psychiatry in Holland and especially work therapy. I was enthusiastic about its results and intended to try to get a job in a mental hospital.

Other professors followed with interest the "experiment" of appointing a female assistant. After I had been in the training program for three years, the professor in gynecology said to my mother, "Your daughter is in the psychiatric department, and to my astonishment, it has worked out very well and everybody is pleased. I'm afraid I too will have to take a girl in the future." And indeed, since the beginning of World War II, in 1939, all clinics have been crowded with women doctors.

In 1935 it was my turn to become a chief assistant. I had intended to leave as soon as I qualified in order to avoid this complication, but my turn came sooner than I had expected. I was sure that my professor would again find it difficult to give leadership to a woman. The entire hospital staff and all my fellow assistants waited tensely to see what would happen. The professor was in a very bad mood. Just at that time a woman friend of mine who was very able and who had been an assistant at the Children's Hospital for years was passed over for a chief assistantship. A young man who had been an assistant for only six weeks was appointed instead. Suddenly my professor called me and said, "You must apply quickly. You deserve to become chief assistant as much as your colleagues do. Now I realize how badly we have treated you." So I became chief of the department. Nevertheless, I had the impression that the professor always expected more from me than he did from my colleagues. And as a matter of fact, this expectation has continued throughout my whole career. A woman doctor has always to be a bit more clever and more active than most of her male colleagues to enjoy the same esteem. I think that is why we women sometimes try to do our work as men would. We often hide our female identity behind a male attitude in our work.

In 1936 I was given the job I had always wanted—head of a department in a mental hospital, combined with social-psychiatric duties. In Groningen I had had the opportunity to gain experience in social psychiatry. I was the only female doctor among twenty-nine applicants, but I was appointed, in the first instance only for one year, since the board was afraid it was too hard a job for a woman.

Work in an old mental hospital with old-fashioned methods was of course a challenge. Everything I was able to change and modernize was a gain and gave satisfaction to me, to the staff, and even more to the patients. The board was very helpful indeed. I worked independently and very industriously among nice colleagues. It was a period of radical change in mental hospitals. We immediately tried out all new approaches and were enthusiastic about the successes. We experimented with active therapy, recreation, early releases with extramural checking, more individual treatment, more aftercare, and shock and insulin therapy. After the war came leucotomy, chemotherapy, and group therapy, such as psychodrama. We tried to avoid hospitalization. Sometimes the results were wonderful.

I believe that working in a mental hospital gives great satisfaction, especially for a woman. At least, this was true in my time. You played and had time to play several roles. You were therapist, general doctor, mother, friend, and sometimes police officer or mayor. Nowadays this attitude has been discarded. Teamwork has come to the fore; the patient is now a "client," and maternalism is considered to be an attitude stimulating hospitalization and dependence. But at that time I felt that I had to be the one who gave the patient safety, sympathy, and self-confidence, with the help of the staff. I am afraid that intensive teamwork will confuse the client. He or she has too many people to identify with.

In 1940, two weeks before the war struck Holland, I was awarded my doctor's degree with the thesis "A Contribution to the Knowledge of Narco-lepsy." After that I underwent a training psychoanalysis for one year. Unfortunately, my Viennese analyst, a pupil of Freud, was sent to a concentration camp and never came back.

In 1941 I married a veterinarian, who later became a professor in anatomy and embryology. Two daughters were born to us, and we had a very happy family life. The first year of my marriage I had a part-time job. I was very strong and had no difficulties in combining my family life, my representative functions, and my work. My mother lived with us, and I had a young housekeeper to look after the children and run the house. I am sure no one suffered from my career. My two daughters are both married, have children, and are working, too, one as a part-time doctor and the other in her home as a translator.

During the war I had a private practice for a couple of years. I left the hospital because the superintendent was a Nazi. During that period I also worked in a child-guidance clinic. But after the war, in 1945, the mental hospital needed me badly and I took a full-time job in a male ward of the county hospital's modern sanatorium, which cares for 200 patients. There I could give all types of modern treatment under very pleasant circumstances. There was much to improve after the war, when hunger, neglect, and danger had reigned.

In 1958 I retired. My health and that of my husband declined. I continued, however, to give lectures and consultations to the staffs of hospitals. In 1969 my husband died. Some years later I became seriously ill, and now I am too old to practice. A psychiatrist, however, is never without work and many friends and acquaintances know the way to my apartment for a cup of coffee and advice.

If I had to choose again, I would go in for the same career and specialty. I have had a wonderful life, which is a great privilege. I am still interested in new approaches in psychiatry, although I do not always agree with them.

During my life I have learned that we women doctors should try to realize that often we will have a different view of human problems from that of our male colleagues, even though we have had the same training. Therefore, we must not always try to identify ourselves with the men. Sometimes it is necessary for our experience as women to be used. There are many subjects in psychiatry, as well as in general medicine, that should be studied from a masculine *and* from a feminine point of view. Problems regarding marriage, the pill, abortion, sex, emancipation, and so forth, which so often color general illnesses and disturbances, can be interpreted differently and frequently misunderstood because they are considered from a masculine point of view in our masculine cultural pattern. There is plenty of work for women doctors. They have to be doctors first but without forgetting that they are also female human beings.

Alma Dea Morani
b. March 21, 1907

The request that I submit an autobiographical account searching for the early reasons that motivated me to study medicine is a real challenge. Such a search requires contemplation and an attempt to recall and chronicle the facts. Here is an honest effort to dig into my conscious and subconscious and to supply factual information without any attempt at analysis or evaluation.

I was born in New York City, the eldest of four children, of Italian parents. My father came from a middle-class Italian family in Reggio, Calabria, near the boot of Southern Italy. Both his father and grandfather were sculptors, chiefly concerned with creating religious monumental figures to adorn churches and castles. My father frequently spoke of his early apprenticeship, in which he helped his father repairing wood and stone carvings, church decorations, and various art pieces commissioned by the local municipal leaders, so much of his childhood was spent working with tools. Because he early demonstrated a talent for drawing and sculpture, he was sent to art school in Naples at the age of fourteen. He became a competent painter, creating lovely landscapes and beautiful realistic flowers. He finally specialized in portraits from living subjects, using both media, the colors of paint for pictures or the forms of clay for busts. He left a wealth of original bas-reliefs in public buildings, theaters, and private homes in many cities in the United States and Canada.

My mother was a language teacher coming from a so-called noble family of Sienna, Italy. I now view her as an intellectual who qualified as a high-school teacher in the province of Tuscany and spent several years teaching in the lyceum in Sienna. She was unusually well educated and spoke four languages—Italian, German, French, and English—having acquired English after she and my father settled in New York. Her strong character and spirit of independence were unusual in her society. When an opportunity for travel arose, she elected to go to Berlin as language teacher to the children of the Italian consulate. She spent several years in Nuremburg, perfecting her German, studying art, and enjoying the social events of her time and station. In addition to teaching, she wrote short stories and occasional poems, some of which were published. She also acquired dexterity with lace-making and needlepoint work, a talent that she used for the rest of her life and that was much admired in America.

My childhood was not extraordinary. I remember nothing before the age of three or four years. Because there were no physicians in the background of either of my parents, I do not recall the subject of studying medicine ever being mentioned during my childhood. My mother insisted that I go to college, and she suggested that I become an interpreter or a pharmacist. My father, thinking I had some artistic talent, felt that I should become an artist, like himself, and wanted to put me in an art school. While I recall considering these suggestions, none of them had a strong appeal for me. I passed through grade school easily, as I was always a good student, and remember excelling in English and art classes. During my last year in grammar school the principal selected me as her personal messenger, and I frequently carried notes from her to various teachers. Although this interrupted my classwork, I kept up my studies without much effort. Reading was my hobby, and my nose was always buried in a book. Dear mother insisted on teaching me Italian at home in the evenings, for she believed in languages, and in a few years I had mastered reading and writing Italian.

Before graduation from grammar school, probably in 1920, when I was thirteen, I heard about Girl Scouts, as this movement had then become active in New York City. I joined Troop 18 in the Bronx and acquired a Girl Scout uniform. The comradeship had a strong appeal, and I was thrilled that one could join such outdoor activities, for my ability to excel in athletics was a source of pride to me. In addition to attending weekly meetings, I spent my summer vacations working in a Girl Scout camp and enjoyed the training offered in nature lore, swimming, and horseback riding. Fortunately, my parents approved of my scouting interests and helped me. My troop had an excellent leader, who was a dedicated intellectual woman of Jewish background. She had a warm, friendly personality and managed to instruct, guide, and inspire her troop of about twenty girls in my age group. This woman was a born teacher and an important influence in my growth and development, for she had the wisdom to make us think for ourselves. She selected me for special attention and advice because she felt that I had high intelligence and was not lazy. She encouraged individual tendencies, and I was soon made patrol leader. I learned many scout crafts that I could teach the younger girls.

At this point the course in first aid brought to my attention the enormous field of medicine and surgery. My scout leader opened my eyes to the possibility of helping injured people through knowledge of first aid. Reading first-aid and anatomy books and understanding the rules for good health and hygiene seemed very worthwhile and exciting. Suddenly the realization came to me that with such knowledge I could help other people stay strong and healthy and, even more important, help to repair people who were injured or to heal those who were sick. In truth, I feel this was the first motivating step that directed my thinking toward the possibility of studying medicine. Most significant was the opportunity to assist the camp nurse during my summer-vacation work, when campers became ill or were injured. Here I was thrilled with the excitement of playing nurse-doctor, and I learned much from the camp nurse about how to examine children and to give first aid. I soon realized the limitations of the nurse's activities, and this confirmed my decision not to be a nurse but to become an actual doctor.

While I was in high school, a woman biology teacher heard of my intention and definitely encouraged my ambition. Studies in chemistry, biology, and geography absorbed me, and I collected specimens from the plant and animal world. Dissection of frogs and lizards fascinated me, and I yearned for the day when I could dissect and study a human body. Fortunately, I had no fear of live or dead animals, and at one time I kept several small, harmless snakes in a box in my bedroom. When the mother snake delivered forty tiny snakes, my parents made me deliver my treasure to the local zoo.

Even after I entered high school, my scouting interest continued—and with it the image of acquiring the ability to rescue the injured, to cure them, and return them to their duties. Yet it seemed an impossible dream—to think of becoming a woman surgeon, something unheard of in 1922. I realized too the years of sacrifice and hard study that would be needed as preparation for medical school. Once again my scouting friends helped me by introducing me to a local hospital, where my Saturdays were spent doing volunteer work in the pharmacy, the clinics, and finally in the operating room. It seemed to me that I was getting closer to my ambition by walking hospital corridors and talking to the surgeons, who, incidentally, were amused by the girl in pigtails who dared to say, "Someday I too will be a surgeon."

High-school studies passed uneventfully, and again my grades were good and my courses easy. I consulted no one but decided to attend evening high school in order to learn stenography, typing, and bookkeeping. This I managed for two years until the authorities caught up with my ambitious plan and I was forced to abandon evening school so that I could graduate from day high school. My next step was to find a part-time job in order to earn and save money to enter college and do premedical studies. Despite my parents' objections, I worked in the afternoons and on Saturdays for a Jewish dentist as an oral hygienist. He had many Italian patients, and I was a good interpreter. I took his plaster impressions and sterilized his instruments. This activity made me feel that I was getting closer to learning to be a doctor.

In 1925 I entered New York University at its Washington College division. This institution is renowned for its premedical studies, and I spent three hard years there, preparing to enter medical school. We were 8 female premedical students in a class of 125, which made conditions crowded, noisy, and competitive. During the first year four of the women dropped out. I remained, one of the four determined women slaving to obtain good grades. My best friend Hilda and I agreed that we must become doctors, for this ideal offered us knowledge, status, a chance to earn money, and most important, the opportunity to help suffering people. Hilda and I remain good friends today, and we both recall that only one male faculty member encouraged us through the premedical examinations. Days there were very long, as my family had moved to Staten Island and I had to travel for an hour and a half morning and evening.

When the time came to apply for medical school, Hilda and I agreed to seek one outside of crowded New York City. With our parents' consent, we chose the Woman's Medical College of Pennsylvania, a grade-A school, at that time restricted to females. As we had good qualifications, we were quickly admitted, and we arrived at the medical college full of hope and enthusiasm. I felt sure then that I would get to be a doctor and later a surgeon.

It is customary for medical students to seek summer jobs to earn good money, so during the vacation months I obtained a position in a state mental hospital in New York State. I was the only medical student accepted, and my duties included examining and cleaning the teeth of the mentally ill. I also assisted at autopsies and became friendly with the pathologist on the psychiatric staff. It was wonderful to gain knowledge in both fields, and I much enjoyed this summer work. Admittedly, I had some fears when examining the violently insane. I thought these patients sad and hopeless, which strengthened my motivation toward surgery, because as a surgeon, I could repair broken bones or removed diseased parts. One of my chores was to sew up bodies after autopsies, and when the chief pathologist noticed my interest, he had long discussions with me. He encouraged me to become a surgeon, although he spoke of the great difficulties that a woman doctor would encounter in getting proper surgical training. "You will be a pioneer," he said, and his words came true.

Medical school studies were a joy because I maintained high grades and obtained a scholarship after the first year. As I had expected, I excelled in the subjects that appealed to me—anatomy, surgery, and pathology. I showed little interest in gynecology, obstetrics, pediatrics, or pharmacology, but by that time everyone knew I was going to be a surgeon. It is amusing how everyone accepted this statement as fact. I must have looked and talked as if there were no doubt in my mind.

After I received my M.D. degree, in June of 1931, the real test began, for how could a female get a male surgeon to train her? However, I had impressed the chief surgeon, who knew of my ambition. I considered it fate when he wrote to me during my internship, saying he was willing to try me as third assistant at a salary of fifty dollars per month. The miracle had happened. I had my opportunity and was ready for the confrontation.

My internship was spent in a Catholic hospital in Newark, New Jersey, full of exciting and wonderful events. I, the first female intern at St. James' Hospital, worked amicably and well with two male interns, soon began to assist the general surgeons, and gained the respect and cooperation of the all-male staff. I actually performed six appendectomies and many minor operations during this time. Even the mother superior, who was hospital administrator, admitted that I would make a good surgeon, although she did not always approve of my behavior, as I kept late hours, smoked, and did not attend Sunday mass regularly. I insisted on being treated as a doctor, despite the fact that I had to live in the nurses' home, and I was not conscious of any discrimination. Gradually I developed a strong sense of responsibility and compassion for the poor and the sick, particularly the injured.

By September of 1932 I was back in Philadelphia in a small apartment near the Woman's Medical College. This was my big chance, as I was given the opportunity to assist the professor of surgery, Dr. John S. Rodman. After two years I became his first assistant, lecturing and demonstrating to medical students. Eventually I was promoted to instructor in surgery, remaining the only woman on the faculty. In 1938 I bought a house, where I lived and had office quarters and considered myself a successful general surgeon. I wrote several papers on treatment of burns and wound healing and qualified for the American College of Surgeons in 1941. When I passed the American Board of Surgery examinations in 1947, I was the fourth woman in the United States to accomplish this, and my family and friends felt that I had now "arrived" and should be satisfied with my success.

Yet, strangely, I felt dissatisfied and even bored. Routine operative procedures became monotonous. They were all "surgery of despair," being the removal of diseased or injured parts. What I sought was the "art of surgery," the surgery of repair or of the creation of new or more normal parts. Gradually I realized that it was cosmetic or aesthetic surgery that absorbed my interest, for here was the challenge of reconstructive work.

Through a woman's club, the Soroptimists, I was awarded a fellowship to do special training in plastic surgery with the celebrated Dr. Barrett Brown of St. Louis, Missouri. Although he had no time for women, he reluctantly accepted me for a one-year residency at the famous Barnes Hospital, which boasted a huge plastic-surgery unit. My training was both wonderful and frustrating. I observed four accomplished plastic surgeons performing amazing facial reconstructions. Their work was frequently original, risky, and inspiring, but although I was anxious to attempt these operations, I was only permitted to observe and assist, never to perform. However, having visited the mecca of plastic surgery, I developed the courage to attempt such surgery on my own. Late in 1947 I became the first female member of the American Society of Plastic and Reconstructive Surgery. This made me very happy, as I could now call myself a plastic surgeon.

In 1948 I fulfilled another dream by building a house near my office and the hospital. My elderly parents came to stay with me for several months a year. My handsome father gave me sculpture lessons, as he felt I could become an artist, as well as a surgeon. These artistic endeavors helped me to refine my surgical technique, as I developed an accurate eye for what is aesthetically correct.

The years from 1955 to 1975 were my years of strength, and I labored in plastic surgery in four Philadelphia hospitals, wrote scientific papers, and gave my teaching services gratis to several medical schools, both in the United States and abroad. I lectured on plastic surgery and burns and performed hundreds of free operations in the United States, Europe, and the Far East. One of my most exciting experiences was in 1964, when I spent six weeks in Taipei, Taiwan, as a volunteer visiting professor of plastic surgery. This was at the request of the National Defense Medical Center, and I enjoyed the prestige and hard work. I helped to create a modern department of plastic surgery for both the Veterans Hospital and the Army General Hospital. Here I had the opportunity to work with the Chinese Medical Women's Association, giving what little free time I had available to assisting in their clinic in Taipei.

Because of these services abroad, the Republic of Italy conferred on me the title Cavaliere of the Order of Merit in 1968. Recognition also came in the form of twenty-two awards and two honorary degrees. The difficulties I encountered as the only woman surgeon in many hospitals faded away; time brought important changes, and the barriers gradually disappeared as more women entered the surgeons' world. Now women have achieved almost equal status.

In 1950 I had joined the American Medical Women's Association and so became a member of the Medical Women's International Association (MWIA). I found that the MWIA meetings were well planned, and the accompanying cultural events contributed to my education in science and art. Active participation brought me to executive level in 1966, when I was elected vice-president for North America. My greatest honor was when I was elected president of this, the oldest international medical organization in the world, and I held this position from 1972 to 1974. My devotion to this group of women physicians brought both challenges and rewards, and I gave generously of time, energy, and money. For two years I traveled extensively and set up new activities, such as public relations, fund-raising, and newsletters. As a result of determined efforts our association received its first large grant in 1971 from the International Family Planning Assistance Fund. This involved me in flying to Manila to help organize the first regional family planning conference in the Far East. Today I feel rich because of my happy friendships with physicians of both sexes all over the world, many of whom remain my close friends and have enriched my life.

I never married despite three opportunities, for my world was full and I kept busy with work, art, and travel. While I avoided medical politics, I served as director and later treasurer of the Philadelphia County Medical Society.

By 1966 I had lost both parents and rarely visited my siblings. All of them lived in New York, happily married and with grandchildren. I remained the independent surgeon-artist who traveled annually, especially to foreign countries in the interest of the MWIA or the American Women's Hospital Service, or to attend congresses for plastic surgeons.

Now in 1976 I find it difficult even to consider semiretirement after 45 years of a rewarding career. The hard work was the best part of it, and it had its share of agony and glory. I was fortunate in that my pioneer efforts in plastic surgery grew to national and international proportions, which broadened my horizon and contributed much to my own development. The building of friendships all over the world has been the greatest dividend. As a result, I recommend medicine as an all-absorbing career that becomes a way of life. The requirements for such a path are determination, good health, a little wisdom, and a great deal of good luck. What joy we receive in giving of ourselves.

INDIA

Sharju Pandit Bhatia
b. June 19, 1907

I was born to an orthodox Brahmin family in a small village in the late princely state of Gwalior in India. The maharaja of Gwalior had given my grandfather property so that he could cultivate the rich black soil and earn his living. My father was the revenue collector, known as the patwari. My parents took a keen interest in the property and both worked hard in the fields producing cotton, wheat, and sugar cane. In those days opium used to be grown in certain areas, and ours were suitable fields. My mother helped my father picking cotton and incising the poppies to collect opium.

I was three months old when an epidemic of plague spread in our area. My father sent mother and the five children to her parents' home. He was to follow, but he became a victim of plague and died. Mother was left with two boys and three girls, the eldest being a son who was fourteen years old. My two sisters married young, and both died of plague soon after their marriages. My eldest brother died at the age of nineteen. Owing to the plague epidemic I was not vaccinated for smallpox, and as a result, I had a serious case of smallpox at the age of five months. I was the youngest child.

My maternal grandfather was an astrologer. Of his three sons one became an astrologer and two studied medicine. After my father's death, mother gave up her farm property and lived with her father in order to educate us children. I was keen to study and by my fifth year had already learned to read and write Urdu.

My brother and I adopted our grandfather's surname so as to identify ourselves with this family. My medical uncle's five children, my brother, and I were brought up together. Mother was very strict with us, and during my school years I was required to help with cooking and other household work.

I watched my uncle's medical work closely and used to play "doctor" with my cousin, who acted as his helper. The maharaja of Gwalior was interested in the education of girls. Whenever he visited my school, I was asked to read in his presence. In 1915 my uncle moved to the medical school at Indore, where there was a girls' school, the Canadian Baptist Mission School. I joined the first class and started to learn English.

In 1916 the Lady Hardinge Medical College for Women was opened in New Delhi. A rich citizen from Indore had paid a handsome donation to this college. My uncle told me that, if I wanted to be a doctor, he would send me to this school. This encouraged me, and I passed my high-school finals at the age of sixteen. I entered the Lady Hardinge Medical College for Women in 1923. Most of the teachers at that time were European women devoted to their work. That same year there was a Muslim student from Delhi, who came in a burka. She was the first Muslim woman to take up medicine. Later I attended the Grant Medical College in Bombay, where my brother was a student. I lived for a time in a missionary hostel for women students.

In 1927 I lost my mother from typhoid fever. This disaster made a great impression on me. I was conscious that it was too much to expect that my uncle bear the expense of our education. The National Association of Women aided the best of the deserving students, of whom I was one. Each year my college fees were paid and some extra money was given to me for books. This assistance and merit scholarships helped me on my way. After obtaining the M.B., B.S. (Bombay), in 1931, I presented myself for the ophthalmology competitive examination. Professor Duggan made fun of me, but I won a gold medal and a cash prize in this subject. My brother completed his medical studies at about the same time.

The Women's Medical Service of India, established in 1914, recruited Training Reserve officers with a view to enabling deserving young Indian women doctors to gain experience under senior officers. I applied for admission to the Training Reserve and soon got an offer of a junior post in a small women's hospital. In those days there were very few hospitals for women and most were run by private organizations and missions. A large number of complicated deliveries were brought in to the hospital from distant rural areas, where they had already been handled by indigenous midwives. There were many cases of difficult and obstructed labor, and postnatal sepsis. It was sad to see the women arriving in that condition. I gained considerable experience under my senior officer and learned to work under difficult conditions and with very few nurses. We dealt with emergencies single-handedly and took full responsibility for getting the operating theater ready.

I was then transferred to Agra, which had a four-year course for women attached to its medical school. I was given charge of the outpatient clinic and the teaching of jurisprudence. The hospital had a good reputation, and the purdah and other women took advantage of the services of well-qualified women doctors. I started antenatal clinics and kept in touch with the women when they came for delivery. The medical superintendent took pride in this work, as very few hospitals in India had well-run antenatal clinics.

In 1933 the All India Institute of Hygiene and Public Health was established in Calcutta with the help of the Rockefeller Foundation and a diploma course in public health was started. The Countess of Dufferin Fund wanted special courses to be provided in maternity and child welfare. There were only three candidates in the first batch of students for this course, and I was one. I had to promise to continue in public health (maternal and child welfare). I pointed out that, unless there were posts in public health for women, it would not be possible to utilize the training fully. The board decided that I should do postgraduate work in obstetrics followed by visits to maternity and child-welfare institutions overseas.

I was awarded a Rockefeller Fellowship for study in the United States. I was the one Indian chosen for the year of 1935 through 1936 to study maternity and child welfare. I reached New York after thirty days travel and then proceeded to Harvard School of Public Health. Professor Stewart made it clear that the child-health department was not yet ready to offer specialization but said that he would see what could be done for me. I attended lectures with M.P.H. students who were doctors from different countries. Among them was one American woman, and we two were the first women at the Harvard School of Public Health. Professor Stewart gave me individual lessons in child health and arranged fieldwork for me. I passed the M.P.H. with distinction in child health. Study visits were arranged to New York, Philadelphia, Chicago, and Washington, and I spent a few weeks in Canada. I was full of enthusiasm and ideas as to how to set up administrative machinery for services in urban and rural areas in India.

On my return to India, at the end of 1936, I was posted to the All India Institute of Hygiene and Public Health in Calcutta to conduct an inquiry into the causes of maternal deaths in this city. Initially I experienced difficulty and had to be careful in my approach, as the doctors, midwives, and relatives felt that they would be blamed if found responsible for the deaths. The inquiry revealed that the maternal death rate in Calcutta was twenty per thousand and that sepsis and anemia were the major contributing factors. The Indian Council of Medical Research then provided funds for further research.

I soon realized that tact and experience were needed in the planning of health services. At first I thought that we ought to replace the indigenous midwife or *Dai* by trained midwives. Later I appreciated the important role the *dai*s play in midwifery services in the rural areas, so I formulated a scheme for their training. Simple equipment, instruction, and supervision of their technique were outlined, and my scheme was adopted under India's first Five-Year Plan.

In 1938 I worked as medical officer for the Indian Red Cross Society in Bengal, and in 1939, when the post of superintendent of maternity and child welfare was created in Bengal, my services were requested for a period of two years to start such a bureau in the State Department of Health. I looked forward eagerly to such pioneering work.

Touring was difficult at that time, as the villages were not connected by roads and the houses were far apart. I had to travel by train, road, steamer, or country boat. In waterlogged areas I had to walk through slush. In some sections the villages were separated by knee-deep water and rice fields. The rest houses were made of bamboo, with no privacy, very little furniture, and no arrangements for meals. I used to tour twelve to fifteen days a month to explain the scheme, assist the local people to appoint a committee, approve of the premises chosen, and judge if people were willing to take advantage of the services. When I visited villages where houses were scattered on both banks of a river, I fixed up a small steamboat to serve as a mobile center. Four trained workers were on the boat all the time. Small rowboats were provided to enable the staff to reach the village homes. Clinics were held on the boat, to which the indigenous midwives were asked to accompany the mothers. They were instructed in simple rules of cleanliness and were provided with equipment. This experiment proved to be a success.

The government of Orissa, a nearby state, then approached the Women's Medical Service, asking for my assistance. I stayed in Orissa for two years, establishing their maternity and child-welfare services.

In 1944 I moved to Delhi as director of the Maternity and Child Welfare Bureau under the Indian Red Cross Society. This bureau was advisory for any voluntary or governmental organizations, and any reference to maternity and child welfare made to the government of India by international organizations or states was referred to us.

I had already been selected for the post of professor at the All India Institute, but the government wanted me to continue the administrative work at the bureau. I explained to the director general the limited scope of the bureau under the Red Cross Society and suggested that the state government assume responsibility and that this important health service no longer be left to voluntary organizations. The post of adviser for maternity and child welfare was created by the government in 1946, and I was asked if I would like to be considered for the position. I requested status and emoluments on a par with allied posts, and the government agreed.

In 1947 I arranged for a year's leave to study in the United States. Just two days before I was to depart and while saying my prayers, an inner voice said that I should not proceed. I remained in India.

In August of 1947, following the partitioning into Pakistan and India, a number of Hindus began to migrate. The government arranged a reception camp. I was called back from leave and asked to see to the 10,000 people who had arrived by then. I took with me twenty young men of the St. John Ambulance Brigade and asked a health visitor, who was a refugee, to assist. The local people got twelve beds and had one of the rest houses opened. A wooden bench borrowed from a shop served as a delivery bed. The health visitor took charge of this maternity section. After a few days another trainful of people arrived with thirty babies who had been born during the journey.

Since children suffer most from altered living conditions, the incidence of sickness among them began to rise. A pediatric hospital was started with 100 beds. As there was difficulty in recruiting nurses, young girls of middle and high-school education were asked to help. As their educational qualifications did not meet the requirements of the Indian Nursing Council, arrangements were made for their education. The public health nurse instructed them in simple procedures, which enabled them to take care of the sick children. Within a month the girls were found helpful in the hospital.

I stayed in the camp for four months and organized milk centers in each township of 25,000 people. The women in each center served as volunteers to assist in the work there. The total population of the camp grew to 3 million. I have often thanked God for giving me the intuition to cancel the trip in 1947, which enabled me to serve my people during the most critical period in the history of the nation.

In 1948 the Indian government appointed me adviser for maternity and child welfare. This gave me many new opportunities. The United Nations' Children's Fund (UNICEF) initiated programs to assist developing countries in promoting direct services for children. My provisional plans were ready, and when I presented them to UNICEF, they were accepted and aid was provided. Assistance was given to expand and improve the Department of Maternity and Child Welfare at the All India Institute of Hygiene and Public Health in Calcutta, which was made the regional training center for Southeast Asia. A demonstration center was set up near Delhi to train doctors and public health nurses, and assistance was given to improve the nutrition of mothers and children.

The first, second, and third Five-Year Plans were put through while I was in office. Under the first we emphasized the training of health personnel by expanding existing schools and opening new ones for health visitors and midwives. Under the second plan we developed pediatric services and training at medical schools and assisted the states to train and supervise *dai*s for rural areas. Under the third we worked out schemes to diagnose and rehabilitate partially deaf and blind children.

During my official years one thing that troubled me was the way family planning programs were being organized in India. After my retirement I asked the health minister to integrate family planning with maternity and child welfare, and this has been achieved.

I retired in 1961 at the age of fifty-eight, having worked for thirty years, and in 1962 I also retired as president of the Association of Medical Women in India. I have had a most interesting and challenging professional life, despite pioneering difficulties. God so planned that one project paved the way for the next. I thus have several "firsts" to my credit. The most important is that I was the first physician to organize the health programs for the women and children of our country. I have tried to encourage young women doctors to enter the field of public health maternity and child welfare.

I was single until the age of forty-four years and had never thought of marriage. In 1952 I married Major General S. L. Bhatia, an officer of the I.M.S. and a highly educated person.

In 1961 I came to Bangalore, where my husband has made a permanent home since 1955. In my domestic life I have been very lucky to have a good home and a fine companion. Although we have no children of our own, I have worked for children and children are always around me.

Since retirement I have kept myself free to take up social work when and as it comes. I have been chairperson of the Social Welfare Board of this state. I am vice-president of the State Council for Child Welfare and am connected with the Cheshire Home and Chinmaya Mission Hospital in Bangalore.

In India medical women have done well, and their success is largely a result of the efforts of senior medical women from the United Kingdom and of missionary doctors. The Association of Medical Women, founded in 1907, has contributed a great deal to the advancement of women in medicine and to maintaining the high status that medical women enjoy.

Health services are not yet in the forefront in our country. The public and even the professional people are not aware of the value of such programs. Women working in public health do not enjoy an equal status in professional circles. They also suffer from financial inequality. There is, however, a great personal satisfaction in public health work, which should attract women.

When I was first admitted to the Training Reserve, a reference was requested of Dr. Balfour in Bombay. She was then working on causes of fetal death, and I used to meet her in the pathology museum. I came to know much later that she had mentioned in her recommendation that I would be useful to the Training Reserve, as I was interested in preventive work. I have often marveled at the judgment of this great person and at the way God led me step by step. He gave me ample opportunity to equip myself for public health work, to gain experience, and to serve. I trust that I have tried to live up to the assessment of Dr. Balfour in my professional achievements.

Chung-en Nieh
b. August 2, 1907

I am indeed fortunate to have been born before 1910 and to have lived during the twentieth century. I believe that more has transpired in my lifetime than in any previous generation since civilization began. The first year of this century saw the Boxer Rebellion, which weakened the power of the Manchu dynasty and paved the way for the founding of the Republic on October 10, 1911. In the following decades the nation was tested by the war with Japan, the Chinese participation in World War II, and the struggle with the Communists.

I was born in Anking, Anhwei Province, China, where my father was a teacher of English. My family was Christian, and my grandfather was a pioneer clergyman in the Episcopal Church in Central China. My father was the favorite son, and being the eldest child, he was expected to preserve the family line and carry on the centuries-old traditions, so he was sent to one of the most famous Christian universities of the time, namely, St. John's University in Shanghai. My mother was a wonderful woman who could have had an outstanding career but received only a high-school education. Her mother died when she was two or three years old, so she was brought up by her grandmother, a very kind woman who, although very stout, was smart enough to run two businesses, duck-raising and a teahouse.

When my mother became pregnant with me, my older sister was only five months old. The sister and brother who came after me both died in infancy. I was such a well-behaved, quiet baby that my mother was anxious in case I might be retarded. My grandfather never worried, for he gave my older sister the name Hsien-en, meaning "First Grace," and me Chung-en, "Repeated Grace."

My mother sent my elder sister and me to primary school. When I was ten, we went to a missionary boarding school, St. Hilda's Girls' School at Wuchang. We were not allowed to go home, but food, such as meat and eggs, could be sent to us on Saturdays. Only blue cotton uniforms were allowed. We stayed at St. Hilda's for five years and then went to St. Mary's in Shanghai. There we did not have to wear uniforms and could dress in silks and satins every day. The food was rich and the tuition much better. About a dozen girls from my hometown

Hankow attended St. Mary's, and every vacation, winter and summer, even if only for a few weeks, we would take a steamship home.

Since I had decided when I was sixteen that I wanted to study medicine, I left St. Mary's and went to another missionary high school in Changsha where more science was offered. I planned to enter the medical college nearby after one academic year at this school. However, there was a good deal of Communist activity, and the college was temporarily closed, with the result that all the students had to stay at home for a year. It was during that winter, when I was eighteen, that my mother died. She was forty-two years of age and near the end of her twelfth pregnancy. She left seven children, five younger than I. Living through the deaths of younger brothers and sisters had strengthened my determination to study medicine, especially as mother often said to us girls, "You must go to college, learn to play the piano, and then go abroad to the United States. Some of you must study medicine; it is the best profession, and doctors can save lives." After her death I stayed at home for a time to care for my younger brothers and sisters. My older sister was very pretty and soon had a boyfriend. According to custom they had to wait one year after a death in the family before marrying. My father remarried at about the same time, and our stepmother had six children, only three of whom survived. Even at that time I tried to help my stepmother by giving her information on the little I knew about birth control. She is now eighty-one years old, but as she is living in mainland China, we dare not write to her.

In 1927 I entered Ginling Women's College at Nanking and registered for premedical subjects. I continued my piano lessons, and whenever I had any leisure, I would spend time at the piano. After my graduation my teacher asked me to stay on at Ginling to help her teach music, but as I had applied to take the entrance examination for the Peking Union Medical College (PUMC), I told her that I could only help her if I did not pass. When I had a physical checkup, Dr. Catherine Chen said to me, "You weigh only eighty pounds and are not even five feet tall. You will be unable to carry even one of your many weighty medical textbooks."

Soon after graduation from Ginling, three classmates and I went to Peking, the most beautiful city in China, where we waited for the examination results. To my surprise and joy, I had passed. PUMC was then one of the eleven best medical centers in the world. The buildings on the campus were like old Chinese palaces, but with modern installations and facilities.

In my first year at PUMC thirty-two students were admitted, nine of whom were women. When we graduated in 1936, there were only sixteen of us, including all nine women. Before I left Peking, I went out to buy some mushrooms for my sister. Soon after my ricksha started, I passed the college tennis court, where I noticed a young man sitting on a wall. When I went into the hospital for my third year I met this same man. He was Dr. Hsien-lin Chang, fourth-year assistant resident in surgery—my future husband. He was seven years my senior and had graduated from PUMC in 1929. He said he did not believe that I was a medical student, as I was so young and pretty and, in addition, so different from other girls because of my pride and dignity.

I had other boyfriends at this time, but Hsien-lin proved to be of immense help when my younger sister developed pulmonary tuberculosis. She was admitted to PUMC for diagnosis, but no beds were available in the medical ward. We approached the surgical ward to borrow a bed, and here Hsien-lin came to our aid. Three days later he advised me to send my sister to a missionary hospital, as PUMC was not a sanatorium. However, my sister soon became semiconscious and passed away. After her death I had to have checkups and chest X-rays every month for half a year.

In my fourth year Hsien-lin was chief resident in surgery. Once he repaired my stethoscope and asked me to go to his office to retrieve it. He then locked his office door and kept me there for an hour, despite my protests, while he told me that he had never had a girl friend and had been waiting twelve years to meet me. He then told me his life story. His father had died when Hsien-lin was seven months old, and his mother was only twenty-eight. She had never gone to school and had no property of her own. After her husband's death she returned with her baby to her own home, to care for her younger brother who was seriously ill with tuberculosis. She liked standing outdoors with her little son in her arms, not realizing that the fresh air and bright sunlight were the best protection against tuberculosis. Some missionary women, seeing her there, befriended her and converted her to Christianity. They helped her to go to Wuhu near Nanking where she found work in a large hospital. Hsien-lin was put in a relative's home. He started school at eight and always got high marks. At Christ's Light High School he worked for half the day making wicker chairs and studied for the other half. As he was anxious to go to college to become a doctor, the American missionaries helped him with a loan, which he later repaid. That was how he got to PUMC, and as he was first in all his classes, he won scholarships every year, which helped him financially and gave him more confidence in his own ability. He told me that, because he was poor and not handsome, he had an inferiority complex and did not want to have a girl friend until he was sure that he was able to support a family. He wanted to marry a woman doctor whom he really loved and was not going to allow his wife to suffer. He proposed to me on Christmas Eve 1935, and we planned to marry as soon as I graduated from medical school in 1936. He was awarded a scholarship at Columbia Medical Center in New York, while I was recommended to the Babies' Hospital there. We were married in Shanghai at my sister's home, and two weeks later we boarded a luxury liner for San Francisco, the first PUMC graduates to go to the United States together after being married.

In New York a small apartment near Columbia Medical Center had been prepared for us. It was on the fourth floor of a building without an elevator, and the rent was seventy-five dollars per month. Hsien-lin's salary was only $150 per month, while I received no pay, although I attended ward rounds. While in New York, I became pregnant and was referred to a young doctor. When I asked him what he thought the size of my baby would be, he said, "What do you expect? You are so small, your baby will be around four or five pounds." In consequence, Hsien-lin forced me to eat meat and eggs and drink four glasses of milk each day. When our son Raymond was born, with the help of forceps, he weighed eight pounds six ounces and was a handsome, round-faced boy with big eyes and shining hair.

War broke out in China that year, and I left with my baby for Shanghai in July of 1937. When we arrived, the Japanese army was fast approaching. Hsien-lin and my sister's husband were both in the United States. My sister was worried, as her apartment was not in a foreign concession, so when the Japanese reached Shanghai, I rented two rooms in the French Concession, in the hope that we would not be bombed. One morning we went out to buy a supply of canned goods. While we were on our way, the Japanese bombers came. Our ricksha pullers ran so fast that all our canned goods dropped off. However, we were lucky, as the store where we had been shopping was bombed ten minutes later.

I began working in the Shanghai Children's Hospital in the French Concession. Hsien-lin returned to China in November, where he was promoted to assistant professor in Peking, but he took over the Red Cross Medical Corps. He went first to Hankow and then to Changsha, while I stayed in Shanghai for a year. He wrote once a week, which was something special, as he did not like writing letters. After a few months my mail stopped, and then I received a letter telling me that Hsien-lin had had a severe attack of typhus and been unconscious for two weeks. He had lost forty pounds and all his hair. My mother-in-law and I were so shocked that we shed tears, but we thanked God that his life had been saved. He had caught typhus when he had traveled in a train so crowded with refugees that even the roof was full of people, some of whom carried infected lice.

My husband decided that we should leave Shanghai and proceed to the interior, so we went by ship to Hong Kong and from there to Changsha. There I called at my home and asked my younger brother and sister to join me. We all boarded a Red Cross ambulance and went to Kweilin, where we stayed for some months. Hsien-lin had to go back to Changsha, where he was very busy during the bombing raids.

From Kweilin we moved to Kweiyang, headquarters of the Chinese Red Cross Medical Corps. The winters were very cold, and I saw many a newborn baby frozen to death and many a child without milk to drink. Every winter I had to sell one ounce of the gold I had bought in Shanghai in order to buy coal. Our headquarters were in a small village, and as there were no houses available, we lived in tents for the first two months. Then we hired carpenters to build a bungalow that we could call home. It had one living room, two bedrooms, and a bathroom, and I designed the windows with two dozen small pieces of glass I picked up. It was our own property, cozy and comfortable. I suggested that we get a pair of pigeons, as they reproduce rapidly. They nested in a nearby tree and soon became so numerous that we were able to eat the eggs and make soup of the birds. With our house comfortably settled, I went to work, treating outpatients for two hours in the mornings, as well as examining children and new personnel. In the afternoons I gave lectures on infectious diseases to army officers in the Medical Training School.

When Raymond was three years old, I became pregnant again. Hsien-lin insisted on an abortion, which was performed by a woman professor of obstetrics. There was no milk for Raymond, so Hsien-lin asked the transportation service to buy two female goats from India, which gave us lots of milk. My mother-in-law prayed every day for more grandchildren. When we had saved ten large five-pound tins of milk powder and our goats were producing satisfactorily, Hsien-lin asked me whether I was willing to have another child. I agreed, and Norman was born in July of 1943. I nursed him for fourteen months. Like his father he was later at the head of his class in school, quiet and fond of classical music and sports.

In December of 1944, while Hsien-lin was in Chungking, the Japanese army reached a small town only 200 miles from us. My supply of gold had been sold, and we had no money, so I had to sell Hsien-lin's fieldglasses, pistol, and typewriter and leave for Chungking. We were to be evacuated to a town between Kweiyang and Chungking. Only old people, parents, and children were allowed to ride on the two trucks. Those with no children had to walk. Each person was allowed only two kilograms of luggage, and we had to draw numbers for seats. Hsien-lin went ahead, and two days later I got seats on a truck. I sat in front with Norman, who was seventeen months old, while Raymond, my younger brother, and the housekeeper sat at the back of another truck with our luggage and our precious milk powder. On the way Hsien-lin met us and said that the refugee quarters were just barns. I decided not to go there but to go to Chungking. Normally, it was an eight-hour drive to Chungking, but our truck took twelve days. When we arrived, we found that our precious milk powder, the housekeeper's suitcase, and $800 were all missing. We went to a high school, where we stayed in the vacant classrooms during the Christmas vacation, and then moved into the surgeon general's headquarters, as we were assigned work in the Chungking Army General Hospital. The weather was far warmer than in Kweiyang; sugar and flour were far cheaper; and the fruit was delicious. We stayed in Chungking until VJ Day, in August of 1945, when the Japanese surrendered after the atom bomb fell on Hiroshima.

After VJ Day we left for Shanghai, where we lived in one of the wards of the Army General Hospital. The surgeon general was Dr. Robert Lim, who reorganized the old Chinese Army Medical School into the present National Defense Medical Care. Dr. Lim had arranged to send 120 medical personnel to the United States for training. I was one of the lucky ones to be chosen. Hsien-lin was a member of the senior staff and did not need to have medical training; I left the two boys with their father while I went to the United States.

I left Shanghai in August of 1946 and arrived in San Francisco two weeks later. I went from there to Brown Medical Center in Houston, Texas, where I received two months' basic training. After that we were divided into groups of seven each. There was one other woman in my group. We wore U.S. Army uniforms, lived two in a room, and received $250 per month from the American medical department. Our group was sent to Tilton General Hospital in New Jersey, where I stayed for only two months, as pediatrics was not taught there. I got permission to go to New York, where I found all the hotel rooms filled. Luckily I met Miss Lin from Ginling, who invited me to stay in her guest room for one dollar per day. My husband and sons arrived on Chinese New Year's Eve, and fortunately, we found an apartment with a private bath and a large kitchen that we shared with others. I attended the Babies' Hospital, while Hsien-lin visited the surgical departments at Columbia Medical Center and took a course at the Memorial Cancer Hospital.

That summer I could have returned to Shanghai on the U.S. *Transport* without cost, but I forfeited my place because Hsien-lin still had another six months' traveling, to visit other hospitals. While he was traveling, we could not afford the $150-per-month apartment, so we spent the summer and autumn ninety miles from New York City at a convent run by the Episcopal church.

At the end of the six months we returned to Shanghai and arrived there on Chinese New Year's Eve. My mother-in-law was waiting for us in a ward of the Army General Hospital, where we stayed for a few months. Then we moved to a small apartment belonging to the hospital and medical-school staff. We were only able to stay there for eight months, as the Communists were then attacking on the mainland. Because of this attack, we moved to Taipei, Taiwan. The surgeon general's office assigned a steamship to help move the staff, with their furniture and other personal belongings. The ship made several trips from Shanghai to Taiwan. My mother-in-law was the first of the family to go to Taipei; she traveled with our male servant and moved into the house assigned to us by the school. We were the last to leave Shanghai, arriving in Taipei on February 28, 1949. The governor of Taiwan, General Chen Cheng, who had been operated on by my husband, allocated a bungalow and a big house for us in the same compound as our director.

I began teaching pediatrics as an associate professor in the National Defense Medical College. Hsien-lin was a full professor of surgery. He started the Center Clinic for civilian patients with only NT $700 as capital, beginning with surgical outpatients and outpatient sessions for medicine, obstetrics, and pediatrics. After my mother-in-law's death in 1951 I requested permission to emigrate to the United States. Raymond was sent there to school when he was sixteen, and I took Norman over in 1959, and returned to Taipei the following year, leaving him to attend school in the United States.

Our professional work and the Center Clinic proceeded smoothly. Hsien-lin had predicted that, as Taiwan was virgin land, there would be much to be done. The island had been occupied by the Japanese for fifty years, and little modern progress had been made medically or otherwise. The surgeons and obstetricians operated and delivered babies without wearing sterilized rubber gloves. They spoke Japanese and a local dialect only. Hsien-lin went to the provincial hospital and the Taiwan University Hospital to teach modern medicine, including sterilization, and to incorporate the house-staff system. The doctors and interns also had to be taught English. At the present time, under the educational system of the Republic of China, every child is taught Mandarin in elementary school and starts English in junior high school.

When the Center Clinic started, I had only a few patients. Then I started immunization, and soon I had much to do. I began work at 10:00 a.m. with outpatients, and sometimes I could not get home for lunch until early afternoon.

Many of the parents of my child patients were illiterate, and it was very difficult to deal with them because they believed, for instance, that when a child has teeth, no milk is necessary. Rice to them was the most important food, and they would not think of eating meat, especially beef. As I had to repeat the same advice many times over, I wrote a booklet, *How to Keep Your Child Healthy.* The first edition of five thousand sold out in a few years, and now there are only a few left of the second edition of three thousand copies.

I was criticized for being impolite to parents who were prone to put too many clothes on their children and who thought that one visit was enough for ordinary children's diseases. However, they soon gained confidence in me and became my good friends, as I had three special beds for children suffering from high fever or convulsions. When the parents saw the young patients getting well so soon, they became very appreciative, and many even wanted me to adopt their children!

After attending the congress of the Medical Women's International Association in Manila in 1954, I founded the Taiwan Medical Women's Association and was elected its first president.

As head of the Pediatrics Department of the Center Clinic and associate professor of pediatrics at the National Defense Medical Center, I was instrumental in starting immunization against diphtheria, whooping cough, and tetanus in Taiwan twenty-five years ago, and I also introduced oral polio vaccine when this superseded the Salk vaccine.

Hsien-lin was full professor and head of the department of surgery at the National Defense Medical Center, head of surgery at the Taipei Veterans' General Hospital, and first director of the Crippled Children's Rehabilitation Center. He was the first president of the Taipei chapter of the International College of Surgeons. He passed away suddenly in January of 1969, at the age of sixty-eight.

Raymond is married, has three sons, and is working in the United States. Norman is also married and working there, having earned his Ph.D. in biochemistry in Los Angeles.

Now I spend most of my time in Taipei and make frequent trips to the United States to see my children and grandchildren, but while here, I still attend to my medical practice and live in my little cottage, although I have retired from teaching.

KOREA

Duck-Heung Bang
b. July 6, 1908

I was born in the country in Korea, the fourth of six children of a modestly successful merchant. My grandfather was an army officer at the end of the Yi dynasty and must have been very patriotic. The Japanese carried through with their policy to annex and make a colony of our country, which had a long and stable history but had gradually become weak at the beginning of this century. Because of his activity as a Korean patriot, my grandfather was executed by the Japanese. As a result, it seems, my father gave up his desire to go into a government career. In the meantime, Korea came under Japanese rule in 1910.

Before I was even 100 days old, our family moved to Seoul, and it was there that I started in the primary school. Education for girls in a modern sense had just begun in Korea—only in Seoul and a few other cities—so I was lucky to be in Seoul when I was. Usually, girls were raised in the family circle in a Confucian manner, without going to school. Even in cities it was a rare thing for a girl to enjoy modern education. Traditionally, girls were discriminated against, and even in upper-class families, they were not allowed to go out. After I finished primary school, my parents sent me to a high school. This was, of course, a great event for me at that time.

During my second year at high school, my brother, only two years old, died of acute dysentery. I believed that his death could have been avoided had he had proper medical care. In Korea at that time, there were only the old-style physicians, who treated diseases with Chinese herbs, and a very limited number of modern doctors, trained in the Western style of medical science.

I made up my mind to become a medical doctor; the tragic death of my infant brother had given me this idea. As a woman doctor, I thought, I could probably help women and children better than any male physician could. Thereafter, this was the main idea that directed my entire life.

There were many difficulties ahead of me in pursuing my goal. First, my high-school training in Korea was hardly sufficient to get me admitted to a medical college in Japan and there was no medical school in Korea that admitted women. Even in Japan there was only one women's medical school, I entered a teacher-training school in Seoul, which qualified me to teach in primary schools. I taught for four years, during which time I was able to save some money for my future medical studies. Meanwhile, I did not neglect to prepare for the entrance examination at the Tokyo Women's Medical College. I cannot forget the moral support of my mother, who, having been brought up in an old-fashioned Korean family, did not fully understand what I intended to do. Nevertheless, she gave me the necessary encouragement to pursue my goal.

In 1929 I succeeded in entering the Tokyo Women's Medical College. The school had a five-year course, including one preparatory year. The savings I had accumulated as a schoolteacher were just enough to cover expenses for the first two years. I was often in serious financial difficulty, but private personal donations saved me. At any rate, I was very happy when I obtained my medical license in 1934 and became one of the very few women physicians in Korea.

At my mother's suggestion I came back to Seoul and began to work at Seoul University Hospital to become a pediatrician. According to Korean tradition, a woman, no matter what she wanted to become, had to marry early. All happiness for a woman depended, after all, on a good marriage. Koreans still think this way, although almost sixty years have passed since intellectual Koreans accepted a modern way of living. I married Dr. Sun Keun Lee, the chief of the pediatric department at the Seoul Municipal Hospital. My marriage brought new problems. My husband had four children from his previous marriage. Their ages ranged from two to eleven years. This meant that all at once I became not only a wife but a mother.

I had been raised from childhood in the Buddhist faith, which says that whatever happens in our present life was predestined in our previous life. This means that there was a supernatural power that made me the mother of those four young children who had lost their own mother. Thus, all at once I had three areas of duty. I had to be a mother, a wife, and a medical doctor. It was not always easy for one individual to fulfill these functions, especially as I later added four children of my own to the family. No one had ever told me anything about family planning. I have thus brought up eight children, and I am proud to be able to say that every one of them has an excellent career, two of them being medical doctors.

My husband started private practice in 1936, but as he continued to teach at the Seoul Medical College, the main load of the private practice fell on me. At the beginning we had only a few patients, but the practice grew until we often had more than 100 every day. The records show that one day I wrote 215 prescriptions. We had fourteen beds in our clinic. These were often filled, and then we had to vacate our guest room and nurses' quarters to accommodate patients. Besides treating the patients at our clinic, we had to make house calls whenever they were needed. It often happened that it was simply impossible to take care of all our patients, and to my deep regret, I had to send some to other doctors. The overwork often caused sleepless nights, but the satisfaction of seeing the children recover made me forget the heavy burden I had to bear. I often wondered what attracted so many patients to my practice. One of the answers, no doubt, was that I, as the mother of eight children, could advise other mothers better than any other pediatrician could.

In 1945 Korea was liberated from Japan. This change brought with it many new political and social problems. The invasion from North Korea, which lasted for three years, resulted in the total destruction of the city of Seoul and in general misery to the population. I managed to keep my practice in spite of the innumerable problems we encountered during those difficult years. My husband died in 1967 after a long illness. He suffered first from tuberculosis of the lungs, from which he recovered almost miraculously. However, his health deteriorated in 1966 and he was hospitalized for many months until death liberated him from his long service as physician and educator.

I kept my practice until 1971, when I decided that I had fulfilled my duty as a physician, wife, and mother. In any event, my health would not allow me to continue my work any longer. I have had diabetes for twenty-one years. It was diagnosed soon after an operation for uterine myoma in 1954. My hearing and eyesight were also deteriorating so rapidly that I had to give up any hope for complete recovery. I have two sons and their families in the United States, and I thought it was high time to visit them. This journey was most enjoyable, and I was treated very nicely by my children.

I realize that times have changed very much in Korea since the days when I studied medicine. There was no medical school for women then, whereas all the medical colleges admit women today. Nowadays we have about 1200 women doctors. When I started to work as a physician, I was often annoyed by being regarded as a nurse. When I examined patients, for instance, they sometimes demanded to be examined by a real doctor and not by a nurse. What a change has taken place when one sees that the current dean of the Ewha Women's Medical College is a woman!

This is a condensed history of my life, but it no doubt represents the life a woman physician had to go through in a developing country like Korea. Looking back over it all, I can see that I had a busy, sometimes hard life, but I have had the great satisfaction to have become a physician and to have worked for thirty-five years as a pediatrician during these transitional periods in the history of my country. I feel that I have accomplished something for our community, although perhaps not on a large scale, and that my life has not been wasted.

Isobel Russell Robertson
b. December 13, 1908

I was born in Cape Town, capital of the old Cape Colony before the Union of South Africa was formed. Our home nestled against Table Mountain, around which the city was built. Both my parents were descendants of Scottish Presbyterian ministers who had emigrated to the colony in the last century. My father was a lawyer, and he practiced in Cape Town until he was appointed judge of the High Court of Rhodesia in 1915. Mother was a university graduate and a keen botanist. She began to teach me botany when I was three years old, and I was soon able to distinguish the flower families.

I remember the excitement of our journey to Rhodesia, which took four days in the train through the desolate Karroo and the edge of the Kalahari desert. Our new home was in Bulawayo, the largest town in the country but with only about 5000 inhabitants. I was at school there up to matriculation. We were rather isolated from civilization, but fortunately, my father had a very good collection of books, and in my early teens one of my main interests was reading. As the books were about places I had never seen and circumstances remote from my experience, it was natural that I developed a longing to travel and see the world.

In addition to my liking for botany, I became interested in the animal life of our tropical environment. I used to watch the large warrior ants, which marched in columns and made war against the soft-bodied termites, which in turn protected themselves by building mud tunnels up the trees. Mosquitoes were a nightly nuisance, and we knew the difference between the malaria-carrying anopheles and the harmless culex. We slept under nets to keep these foes at bay. We knew too that streams and pools, often thick with water lilies, were infested with bilharzia, and were therefore dangerous places in which to paddle.

It was taken for granted that all four children would have academic careers. There was no university nearer than Cape Town, but fortunately, there were very good scholarships available. In 1926 my brother Fraser and I, both scholarship holders, started at the University of Cape Town. He took up medicine, while I aimed at a science degree, with the intention of specializing in bacteriology and working in the Tropical Research Institute in Rhodesia. I romped through botany, thoroughly enjoyed zoology and Latin, and struggled with physics and chemistry. In zoology we did much comparative physiology, contrasting the basic metabolic rates of wood lice and actively running beetles, finding the oxygen concentration of the blue blood of rock lobsters, and staining the chromosomes of grasshoppers. In my second year a friend who was a medical student urged me to change to medicine, and I began to think along these lines. She took me to see the anatomy laboratory, which did not upset me, and then smuggled me in to a postmortem. This was a near disaster, as the room was small and crowded and we stood on a rickety table at the back. When the proceedings began, the room started to spin. My companions were terrified that I would be detected, as I had no right to be there, so they gave me a cigarette to inhale, which only made matters worse. Fortunately, I managed to escape in time. This experience cured me of any desire ever to smoke but did not put me off medicine. I made the change in curriculum the following year, when I discussed my course with the professor of bacteriology, who strongly advocated a medical degree. I was able to take physiology as a B.A. subject and anatomy as an extra. At this juncture Fraser and I decided to finish our medical courses in Edinburgh. Fraser had missed a year due to rheumatic fever, so we were in the same class there.

Edinburgh medical school was very competitive; we knew that only half the class would qualify, and so we worked very hard. We did in three years what we would have taken four years to do in Cape Town. Life was a long grind, with intervals for golf and tramps over the moors. This was the middle of the depression, and some of the patients we saw had been on the dole since leaving school, having married and produced children without ever working. The seriousness of the position was brought home to me when I heard that out of 700 arts graduates of 1931, only 100 had managed to get work a year later.

I did midwifery at the Elsie Ingles Hospital, which was founded and run by women. My first district confinement was done in a box bed built into the wall. The family waited on the landing until we had finished and then climbed into bed over the mother. Someone rolled over onto the baby and suffocated it during the night.

During a short vacation I stayed with a friend at a hospital for puerperal fever near Sheffield. The hospital produced antistreptococcal serum from goats and gave it to the patients. By today's standards the results were lamentable.

When we qualified, Fraser was appointed house surgeon at Salisbury, while I went to Bristol Royal Infirmary. My arrival there is worthy of record. When I entered the infirmary with all my possessions, at 7:00 p.m., the senior resident officer greeted me by saying, "I want to tell you something. You need not stay if you do not want to, as you will be the only woman here." I was much taken aback and asked if I might at least stay the night. After dinner I went up to the women's sitting room, where I met a medical woman who was leaving the next day. On hearing what had happened, she said, "Don't let them bully you and you will be quite all right. You stay." I was there for a year, one of the happiest of my life; I enjoyed the work, loved Somersetshire, and got along well with my colleagues.

This happy life was dimmed by an incident that affected the future of my career. During an eye operation at which I was assisting, the patient, a normal child of four, died under the anesthetic. This tragic event focused my interest on work with children, and bacteriology lost its glamor. My first experience of the social side of medicine was the problem that arose when the seven-year-old son of a vagabond was brought in, unconscious, in diabetic coma. When the boy recovered, the question of his future had to be considered, as the tramp could not be trusted to give him insulin.

At the end of this year I returned to Rhodesia, and early the next year I married Donald Robertson, a civil engineer, and started my married life in Durban. Here I worked for a while in a Zulu hospital, where my main task was examining specimens for tuberculosis and amoebic dysentery. Some of our patients had been previously treated by Zulu herbalists, who made small incisions in the skin over painful spots and rubbed infusions of herbs into these cuts. This caused keloid formation, and these keloids often gave a clue to the problem. On a number of occasions a needle plunged through the skin in the center of a cluster of keloids would strike an amoebic abscess in the liver. The Zulu population had practically no resistance to tuberculosis, and at that time, prior to chemotherapy, our patients died within a few months despite conservative treatment.

After our first daughter was born, we moved to a small inland town, where I started general practice, mainly among the Coloured population. Midwifery services there were very inadequate, and a patient was admitted to the hospital only if a Caesarean section was necessary. I had the experience of doing a forceps delivery in a small hut, with the patient lying on the floor. The forceps were boiled in a three-legged pot outside. We could not even have a lantern, as my colleague was giving the patient ether, so the delivery was done by the light of an electric torch. About this time I received a sample of Prontosil Rubrum, the first of the sulfonamides. It happened that I was called to a patient desperately ill with puerperal sepsis. Remembering what I had seen in Sheffield, I was in despair. However, I decided to try the Prontosil—and what a miracle it was to find the woman up the next day, with a normal temperature.

Our second daughter was born in 1939, shortly before the outbreak of war. Donald and both my brothers went "up north" with the South African forces, first to Abyssinia and then to Egypt and Libya, where Fraser was killed in 1941. This was a bitter blow to us all.

After Fraser's death I took over his practice in Cape Town, my parents having retired there shortly before that time. I continued in general practice until the end of the war, but it was never really a success, as I was working alone, therefore always on duty. I did not like the diverse types of cases with which I had to deal, varying from midwifery to treating a British Tommy in a pea-green stupor as a result of consuming rock lobster and Cape brandy on his first shore leave on the way to the East. The worst aspect was that the patients liked evening surgery, and this was the time when my children needed me most. When Donald returned from the army, he encouraged me to specialize in public health.

After obtaining a diploma in public health, I joined the Cape Town City Health Department in 1946 and worked in the Maternal and Child Welfare Branch, of which I became head in 1956. Our system of working was modeled on that of Great Britain as it had been before the introduction of the National Health. We had clinics scattered throughout the residential areas of the city, and in addition to the medical staff, we had health visitors, who assisted in the clinics and made home visits.

Apart from the routine day-to-day work, we undertook surveys into such conditions as rickets, anemia, and gastroenteritis and investigated means of prevention of these conditions. Nutrition was one of my biggest preoccupations, since in this country, as elsewhere in the world, malnutrition in infants and young children remains a pressing problem that is difficult to deal with adequately. Over the years we did make progress in teaching the mothers to feed their children properly, but there remain the problem families, the young unmarried mothers, and the alcoholics who go their own way and whose children develop marasmus or frank kwashiorkor if a strict watch is not kept.

We saw tangible results with prevention of infectious disease. When I started, the only immunization we gave was against diphtheria and smallpox. In 1951 we included whopping cough and shortly afterward tetanus and BCG vaccination to prevent tuberculosis. After a severe outbreak of poliomyelitis, in 1958, we introduced the oral vaccine, initially by a mass campaign to get everyone under forty immunized. Since I retired, measles vaccination has been introduced, as measles has been a great scourge, particularly among poorly nourished children. It was gratifying to see the various diseases fading away year by year, particularly tuberculous meningitis, which used to attack over 100 infants in Cape Town every year until BCG vaccination of the newborn was commenced.

Education formed an important section of my work. There were lectures to medical students and postgraduates, as well as to nurses doing public health work and training for our staff. Associated with this work was membership in a number of organizations: the National Council for Child Welfare, of which I was chairperson in 1971; the South African Paediatric Association, the Nutrition Society of Southern Africa, and the Cape Child Health Association. The last has been my special "baby" for the past fifteen years. We started in a small way with a home for babies convalescing from gastroenteritis and then were given the use of trust funds, which enabled our committee to build a convalescent home for sixty-eight infants and children.

In 1951 a group of local colleagues started the South African Society of Medical Women, which became affiliated with the Medical Women's International Association (MWIA). This society has done a lot to improve conditions for medical women in the various services in the country. In 1957 I attended a meeting of the MWIA in Burgenstock, Switzerland. This was the first time I had been back to Europe since I left England in 1934. After the congress I went to Britain, where I visited various health departments, including that of Birmingham, where I was shown their system of domiciliary care of premature infants. On my return I started a similar service in Cape Town, and the service is still in operation. I also initiated a rather primitive system of heated boxes for transporting premature infants by ambulance. This has developed, I am glad to say, into proper ambulance incubators. In all, I have attended four MWIA congresses, all of great interest. In 1972 I was elected MWIA vice-president for Africa and the Near East. When I faced the problem of tackling the fifty-seven countries in my region in order to enlist new members for the MWIA, I realized that the difficulties of communication were considerable. I visited three neighboring countries, namely Lesotho, Rhodesia, and Swaziland, but for the rest I had to rely on correspondence. The average time it took to get a reply to a letter was two months, while often none was forthcoming. However, eventually I managed to contact a number of colleagues, one of whom, a Nigerian, became our guest at Rio de Janeiro and subsequently inspired her colleagues at home to form the Nigerian Medical Women's Association, which is now affiliated with the MWIA. In some of the African states where medical women are few in number, certain doctors have become individual members of the MWIA.

I retired from full-time work in 1970 but have continued with part-time clinic work and teaching. Neither of our daughters showed any interest in medicine. Both are married, and now that their children are in school, they have gone back to their professional work as teachers of biology. My eldest granddaughter, who is fifteen, expresses the wish to become a doctor, which I trust has a more solid foundation than the desire to follow in her grandmother's footsteps by traveling to exciting foreign places.

Minerva Smith Buerk
b. February 4, 1909

I was born a healthy, happy child to William and Sarah Russell Smith at their farm in Brant County, Ontario, Canada. I was the seventh in a family of ten children.

My mother had been a schoolteacher. My father, however, had not had the opportunity for higher education, and this helped to motivate his insistence on higher education for all his children.

We children were reared under a firm disciplinary code and with strict religious training, which served as a basis for character-building. Our Sundays, for instance, were devoted to the activities of our Anglican church. At an early age each child was assigned responsibilities for the maintenance and improvement of our environment.

The preschool days were idyllic for us children. On our large farm we were able to hike through our own forests and meadows and to fish in our own streams. In the spring we gathered lovely spring flowers and explored the ponds and marshes for the return of migratory wildlife. In the summer we experienced the wonders of wild berries and plants and enjoyed picnics in our own oak grove. In the fall we had the joy of gathering fall fruits and nuts. In the winter we had delightful sleigh rides and were warm under the buffalo-fur robes as we sang under the bright stars that shone in a midnight blue sky. Thus, at a very early age we were exposed to the magnificence of the flora, fauna, and environment and were imbued with a reverence for life of all nature's gifts and creatures, great and small. It was a simple, stable, and happy life.

At the age of six I attended a primary school two kilometers away from my home. I can recall trudging off to school through the rain or sleet or walking over the snowbanks that completely covered the fences. It never occurred to us to feel deprived or disadvantaged. Our school was a one-room schoolhouse; our one teacher taught all grades; and decorum in the school was exemplary. I was an alert student with original ideas, and the teacher would relate to my parents my amusing, frank, and forthright remarks.

It was during these early years that my initial desire to become a doctor occurred to me. Our local doctor was a frequent visitor in our home. He had been a career army officer in India and faraway lands, and on these visits he would often relate his experiences. I would listen with rapt attention, and it became apparent to me that there was a great world of experience and work out there in which I wanted to participate. At about the same period my handsome, sixteen-year-old brother, away at a boarding school, drowned among the ice floes of a flooding river. I recall vividly my feeling of utter helplessness and futility when the messenger related the sad news to my mother. This feeling of helplessness was an impetus for me to do something worthwhile and to be of help in the future.

As we became older, we children were all sent off to the city schools. The girls were encouraged to participate in extracurricular activities, such as sports, music, drama, and art, as well as to study. I was never interested in sports, but I was more enthusiastic about drama, piano, and particularly, about dancing. I participated in all the plays and concerts at church and school and was the family comedian. However, my love of dancing had a deleterious effect on my school grades and I was never a valedictorian of my class. When the subject of careers was discussed, it was assumed that all the girls would be teachers, and I rebelled at the prospect of being a staid teacher like my older sisters. My desire to become a doctor was not considered because my parents had too many children to educate. In those days secretarial work and teaching were the only acceptable careers for girls.

After high school I left home to enter a school of nursing in New York State, much to the consternation of my father. After a year romance entered my life and I was convinced that home life in suburbia would mean happiness ever after. In a strange town, without friends and family, I found that suburban life held no great challenges, so I sought many outlets to utilize my energies. There were gardening to the point of creating a prizewinner of the area, expertise in flower arrangement, oil painting, ceramics, antiques, and concert piano work. After six years my husband's lingering terminal illness made me realize more acutely the desirability of medical training.

At the age of twenty-seven I was a widow, alone, unskilled, and again on the threshold of a new life. After weeks of soul-searching, I awakened one morning with the firm conviction that I would fulfill the one desire of my lifetime—to study medicine—and nothing would deter me. Only one family of my circle of friends encouraged me and had confidence in my ability to execute my plan. I lost no time. I went to the University of Buffalo for the entrance requirements. The pursuit of medicine seemed a monumental task and beyond my wildest dreams. Nevertheless, that summer I studied and passed all the necessary examinations and qualified for entrance. Thus, at the age of twenty-eight I began my first year of premedical studies. Studying occupied my entire life, and it was very difficult, as I had been out of school some nine years. During my last year at the university I majored in medical technology, and in 1941 I graduated as the first candidate with a B.A. degree in medical technology.

At the age of thirty-two I entered the Woman's Medical College of

Pennsylvania in Philadelphia. Luckily, this hospital needed a night laboratory technician at the time. The dean was sympathetic to my situation and arranged for me to do emergency laboratory work at night, to be housed in the hospital, and to attend medical school part time. The next two years were critical ones for me, and my frail being succumbed several times to pneumonia. It became apparent to me that, if I were to continue in medicine, I would have to specialize in a field that would be more compatible with my physical capabilities. At the end of two years I was assigned the managership of the college bookshop and was able to attend medical school full time. I graduated in January of 1946 with my M.D. degree. My goal of a lifetime had been reached.

In 1946 my postgraduate training began with an internship in Detroit City Hospital, which gave me an awareness of the rapid social change in a postwar society and an appreciation of the complex workings of a large urban hospital. It was not unusual for us to work steadily for twenty-four to thirty-six hours.

My specialization training in dermatology and syphilology began at one of the leading medical centers, the Johns Hopkins Hospital in Baltimore. At the time the various treatment schedules of the new antibiotic penicillin were being designed and tested for all phases of syphilis. This was another year of intellectual challenge, long hours, and endless research projects.

From 1948 through 1950 I had a fellowship in dermatology at the Hospital of the University of Pennsylvania in Philadelphia. I was the only woman in a group of thirty-one residents, many of whom were being trained after their World War II service. Finally, in 1950, after thirteen years of study, I completed my training, passed my specialty boards, and qualified as a certified dermatologist.

Eventually I opened my own office for private practice in the small town of Bryn Mawr, Pennsylvania, avoiding big-city life and traffic. It took some time, and it was difficult to establish a practice because very few women physicians were in the area and patients were not accustomed to medical women. However, after a few lean years my practice grew steadily to the point where I wanted it. My practice was highly individualized and personalized; thus it grew mainly by patient-to-patient referral. It was a most rewarding and gratifying career for a total of twenty-three years.

During my professional life I was instructor and associate in dermatology at the University of Pennsylvania in Philadelphia and visiting associate professor in dermatology at the Woman's Medical College. At my own suburban Bryn Mawr Hospital I became chief of the dermatology service after a very few years and held that position for ten years, relinquishing it before retirement to give younger persons an opportunity to serve. Later in my career I was appointed a consultant to the Federal Drug Administration in the United States Department of Health, Education, and Welfare for the purpose of reviewing the safety and efficacy of some topical over-the-counter drugs. This was a very challenging assignment.

In addition to my active professional life, I had many extracurricular activities. I maintained my study of the piano. Other consuming interests were antiques, traveling, photography, and shell-collecting (conchology). I spent my free days as a volunteer in the mollusk department at the Academy of Natural Sciences of Philadelphia. Because of my keen interest, I was invited to participate in several of its scientific expeditions to the tropical waters of the Pacific, the Indian Ocean, and the Caribbean to collect living marine mollusks. Thus I gained expertise in the collecting field and in snorkeling and skin diving. It was always a great thrill to goggle over the coral reefs and explore the magnificence of the sea world. Our specimens have gone to the academy's collection and to other world-famous museums. To this day I still maintain my active interest in malacology and am now a research associate at the academy. At present I am engaged in describing the anatomy and microanatomy of marine mollusks never before described or even seen by the human eye. Microanatomy is a vast new area that we are just beginning to study and report.

During the midpoint of my professional career I was asked to serve on the scholarship committee of the American Medical Women's Association. This assignment touched a resonant chord in me because it took me back to my spartan days as a medical student. It was easy to assume greater responsibility in the various offices of the organization and eventually in 1971 to become president of the association. I felt privileged to serve in this capacity. My presidency focused chiefly on three projects: greater visibility and participation of the woman physician in organized medicine, equal rights in educational opportunities for women in medicine, and scholarship funds for our women medical students. By the end of my presidential year I was gratified to have obtained a $100,000 gift to the scholarship fund from the Sears Foundation, as well as an additional $10,000 from private donors.

It was during my presidency that I was selected as one of "six distinguished American women" who were invited as guests of France, under the auspices of their Cultural Division of Foreign Affairs, to visit for two weeks and to meet our counterparts in business, banking, sciences, and the professional fields. This honor of a lifetime was a most broadening and rewarding one.

In 1972 I became national corresponding secretary of Medical Women's International Association (MWIA) for the United States. In 1974 I was elected and in 1976 reelected as vice-president of MWIA for North America, representing women physicians of Mexico, Canada, and the United States. My office expires in 1978. In the past I have enjoyed attending numerous congresses of the MWIA, which have enriched my life immensely through the numerous contacts with such outstanding women from all nations.

In 1976 the Alumnae Association of the Woman's Medical College of Pennsylvania presented me with their highest honor, the Achievement Award for being "spokeswoman and model of the concerned physician . . . vice-president of North America for MWIA . . . for accomplishment as a practicing dermatologist in both patient care and research . . . [and for] contributions to Alma Mater and women in medicine the world over."

Recently, in March of 1977, I received the highest national award given by the National Society of the Daughters of the American Revolution—The

Americanism Medal. This medal is awarded to the naturalized citizen who has demonstrated "outstanding leadership, trustworthiness, patriotism, and service following naturalization." This award was presented at the first university on the North American continent—The University of Pennsylvania. I was deeply touched by this recognition and high honor, and I treasure the medal and honor to this day.

My story is one of an older person returning to college, studying, and initiating the practice of medicine at the mature age of forty-three. It is a story of many hurdles and barriers that had to be overcome. Medical educators still reject and discourage the older candidate in medicine and frequently refuse to accept the mature student despite competence and motivation. I strongly urge the qualified older student who has a sincere wish to study medicine to pursue the dictates of her desires. Medicine can be for her, as it has been for me, a most gratifying and rewarding career, above and beyond all expectations.

In 1864 a Boston preacher, Phillips Brooks, wrote:

Education is a companion
No misfortune can depress
No clime destroy
No enemy alienate
No despotism enslave
At home a friend
Abroad an introduction
In society an ornament
And in solitude a solace.

Medicine is all of this and more. It can be yours for the effort.

Agnete Meinert Braestrup
b. July 10, 1909

My parents grew up in a small, historic Danish town sheltered beside a picturesque lake. My father's family had for generations been "free" farmers, owners of their own land. They were educated people, and the sons were sent to the Latin grammar school in a larger town. My father was no exception; he left his parental home at fourteen and never lived in it again. He had to make his own decisions and so became mature and independent. My mother's family were townspeople, and both her parents' families were army people. Her father became an engineer and settled on the mainland, where my mother was born. My grandfather soon became established socially and culturally. He constructed new railroads and was a good amateur actor, able to sing and dance.

My parents said that they always belonged to each other, but the attachment was not encouraged by their families and they were forbidden to correspond. At the age of sixteen my mother was allowed to go as an au pair girl to another town, and she thus escaped parental control. As an antimilitarist, my father had to leave Denmark before he was eighteen years of age. He went to Zurich, Switzerland, where he had to pass the Swiss general certificate before he was accepted at the Polytechnic College. My mother followed him and stayed in various homes, in all of which she was introduced to endless matrimonial problems. Everywhere she went, the wives opened their hearts to this young girl of nineteen.

However, my mother's experiences did not in any way interfere with her happy relationship with my father; they looked forward to the day when he would get his diploma and they could marry. On the wedding night, nevertheless, he gave her a slight shock by saying, "I give myself to you pure." After all, she knew nothing about venereal diseases and the prostitution of those days. This young couple were better prepared than many to found a family, as they belonged to each other and loved and respected each other's personalities.

I was the first of three children born into this family and was delivered in Berlin by a woman obstetrician. My grandmother came to stay with us for six weeks, and when I cried at night, she would pick me up and lay me on her stomach. My mother would tell her that babies should only be picked up at regular hours, but her reply was, "I know that babies must have warmth"; so we slept contentedly together.

From the first day of my life, emotional security, love, and acceptance of my personality were granted to me. My parents' attitude toward my brother was always different. They lost their second child, and when my brother arrived, there were difficulties in rearing him. My mother was afraid of losing him, too, and this anxiety, which never left her, later affected his general behavior. I remember a number of events that happened in the first five years of my life, all connected with the atmosphere of anxiety or tension, and relating to things rather than people. The first is the memory of the overwhelming pain that resulted when I stepped on a big carpet tack when I was two and a half years old and we were moving from Berlin to Austria. The whole scene, the colors and everything in turmoil, are perfectly clear to me.

An episode that occurred during the summer when I was five shows a characteristic feature of my makeup. My mother later told me that I was walking along a country road and came to a wayside crucifix where some workmen were playing cards during their noon break. I left our housekeeper, went quietly up to the men, and said, "You cannot play cards below a crucifix," whereupon they rose and left without a word. I have acted in a similar way on other occasions, using all my accumulated experience and thoughts to express my attitudes or conclusions on matters in which I was previously unaware of my competence.

World War I was declared, and for the first time in my life, I was confronted with evil. Life was completely changed; my mother and her friends met in the afternoons to knit warm helmets and socks for the soldiers, whom we could hear marching in the streets below and singing patriotic songs. The noise of their heels still sounds in my ears. I asked my mother endless questions about where they were going, what they were doing, and where they could sleep and eat. About six months later my father accepted a professorship in Denmark. Fortunately, he had just turned thirty-three, which put him above the age limit for military service.

The most exciting experiences of my childhood took place during the summer vacations in my parents' hometown. My "old" grandfather loved gardening and had a very neat, old-fashioned garden with lots of different types of flowers and plants, but he did not want children playing in this paradise. My mother, however, did not allow me to play outside the garden, in the park, with unknown children. One day she caught me in the forbidden park while I was performing mystical rites, with some ten children solemnly following all my directions.

In the house of my "young" grandparents something was always happening. When my grandfather went on his veterinary calls in his three-wheeled car, I would often go with him, and I used to observe the anxiety of the farmers when he arrived. Once he had dealt with the sick cow or horse, there would be a change to relaxed gaiety, with coffee for the grown-ups and something for me, as well. Sometimes grandfather himself was ill, and I would nurse him, bringing him chamomile tea and comforting him. My most exciting experience was accompanying him to the basement, where strange odors met us. Here he had his pharmacy with endless shelves of bottles filled with the chemicals and herbs from which he produced medicines.

After our return to Denmark I started school in the middle of the first grade, together with one other girl. I was not at ease in this large schoolroom with all its empty desks; nor did I like the recesses because children often came up to me and said, "Say something in German." I knew very little German but would recite a children's rhyme. When I finished, they would all laugh. From that moment I began to feel I was different, and this idea has remained with me all my life. As a result, I became withdrawn, although observant. I studied my teachers and classmates and noted their behavior and appearance and the apparent disparity between what they said and what they really meant. It seemed to me that they were not really sincere. School was terribly boring, although my teachers were good and I did well, so I had plenty of time to occupy myself with my thoughts in relation to those around me and to the few books I was able to read. I worked slowly because I was—and still am—dyslectic. I read my first book at the age of nine. This was Dickens' *Oliver Twist*, which introduced me to a new world of poverty, misery, and cruelty, so unbelievably different from my own. The next year I learned more from a twelve-year-old Viennese girl who, like so many other children, was welcomed into a Danish home after World War I. Despite all they had suffered, she and her friends introduced me to gaiety and happiness through singing and playing the piano.

A year or two later we had our first male teacher, and I immediately "fell in love." I can still see him at morning song in his elegant black suit with white stripes and mahogany red shoes. He taught natural science, and for the first time in my life, I enjoyed school in the classroom, as well as on excursions in the neighborhood. This teacher taught me many things, especially in the laboratory in the school attic, where he "was just about to demonstrate how life begins."

From then on, the future began to occupy my thoughts. I soon decided that I would never aim at becoming famous, as this did not seem worthwhile when a man like Erasmus of Rotterdam, who had been the father of humanism, was practically unknown just a few hundred years later. I wanted to do something for people. Then, suddenly, I knew what to do—I wanted to become a doctor. I can even remember the spot where I made my decision.

The years of puberty and adolescence were very perceptive. I enjoyed reading the books of great explorers of the Himalayas and Greenland and became acquainted with different cultures and religions. The philosophy of Taoism fascinated me, as did the life and work of Mahatma Gandhi. When I visited India for the first time, in 1958, I had the feeling that I had come home. During the summer I enjoyed mountaineering with my family in Switzerland. When I was sixteen, I asked whether I might go with a group of Danish teenagers to Norway. My parents, in order to evaluate the sincerity of my wish, said that they would permit me to go provided I pay half the costs myself. This I did, and I had many wonderful experiences—but in addition, one alarming one. In the heart of the bare, majestic mountains, the group leader made a speech to all of us. As it happened to be my seventeenth birthday, he addressed me, giving me a brooch depicting Pillargure, a girl who blew a horn to call her people to fight the invading Scots, and saying that I should become a woman like her. How could he know? And how could another of the leaders have written in my book, "It is your vocation to help the masses"? This was certainly bewildering to one who wanted to hide and remain anonymous but who nevertheless had made the decision to help people. Why was it that the group I was in chose me as their leader?

My years in the medical faculty of the University of Copenhagen were as lacking in interest as my school years. The subjects were exciting but were only the tools through which I could reach my objective. Gradually it became increasingly obvious to me that the prevention of medical and social evils would have a much greater impact than curing individual diseases. But how could this be done?

Someone told me that medical students could work their way from Copenhagen to New York once they had passed their basic sciences, so I went to see the director of the maritime company and asked for employment. There was dead silence. He looked me up and down and then said, "We cannot take women for that job." I must have looked very disappointed because after a while he continued, "Would you take a job as a children's nurse?" Off I went, and this opportunity opened up a new world to me, with the many social classes among the passengers and crew. Fortunately, I was accepted by a group composed of the first steward, the deck steward, and the hairdresser. No one knew that I was a medical student. During my week in New York I found out what I could about institutions dealing with preventive medicine and decided not to marry until I had been on a study tour of the United States.

As I always had good relationships with the opposite sex, I had many offers of marriage, but I never wanted to marry anyone except the man who became my husband. We married almost forty years ago and went to America together. He did research while I visited all kinds of institutions involved in preventive medicine. Soon I found out that my basic knowledge was much the same as that of American students but that the practical application was different. This strengthened my resolve to use my knowledge for the benefit of people in general.

On returning home, we started our family of three children. My husband continued in a hospital career in pediatrics and became chief of the pediatric department when he was thirty-six years old. I decided to confine myself to part-time work within my field of interest and have been doing this for thirty-five years. I have worked in schools, kindergartens, and nurseries in our established health system. In addition, I have taught hygiene to both teachers and children and written articles on research for medical journals and for the general public in magazines and newspapers.

As I have always had difficulty in putting my thoughts on paper, I wrote only when I had something new to communicate, which often changed the established belief on a subject. I was always seeking the best way to make an impact.

Although I was little involved in the resistance movement, I worked hard to repair the ravages of war. In July of 1945 a colleague and I led the first convoy through northern Germany to Arnhem in Holland to collect 500 children and take them to Danish homes. On the way we passed Hamburg after curfew. The city was bombed out, with no living being anywhere in sight. A story from the Bible that I had not heard since I was a small child at school suddenly came alive for me. I saw Lot and his wife and understood that we could not look back or we would not survive but that we must work for the future. As an executive member of the Danish Save the Children's Organization, I traveled all over Europe in the years that followed, organizing and supervising feeding projects for children.

I was called to serve as chairperson of our small group of Danish medical women on account of my special talents and experience rather than my medical skill, which I had not used since starting my family. We became aware that the abortion problem was on the increase and decided to do something about it by opening a number of pilot clinics in Copenhagen in 1947. And what happened? The Danish Medical Association announced that this was not allowed! Immediately the newspapers reported that war had been declared between the mighty general medical association and the Medical Women's Club. It was a mean war and a long one, but we won, perhaps because I was able to counter on the spot the many attacks that were made on us. These were allegations that we had neglected formalities and that, in general, medical women's qualifications were poor. When this approach did not work, the medical association attacked me personally. Our victory here should make all medical women realize what a fantastic instrument a medical women's organization can be. It can bring solutions to sociomedical problems, which no other body I can think of is able to do.

At this time I introduced the concept of family planning in a newspaper article. From the late 1950s I sacrificed more and more of my professional work to the cause of planned parenthood, sex education, and population problems. In 1956 the Danish Medical Women's Club, the Danish Medical Association, and the Danish Pharmacy Proprietors Association, together with a representative from the Ministry of Justice, founded the Danish Family Planning Association, which is a member of the International Planned Parenthood Federation (IPPF), and in this sphere I served on the executive committee of the European and Middle East regions from 1958 to 1970. For six of these years I was president of the Danish Family Planning Association. From 1969 to 1971 I was president of the IPPF. In 1970 I gave up my other professional work, and since then have devoted all my time to family planning.

Khunying Cherd-Chalong Netrasiri
b. August 27, 1909

My first vivid recollection is of the cool, calm late afternoons spent on the little beach at Tungka Harbor, in Phuket, with my sister and my childhood friend Khun Ampha, accompanied by our nurse. That was the year 1913. At that time my father, who was then chief justice of Phuket circuit in the south of Thailand; my sister, who was seven years of age; and I, three years younger, were living with a close friend of my father's, also a government official; his wife; and their dearly loved adopted daughter Khun Ampha, a girl of my own age. This rather unusual domestic arrangement was a consequence of my mother's untimely death when I was four years old and my father's decision to accept his friend's offer for us to temporarily make our home with him and his family. His wife, the kind-hearted woman who took charge of my sister and me, was well educated and was at that time the principal of the girls' school of Phuket Province. Thus, motherless though we were, my sister and I did not suffer unduly thanks to these kind friends and my father, whose love and intense care for our welfare were evinced by the fact that he did not remarry until ten years later.

My schooling began quite early, when I was five, at which time I learned to read and write Thai at the Phuket Girls' School. Two years later, in 1916, my sister and I were sent to school in Bangkok, the capital city. There my father entrusted us to the care of an eminent government official, who then held a far higher position than did my father but who had been a close friend of his from school days. We two sisters were warmly received into that household and were well taken care of, along with our host's eldest daughter, although, in his characteristic way, my father provided us with a trusty maid of our own. The school we went to was the Assumption Convent, a girls' school of high repute run by Roman Catholic nuns.

Two years later, when I was nine, my father was transferred to Bangkok and so we were reunited. We were overjoyed. At about that time we moved from the Assumption Convent to St. Joseph's Convent, another good Catholic school.

When I was fourteen, my father remarried. My stepmother was a daughter of a high-ranking official of the ministry of the royal household, a highly educated woman, well known and esteemed in the society of those days.

Although I was quite happy at St. Joseph's Convent, after finishing secondary grade five, I decided to leave and enroll in Rajinee School, which followed the curriculum of the public instruction, for I wanted to work toward the secondary-school diploma. Altogether I spent two years at this school, and my record was consistently good. I was always at the top of my class in each year's final examination. As luck would have it, at Rajinee School I was reunited with Khun Ampha, my dear friend from Phuket days. She turned out to be a great character, with a tremendous sense of humor, and she was very popular with everyone.

Toward the end of the final year the topic that cropped up most often in our conversation was the question of what we would do after leaving school. At that time coeducation was unknown in Thailand, and Chulalongkorn University, the only unversity in the country, was still very much in its formative stage, as yet with no women students. Girls who completed secondary grade six or eight, if they were adverse to the idea of staying at home, either became teachers or took up training to be nurses. Neither profession attracted me, although I really did not have any clear idea of what I wanted to do or to become. My friend Khun Ampha, on the contrary, knew and spoke her own mind. She said again and again that she wanted to become a doctor, and this characteristically wild plan of hers was well known among us all. Although the idea appeared impractical to me at the time, I felt rather drawn toward it. When I had typhoid at the age of fourteen I was attended by a modern physician who had been on observation tours of modern medical practice in Western countries, and the respect, deference, and awe this marvelous man inspired in everyone around made a deep impression on me. I was all the more strongly impressed with the "modern medicine" when I remembered the traditional treatment of unpalatable pills, powders, and potions that I had had to take in large quantities in my childhood when I suffered from a common ailment, such as measles or chicken pox. It occurred to me that the medical profession would be a noble course to follow, but I dismissed the idea as an impossible dream.

Then something quite miraculous happened. I chanced one day to accompany my stepmother to pay a visit to Her Highness Princess Chandranipa Decakul, a granddaughter of King Monkut and at that time principal of Benjamarajalai School for girls. Her Highness, whose intelligence, fine character, and perfect grace were widely admired, asked me kindly, "What are you going to do next year?" I said, "What I really should like is to study medicine and become a doctor, madam. But I fear it's rather a hopeless wish."

Shortly after that brief exchange, this kind and visionary princess sent a message to my father. The gist of that message was that Her Highness had discussed the question of admitting women students into our university with His Highness Prince Dhaninvat, minister of public instruction, and His Highness had decided that the time had come to make the university coeducational. However, there was one point he insisted on: that we make sure there were a reasonable number of women in the first year.

So in 1927 coeducation began in Thailand with the admission of seven women undergraduates into the Faculty of Arts and Science. Without exception we women had outstanding academic records and were daughters of fairly well-to-do senior government officials. Among the seven was my friend Khun Ampha, the originator of the whole idea of entering the medical profession, but most unfortunately and ironically, she found the science subjects utterly unbearable and had to relinquish the course during the first year.

At the university we studied the basic sciences for two years. Then, after passing an examination in 1929, we embarked on the medical course proper, at Siriraj Hospital Medical School. Five out of the total enrollment of twenty-four starting the course that year were women. Life across the river, at Siriraj, was quite different from what we had been accustomed to. At the Faculty of Arts and Science of Chulalongkorn University, we had been kept under strict surveillance, and although the men and women students attended lectures and laboratory sessions together, we were completely segregated outside those hours. At Siriraj we were left entirely to our own devices, but there was no evidence of unseemly or reproachable conduct anywhere at any time.

The year of 1933 was our year of triumph. We—that is to say fourteen of the original twenty-four—successfully completed the course and were awarded the degree of Bachelor of Medicine. Three out of the fourteen graduates were women, the first three women medical graduates in the history of our country— and I was one of them.

I had further luck in being selected for the post of a house officer in the medical department of Siriraj Hospital, and a year later, in 1934, I was recruited for a permanent post there. In other words, I was the first woman to become a house officer and a physician in a teaching hospital in Thailand.

In those days the medical department treated both adults and children. The head of the department decided that, as a woman, I should be given the responsibility of taking care of the children, and I was also required to do some teaching in pediatrics.

In 1938 I was awarded an Alexander von Humboldt Fellowship to pursue further studies in medicine in Germany. My chief suggested that I spend one year studying pediatrics and the remaining time in tropical medicine. Luck was not on my side this time. After working for a year at Leipzig University Hospital under Professor Catel, a prominent pediatrician in those days, I applied for admission to the Institute of Tropical Medicine, only to be told that Germany at that time needed all the institute's specialists in tropical medicine and therefore was not in a position to admit foreign students. I had no choice but to return home. However, I did stop in the United States, where I spent just over one month observing at the Children's Hospital in Philadelphia.

In 1940 I married Dr. Arun Netrasiri, a colleague at Siriraj Medical School. We had met, in fact, thirteen years previously, when I was a first-year student at the Faculty of Arts and Science and he was in his second year. Soon after that, however, Arun won a Ministry of Education Scholarship to study abroad. He chose to study medicine in Germany, where he spent eleven years and obtained a degree of Doctor of Medicine, specializing in pediatrics.

On his return to Thailand Arun joined Siriraj Medical School, and from that time until his retirement, in 1968, we worked closely together. In 1946, three years after the establishment of the Department of Pediatrics, Arun was elected chief of the department. At that time our staff included the head, myself, one senior house officer, and one house officer. Our two junior colleagues, apart from being remarkably able professionally, were tremendously hard-working and totally devoted to their vocation. It gives me great pleasure to think that our colleague who was the house officer then is now head of the department. Under the able leadership of Arun and with the superb cooperation of all our colleagues, we were able to build up the department and to watch it grow in strength until it achieved standards comparable to those of any institution of its kind in this region.

In addition to his career at the Department of Pediatrics, my husband had the great honor of serving as the attending physician to Their Royal Highnesses the crown prince and the three royal princesses, and subsequently the king, in his great bounty, made Arun knight grand commander of the Most Illustrious Order of Chula Chom Klao, and me companion of the same order, which explains my title Khunying.

As one of the first women to enter the medical profession in my country, I suppose I could be called a pioneer of sorts. But for almost the whole span of my career my role was one of the proverbial "elephant's hind legs," working for over twenty years under my husband's leadership. I make this statement without the least resentment. On the contrary, it gives me great satisfaction to contemplate the growth and the publicly acknowledged achievements of our Department of Pediatrics. Whatever my own contribution may have been, I am happy and proud to think that, during those long years we spent building up the department and this branch of medicine, my husband could always count on me not only for a loyal colleague's professional cooperation but for a wife's understanding and moral support. Arun and I have one daughter.

In 1954 the University of Medical Science awarded me the honorary degree of Doctor of Medicine. In 1968 I succeeded Arun as head of the Department of Pediatrics. I held the position for one year and then retired. Now, in our retirement, one of our greatest sources of joy is our two grandsons. Our daughter, who holds a degree in economics from Chulalongkorn University and a master's degree in public administration from Kent State University in Ohio, is a lecturer in the Faculty of Commerce and accountancy, Chulalongkorn University. As it happens, our son-in-law, who holds a diploma of the American Board of Pediatrics, is a staff member of the Department of Pediatrics at Siriraj. Thus, to our immense satisfaction, we are kept in close touch with our dearly loved old department, and we watch with keenest interest its progress and prosperity.

CANADA

Enid MacLeod
b. September 16, 1909

I was born in Jacksonville, Carleton County, New Brunswick, Canada. My father Reverend William H. Johnson, born in London, was a Baptist minister. He was trained in the manual trades, as well as the ministry, as he had since early in his life intended to become a missionary in Africa. When he graduated from Spurgeon's College, his physical examination revealed that it was not safe for him to go to Africa, but he was advised to leave England for the sake of his health. At that time Canadian Baptists were seeking more preachers, so he emigrated to Canada.

My mother, born in London, was trained to be a missionary's wife with a special education in midwifery and sewing. She arrived in Canada one year after my father. They were married in Saint John, New Brunswick, and settled in a country parsonage in 1908. They had three daughters and one son, of whom I was the first child.

We moved frequently, living in small villages, and I attended five different schools before completing high school. This was unusual in my day, although it is more common now. I enjoyed going to school and usually did well in comparison to my schoolmates, although I was never motivated to work hard. At about ten years of age, when my future education was being discussed, I asked my parents what my best choice would be and was told, "To become a medical missionary." That settled the matter. My future was never discussed again. When we were children, we often played "hospital" or "operating room" or similar games, and it was I who always played the part of doctor. Being a woman doctor was never considered "odd" in our family, but I had the strong feeling that I was expected to remain single all my life if I became one, so I never thought that I would marry.

In 1927, after taking a business course, I started to work as a secretary to earn money for college. I had never worried about where all the money would come from, although I knew my father was making less than $1000 a year and could not help me financially. We were brought up to believe that something would turn up and that the Lord would provide.

In 1929 something did turn up. I was offered a bursary by the Missionary Society to study at Acadia University. After I received a B.A. in biology and chemistry, I applied to and was accepted at Dalhousie University in Halifax. Money for my medical studies was loaned to me by persons interested in me personally and by several interested in medical missions. I graduated, M.D., C.M. in 1937.

In medical school, I was the only woman in my class of twenty-nine. At that time there were few women studying medicine at Dalhousie, but during my years, there was one in each class. As students, we were accepted, but as interns, we were not allowed to serve in the Victoria General, the main teaching hospital, so my internship was limited to small hospitals in small towns where I was often the only resident. In those days we were required to intern for one year before our final oral examinations for our medical degree. It was customary however, in front of patients, for us to be addressed as "Doctor." In one of the small hospitals where I interned, the superintendent always addressed me as "Miss Johnson," although she addressed the male interns as "Doctor." I was amused by this injustice, but some of my female predecessors had strenuously objected to it. This type of petty discrimination has largely disappeared; today nearly one-fifth of the doctors in our province of Nova Scotia are women, and they are welcomed and treated with respect in any of our hospitals.

After graduation I started looking for a hospital where I could be a resident to gain some experience. I found myself doubting my fitness for the life of a missionary doctor. I was not wholly committed to religion or to the thought of remaining single all my life. I decided to get away from familiar places and use the next few years to gain experience in as many medical fields as possible. It was difficult at that time for a woman to get a post as resident in either a specialty or a rotation. I was finally accepted as the sole resident at a small general hospital in Ontario. Later I learned that my application had been accepted only because the previous resident had been a fiery-tempered Italian and the administration thought that, as a woman, I would be more subdued; even so, most of the medical staff had had reservations about appointing a woman resident.

A year later, after considering my own motives and consulting my family and many others who had encouraged and helped me, I resigned from the mission board and made plans to enter a specialty to earn enough money to pay back the Acadia bursary and the money loaned me while I was at Dalhousie. This money had been given with the understanding that, if I became a missionary, I would never need to repay it.

In 1939 I was fortunate enough to meet Dr. Harold Griffith, an anesthesiologist in Montreal who was looking for a resident. He offered me the position, and after three years with him, I became a certified anesthesiologist. During this period I worked with Dr. Griffith in the introduction of the use of curare as a muscle relaxant in anesthesia.

After I had been in Montreal for two years, the Montreal Hospital Unit for Overseas Army Service was organized. The unit needed an anesthetist, and Dr.

Griffith recommended me, but I was not accepted because I was a woman and there were no residential provisions for women in the medical unit. When Dr. Griffith asked whether I could be put with nurses, the reply was, "Of course not. She would outrank them"! This policy was changed later in the war, when women's corps were organized, but by that time I was married and beginning a practice in Sydney, Nova Scotia.

In 1942 I married a lawyer, Innis MacLeod, who was practicing in Sydney. I practiced anesthesia for the next six years and was accepted on my own terms by other doctors and many surgeons. This was mainly because the general practitioners there were used to giving anesthetics and not because I was a woman. Patients needed a little education, as they were not used to female doctors and sometimes refused to pay my bills. After a few years I became known, and some patients even asked their doctors to call me in for the anesthetic. While the war was on, I was the doctor for the blood-donor clinic in the area. This volunteer work gave me an opportunity to meet the local people.

In 1948 my husband took a position with the Nova Scotia government in Halifax, so we moved. Having two children, I preferred to work part time for the next few years. Such things as school inoculations and work in clinics, along with raising my children, kept me busy until 1960, when I began working at Dalhousie Medical School in the physiology department. I have been in this department ever since and am now an associate professor, teaching paramedical and medical students and enjoying the life of a full-time teacher.

Our children did not follow in the footsteps of either of their parents. Our son is an economist and our daughter a social worker. Both are happily married. At present we have no grandchildren, but perhaps there will be a lawyer or a doctor someday!

As time goes on, more and more women in Canada are studying medicine. There are as many reasons as there are women, but the future looks bright for them, as they can now enter any specialty with ease. The availability of good household help, although still inadequate, is improving; thus, it is not such a problem to raise a family and practice medicine at the same time as it was thirty years ago.

Having had the experience of both practice and the academic life, I would never discourage a woman from studying medicine. Only recently I talked to a graduate of a Canadian medical school who is finding clinical work uninspiring. She is now considering the academic side. There are other openings for those with M.D. degrees, including research, administration, or preventive medicine. Women are welcome in all these fields in Canada today. We have come a long way since I graduated in 1937, when a woman could not even do an undergraduate internship in the teaching hospital of the medical school she had attended!

Marianne Lindsten-Thomasson
b. October 6, 1909

I was the eldest child in a Swedish teacher's family; my two brothers and a sister came later. My sister, who was the youngest, is nearly fifteen years younger than I. For generations, as far back as they can be traced, my father's family have been farmers in Småland, Sweden, with an odd university graduate, usually a minister, here and there. My father had four sisters, all of whom emigrated to the United States, and two brothers who, like himself, became teachers. My maternal grandfather was a bank official and died young of pulmonary tuberculosis, leaving my grandmother to bring up three small children, of whom only my mother reached adulthood. She was trained as a language teacher but taught for short periods only. One of my ancestors on my mother's side was a general practitioner at the end of the eighteenth century, but I know of no other doctors in my family. On the other hand, both my parents were interested in botany and passed on this interest to me while I was very small. Throughout my schooling I was most attracted to the natural sciences.

I have no early memories that are medical in nature, apart from my smallpox vaccination, which was probably performed when I was four years old. We were living in Göteborg at the time, and the vaccination was done in the doctor's home, as he was a family friend. The doctor's son and another playmate were ritually "scratched," despite their vociferous protests. I had whooping cough when I was eight and was treated with syrup of thyme, which I thought tasted awful but swallowed without grimaces. My two-year-old brother had first been fed the same remedy to set a good example for me.

I learned to read at home at so early an age that I do not remember how it happened. Probably I was four years old. Gradually I read everything I could get my hands on—mythology, travel, popular science, and adventure. My favorite author in my early teens was Jules Verne. But I always glanced quickly through bloody or macabre stories because they upset and frightened me.

As I learned to read and write at home, I did not start school until I was eight. I then began in the third grade at Skara Girls' School. After two years the family moved to Landskrona, where my father was appointed lecturer at the high school. I was ten at the time and had to change schools in the middle of the autumn term. I was unhappy about the change, and later, as a school doctor, I felt great sympathy for children who had problems adjusting to a new school. I came to a class where the groups were already formed; my dialect differed from that of most of the pupils; and in addition, I was a teacher's daughter and thus never really accepted. After three years I had the opportunity to transfer to the local gymnasium, or high school, in Landskrona, which had just been opened to girls. Otherwise, girls who wished to earn a diploma and go on for university studies had either to do so as private entrants or to apply to one of the few high schools for girls in Sweden.

At home it was regarded as inevitable that the four of us would go on to the university; in fact, no other possibility was considered. Certainly, my father's income was not large—teachers' salaries in the 1920s and 1930s were by no means substantial—but we lived modestly and he helped all four of us children to graduate without debt. When I was fourteen and entered the gymnasium I did not really know what I wanted to do, and indeed, I have no memory of having thought much about the future. I chose the Latin line, perhaps guided by some influence from my parents. At that time none of the family had chosen the "modern" line. I found greater satisfaction in my years in the gymnasium than I had at the girls' school, although I still had comparatively little contact with my classmates. We had the great fortune to have the same teacher throughout our four years of study, an advantage that seems to be very unusual nowadays. In the spring of 1927, when I had passed my matriculation at the age of eighteen, I decided to study medicine. I was still interested primarily in the natural sciences but did not wish to become a teacher, so I chose to try to be a doctor. During the summer I succeeded in filling in my educational gaps with the courses in physics and chemistry. In the autumn I enrolled for a course in general chemistry, which was then the first step in medicine. We gathered outside the Institute of Medical Chemistry in Lund and found that there were thirty-one candidates for thirty places. However, no elimination competition was arranged, and an extra place was arranged for number thirty-one.

Anatomy studies began that same term. Before I started, I had been more than a little nervous about what my reaction would be, considering how squeamish I had been earlier when reading or seeing pictures of macabre events. But at Anatomicum it was quite different, as dissection was part of the job and became wholly natural. The preclinical courses followed in due order, each opening doors to new fields with wide horizons. When the clinical studies began, I at first felt disturbed and worried. It was difficult to be assigned patients who had often gone in and out of the Department of Internal Medicine and "belonged" to several courses of medical students. I had a feeling that they knew considerably more about their ailments than the poor medical students and that we were scrutinized by very critical eyes. However, as the months went by, we were able to treat patients at the primary stage and the work seemed more meaningful.

One course that I particularly remember was at the beginning of the clinical studies, when we were assigned to the orthopedics department under Dr. Frising for one month. He taught us much about psychosomatic medicine long before the term was coined. Two books that made a deep impression on me were Erwin Liek's *The Miracle in the Art of Healing* and Axel Munthe's *The Story of San Michele*. During my studies I never felt discriminated against on the basis of my sex, but I was forcibly confronted with the problem in my first temporary post in the summer of 1933, when I was assistant locum tenens at the hospital in my hometown. The salary included free board and lodging, but I was asked not to eat in the doctor's dining room because "one of the assistant doctors does not wish to see women at the dining table." As I could eat at home, I willingly refrained from eating there on the condition that I be reimbursed.

In 1936, when I had completed my studies and was a qualified doctor, I tried to find work, but at that time there were many doctors and few posts. It often happened that, when I applied for a locum tenens I was told that women were undesirable. Indeed, women doctors were rare at that time, and in 1939, when I won my first permanent position as assistant doctor at Gällivare Hospital, patients generally were not even aware of my status. Many times when I was on emergency call and had finished suturing a wound or setting a fracture, the patient would ask, "Isn't the doctor coming soon?" A few years later, in 1945, when I was locum tenens for a general practitioner in Tranas, the telephone rang and the nurse said the call was for me. I took the receiver, said my name, and the voice at the other end said, "But I want to talk to *the doctor*." I explained that the ordinary doctor was away and that I was taking his place and asked what the matter was. After a long silence the voice said, "But I still think you sound just like a woman."

Fairly early in my university years I began to ponder whether to try to become a general practitioner or a specialist in pediatrics. In both fields the doctor treats the whole person, a fact that appealed to me more than specializing in a part of the body. I remember that once, when a group of colleagues were sitting talking about what they would do when they "grew up," I said I would like to be a district general practitioner. "Pooh," said one of the others, "There are no women general practitioners." I naturally retorted, "Someone has to be first." Little did I realize then that it would be I, and I must admit that I was happy and proud to hold the authorization in my hand a good ten years later. A somewhat older colleague also decided to become a district practitioner, and she had even decided which district she preferred, but the post was not vacant until a few months after mine. I went to Vilhelmina in southern Lappland, where one doctor had previously looked after the parish single-handedly from a small cottage hospital. He would have preferred not to divide the district but to have an assistant at the cottage hospital. Yet we always had an extremely good relationship, substituting for each other on holidays and leaves.

I never thought that it would be possible to combine the job of rural medical officer with family life. Sometimes I thought of adopting a child, but it was never more than a thought. I set a higher value on my independence and had many opportunities for receiving visits from my father, brothers, sister, and close friends. Nevertheless, in 1950 I married as suddenly and as naturally as I had decided to study medicine. My husband was the district judge in Lycksele, 120 kilometers from Vilhelmina. He was a widower with five children, aged four to fifteen. The family had a summer cabin in my district, so we had already met on several occasions. We lived apart for the first five years of our marriage, meeting on holidays and weekends. This situation worked to our advantage, at least in the first one or two years, as the children and I were able to get used to one another. I soon understood that one need not have given birth to a child to regard him or her as one's own. We increased the family by two, a brother and a sister for the one girl and four boys who already formed part of it. When my son was born, the youngest of the first five, (then aged six) went around saying, "I have a little brother. Now I'm not the youngest anymore." The youngest girl grumbled, however, when she was five, "It is so unfair in this family. Everyone has a little sister except me!"

After I had been in Vilhelmina for ten years, one of the rural district medical officers in Lycksele retired. I applied and was then able to combine job and family in the same place. My new district was only half the size of the old one, but with double the population and harder work. Indeed in all probability, I was able to cope with both family and career only because I was blessed with good health. Another important factor was that the retiring doctor willingly lent a hand as long as he could and that, while the children were small, I had an excellent elderly and experienced housekeeper. Her weekly working hours and mine exceeded those now laid down by law. She stayed with us for twelve years, by which time the older children had left home, the smaller ones had grown up, my husband had retired, and we had moved to a smaller house.

After almost twenty-seven years of service as a general district practitioner, at the age of sixty-three, I was entitled to retire on full pension, and I did so with some relief. After working in my own surgery with two assistants, one of whom had helped me for nearly seventeen years, I was compulsorily transferred to a newly built medical center, serviced by three doctors associated with Lycksele Hospital. It had supermodern accommodations and first-class equipment, but the work there was heavier going and rather impersonal, and I found it difficult to adjust. Several successors would seem to have felt the same way, as my post is no longer a permanent appointment. Indeed the other two posts are also still held by temporary staff. I myself am delighted with my present situation. I am the doctor at the local school (ages seven through sixteen), as well as the physician for two small old-people's homes and a small outpatient clinic for alcoholics. I have a very small private practice, limited to cases that can be treated without extensive equipment.

I regard it as self-evident that women have the same right as men to choose their career—be it medicine, the ministry, seafaring, science, or whatever—according to their own wishes and talents. I only wish all individuals were able to do so and to fulfill their desires. If I were choosing a career today, I do not know which one I would decide on, as there are now so many possibilities. University studies no longer lead to an assured status or a job for life—if indeed, such is to be desired. When my daughter and I were talking one evening of what career she planned to follow, she said that she could not imagine choosing a profession that she would pursue all her life. She intended to change professions every few years. Formerly such an idea would have been considered absurd. I myself could not think of retraining at regular intervals and am grateful to have had the opportunity of working in a profession that I have so far enjoyed.

AUSTRALIA

Lorna Lloyd-Green
b. February 4, 1910

I am Australian-born, the eldest of four children; I have two sisters and one brother. My paternal grandparents came from England and Wales and my maternal grandparents from Scotland and Northern Ireland. My father was the younger son in a family of four children, and my mother the middle daughter of a family of nine children. My father's parents were reserved, conventional, and conservative, but my mother's were more outgoing and community-minded. Both grandfathers were storekeepers—a common occupation in the days of the "goldrush" in Australia if you were not a miner. My maternal grandfather was twice mayor of Castlemaine, a city in the heart of the goldfields. My father was a veterinarian and my mother a schoolteacher prior to her marriage. We had no relations who were medical practitioners, but my mother's youngest sister was a nurse.

My earliest recollection is awakening at night and wandering around my cot, trying—often unsuccessfully—to find the pillow end. I spent my fifth birthday in bed with chicken pox, but I was overjoyed at being given a beautiful three-tiered pencil box. At the age of six I began to play badminton and I learned to spell at school with large block letters on my desk. I went to school at seven o'clock every morning in order to practice the piano, as we did not possess one and I was keen to play well.

I don't think I ever stated that I would go into medicine, but I often "helped" my father with his veterinary treatments, particularly with the anesthetic for operations. At the age of eleven I gave a talk to my classmates on hydatid disease, a self-chosen topic briefed by my father and complemented by additional reading in medical books. My mother's attitude was that every woman should have an occupation of her own choosing. In contrast, my father gave me no encouragement, for he felt that a woman's place was in the home and that medical education was a ridiculous waste of money, for I would be certain to marry. My teachers knew that I had no training in physics and chemistry at all and therefore could not study medicine but could be a teacher. My music teacher was dumbfounded when I told him that I intended to study medicine, and he cherished the idea for years that the courses would be too much for me and I would return to my music. My mother had a strong religious conviction that "more things are wrought by prayer than this world dreams of," and I believed that, if you wanted anything badly enough, you would get it, provided it was God's will.

I had a keen interest in biology and botany and at school was a "big fish in a little pond." I was always first or second in my class and was captain of the school and captain of the basketball team. I always had to work but was aided by a "Pelmanistic" memory.

My medical course was financed by my mother with income from property. My father played no part in this venture. The first year of my studies was not easy, as I had no prerequisite subjects for medicine, but the tutors considered my efforts so unusual and amazing that they helped me at every turn and I achieved success. I had an uninterrupted course, passing each year's examinations. In the finals I obtained honors and finished thirteenth in a class of sixty students in 1933.

I never married, partly because I considered that it was not possible to make a success of two occupations and medicine was a full-time job.

My decision to specialize in obstetrics and gynecology was related to the encouragement of a professor, who was keen that I should do so. Since I was the only woman who had been granted a resident medical job in obstetrics and gynecology for some years, I felt I owed it to my own sex to show that I had made the most of this coveted post.

I consider that women doctors have a big contribution to make to the community. A large number of women prefer a woman doctor and often keep their personal problems to themselves until they find a medical woman. After all, one-half of the adult population is women, and they should have the opportunity to choose one of their own sex.

To be successful, a woman needs to be better than the average man and must watch her step more closely. Had I been a man I would have secured a post at the Women's Hospital, but I was told not to apply because I was a woman and would not be successful. In Australia the average income of medical women is about fifty-six percent of that of men. I have always done full-time work, and I was president of the Medical Women's International Association from 1968 through 1970. I did two years in general practice before specializing in obstetrics and gynecology. Those were very valuable years and laid an essential foundation for treating a patient as a whole person.

If I were beginning again, I would select medicine and the same specialty. Medicine is a very rewarding occupation, and it opens all kinds of interesting avenues in the community sphere.

Mollie Barlow
b. February 20, 1910

I was born in February of 1910 in the town of Bloemfontein, in the Orange Free State, South Africa. Eight years before my birth, the Boer War—three years of fighting between the British and the Boer republics of the Transvaal—had ended, with the British victorious. At the time of my birth, there was a reconciliation among the various countries of South Africa, and the Union of South Africa was born.

My father, a member of the Anglican church, was born in Bloemfontein in the Orange Free State Republic. My paternal grandfather and grandmother were English by birth. Grandfather had come to South Africa in 1849 and helped to found the local English newspaper *The Friend*, of which he later became editor and owner. He was also a member of the Volksraad, or Parliament of the republic.

My mother was born in Dublin, Ireland, and was educated there and in London. She was Jewish by birth, the daughter of a cantor, but never practiced her Jewish religion. She was brought up by a sister, as her father and mother died when she was very young. Mother came to Bloemfontein at the end of the Boer War, in 1902, and was personal secretary to Sir Hamilton Gould-Adams, who had been sent out from England as governor to the captured Orange Free State. She was a highly intelligent and vivacious person.

My father was a farmer, a journalist, a member of Parliament, the editor of one big newspaper, and the founder of another. He was successful in his career and a well-known South African personality. Although fairly well-to-do, his large family of five children, of whom I was the second, kept him poor, as he sent each child to expensive private schools and gave us all professions.

There had been doctors in my father's family for several generations. My great-grandfather, great-granduncle, and an uncle were all doctors. I have two younger sisters and three younger male cousins who are also doctors.

My only brother is severely crippled by cerebral palsy caused by a forceps injury. He is highly intelligent, holding, among other degrees a LL.D. He is also a state counsel, which is equivalent to a queen's counsel in Great Britain, and is a judicial writer of some note. He walks and talks with difficulty and writes only with a typewriter. He is married to a slightly spastic woman. My nonmedical sister is a journalist and politician.

I have always been interested in nursing and looking after the sick. Perhaps it was the years I spent with my brother that taught me to sympathize with people who are not well. We went to school at the same time, although he was four years older than I, and while I protected him physically, he helped me to learn to work and interested me in books and reading. He took special care to see that I did my homework every day and helped me to develop far beyond my years. In standing up for him when other children called him mad, I learned to fight and to answer people back. This facility has helped me greatly in my career.

I was lucky in my parents, who believed implicitly that girls could do anything as well as boys and felt that we deserved equal educational opportunities. When I was five or six, I expressed a desire to become a nurse when I grew up, but my father suggested to me that I become a doctor instead. From that time on, I never wished for any other profession, and as a teenager I was already taking a great interest in anything remotely related to medicine, such as giving an injection of antitoxic serum for snakebite to one of my father's cows and helping to look after my sisters when they were sick. When I myself was about eight years old, I was hospitalized with a pyrexia of unknown origin. I tried so hard to understand my temperature chart but was too shy to ask anyone what it meant.

At ten years of age I went to a government primary school in Bloemfontein, and then continued in boarding school in Johannesburg. I did not like boarding school, but this was my own fault, since I was "agin" the government and was always doing something I was not supposed to do. Nevertheless, I did well scholastically, matriculating at the age of fifteen. My headmistresses wanted me to pursue a mathematics degree at Cambridge, but I was set on studying medicine and so went to the University of Cape Town, where I qualified with the degree of Bachelor of Surgery and Medicine at the age of twenty-one, in 1931. After a residency in gynecology I spent nine months in Pretoria as a medical officer.

During my teens I was shy and not interested in boys or men. I never bothered to think of marriage and was quite astonished in my fifth year of medical school to hear the other women discussing what they would do about their careers when they married. Up until the time I qualified, I was quite happy and contented to spend my free time with my family and women friends and my holidays riding and swimming and making a fuss over my younger sisters.

By the time I qualified, I realized that men were really rather nice, and after I had completed my first house appointment, I met my future husband. I was twenty-two, and he was twenty-six. He was a university graduate, an attorney by education but engaged in journalism, and he later became a publisher. There was a depression in South Africa when we met in 1932, and we could not afford to get married. I therefore went to Great Britain in mid-1933 to learn about anesthetics and left him behind. He chose anesthetics for me as a specialty, as he felt it would fit in with married life. If I had been a man, I would have become a urologist.

I was twenty-five when we married, and I had been practicing as an anesthetist for a year. There were only five other anesthetists in Johannesburg at that time, in 1934. Now there are eighty, and several of them are women.

I waited to obtain a hospital appointment before announcing that I was getting married, since married women doctors were frowned on and were not given appointments. Fortunately for me, the head of the anesthesia department realized that marriage and children did not affect proficiency as a doctor and managed to talk the hospital committee into keeping me on the staff and into giving me maternity leave.

My husband and I have been happily married for over forty years, and we have two children, a boy and a girl, with nineteen months between them. I stopped working only when I was pregnant. After the children were born, I stayed at home with them for three months and then went back into part-time hospital work and a minimal private practice. During the period when my children were small and my husband was serving with the South African forces in World War II, I employed good children's nurses. When my son and daughter were of school age, I sent them to private schools, at first to day schools and later to boarding schools. When the eldest child was eight years of age, I went into full-time hospital practice. During this period I did a great deal of night duty in order to leave my days free for my children. In this way I never missed school events or birthdays and my son and daughter grew up in a happy and well-balanced family. Both my children are university graduates and happily married. Neither feels that I neglected them when they were children.

On my return to South Africa from Great Britain I obtained a part-time honorary position in anesthesia at the general hospital of the University of the Witwatersrand in Johannesburg. During this period I went into private practice as a consultant anesthetist and continued at this work for nine years. I then joined the full-time staff and was appointed head of a department of anesthetics at one of the three teaching hospitals attached to the University of the Witwatersrand. I was the first woman to be made head of a medical department within the university. Eventually I became associate professor of anesthesia.

I retired in 1974, a year earlier than necessary, because my husband has become a chronic invalid and I wished to be able to spend some time with him. I am, however, still engaged in anesthetic practice at two hospitals, and I also do some private practice.

I recently took a course in family planning, so that I could continue in the medical field in a less harassing branch as I became older. I plan to practice medicine as long as I am mentally and physically capable of doing so.

During the years when I was attached to the hospital on a full-time basis, I published a number of papers. I also did original research on malignant hyperpyrexia. My work in conjunction with Dr. Hyam Isaacs on creatine phosphokinase in malignant hyperpyrexia has been the breakthrough in this condition. In 1962 I was awarded the Fellowship of the Faculty of Anesthetics of the Royal College of Surgeons of Ireland.

I have been active in medical affairs, and I founded the South African Medical Women's Association, of which I am a past chairperson. I am a founding member and a past president of the Association of Anaesthetists and a founding member of the College of Physicians, Surgeons and Gynaecologists of South Africa. I was also chairperson of the full-time officers' group and a member of the Branch Council, Southern Transvaal, of the South African Medical Association.

In my career, I owe much to my husband, who understood my wish to be a person in my own right and to be independent, and to my parents, who held that girls were the intellectual equals of boys. My sex has been no handicap. In this country the majority of medical men accept women doctors easily. At the commencement of my career the state authorities had many antiquated rules. If women doctors married, they were not allowed to continue in the positions they held when single. They had to retire earlier than men, and for many years benefits given to full-time medical men were not available. Over the last forty years, however, the position of medical women has improved to such an extent that there are now no positions or benefits that married or unmarried medical women may not enjoy. The reason for this is two-fold. First, during World War II, before I took a full-time position, the state realized that medical women (and nurses) were needed to fill hospital positions and that these women worked just as well if they were married. Second, I personally managed to get the pension age of women raised to that of men. Through my family connections, I was fortunate enough to have access to offices of members of Parliament.

Women in state employment are now permanently employed even if they are married. They are entitled to maternity leave (unpaid), and they have similar benefits to those of men (leave rights, pension, and sick leave). If for any reason state-employed women have a dependent to support, they are given the same grants as are the men.

When I first became a staff member of a hospital, I had to sleep away from the hospital, as there were no quarters for women doctors in the building. In my second appointment I slept in the nurses' block. It was only in my third hospital, in Great Britain, that I shared the same quarters as the men. Nowadays women are such an integral part of the hospital staffs in this country that there are many women heads of departments with men subordinate to them.

In private practice, where an anesthetist depends on a surgeon for work, any good woman anesthetist has plenty of work, most of the cases being given to her by men, as there are still few women surgeons in South Africa.

My advice to women wishing to take up medicine as a career has always been that, if they are interested and willing to work hard, they can easily practice medicine proficiently and still get married and have a family. But they must have both the absorbing interest needed for medicine and the ability to work long, hard hours; otherwise, their career will fall by the wayside. The clever daughter pushed into medicine by a proud mama is seldom happy in her career and often gives up practice on marrying. Also, if she does choose the married state and wishes to continue in medical practice, she must have a cooperative husband who is proud to have an intelligent wife and who will not hinder her in her career.

Beryl Dorothy Corner
b. December 9, 1910

My father came from a long-established family of landowners in North Yorkshire. In the mid-nineteenth century my great-grandfather came to Bristol as a tea merchant with a considerable interest in shipping; another branch of this family has included several generations of medical men. My great-grandfather was prominent in Bristol nonconformist church circles and was a justice of the peace. His only son, my grandfather, became a professional musician, but died from hemophilia at the age of thirty years, leaving one son, my father, and two daughters. My father was brought up largely by his grandparents in a little village on the Bristol channel coast. After being educated at an independent boarding school in Somerset, father became a theological student at London University for the ministry of the Congregational Church. Unfortunately, ill-health interrupted his studies after two years, so he returned to Bristol, where his love of the sea and ships led him to become a local government officer with the Port of Bristol Authority.

My mother came from a Scottish family who lived in London. Her father was a businessman, a natural mathematician with strong scientific interests, particularly in biology. Both her parents were concerned with social reform and were involved in much public activity. Mother's two sisters were London University graduates, one in science, who became head of two well-known girls' schools in Canterbury and London. My mother was educated at a public day school for girls in North London; her abilities were artistic and musical rather than academic. She always showed tremendous concern for people and hoped for a career in nursing, but before she was old enough to start training, she became engaged to my father, whom she met at the church in London where her family worshipped.

I was the first of three siblings, and I spent my childhood in a small villagelike suburb on the outskirts of Bristol, surrounded by fields and woods. Our social and cultural life centered around the local Congregational church, where my parents were very active workers. I had a very happy childhood in this atmosphere of Christian ethics and strong sense of responsibility for caring for people. I was educated at an independent girls' day school, where, from the kindergarten upward, I was always at the top of the class and gained most of the available prizes without any undue effort. At eleven years I won a scholarship in open competition, and this secured me free education for the rest of my school life. I also learned to play the piano, became very competent in elocution and dancing, and was particularly interested in amateur dramatics from quite an early age. My speech training undoubtedly has been a great asset to me in my career. As a teenager, I was described as a "good all-rounder," but possibly the scientific interests of my mother's family led me to believe that I would follow a scientific career; so I chose to study chemistry, physics, and mathematics to an advanced level. Unfortunately, there were no available courses in biology. Science teaching had been my original objective, but I became uncertain about this and began to desire a career in scientific research. While my ideas were vague, a university career seemed a certainty.

One of my childhood longings was to play the violin, so when I had passed the lower school certificate examination at sixteen years, one of my aunts gave me a violin. During the following summer my violin teacher suggested a career in bacteriological research. Of course, I knew nothing about this field, but inquiry from my principal indicated that it would be necessary to obtain a medical qualification to make this a satisfactory career. Such an idea had never occurred to me, as all my life, although I had only minor infective ailments, I had intensely disliked and feared anything to do with illness. My father was "delicate" and had had several operations, but I was always too afraid to visit him in hospital. Despite these emotional obstacles the seed had been sown and the possibility lurked in my mind that this was just what I should do with my life.

Then a remarkable coincidence occurred. During the summer holidays I went to a schoolgirls' holiday camp with a friend who became ill almost at once. The camp medical officer was a charming young woman who had qualified about three years previously at the Royal Free School of Medicine for women and had recently started in general practice. I watched her tender care of my friend for a few days and then plucked up courage to mention to her that I was considering medicine as a career. We talked a little, and I went home with my mind made up that this was the only thing I wanted to do. My parents were flabbergasted, but they quickly discovered my determination and set inquiries in motion. My principal considered me too young and immature and urged me to remain at school for at least another year to complete my science course. However, as no biology course was available, university friends advised me not to waste time but to leave school at once and become a medical student. My parents were not well off and were still educating my younger brother and sister; the financial implications were formidable for them. However, my mother was very tenacious, and both parents had faith that I was making the right decision. My principal, although disapproving of my determination to start immediately, urged my parents to send me to London, as she thought that this would give me the best chance of an academic or research career. My mother was interviewed by the registrar of the Royal Free School of Medicine, and I was accepted for the term that started the following week. In October of 1928, at the age of seventeen years, nine months, I found myself a medical student. My grandmother offered me a home in London, and my aunts gave some financial support.

My career as a medical student was as successful as my school life; in due course I won scholarships, bursaries, and prizes and also participated actively in many student clubs. I played hockey and netball for the medical school, was secretary of the dramatic society for several years, and helped at an East End girls' club some evenings. When the exciting moment arrived to start clinical work, I had completely overcome my early fears and I threw myself enthusiastically into caring for patients.

I had always loved children and as an adolescent had seized every opportunity of teaching or caring for them, so it was fortunate that I was able to spend three months of my undergraduate course in wards for sick children. At the Hospital for Sick Children at Great Ormond Street I was immediately impressed with the wonderful tenderness and diagnostic skill of the physicians and the superb nursing techniques for extremely ill children. This inspired me to want to specialize in children's work, but at that time there seemed no possibility of doing this, as the only medical careers open to most women then were in general practice or public health clinics. Most junior-resident hospital posts were closed to women, and I had neither money nor influence, which were then essential for securing senior-staff hospital appointments and the necessary training for higher qualifications. I was, however, very fortunate in securing a house-physician post at my teaching hospital, where I worked under Dr. Dorothy Hare immediately after graduation, in July of 1934. It was my ambition to obtain the Membership of The Royal College of Physicians of London (M.R.C.P.) and the London M.D. degree by examination in the shortest possible time: then two years.

When I left the Royal Free Hospital, I had no job, but within two days after I arrived at home, a neighbor, an honorary surgeon at the Bristol Royal Infirmary, invited me to be his house surgeon there. This post gave me wide experience in all branches of surgery, anesthetics, casualty, and even occasional emergency obstetrics. My chief Wilfrid Adams discussed my career intentions and persuaded me that Bristol needed a consultant for children's diseases and that I seemed to be just the person for this post. There was an old children's hospital, still partly staffed by general practitioners, which obviously had great scope for development. He warned me that it would be a very uphill task in the early years but also pointed out later rewards seemed inevitable. Once more I decided to accept the challenge and became resident medical officer at Bristol Children's Hospital. Continuing in that post, I obtained my M.R.C.P. (London) and M.D. (London) exactly two years after graduation, receiving both honors on the same day!

The difficulties of obtaining further specialist training then seemed insurmountable. I applied hopefully for many jobs in London and provincial hospitals, only to be told by the administrators that, although I was the best-qualified candidate, they were not prepared to accept a woman. At last I was appointed house physician at Brompton Hospital for Diseases of the Chest in London. This seemed an opportunity to obtain some special experience, and although there was considerable competition, my sex did not seem to matter! The following six months proved to be one of the most profitable experiences of my life. I made permanent friendships among my resident colleagues, all of whom were men, and I received a great deal of support from my consultants throughout my career.

Near the end of this period an unexpected retirement of an honorary physician at Bristol Children's Hospital occurred. My friends urged me to apply; although I was just twenty-six years old, with relatively little experience, it seemed unlikely that there would be another vacancy for a long time. I was appointed and then entered on five years of real frustration and difficulty. I continued to train myself by attending meetings, lectures, and conferences, and earned my living with the hard uphill task of establishing a private consulting practice, with student tutoring, lectures for nurses, and all the other means by which, before the National Health Service, it was possible to pick up small fees. My major task was to develop facilities for diagnosis and treatment at the children's hospital and to establish consultant-referral outpatient clinics. These aims were facilitated when I became an energetic secretary to the Medical Staff Committee and in due course a member of the Lay Board of Management. Bristol University appointed me clinical teacher for diseases of children and subsequently lecturer, and also awarded me a fellowship for research on rickets in childhood in 1939.

Then came World War II. The children's hospital was heavily bombed, and the children had to be evacuated to an emergency hospital at Weston-super-Mare, where I continued to work and teach undergraduate students. My wartime activities included a diversity of tasks, such as care of evacuated sick children and first-aid work at the Bristol Aeroplane Company.

In these early years I was beset by three big difficulties: first, my youth; second, my sex; and third, my area of specialization. Pediatrics was not generally regarded as a separate specialty from general adult medicine in Britain. Pediatricians were extremely few in number, and all found it difficult to make a living solely in children's consultations and to get the specialty recognized as distinct from adult medicine. However, by 1943 work poured in to me from all directions and I was asked to take up many more appointments than I could possibly manage. The care of virtually all babies born in Bristol consultant-staffed maternity hospitals had been allotted to me, and schemes were well advanced for special teaching in newborn care and for the first premature baby unit, which opened when resources allowed, in 1946. In late 1947 the Department of Child Health was established at Bristol University, so that my load of teaching as part-time lecturer greatly increased and I became extensively involved in academic work.

In 1948 I became a maximum-part-time consultant pediatrician with the National Health Service on the staff of the Bristol teaching hospitals and several other hospital groups in the area. At the same time I maintained a considerable private consulting practice. All my problems with professional status and finance were over, but my clinical work and teaching were so demanding that I had insufficient time for research and writing, which seemed essential for professional advancement, and virtually no spare time for any social life or activity outside medicine. I had also become involved in medical politics, as this seemed the only way to get changes made in professional life and to obtain the facilities for patient care that appeared so essential to me. I was a member of the local executive committee of the British Medical Association, of the regional and central committees for consultant services, of two hospital-management committees, and of various specialty subcommittees.

In my professional life my particular interests included responsibility for research trials of the first antibiotic treatment of tubercular meningitis in Southwest England and during the fifties for the development of comprehensive services for care of newborn and especially premature infants, a program that gradually gained national recognition. My travels abroad included a study period in the United States and Canada and visits to a number of European centers. My first contact with the World Health Organization (WHO) was in 1961 in the European region. Since 1968 new horizons opened up when, as a consultant neonatologist for the WHO in Southeast Asia, I visited many medical colleges and undertook teaching courses and seminars for pediatric teachers.

My early professional difficulties and frequent later experiences as the only woman doctor on hospital staffs or at committee meetings made me very sensitive to the problems of women in medicine, so that in my later years I have become involved in the British Medical Women's Federation and in the Medical Women's International Association. At the time when there were relatively few women medical graduates, they were easily absorbed into general practice or public health clinical work, provided the necessary finances were available to them, and they were highly regarded by the public for their competence and care for patients. However, for ambitious women and those of high academic ability, life was extremely difficult, because there were so many barriers and so much prejudice against them on the part of men in the profession and of most professional academic bodies. The greatest thrills of my professional life were when I was elected a member of the British Pediatric Association in 1945 in the first batch of four women to be so honored and when I was elected to the Fellowship of the Royal College of Physicians of London in 1953, the twenty-third woman Fellow in a college founded as long ago as 1518! Only in 1969, after twenty-five years of existence, did the Bristol Scientific Club decide to invite me to be the first woman member.

In the early years of the National Health Service there were many men whose careers had been interrupted by World War II, and the relatively slow expansion of the hospital-service and university clinical posts caused undoubted discrimination against women in competition for these posts at a time when the number of women graduates was steadily increasing—hence, the disproportionately small number of women now in attractive consultant or academic appointments. To achieve these meant for most women an extraordinary degree of tenacity and dedication to the task, an ability to withstand snubs and disappointments with humor, and a willingness to accept challenges with faith that these would lead ultimately to the desired objectives.

In my later years my lack of involvement in the life of the community outside the limited sphere of the health professions has concerned me. For this reason, in 1962 I accepted an appointment as justice of the peace for Bristol, and this has opened another realm of intense interest in the human need for which my professional life seemed to fit me well, especially in the sphere of probation and prison welfare. My retirement in 1976 from the National Health Service enabled me to devote more time to this work and to the arts, particularly music, as well as to the church where I have been a somewhat inactive member.

I have always been grateful for the challenges that came to me in my youth and that determined my career in medicine. I am also thankful for my relatives and professional and other friends who stimulated and supported me, especially through troubled times. I have no regrets about any of the decisions I made, for I have enjoyed a life that has been rich in opportunity and experience and that has brought me many rewards. It is to be hoped that changes in the general attitude toward women in professional careers will be of enormous benefit to future generations. However, the modifications needed if professional life and medical postgraduate training are to meet the desires of the vast majority, who will also be wives and mothers, still require negotiation with all the wisdom and perseverance that can be brought to the task—and this negotiation in turn requires the help of the older generation of medical women, who have experienced so many problems that are still not far below the surface.

Gertrud Dina Schachenmann
b. December 18, 1910

I was born in Schaffhaussen, the second of five children. My father owned a wineshop inherited from his ancestors. Since 1568 the members of the family have been citizens of the town of Schaffhausen and have belonged to a trade guild. For 400 years the professions of the family have always been related to the grape and to wine. My mother also grew up in Schaffhausen. Her father came from a little village near the German border, where he was a customs official. My maternal grandfather was an accountant, then a civil servant, and finally a judge of the civil court. My maternal grandmother was German and came from Michelstadt in Odenwald. In her family there were tradespeople, doctors, judges, and engineers. My mother had two brothers. One was a lawyer, and the other became an engineer and later studied medicine. My father and mother were both interested in the arts. Mother had wanted to go to an art school, but she married instead. Later on, she enjoyed painting. I have four brothers and sisters. My oldest and youngest brothers took over my father's business, and they run the winery in Schaffhausen. My third brother is an electrical engineer. My sister is a nurse and is married to a professor of physiology in the United States.

My first years of childhood were spent with my parents and brothers and sisters in an old townhouse in the middle of Schaffhausen. My mother was very much attached to her parental home and took us out to the big garden there every day. When I started school, at six, I fell gravely ill and the doctors suspected diphtheria. After that my parents decided it would be healthier for me out in the country with my grandparents, where I also could go to school. I stayed with them for five years, until my grandfather died. Although I saw my family almost every day, I was brought up as an only child. My grandfather gave me a lot of attention, teaching me natural sciences and helping me with my schoolwork. My father often said, "Leave the child alone. She will be stupefied by all the studying." As I was quiet, well behaved, and very introverted, I did everything I was told to do and was a good pupil, but I did nothing creative. I did not even read books. After the death of my grandfather I was allowed to go to a modern private school with my oldest brother. The school was governed by the pupils and had a very free spirit, which really liberated me. After two years, I started high school, choosing classical studies. While I had been living at my grandparents', one uncle was studying medicine and I heard a lot about medical school at the dinner table. This uncle is still alive. We have always had a very close relationship and have many things in common. After grandfather's death my grandmother, who was always sickly and neurotic, fell ill with an old-age psychosis. She was easily excited and had feelings of being persecuted. She spent most of her time at home with a private nurse. Although she did not like me particularly, she always quieted down as soon as I entered her room. I do not know the reason, but I have often felt I have some soothing effect on people. I was twelve years old, and this was the reason why I decided to study medicine. My classmates were amazed because I had always been very shy and retiring.

When I was taking my matriculation examination, my father was in the hospital in Schaffhausen with several fractures he had suffered in a riding accident. Because he was well known in town, many citizens and also my teachers visited him in the hospital. They all urged him not to let me study medicine, for they thought that I should get married. Father also opposed my studies violently. His prejudice dated back to the first Russian female students who studied at the polytechnic in Zurich during his time. They were rejected and disliked because of their emancipated behavior. My father was afraid I would lose all female charm. In addition, he was very concerned about me because he feared I would break down psychically when confronted with illness and death. Despite all this, I started at the Soziale Frauenschule after my matriculation. Father did not speak to me for three weeks. After I had started, he did not oppose my decision anymore except for his remark, "If you don't pass your first examination, you know what you must do." Later he was very proud of me and had a lot of confidence in my work. Mother always supported me and was in favor of my studies. A tragic fate arranged that father was my first patient to die from cancer just after I had taken my medical examination.

I took my matriculation in Schaffhausen, pursued my medical education in Geneva, Zurich, and Paris, and graduated in 1935. I then began my internship at the Canton Hospital of Schaffhausen. I was the first woman to be an intern in internal medicine. The young chief employed me just as an experiment. This internship was an elating experience for me, and I was able to open up for the first time. Nothing seemed to be impossible. I planned to concentrate on internal medicine and pediatrics and started to work on my dissertation on primary tuberculosis of the skin with Professor G. Fanconi at the Children's Hospital in Zurich. In spite of his deep-seated reluctance to employ women doctors, Dr. Fanconi instantly offered me a salaried post as an intern, which I accepted.

From the day I began internship, more or less everything was handed to me, in great contrast to the experience of most women at that time. I never had to fight for a position, as most of the time I did not want the position and I frequently only accepted offers under pressure. Why this was so, I cannot say. Perhaps the reason was that I gave the impression of being a mother and I did not seem to have the "male" sense of competition. People always trusted me and gave me their confidence, not only my little patients and their parents but especially my own colleagues and professors. To the outer world I appeared to be composed and confident despite a lot of personal anxiety and a tendency to be overscrupulous. I think the important point is that I have always been totally involved in my work and that I have lived intensively and exclusively for my profession.

At first I was undecided about whether pediatrics would suit me. It became, however, my beloved profession. Because the chief of internal medicine was an army officer, he predicted war in 1937 and made an agreement with Professor Fanconi and me that, in case of war, I would direct internal medicine and at times gynecology at the Canton Hospital in Schaffhausen. Nearly all doctors had to serve in the army. Suddenly I had to leave the university clinic in Zurich in order to direct the clinic at the Canton Hospital in Schaffhausen. As I was not yet twenty-nine years old, this was a formidable task, but my strength and my ability grew in this position. After three months I decided to go back to the university clinic in Zurich, where during the war we were only a small number of interns. After three more years in pediatrics, although I was still Dr. Fanconi's youngest intern, he made me his chief assistant. I remained there from 1941 to 1945, at first with Professor H. Wissler as chief and then for two years supervising 300 to 400 patients on my own. Besides performing medical and managerial work, I had to guide the interns and teach the medical students. The workload—day and night—was immense.

When the war ended, I decided to open a private practice for pediatrics in my hometown, Schaffhausen. Again the work was very strenuous, and I almost broke down under the burden. At this point I was elected chief of the pediatric hospital at the Swiss School of Nursing in Zurich. From 1950 until the beginning of 1971 I directed the fifty-bed pediatric hospital, taught nutrition to the nurses, and in addition, had a private practice. In 1968, when medicine and neonatology had become increasingly technical, I decided to resign in my sixtieth year. I did so, and I am glad that I was able to take this step so easily.

The Swiss School of Nursing, with its hospital in Zurich, was founded in 1901 by some of the first Swiss women doctors in order to give them an opportunity to fill leading positions and at the same time to start a free school for nurses. In the founding documents it was laid down that the director of the hospital must always be a woman, while the head doctors of the departments of Internal Medicine, Surgery, Pediatrics, and Gynecology, with about 2000 births a year, could be male or female. Unfortunately, no woman doctor could be found to succeed me. I was the third doctor in the pediatric clinic after the school's foundation. The first was Dr. Maria Heim-Vogtlin, the first Swiss woman doctor.

After my retirement I spent two years of intensive study in the fields of organic malfunctions of the brain, cerebral palsy, behavioral sciences, and child development. In the rural surroundings of the town of my birth I now have a small consulting practice and I direct the center for cerebral palsy at the Children's Hospital in Schaffhausen. I enjoy this work very much; I am not under stress any longer, and I am free to open myself to new perspectives.

Kaisa Turpeinen
b. May 14, 1911

I am the fifth child in a family of six children. My oldest brother became a teacher of mathematics. To our great sorrow he was killed in the war with Russia. My oldest sister Liisa also became a teacher of mathematics. She became head of a well-known girls' high school in Helsinki and helped my youngest sister and me to finance our studies at the University of Helsinki. Then came my brother Heikki, who died of enteritis as a child. The fourth child was my sister Maija. To the surprise of the family, she studied English at the university and became a teacher of languages. My youngest sister Kerttu became a pharmacist and has written the history of Finnish pharmacy.

When I was a child, I was always told that I was born when it was a boy's turn to arrive. In my family boys and girls had been born alternately until I came along. As I did not understand this theory and it was not explained to me or I did not ask, it became a problem for me and the thought was often in my mind in my childhood. I believe it was also very important to me and explains why I became interested in biology very early. That in turn led me to choose a medical career and a specialization in gynecology and obstetrics.

My father was the stationmaster in my hometown, Tampere. He was actually holding down two jobs, for he also conducted the two military bands in Tampere. He had been educated and trained in the music school for the military bands in Saint Petersburg (Leningrad) at the time when Finland was a part of Russia.

My mother came from an old seafaring family that, however, had owned a bookbinding firm for two generations. According to custom, my mother had gone through a cooking and a sewing school before her marriage. She made all our dresses with good taste and cared for us very well. My father had very little time to be with us. Whenever he was at home, he was working on the arrangement of the pieces of music to be played by the bands.

Our home was in a group of wooden houses that filled a whole block and left a large playground for children in the middle. My parents had bought the house before I was born. It had at first only one floor, but as the family grew larger, three small bedrooms were added on above. There was still enough space in the attic for our theater performances.

My father had an excellent memory and was very interested in mathematics. As we children were all good in that subject in high school, he hoped that we would study it at the university. Thus, when my older brother and sister started university mathematics, some of my father's wishes were fulfilled. When my turn came to begin my university studies, father thought that a medical education would be too long if I planned to marry right away. I had a steady boyfriend at that time. I started my studies in biology and chemistry, the same courses that the medical students had to work through. After one semester the boyfriend was forgotten and I joined the medical students.

As I was very young when I finished high school, I became a doctor and got my license to practice medicine when I was only twenty-three years of age, which was a record at that time.

During my studies I had married Dr. Osmo Turpeinen. On his graduation in medicine in Helsinki, he was awarded a Rockefeller Foundation Fellowship and a Finnish State Fellowship for research work in the United States. I accompanied him to America and thus was able to do two more years of medical studies, as well as some research, at the University of California at Berkeley, and at Johns Hopkins University in Baltimore. I started to work on my thesis in Baltimore and finished it in Finland in 1941. The title was "Delayed Pregnancy during Lactation in the Mouse As Influenced by Certain Hormones."

After returning from America, we thought that we were ready to start a family, so we had four children between 1939 and 1945. Many things happened during this same period. First, I finished my thesis. I had chosen the speciality of gynecology and obstetrics and finished that training in 1945. During those years Finland was going through its two wars with Russia. In the second war the women's clinic where I worked was moved to the country; thus I moved with the children to the country. My husband was working with the Ministry of Defense. At that time our marriage deteriorated, and we were finally separated in 1952. The four children were put in my custody.

After World War II I started my private practice in Helsinki as a gynecologist. At the same time I was a consulting gynecologist at the tuberculosis sanatorium in Helsinki.

In 1957 I was asked to become the chief of the marriage and social-guidance clinics of the Finnish Family Welfare League. At that time the league had four clinics, which gave advice on family planning and marriage guidance and was doing genetic counseling, as well as making decisions on abortion. Again I spent three months in America to see and learn what was being done over there in those fields. The work at the marriage-guidance clinics was very much to my liking, and there I found my life work. During fourteen years I was busy founding nine new clinics. In the beginning, family planning was not well known or well accepted in Finland. When I retired from that job, at the age of sixty, family planning advice was being given free of charge in all health centers of the country. A new abortion law came into being during that time. The experiences we gained at the clinics were used in making the abortion law.

After I had finished my job at the marriage guidance clinics, I turned to private practice again. It did not take long, however, before I was asked to be a candidate for the Conservative party, to sit on the city council. I was elected. At present I am chairperson of the Board of Health of Helsinki. As I have always been interested in preventive medicine, I was also chosen to become the chairperson of the Health Education Council of Helsinki.

My life story is not complete if I do not tell about my children. I have two daughters and two sons. My oldest daughter is a nutritionist and is teaching in a nursing school. My second daughter is a psychiatrist and working in a mental hospital. My oldest son is an electrical engineer, working in a fiber factory. My youngest son is a dealer in the valuta department of a big bank. All my children have married nice spouses. I have eight grandchildren, four girls and four boys. My mother used to say, "Small children cause small troubles, while big children cause big worries." For the present I have been spared these sorrows.

Remedios Goquiolay-Arellano
b. November 1, 1911

I was born to a family of moderate means in the city of Manila in the Philippines. My parents Gonzalo Goquiolay and Peregrina Francisco were both in the business world. My father was a Chinese citizen who became a naturalized Filipino shortly after my birth. We were a relatively small family, and I had two brothers and a sister who were all younger than me. I was the only one in our family who was able to finish college.

My early years were spent in Manila. They were happy years. My parents used to say that I was the naughtiest and the most active of all their children. I remember enjoying the company of my younger brothers, a relationship that extends up to this day.

At a very early age—I think I was four or five years old—I was enrolled by my parents in a Chinese school. I stayed there for two years. Later I was transferred to St. Paul and then to St. Scholastica College, where I finished my high-school education. I vividly remember the wonderful times I spent in school. Being one of the youngest and obviously the most active of the students, I was considered the life of my class. I was always involved in extracurricular activities, sports, and drama. I can remember the nuns who were our teachers. They were strict disciplinarians and often had to call me to attention because of my naughtiness. I loved life and enjoyed it. During this period I found myself being attracted to science subjects; in fact, I had a strong desire to become a scientist. My final choice of medicine for my life profession was influenced by Dr. Luis Guerrero, our family doctor, considered by most of us to be the greatest Filipino physician of all times. With his humble and unassuming manner, he struck me as the epitome of the perfect medical scientist. I dreamed that someday I would follow in his footsteps and make a name for myself in the medical world. He was a pediatrician.

On graduation from high school at the age of seventeen, I came to the first major crossroad of my life. I wanted to take up medicine, but the University of Santo Tomas did not offer this course to women. I thought about the University of the Philippines, but I felt that I would rather enroll in a Catholic school, probably because of my pleasant experiences during my early school years.

I found pharmacy to be a challenging study, and I had no difficulty. I managed to graduate at twenty years of age with highest honors, but my restless soul was not satisfied. I still wanted to take up medicine. Fortunately, at this time the university decided to admit the first woman students to the Faculty of Medicine and Surgery. Then came another crossroad in my life. I was in the midst of preparation for the government examination for pharmacy licensing, which was due a month after the beginning of the school year. I had to prepare for the examinations and yet I wanted to enroll in the Faculty of Medicine. After due deliberation and with divine guidance, I decided to enroll in the Faculty of Medicine and at the same time prepare for the government examination. Because of this, I was late in my entrance to the medical school, and I had to work hard to catch up with the rest of the class. Nevertheless, I managed to top the government examinations.

I do not regret my struggles during the first months of my medical studies, for they opened my eyes to the need for conscientious and diligent work in medicine. I developed and maintained this attitude, which culminated in my being magna cum laude. I am happy to say that I likewise topped the medical examinations that year. My medical studies were not purely hard work. My excessive energy led me to join in many extracurricular activities in the college, and I consider the period of my medical education the happiest time of my life. I am proud to say that I was not only one of the first woman graduates in medicine at the University of Santo Tomas but among the top students in my class and in the medical board.

On graduation I encountered yet another crossroad. Women doctors were very rare, especially in clinical medicine. I was offered a job as a faculty member to teach pathology, tropical medicine, and medical science. Should I accept this and forget about pediatrics? My strong desire was to emulate the great Dr. Luis Guerrero, and this prompted me to obtain a position as a resident physician in pediatrics at San Juan de Dios Hospital, where I topped the competitive examination for the post. I thus became the first woman resident physician in pediatrics. At the same time I joined Dr. Luis Guerrero's Department of Pediatrics as an instructor, as the first woman instructor there. My choice of this specialty was a correct and happy one. Finally, in 1970, I was appointed professor and chairperson of the Department of Pediatrics.

I am involved in many medical societies. I was a founding member of the Philippine Medical Women's Association (PMWA) and the Philippine Pediatric Society. I have held various positions in the Zonta Club and the Philippine Medical Association. I have been president of various medical associations: the PMWA, from 1954 to 1956; the Philippine Pediatric Society, from 1966 to 1969; the Clinica Arellano (a hospital my husband and I founded, incorporated in 1963), from 1963 to 1973; the Catholic Physicians Guild of the Philippines, from 1971 to 1977; and the Asian Federation of Catholic Organizations, from 1972 to 1976. I am currently vice-president for Asia of the Federation of International Catholic Physicians.

Undoubtedly, I feel that life has been kind to me by showering me with these opportunities for achievement. As to my family life, marriage came shortly after graduation. I married Servando Arellano, then a promising resident physician in obstetrics and gynecology. Two careers in medicine in our family did not affect our marital relationship. I have a most understanding and liberal husband. We both decided that raising a family and pursuing our medical careers could be achieved simultaneously. Our decision, a difficult one, proved to be the right one for us both. Life was kind to us. My husband became a most successful obstetrician-gynecologist, and department head and professor of obstetrics and gynecology of the Faculty of Medicine and Surgery of the University of Santo Tomas. He has recently retired from this position. We were able to own a small hospital in Manila, which is operating successfully. What I consider the greatest gift that divine providence has given us is our children. Eduardo, like his father an obstetrician-gynecologist, is married to a pediatrician, Coarzon Porciuncula, and has four children. Roberto is a radiologist and is married to Gloria Nuval, a commerce graduate. Milagros is a medical technologist. Antonio is a commerce and law graduate. He is actively practicing law in Manila and is married to Bernadette Estrella, a commerce graduate; they have two children.

I believe that women choosing medicine as a life career have to make clear-cut and firm decisions. Marriage can deter or hamper their professional growth. Some women have rejected marriage in favor of the profession. I believe profession and marriage can thrive together, provided that both spouses make up their minds to this. I am most thankful for my wonderful husband, who besides permitting full development of my potential as a professional woman, has encouraged me all the way.

Were I to choose a life profession again, I would without hesitation select medicine. It is true that the sex of a professional may affect the choice of a specialty. It must be realized that certain specialties demand attributes that may be present in one sex more than in the other. However, success and acceptance in a specialty depend more on the person than on the sex.

As I look back, I cannot help but be thankful to the Lord for His bounty. He gave me a chance to achieve in life and to help others achieve. I close this short story of my life, hoping that I may be permitted a few more years of service to the children of my country.

Fe del Mundo
b. November 27, 1911

I was the sixth of eight children and lived for the first ten years of my childhood in Intramuros ("the Walled City"), also called Old Manila, where the Pasig River joins the Manila Bay. In this locality there was still much Spanish influence from the 400-year Spanish regime. Narrow cobblestone streets lined by adjacent two-story wooden houses with inner patios to brighten and ventilate interior rooms were from that epoch. Spanish was the language almost everyone spoke. Six cathedrals and five chapels in prestigious Catholic colleges greatly influenced the life and culture of the people in this historical district.

My family rented a typical house located just across from the Manila Cathedral. As a result many of our daily chores were in some way associated with this church. We were poor and simple in our way of living. My mother did all the household chores, kept a small pastry store, sewed all our dresses, and went marketing every day at dawn. She was noted for her industry and simplicity. My father was educated in a Jesuit school. They say he was a bright and good lawyer. He was twice elected to the assembly of his province, the little island of Marinduque. I had the impression that his political career made us poorer each year. He was not much of a businessman, and I recall the business reverses that made all of us unhappy. However, he succeeded in procuring farmlands in the island of Mindoro, but his family did not begin to benefit from these until long after his death—in fact, only in the past few years.

My father chose to have us educated in government schools, which at that time had high standards. We had many financial problems and were wanting in comforts and amenities that the other children enjoyed. I recall that most of our toys were homemade or improvised. An allowance was a luxury, and so we seldom enjoyed such a privilege.

My elementary-school days were uneventful. I was very shy and quiet and an average student. We were reared the Spanish way, with much discipline, even to the point where we were often spanked. An unmarried aunt who lived with us was very particular about our manners. We were taught that in the presence of adults we were only to listen and not to be heard. Respect for elders, thoughtfulness, and obedience were deeply inculcated in our young minds. Much of what I learned in my early childhood, from both my parents and my teachers, has left a deep imprint on me, so that even now I continue to observe and practice many of their teachings. I was always guided by my father's words to the effect that our education was the only legacy he could leave us and therefore we should make the most of our studies.

There were eight children in the family, which at that time was the average number, but only four grew to adulthood. Three died early in infancy and one passed away when she was in the third grade. This little girl left a note wherein she stated her plan to study medicine in order to take care of the poor. Her death caused much grief in the family, and I decided that one day I would carry out her plans and wishes. Of the four remaining children, the eldest was the brightest and very famous for his scholastic records, being the first summa cum laude graduate in the state university. He was a chemist, pianist, linguist, and inventor. The second finished pharmacy and a Ph.D. in education. I was the third. The youngest became a dentist.

I remember being elected class officer in the third grade, and at the induction ceremony I recited Longfellow's "Great Wide Beautiful Wonderful World." No wonder I continued to love the world and nature. I enjoyed letter writing very much, and in the seventh grade, when the principal, who was substituting for our sick teacher, asked us to write a letter of application, she was most encouraging; in fact, she commented that she would readily employ me on the basis of my letter, which was displayed on the bulletin board.

I graduated with honors from high school, but just then we suffered the loss of my mother, which greatly affected all of us. I recall that she was most concerned about me, and during her critical moments she expressed her worry that I would find it difficult without her. She was so pessimistic about my future that she asked an aunt, who later became my guardian, to give me special attention and care.

The choice of a profession was a problem, but I remembered the wish of my deceased sister. The family felt that the study of medicine would be too long and too strenuous for my health. I was, however, rather determined, and my elders gave in to my choice.

At first I felt lost in the University of the Philippines. The liberal arts classes were big, and then we had to move from one building to another, rubbing elbows with students of different disciplines. Somehow I did not seem to adjust well. I was one of the younger students, and as a premedical student, I wore short socks and had ribbons in my hair. Two years of preparatory courses passed. I enjoyed most of all physics, mathematics, and English, the very subjects I had not particularly cared for in high school.

Entrance into medicine proper involved stiff competition, with high school top-notchers vying for admission. Only about 100 were to be chosen from 250 applicants. Happily, I came out first on the entrance examinations. As I had been forewarned, the courses were difficult, requiring long hours in school and more hours of study at home. On three occasions I was almost ready to quit, but I always remembered how everyone had been against my choice and realized that I had to bear my difficulties quietly. We had further financial problems. My father was often ill, and our chemist brother was on a fellowship in Germany. Our pharmacist sister was the only one who could help with the family expenses. I could hardly buy the necessary books and had to resort to borrowing them from former students or from my own classmates. Somehow I did better than those who had the books. I almost had to stop in my fifth year, when I did not have the matriculation fee of 174 pesos (the equivalent of 22 American dolars). Fortunately, my guardian aunt came to my rescue, and I managed to continue. Immediately after final examinations each year, I would be ill. This was probably a result of exhaustion, the tension of competition, and the walking to and from school. Still more important was the fact that I did not care for nourishment. At any rate, I went through the five years with no failures and finally graduated in a class of seventy in 1933. Happily, amidst all odds, I topped the class and received the Most Outstanding Award for 1933 Medical Graduates, which was granted by the Colegio Médico-Farmacéutico de Manila. This was my first significant award and the first recognition I received for achievement.

The same year I took the national medical board examination, and I wept as I obtained third place, with a difference of only 0.5 and 0.4 from the first and second places, respectively. As I put away my books, I wept again, for I did not want to be separated from them. My guardian, however, reminded me that graduation did not mean that my education had ended.

The choice of a specialty was the next problem after graduation. I immediately had an opening in the private office of my uncle and guardian, who had a clinical pathology laboratory and a dermatology clinic. I was his assistant for three whole years, by necessity rather than by choice. I looked for opportunities to go abroad for postgraduate studies, preferably with a grant. Happily and unexpectedly, I received a call one evening informing me that the president of the Philippines was offering me a scholarship and that I should report the next morning at the palace. This was what I had prayed for—a scholarship that would allow me to go to the United States with the privilege of choosing and learning a specialty for four to five years. I felt this was to be manna from heaven and could hardly believe my luck.

I left for the United States in November of 1936, having decided to take pediatrics, since there was only a handful of pediatricians in the country and I had seen so many children who were almost without medical care, particularly in the island of Marinduque, where I had done a term paper for our public health class.

As one of the first to qualify in this specialty and as the recipient of a government scholarship, I had enviable opportunities and I made contacts in the United States, all of which have become valuable assets to my career. I spent three years of my postgraduate studies at the Children's Hospital in Boston and at Harvard medical school, one year at the University of Chicago, six months at Johns Hopkins Hospital, and short terms in various pediatric institutions, all to round out my training. Late in 1940 all scholars were recalled home because of impending World War II. Unfortunately, on the way home I had an automobile accident in Honolulu with my sister, which delayed our return by four months. Finally, in 1941, I reached Manila to resume work, this time as a pediatrician. I was able to visit my benefactor, President Manuel L. Quezon, who advised me that I did not have to pay for my scholarship in terms of service in an assigned institution, as was the usual procedure for Philippine scholars. The president felt that, wherever I worked, I would be rendering service to our people. That was the last time I saw my distinguished benefactor.

Soon World War II broke out and changed my plans for the future. Little did I suspect that the war years would allow me to continue the practice of pediatrics. Conditions were very trying and discouraging, in contrast to what I had been used to in prestigious American hospitals. My activities started early in 1942 with the care of children prisoners of war at the University of Santo Tomas Internment Camp. For them I opened a children's home at the Holy Ghost College, under the auspices of the National Red Cross. Somehow we managed fairly well, notwithstanding war conditions, tension, and privation, and the youngsters were happy until precarious conditions required their return to the camp. My records show that altogether 400 youngsters from five months to fourteen years of age were cared for in the children's home.

My next endeavor was a children's hospital under the auspices of the City of Manila in 1943. The hospital was established in an improvised school building close to the University of Santo Tomas Internment Camp, and it functioned until the liberation of Manila, in 1945, when with the support and assistance of the U.S. Army, this hospital was converted into the North General Hospital for civilians who had to be transferred out of U.S. Army general hospitals. It was my feeling that organizing a 500-bed general hospital with 300 employees amid privation and all kinds of difficulties was a real test of endurance, determination, and resourcefulness. Happily, this became a successful emergency hospital, thanks to the U.S. Army officials, through an energetic colleague, young Filipino physician Major Manuel Escudero. The institution soon became a departmentalized general hospital, which rapidly developed into one of the largest government general hospitals under the Department of Health in the northern section of Manila.

As the ravages of war started to dissipate and rehabilitation went on at a rapid pace, I found myself deeply involved in institutions, organizations, project or service programs, and medical associations. It was my privilege to organize the Philippine Medical Women's Association, and at about the same time I became one of the founding members of the Philippine Pediatric Society. Soon I was president of the Manila Medical Society, but I had to decide how far to go, as I knew I was spreading myself too thin. In addition, I was director of one hospital and then another, teaching medical students, first at the University of Santo Tomas and then at Far Eastern University. My regret was my inability to join the faculty of my alma mater, the main reason for which was my sex.

Through the years I worked very hard to deserve the many and unusual opportunities I have received in life, and I have not forgotten the challenge

President Quezon provided when he remarked that I could render service to our people wherever I would work. I made use of each opportunity, guided by the memory of my mother's conscientiousness and industry, my father's righteousness and determination, my guardian's resourcefulness and initiative, and my teachers' helpfulness and unselfishness.

The momentum of my work and activities never faltered. The twenty-four hours of each day have always seemed insufficient. The pressure of work, however, rather detached me from my family, for my two sisters were married and they had their own families. I have remained single, which is a puzzle to many. This was neither by choice nor by conviction. I have refuted the claim that I was married to my profession, for I believe that I could have fulfilled the requirements of both marriage and my profession as successfully as many others have done. As in the case of my contemporaries, I was not devoid of suitors. My present status, I surmise, is the result of many factors, and all I can say now is that marriage was not meant to be and that I am closer to what I have longed to do.

I have traveled both locally and internationally far more than I ever expected to, almost every time on a grant. These trips have allowed my education to continue and have increased my contacts. As president of the Medical Women's International Association from 1962 through 1966, I visited component branches in 34 countries. In the Philippines, as president of the Philippine Medical Association, I visited 77 component provincial societies. And as project director of the Institute of Maternal and Child Health and its Family Planning Project, I saw over 200 Maternal and Child Health (MCH) centers spread over the country. I recall how deeply moved I was by the standing ovation I received when I gave my valedictory reports in both associations. My involvement in family planning was classified as pioneering and was considered helpful; so this work was recognized with a significant project grant from the U.S. Agency for International Development and later from the Commission on Population, which culminated in a presidential appointment as commissioner. These events, I shall never forget.

Ever since I received my first award in 1933, when I was fresh out of medical school, I have been conferred awards, citations, recognitions, and honorary degrees, which I never expected to receive in my lifetime. As I review this list, I cannot but believe that people have been very kind and generous to me.

Dr. Edward Park, a mentor and benefactor, now professor emeritus in pediatrics at Johns Hopkins University, was most encouraging when he wrote me the following words:

> From the standpoint of recognition of values in life, there are advantages and disadvantages in being a woman. Women do not have the opportunities of men, but when they succeed in spite of that lack, they suddenly become more conspicuous than men who might have done equally important things, just because they are women and what they

have accomplished is not expected of them. Then too, when they succeed in passing the preliminary stages which are often wrought with difficulties, they reach the point when their work will be so recognized that honor will be showered upon them. Such was the case of Florence Nightingale and Madame Curie, such is what you experience now.

I shall always be indebted to numerous individuals for what I have attained. I thank them through prayers and services that I can still render help to other human beings, particularly to children. In turn, I am happy that I leave behind a few tangible expressions of gratitude: a legacy to the children of the land, to whom I bequeath the Children's Medical Center, Philippines; a textbook of pediatrics, which was accomplished with the cooperation, sacrifice, and determination of my coeditors and various contributors; two organizations that I had the privilege of organizing, namely, the Philippine Medical Women's Association and the Maternal and Child Health Association of the Philippines (1972); a number of physicians whom I helped train toward their specialization in pediatrics; a compilation of my twenty-years' weekly "Baby and You" column for parents in the *Sunday Times Magazine*; and last but not least, infants and children in the country who have grown up with whatever medical care and health guidance I was able to extend to them. These are what I can now look back to with satisfaction and what make me feel that altogether my own life story was not in vain.

Index